PURITANS AND
REVOLUTIONARIES

PURITANS AND REVOLUTIONARIES

Essays in
Seventeenth-Century History
presented to
Christopher Hill

Edited by
DONALD PENNINGTON
and
KEITH THOMAS

OXFORD
AT THE CLARENDON PRESS
1978

Oxford University Press, Walton Street, Oxford OX2 6DP

OXFORD LONDON GLASGOW
NEW YORK TORONTO MELBOURNE WELLINGTON
KUALA LUMPUR SINGAPORE JAKARTA HONG KONG TOKYO
DELHI BOMBAY CALCUTTA MADRAS KARACHI
IBADAN NAIROBI DAR ES SALAAM CAPE TOWN

ISBN 0 19 822439 7

© *Oxford University Press 1978*

*Printed in Great Britain
at the University Press, Oxford
by Vivian Ridler
Printer to the University*

FOR CHRISTOPHER

WITH

GRATITUDE AND AFFECTION

Preface

CHRISTOPHER HILL has been teaching and writing on seventeenth-century English history for more than forty years. Few British historians have a reputation so truly world wide, and none has had a greater influence upon the study of his chosen period. A work which included contributions from all the scholars who have benefited from his teaching and example would require many large volumes. This is a much smaller offering, intended to mark the occasion of his retirement from the mastership of Balliol College, Oxford. The contributors are drawn only from those present historians of the seventeenth century who were once his undergraduate or graduate pupils. Even so, it has proved impossible to find room for everyone who falls into this category and the fifteen contributors have had to accept a stringent word-limit.

Most of the contributions relate to the two themes which have always been central to Christopher Hill's work and which he chose as the title of his first collection of essays, *Puritanism and Revolution*. But the contributors have dealt with many different aspects of the period and exemplify many different ways of investigating it. For Christopher Hill has never sought to create a 'school' of disciples. Indeed nothing testifies more to his stature as a historian than his success in developing a profoundly original and independent view of seventeenth-century England while maintaining the respect and affection of historians of so many different persuasions.

Neither he nor his admirers would enjoy the formal eulogy which a Festschrift sometimes includes. In any case it is much too early to assess the work of a writer who is still at the height of his powers. We have therefore merely asked five people who knew him well at different stages of his career to provide some personal reminiscences. An interim bibliography has also been included. It is not intended to be comprehensive, but it gives some idea of the prodigious output of this most fertile and creative historical writer.

We should like to thank another of Christopher Hill's friends and colleagues, Mr. Dan Davin of the Oxford University Press, for his help in the various stages of publication.

D. P.
K. T.

Oxford, March 1978

Contents

Abbreviations

Add.	Additional
AO	Archives Office
BIHR	*Bulletin of the Institute of Historical Research*
BL	British Library
Bodl.	Bodleian Library
Cal. Comp.	*Calendar of the Proceedings of the Committee for Compounding, 1643–1660*
CJ	*Commons Journals*
Clarendon	Edward, Earl of Clarendon, *The History of the Rebellion and Civil Wars in England*, ed. W. D. Macray (Oxford, 1888)
CSPD	*Calendar of State Papers Domestic*
Debates 1621	*Commons Debates 1621*, ed. W. Notestein, F. H. Relf, and H. Simpson (New Haven, 1935)
Debates 1628	*Commons Debates 1628*, ed. R. C. Johnson, M. F. Keeler, M. J. Cole and W. B. Bidwell (New Haven, 1977)
D'Ewes, ed. Coates	*The Journal of Sir Simonds D'Ewes from the First Recess of the Long Parliament to the Withdrawal of King Charles from London*, ed. W. H. Coates (New Haven, 1942)
D'Ewes, ed. Notestein	*The Journal of Sir Simonds D'Ewes from the Beginnings of the Long Parliament to the Opening of the Trial of the Earl of Strafford*, ed. W. Notestein (New Haven, 1923)
DNB	*Dictionary of National Biography*
EcHR	*Economic History Review*
EHR	*English Historical Review*
Firth & Rait	*Acts and Ordinances of the Interregnum, 1642–1660*, ed. C. H. Firth and R. S. Rait (1911)
HJ	*Historical Journal*
HMC	*Historical Manuscripts Commission Reports*
LJ	*Lords Journals*
Nalson	John Nalson, *An Impartial Collection of the Great Affairs of State from the beginning of the Scotch Rebellion in the year MDCXXXIX to the Murther of King Charles I* (1682–3)
P. and P.	*Past and Present*
PRO	Public Record Office
RO	Record Office

Rushworth	John Rushworth, *Historical Collections of Private Passages of State* (1721)
S. of R.	*Statutes of the Realm*
STC	A. W. Pollard and G. R. Redgrave, *A Short-Title Catalogue of Books printed in England . . . 1475–1640* (1926)
Thurloe	*A Collection of the State Papers of John Thurloe*, ed. T. Birch (1742)
TLS	*Times Literary Supplement*
TRHS	*Transactions of the Royal Historical Society*
VCH	*Victoria County History*
Whitelocke	Bulstrode Whitelocke, *Memorials of the English Affairs* (Oxford, 1853)
Wing	D. G. Wing, *Short-Title Catalogue of Books printed in England . . . 1641–1700* (N.Y., 1945–51)

Unless otherwise stated, all works quoted were published in London.

Christopher Hill
Some Reminiscences

John Edward Christopher Hill was born on 6 February 1912. His father was Edward Harold Hill, solicitor, of The Lodge, Huntington, York; his mother was Janet Augusta Hill, formerly Dickinson. From 1923 to 1931 he attended St. Peter's School, York, first as a day-boy and later as a boarder. In 1930 he won a County Major Scholarship, and the Headmaster's Prizes for History and for Latin Prose; and in 1931 he entered Balliol College, Oxford, as Brackenbury Scholar.

SAMUEL H. BEER, *Rhodes Scholar at Balliol and from 1953 Professor of the Science of Government at Harvard, writes:*

CHRISTOPHER HILL came up in Michaelmas Term 1931, a year before me. He took the scholarship exams at Balliol, but by the time the dons decided they wanted him he had accepted an offer from Cambridge. Kenneth Bell, a history don, motored all the way to York to dissuade him. Informed by Mrs. Hill that her son was preparing to go to Cambridge, Kenneth replied that, no, he was coming to Balliol. And so he did.

He was small, but wiry and strong. I remember V. H. Galbraith, a tremendous admirer, reciting Hill's exploits of the previous day on the rugger field, where he had tackled large, bony opponents without flinching. His wit told you a good deal about him. Although very bright, and known to be, he was not clever at other people's expense. He could be sardonic, but the objects of his ridicule were not personal. When the first three volumes of Toynbee's *Study of History* appeared, Christopher delivered his judgement to Galbraith: 'p-p-platitude', he said, the stammer heightening the effect, 'supported by great learning.' His pervasive sense of the ridiculous made him great fun to be with. But humour also served a defensive function, helping him to avoid any serious discussion of his personal feelings or thoughts about the world.

As for his politics, Hill was not a member of the Communist Party while an undergraduate—he was recruited some time later after going to All Souls—nor was he an active member of the October Club.[1] In this Oxford the spirit of Waugh was still stronger than the spirit of Auden and Spender.

I don't recall Hill ever taking out a girl, although later he did bring Cordelia Saleeby, a good-looking Lebanese, to our wedding. But unlike many of our English contemporaries he was not afraid of girls. My wife, Roberta, who also knew him in those days, describes him as 'nimble, witty, warm, and handsome'. But the University rules, not to mention the social norms, did not encourage close contact between the sexes.

The Spring of 1934 was glorious. There was a drought. Less serious people enjoyed the sun. Roberta had a flat in Norham Gardens and often in the afternoon our friends would come round and we would all go for a swim in the Cherwell: Tristan Jones, with a towel around his head, David Astor, the handsomest man in Oxford, Derek Kahn, the second most handsome, later killed in the war. The relevance to Hill is that he rarely if ever came by. It was the term before his Schools and he was working very hard. For in spite of his gaiety there was no frivolity in Hill. He spent his time not in politics or womanizing or chit-chat, but working. Moments of self-revelation were rare with him. The only one I remember was in the living-room of his home in York when he pointed to a window-seat and remarked with emotion, 'That is where I spent all those hours reading'.

He took his top first in the History Schools in Trinity Term 1934; then in the autumn lived in digs off Beaumont Street—straight out of Orwell's *Keep the Aspidistra Flying*—with C. E. Collins, a Balliol contemporary, while preparing for his exams for All Souls. After winning the Fellowship, he moved into that sybaritic life, but continued to work. In February 1935, I wrote to Roberta in London, 'Poor Christopher Hill fainted the other day after one glass of sherry—fell into a dead clammy sweat from overwork.'

---

[1] The October Club was an undergraduate club which took its name from the October Revolution and consisted of a mixed bag of Communist Party members, fellow-travellers, and the merely curious. Nominally, it was for the 'study' of communism, since according to the University rules undergraduates were not permitted to form a club for political action. Actually, it devoted most of its energies to bringing speakers to Oxford—perhaps to expose their 'petty bourgeois socialism', as in the case of H. G. Wells, whom I recall hearing at a meeting of the club in Michaelmas Term 1932.

I don't mean to suggest that he could not handle alcohol. I was seeing a good deal of him at this time and one night in Trinity Term, 1935, we had dinner in a little second-floor café near Carfax, intending to go on to a lecture by Laski. At that time Laski had entered his strongly Marxist phase, publishing a year later his historical study, *The Rise of European Liberalism*. As we drank our second bottle of wine, the time and inclination to hear Laski passed, so instead we went to Hill's rooms in All Souls to listen to records. About eleven A. L. Rowse, then a left-winger, poked his head in the door. I vividly remember his hair-do; today we would call it an Afro. He said Laski was upstairs and would Christopher like to meet him. Looking at me, he asked, 'Is your friend a good Bolshevik?' Being assured of my credentials, he took us up to Laski.

The idea of using Marx to study history was still new in England. I recall my sense of daring and novelty when, during a tutorial with Humphrey Sumner in Hilary Term, 1935, I blurted out something to the effect that I thought the conflict of the seventeenth century was 'a class war'. 'Of course, but what else?' was Humphrey's sensible rejoinder. This was six years before Tawney's 'Rise of the Gentry' and there was virtually nothing for an undergraduate to read along these lines.

By the Spring of 1935, however, Hill was already a Marxist and beavering away on the Civil War. My impression is that his interest in the Civil War came first and his Marxism later. At any rate, his reason for going to Russia the next year was to get in touch with Soviet research, e.g. by Arkhangelsky, on Cromwellian England. The Warden, Professor W. G. S. Adams, favoured his studying abroad, but showed disappointment at the choice of country and asked whether Christopher might not prefer one of the more rapidly developing countries—Germany, for instance. It was in Russia during the winter of 1935–6 that he got the infection that led to his mastoid operation.

Roberta and I were married in a civil ceremony in the Spring of 1935 after Schools. Christopher, who was one of the witnesses, asked us to come for a visit to his home in York as a kind of honeymoon. Another reason was to help persuade his parents to let his younger sister travel alone on the continent. We knew little of Christopher's social background. In manners he was, to our perceptions, remarkably classless. In fact, we thought he was probably not very well-off and wondered if our visit might put a strain on his family's resources. This apprehension was strengthened by his mother's appearance, hat askew, in a rattle-trap car for the drive North. Our surprise could hardly be contained when we drew up at a magnificent residence toward the outskirts of York. A high wall stretched around grounds which ran down to a little river and had a tennis-court. A servant brought us lunch at a table on the lawn.

The centrepiece, however, was Father. A Methodist, he had retired after a career as a successful solicitor with a fair amount of money to do good works. He was handsome, sandy-haired and tallish—Christopher took after his mother in physical appearance—quiet in manner in contrast to Mrs. Hill's talkative vivacity, but agreeable. Given our age, Roberta and I were connoisseurs of parents and, compared with our judgements of other parents, our rating of Mr. Hill was high: I would call him a strict, but genial Puritan. The strictness was fairly severe, even for those days: no drinking and no smoking—and no evidence, e.g. on the breath, of having indulged in either. So when we surreptitiously went out to a pub, we took care to eat some Sen-Sen[1] before returning to dinner, where, as Roberta recalls, 'Christopher's innocence was beautiful'.

From York we went with Mrs. Hill to a cottage in the Lake Country. Here we climbed hills and enjoyed the sun and rain. I think it was also here that I learned of Christopher's love of Wordsworth, especially *The Excursion*. This surprised me. I had never suspected a romantic streak in the sardonic Hill.

After I got back to the States, we corresponded for a while. Then came the Moscow Trials and in some perturbation I wrote Christopher asking what it was all about. I did not receive a reply and we did not get in touch again until the War.

In September 1936 Christopher Hill became a Lecturer in History at Cardiff. One of his colleagues there was GWENDOLYN B. WHALE, *Lecturer, and afterwards Senior Lecturer, in History from 1925 to 1958.*

Hill's formal appointment was made in mid-June 1936; but the matter had really been settled earlier, when Principal J. F.

---

[1] A liquorice-flavoured sweet.

Rees and Professor William Rees (Head of the Department of History) paid a visit to him at Oxford. Professor Powicke recommended him as an extremely able man, for whom a spell at a provincial university would have a mellowing effect. He was appointed for two years, and the tacit assumption was that he would then be returning to Oxford. J. F. Rees was extremely keen to get a Fellow of All Souls on the staff of the College. He himself had been at Lincoln College well before the first war, and still saw Oxford in pre-1914 terms. He probably had no idea that a Fellow of All Souls could be sympathetic to post-1917 Russia.

Some of his colleagues did not take immediately to the self-assurance of this young man from Balliol and All Souls. But many of us began very soon to develop a lasting affection for him. The normal relationship between students and staff was a distant one. Christopher's more intimate Oxford manner was appreciated by his students, especially by the best of them. He got to know them well, and impressed his colleagues at departmental meetings by his ability to report succinctly and perceptively on the qualities and attainments of his pupils. He said later how much he had appreciated their pleasant and unsophisticated manner, and how grateful he was that they had helped him to find his feet. Balliol men on his return proved a bit of a trial.

The appointment was in post-medieval constitutional and political history, with special reference to the seventeenth century. In his lectures on the Reformation to first-year students he seems to have made it clear that he rejected belief in revealed religion. 'Does he believe in God?' was a question floating around this elementary class. Some of us assumed that he was reacting against a strong religious background. But what impressed me was his deep and deepening knowledge of the sermons and theological writings of the Puritans. It was only a few weeks ago that I learnt from Ivan Roots of Hill's Lothian Prize essay in 1932 on Jansenism. At once I seemed to perceive a continuous and almost personal concern for the Protestant type of religious thought running through his work. He chose the Puritan Revolution as his main field of teaching at Cardiff: the social, economic, and intellectual dimensions of the conflict seemed to provide the perfect blend of interests.

He was known to have left-wing ideas, but was careful not to upset anyone in the College. He lived in digs on a housing estate in north Cardiff with the Awberrys, a family closely connected with the Communist Party; but the extent of his commitment to communism was not common knowledge. He addressed meetings of the Left Book Club; and he devoted a lot of time to work for the Basque children who had come to Cardiff as refugees from the Spanish Civil War. When, after his return to Balliol, the appearance of *The English Revolution, 1640* revealed how much of a doctrinaire Marxist he was, some of his former Cardiff colleagues were shocked, and even pressed hard to know whether information about this had been concealed when he was appointed. The Principal himself was certainly upset, but the warmth he felt for Christopher was not dissipated by the incident.

In spite of his friendliness and accessibility, there was a feeling that there was a withdrawn and deeply secret Christopher—perhaps more so then than later. But after forty years the impact he made and his intellectual power are still remembered.

In September 1938 Hill returned to Balliol as Fellow and Tutor in Modern History. RODNEY HILTON, *later Professor of Medieval Social History in the University of Birmingham, had just graduated and was beginning research.*

I became aware of Christopher Hill (not indeed under that name) by reading an article entitled 'The 250th Anniversary of the "Glorious" Revolution of 1688' in the *Communist International*, vol. xvi (November 1938). The name given to the author was C. E. Gore, for already in those days it was prudent for someone in the early stages of a career as a university teacher not to blazon attachment to a political organization still considered to be revolutionary. The article was attractive to a young student of history who was also immersed in an early reading of Marx, Engels, and their followers, because it was incisive, witty, densely packed with suggestive lines of thought, obviously based on considerable erudition, and refreshingly free from jargon. And this was to be Christopher Hill's style, as we can see from his essay in the tercentenary volume, *The English Revolution, 1640*, onwards through an ever-increasing flow of fine interpretative works devoted to many of the themes of the 1938 essay, especially the irony of the fate of petty bourgeois radicalism within a revolution made in the interests of a great bourgeoisie of landed property, finance, and commerce. In those days a Marxist intellectual could not fail to be involved in politics and the almost inescapable choice in the late 1930s was the Communist Party. As an obscure activist in that Party, I first met that older and already prestigious activist, Christopher Hill, some time after he had moved back to Balliol in 1938.

I suppose that, although younger than Christopher, I had had some experiences similar to his. Both of us were from the North, (he from Yorkshire, I from Lancashire) and neither was a product of those exclusive public schools whose pupils were then very much in evidence in Oxford. The Communist Party group in Balliol in those days, as I remember it, had a social composition not at all like some writers' reconstruction of the Communist intelligentsia of the late thirties as coming characteristically from upper-middle-class backgrounds. Our members were predominantly from grammar schools and from lower-middle-class families, even with working-class ancestors one or two generations back. I think that many had a strong Nonconformist upbringing, or (as in my case) deliberately irreligious, though with all the cultural attributes of Nonconformity. In fact it was not difficult for people with this sort of background to become Communists.

Christopher was regarded with some awe in our circle. He had held a fellowship at All Souls, naïvely considered by some of us (in spite of its Munichois connections) to be a genuine centre of intellectual, even if bourgeois, excellence. Moreover he had, at the same time, committed himself in an entirely different direction by spending a year in study in Moscow. Before going there he had been interested in Port Royal and Jansenism, but the time in Moscow would no doubt have confirmed his shift in the direction of English Puritanism, studied in the context of the growth of a capitalist agrarian economy. Marx had already given the lead (e.g. in the final section of *Capital* i) by emphasizing the importance of shifts in the English economy between the fifteenth and eighteenth centuries as a preparation for the development of industrial capitalism. Moreover Russian agrarian historians from Vinogradoff to Kosminsky and his pupils had long been interested in English agrarian history. One of Christopher's earliest post-war historical writings was to be a short article summarizing a study of the Manor of Barrow-on-Humber made by the Soviet historian V. M. Lavrovsky, on the basis of notes of Alexander Savine. It would be difficult to imagine two more contrasting places than All Souls and Moscow in the 1930s, and these experiences may have developed that sense of irony in life and history to which I have already referred. It could not but have been intensified by the contradictory commitments which Communists experienced between Munich and the invasion of the Soviet Union by Hitler.

The war scattered everybody, though in Oxford call-up was sometimes delayed for a few months, which allowed some meetings, including contacts with German and Czech Communists in exile. Eventually Christopher's knowledge of Russian and of the Soviet Union was used officially. He went from the army to the Foreign Office where, under another pseudonym (K. E. Holme), but now under highly respectable auspices, he produced a booklet on England and the Soviet Union entitled *The Two Commonwealths*, another occasion no doubt for private ironical reflection. By that time, however, a thousand miles of distance had ended my contact with him. This was renewed in 1946, the beginning of a period of some difficulty for Marxist intellectuals. The Communist Party had expanded during the war and had held many of its recruits from the intelligentsia. With the development of the Cold War in the late 1940s, not to speak of the irrationalities of the Stalin regime, some not only left the party but rather easily discarded what was only a superficial employment of Marxist concepts in their intellectual work.

However, it would be quite wrong to present the decade before 1956 as one of either siege mentality or disorientation among English Marxist historians, among whom Christopher was an outstanding figure. It was the period during which an active group of Communist historians took part (whatever their period or subject specialization) in practical and theoretical discussions on a wide range of issues, from the relation between ancient slavery and commodity production to the complexities of the political and social genesis of the working class. As one would expect in the Marxist perspective of English history, the meaning of the bourgeois revolution was considered crucial. Was it a bourgeois revolution or the defeat of a counter-revolution? Had the bourgeoisie not become masters of the economy and the state a century earlier? There were some excellent and persuasive papers presented which argued the latter case, but those who regarded the English Civil War of the mid-seventeenth century as a bourgeois revolution won general conviction by their arguments. It was Christopher Hill who inspired the debate. The mastery of the historical evidence and the ability to conceptualize, whilst seeming to remain within the British empirical tradition, which has been characteristic of his work, was already evident. It must be said that the conclusions that were reached were the outcome of a genuinely free debate, as one would expect when the tone and the high scholarly level were set by Christopher Hill. It should also be said, in fairness, that in the period of the intellectual bludgeoning in the international Communist movement, associated with the name of Zhdanov in the Soviet Union, the political leadership of the CPGB, at any rate as far as the historians were concerned, made no attempts to impose ideological purity and at one meeting (through John Gollan) stated this as conscious policy.

I have heard it said that the great period of Christopher Hill's fruitful historical work began only with his departure from the Communist Party, as if this were a demonstrable effect of an obvious cause. Who can answer this but Christopher himself? I, however, do not believe it. The historians' discussions to which I have referred were not made to order, but emerged spontaneously and were a great stimulus to research. Nor was political activity forced, but entered into voluntarily. As far as Christopher is concerned, continuous political activity went on until the Party Congress of 1957, when he battled on for the democratization of the Party.

He had shared the hopes and the consequent disillusion of many English Communists, resulting from the apparent renunciation of Stalinism by Krushchev at the twentieth Congress of the CPSU, followed swiftly by military intervention against the attempts at Communist democracy in Hungary. There was enormous disgust at the official repudiation of the on-the-spot reporting (favourable to the Hungarian anti-Stalinists) by the *Daily Worker* correspondent, Peter Fryer. Anger and disappointment were directed not only against the Soviet action but also against the British Party bureaucracy, which at that time seemed incapable of the independent political judgement which, to some extent, it later showed when the Soviet Union again imposed its will by military means on Communist democracy in Czechoslovakia. Consequently it was for inner-party democracy that Christopher Hill was fighting at the 1957 Congress, some considerable time after many intellectuals had left. That battle was lost and he left the Communist Party after nearly a quarter of a century's membership. The stand he took was of course the only one that the historian of the Levellers and the Diggers could have made, but that stand and the works that were to come had already been well prepared.

One of Hill's first pupils after the war was HUGH STRETTON, *who graduated in 1948 and immediately became a Fellow of the College. He returned to Australia in 1954 as Professor of History at Adelaide.*

I love and admire Christopher Hill and am glad that this book praises him as well as laying scholarly tribute at his feet. But we who write the praise have to be forgiven a good deal of bad taste. It is rude to print obituaries of the living, but we are not allowed to stick to safe formalities. We are supposed to write about the man in a personal, penetrating way, i.e. to write things which it would be thought ill-bred to say in his presence. The task is specially hard for a foreigner who cannot have his more embarrassing thoughts uttered for him, as educated Englishmen can, by an impersonal Chinese accomplice named Wun. Another incapacity is shared by us all. As professional academics we have to write many references, without realizing quite how habit-forming that duty is. Will Dr. Hill prefer to be done in the style which recommends a student for a scholarship, a professor for a vice-chancellorship, or a back-slider for a second chance? Reference-writers know that praise is apt to be discounted if it is not salted with criticism, so an experienced wisdom distinguishes the Confidential Assessment from the Open Testimonial as quite different art-forms. Festschrifts unwisely ask for both at once. Perhaps—like the critics of motor cars who always abuse the ash-trays—we should mention the candidate's harsh wit or excessive generosity but draw a veil if he happens to have raped the help or robbed the till. Anyway, pity us—Christopher certainly will. And however we tarnish our reputations they will be well spent in paying tribute to his.

In 1948 an African student who knew only the English history he had learned at Balliol wrote a mock schools paper on English History from A.D. 285 to modern times. From his script his examiners discovered how simple the pattern of the English past had really been. After the Romans left, there were a thousand years of orderly economic growth and spiritual self-discovery, with most innovation in both fields coming from the public sector. Then for two hundred years the nation was bloodied by religious and class war. In the eighteenth century it was reunited by a single-minded pursuit of naval supremacy; but new dissensions set in after 1815 as Westminster joined the Courts of Europe in an orgy of mistresses and secret diplomacy, with much steaming-open of each others' letters.

Arriving in 1946, I had personal as well as intellectual benefit of those diversities. Richard Southern dispensed a bewitching mixture of astringency and kindness. Paul Rolo introduced me (with all relevant protections) to the delights of hitch-hiking, the Dorset coast, and the Rue Pigalle. A. B. Rodger bent his decanal rules very tolerantly to returned soldiers. Christopher Hill seemed to be a man for all seasons, a helpful human without any barriers whatever. All four were marvellously accessible. To pupils wanting their time or company they never appeared too busy, bored, important, or condescending. From affectionate interest as well as duty the college did seem to exist for its undergraduates, as its rhetoric alleged.

Maurice Keen writes below about Christopher as tutor. I am as grateful as he is for that teaching, but cannot add anything to his most perceptive description of it. That reserved, attentive prodding and direction-finding seem to have continued as helpfully as ever after the publication of Christopher's first major works. Not all scholars—especially controversial ones— survive success so well. They become committed to published

positions, concerned to defend them, less interested in other
people and other questions, busier travellers and generally less
accessible. Success does not seem to have spoiled Christopher
Hill in any of those ways. But it was still a special pleasure to be
present during the years that produced *Economic Problems of
the Church*.

How it was produced remains mysterious. He had enviable,
unusual, but almost invisible habits of work. In those years of
post-war austerity paper was scarce. It also had to be paid for—
the college was not generous with perquisites. It was more
generous to undergraduates, so examiners used to supply themselves with paper by tearing the unused pages out of the backs
of marked examination books. Christopher then cut his ration
into squares of various small sizes. On some he wrote his letters
in a large illegible scrawl; on others he wrote his working notes
in a very small illegible fly-track. I suppose the money he saved
helped to buy some of the beer he gave us, or the books which
lined his room. The back endpapers of many of those books
were covered from edge to edge with minute, orderly, illegible
references to their contents. His big desk was always bare
except when it carried barrels and glasses for his regular
parties; perhaps its locked drawers were accumulating ever-
increasing stacks of those closely written squares of examination
paper; or perhaps they were piling up at home, where he also
entertained pupils and friends often enough.

He gave endless, good-natured time and company and
pastoral care to scores of us. He also spent plenty of time with
his family and did a lot of washing-up. He tolerated all the mess
his family and visitors made but he never made any of his own.
He somehow defied that comfortable belief which had excused
the self-indulgences of dons like Urquhart: the belief that
academics could attend to pupils, administration, research, or
marriage but never to all four, or even three or two. While he
was spending so much time doing so much for so many of us he
was also managing to learn more than anyone alive about the
seventeenth century. I suppose, perhaps unjustly, that through
those years the American critics who now find the quantity of
his erudition so unbearable were secure in their library carrels
padding their microfilm budgets, earning twice Hill's pay
while teaching half his hours, and avoiding undergraduates as

the central enemies of academic advancement—still happily unaware of the block-busting hostilities in store for them. Besides surviving success he has also survived other ordeals, including some political discrimination, and nearly half a century in the same college. Individuals differ, but many do not want to stay so long in one place and some are not improved by it. Against any cocooning, ingrowing, or pettifogging effects of Oxford life Christopher has doubtless been protected by his wartime experience, his political activities and commitments, and his personal nature and values. But he did want to move at least once during those post-war years when the British compromise with the Cold War tended to mean that universities did not sack Communists, but did not very willingly hire them. He applied for the foundation chair of history at Keele. Its Vice-Chancellor was his old Master Lindsay. Christopher was an affectionate and cynical observer of Lindsay's mixture of high conscience and low cunning, and is still its funniest expositor. Lord Lindsay was moved to announce officially that Mr. Hill had been rejected because he was a Communist: not because there was anything intrinsically wrong with that, but because his appointment might prompt wrong-headed outsiders to make difficulties for an experimental university through its early years. That was not the only injury he suffered for political reasons, at the hands of publishers and others.

Within Balliol Christopher was a political leader with an unusual capacity to act like an equal brother-in-arms. Some radicals are chiefly concerned with political and intellectual position, consistency, posture; others with end-results. Christopher was of the latter, useful, honest sort.

In a college governed by its fellows, policy-making occasioned fluctuating amounts of personal feeling and party organization. There was a sort of Left and a sort of Right, though both were somewhat unstable and frayed at the edges, dividing differently on different issues. On a great many matters there was nevertheless consensus. Except for what the kitchen did to some of the food, everybody agreed on low living and high thinking. The college-as-hotel must pay its way, however uncomfortably. Its rooms were rearranged (cheaply) to sleep 250 where 150 had slept before; only caverns too unhealthy for undergraduates were left as guest rooms. Endowment and academic income must go exclusively to scholarly uses. (Other colleges were suspected of spending endowment on claret, gardening, and central heating.) As much teaching as possible should be done by the Fellows, as little as possible by lecturers or part-timers. Except for a few whose teaching was limited by their university appointments, teaching hours were high, variable, and traded between tutor and tutor with much more generosity (in my experience) than meanness. It was agreed that scholars should be attracted and scholarships awarded with ruthless attention to scholarly promise and nothing else. The college must continue to get most firsts in Mods and Schools.

For party-political dispute there remained chiefly the creation of jobs and the selection of commoners, Fellows, and (when necessary) Masters. There was rarely much disagreement about commoners and Fellows when it came to electing them, but there was plenty at other times as the factions discussed the general principles which ought to apply. Right suspected Left of ideological bias—of applying political tests which should properly have nothing to do with criteria of academic merit. It was also feared that the Left would narrow the education of undergraduates, damage the reputation of the college, and dry up its sources of scholars and funds by under-valuing traditions, sporting and social activities, old members, and fruitful connections with Church, State, City, and Public Schools.

Symmetrically, the Left suspected the Right of reactionary tendencies which would damage much the same good things. In a changing society the college would not prosper by refusing to change. In detail, the Right might grovel to the *wrong* Etonians—oarsmen and old members' nephews, instead of scholars. They might try to equip the college with too many chaplains, classical dons, and other exotics when the need was for more social or natural scientists. In selecting Fellows they might look for conservatives. In selecting scholars they might make too little allowance for unequal advantages of family and schooling.

It tended to be the selection of commoners that prompted the factions' wildest fantasies about each other. The Left suspected that the Right's idea of a decent commoner was an amiable, well-connected public-school dunce, keen on rugger and beagling but usually too drunk for either, likely to pass without effort (or qualifications) into the upper-middle ranks of government or business, to the ultimate detriment of British power, prosperity, and social justice, but sure to turn up to Gaudies and quite likely to donate silver or endow a trophy or two. The Right suspected that the Left's idea of a decent commoner was a bespectacled black beetle from a nameless secondary school who would speak to nobody, swot his solitary constipated way to an indifferent degree, then forget the college the day he left it for a job in local government where his chief effect on the national life would be as a chronic claimant on, and voter for, the National Health. From those positions of principle it was always a pleasure to watch the conservative Dean voting in practice to admit Maltese Marxists, and Christopher Hill voting to admit a dapper, well-connected midshipman chiefly because he said, with a simplicity quite unusual at the time, that the function of the navy was 'to sink the enemy's ships, sir'.

Some issues were intrinsically difficult for the Left. They were against privilege—but they were employed in Oxford. Faced with the usual dilemmas of affluent radicals, hard-liners wanted to reduce Oxford's privileges, while soft-liners wanted to open them to more working-class students, to radicalize more research, to apply the privileged resources to improving equalities in the society around them. Christopher Hill wanted all those things. That was not necessarily inconsistent in principle but there could be tension between particular policies in practice. He was a tough, responsible thinker about those dilemmas. However big or little the issues, his view of them was always thought-out and high-principled. If it is appropriate to criticize some ashtrays he may sometimes have been less charitable to opponents' motives than their misguided sincerities really deserved. But not often. He tended to divide opponents into three classes, with full respect or affection for the first two. There were natural conservatives, born and bred. There were very decent idiots, including some scientists and many professors. And there were a few spineless, morally disgusting Hamlets—usually unpolitical self-seekers, or Left deviants who should have known better.

I doubt if he felt the need for such holy conscience or such unholy tactics as he sometimes ascribed to Lord Lindsay, though he admitted to learning a good deal from the old

Master. When he had decided what was right and how much
of it was practicable, his own methods were more straight-
forward: talk with people, use persuasions appropriate to their
concerns, look for bases of agreement; accumulate the numbers,
keep them herded, get them there on the day; see to the wording of motions and order of agenda; don't be secret or treacher-
ous or too clever; with an eye to the long term, be consistent and
dependable. Altogether he was an able, courteous, combative
politician in a time-honoured way and I don't think he lost any
friends by it, however his colleagues might disagree about his
principles and programmes.

In another area it was harder to avoid personal hostilities.
Those years saw the gradual crumbling of a particular code of
sexual behaviour. Crudely speaking, academics could do what
they liked across or outside the bonds of marriage as long as they
kept it out of the courts, the newspapers, and the official notice
of academic authorities—but for breaking those latter rules
people could still be barred from fellowships or (more rarely)
sacked from them. During and after the war Balliol had half a
dozen disputed cases. One Fellow resigned, one was dismissed,
one tutor's election to a fellowship was delayed, another's was
barred, and one fellowship was allowed to lapse for long enough
to see whether the newspapers would notice that its occupant
had appeared in somebody else's divorce case. The offenders
came from all political and religious parties, but with some
individual exceptions the Right voted to enforce the old code
and the Left voted against it. Left offenders whom the Right
had tried to bar or sack would vote, generously in the circumstances, to defend the jobs and liberties of the Right offenders
who had tried to sack them. Christopher was a consistent and
generous leader of the Left on those issues. In private, unpolitical ways he was also on occasion a powerful friend to
people in that sort of trouble.

Altogether he was the puritan that cavaliers always under-
estimate: loving and loved, witty, funny, perceptive, delighting
in life and genuinely fond of an extraordinary variety of its
human representatives. Too many of these pages have been
about his policy-making activities. Able, disinterested academic
politicians are not too hard to find. It was a rarer experience,
for which I remain most deeply and affectionately grateful after

a quarter of a century, to know such a scholar and teacher and such a constant, engaging, effective comrade-in-arms.

Another of Christopher Hill's pupils who became a Fellow of Balliol was MAURICE KEEN.

The first thing that I remember registering about Christopher Hill when I came up in 1954 (I was not yet his pupil, since I only changed to history later) was that he possessed a bright red tie. It was the only outward and visible sign of what one knew in advance that he was, a loyalist of the Communist Party. One had also been told that he was probably the most distinguished Marxist in Oxford. A figure of controversy he was then, and will I imagine always remain: and I think maybe he still is the most distinguished Marxist in an Oxford where there is a good deal more competition for the title than there was in the mid-fifties. And here I must make it clear that for just that reason I face a difficulty in offering my contribution to his *laudes*. On almost every really significant matter where there is room for controversy, religion, politics, social *mores*, and moral values—on all the sorts of matters that seem to demand capital letters to match an importance that one would like to laugh away but cannot—Christopher holds and affirms views that make him and myself opposed people. This, as I say, makes it particularly hard for me to write about him, in a way that will do him justice. But perhaps it also gives a measure of him, that he can command and always has commanded not only respect but real affection too among people between whose views and his there can be no question of reconciliation.

I first came to know Christopher properly when I was taught by him: later I was to know him as the senior history tutor in Balliol when I was the junior one, and then as a fellow when he was Master. I do not think that it was in tutorials that his influence came across most sharply. If one said something very Royalist in an essay on the English Civil War he might suddenly become animated: more often he seemed laconic, rather withdrawn, curled in his big, curiously shaped armchair on the other side of the room. As a teacher his gift seemed rather to be knowing how to send people to the subject and the book that would make the past come alive to them. His reading lists were not very long, but they always appeared to take one pretty directly to something that would not fail to strike one as significant. In time one came to realize that what one was being encouraged to look for were new ways of looking at things: one was being made aware of history as a subject on the move where everything was open to reassessment if one could meet the standards required for that exercise. I suspect that is something that has been even more apparent to Christopher's research students, of whom I was never one, who have been so many and so distinguished.

There was another side to Christopher as a tutor, of course, and one which even more will remember. On Monday evenings he was at home to all historians. No one had to answer the invitation: we simply knew that Christopher and Bridget, a barrel of beer, and a large number of people would be there in his college room. It was a superb way of making sure that one met the people who were reading history in the years senior or junior to one, and for a good many, I suspect, of making sure simply that one met people. And it also made sure that one did not think of this tutor at any rate as someone on the other side of a barrier of status. No other tutor in my time, then or since, has ever done anything like it: the nearest parallel I can think of is stories from an older Balliol generation of Cyril Bailey and Urquhart keeping open house to undergraduates; but that was in a different age and offered, unless I am gravely mistaken, an atmosphere to breathe that tasted different from the air of Christopher's parties. Those parties, I am sure, are one main reason why he has been the lifelong guide and counsellor of so many people who were never seventeenth-century specialists (or Marxists for that matter): the people one remembers and has been surprised to see on an S.C.R. sofa with the Master, taking coffee early and in deep discussion. One thing about those parties has always puzzled me, though. If one took a pint glass before one's third year one would be chided. I have never understood why so committed an egalitarian as Christopher should have given the impression of caring about such a curious status symbol. It was nothing to do with a ration of quantity: one might refill a half-pint glass as often as one wished, and many of us wished rather often.

As a colleague, when he was the senior history tutor in the

college, one saw Christopher at his very best. One came to be aware of the infinite trouble that he was prepared to take for people in difficulties or with a problem: of his ability to stand apart, when dealing with people, from all his own prejudices; and of his immense fund of practical wisdom. In a senior common room which was not exactly welcoming to the young newcomer he was noticeably more approachable than most of the senior fellows—and not just for a young historian, either; a fact that, I suspect, had more than something to do with his becoming in due course the Master. One knew Christopher then as someone who, whether in College meeting, or when one was examining candidates for entrance, or when this or that problem arose in the faculty, seemed always to be completely independent, firm, and fair. It was a time when there were a lot of nicknames being coined. To the historians, senior and junior, he was 'Super God', and to most of them and us that was just about what he seemed to be.

I remember going to see Christopher to tell him that I very much hoped he would stand for the Mastership. 'But you do realise, Maurice', he said at the end, 'that if I was elected I'd want to do a whole lot of things that you would absolutely hate.' Of course it was much truer than I realized then, or when I voted for him. The years that have followed have revealed, to me at least, facets of Christopher that I did not see when he was my more immediate 'boss'; above all, the politician with a lot of know-how when it has come to management, ruthless in making sure that his man or matter carried the day if it could be done within the rules. This cannot be the place to write about that side of things, but one thing there is that must be said. Very few of those who elected Christopher to be Master in February 1965 can have foreseen 1968, the year of student revolution. That year and what has happened since then have made sure that the headship of an Oxbridge College must carry with it strain, difficulty, and immersion in controversy. For Christopher Hill the problems must have been much harder than for almost anyone else. On the one hand his deep-seated views, feelings, and loyalties must have drawn him strongly toward the radical side, graduate and undergraduate: on the other the office of Master in itself has put him in the 'establishment' that radicals would wish to undo: and he has had a college and a governing body to preside over in which every shade of opinion, to right or left, has had passionate and engaged partisans. His part has been one that could not be played without becoming involved in uncomfortable debate, or without incurring harsh criticism from one quarter or another. To have carried the office of Master amid these difficulties and to have remained at the same time a scholar as productive and as unquestionably distinguished as he has been is an outstanding achievement.

There can be no point in trying to make a judicious assessment of Christopher's Mastership: it will be some years before it will be possible to see that in perspective. But certain things which have been obviously good about it I feel I must be allowed to mention. Certainly the Senior Common Room of his College has come to be a more friendly and welcoming place than I remember it fifteen years or so back, and that this is so has much to do with the Master. Through Christopher's time undergraduates at Balliol have seen more of the inside of the Master's lodgings than they would have done at—let me say for the sake of caution—most Oxford colleges. The fears expressed at the time of his election, that he would neglect old ties and that the close relations between old members and the contemporary College would become looser, have proved quite false. No doubt the reason for that is that if Christopher Hill is a revolutionary he is one who has a lot of understanding of tradition and has long known how to make room for it where he thinks appropriate. If this had not been so, and if he had been less strikingly innocent than he is of any penchant for the fashionable gimmickry that often goes along with radicalism, he would have been a much less good Master.

When Balliol College's chroniclers come to cast up his account, they will not be surprised to find suggestions that traditionalists like myself often found things to grumble about when he was Master. But they may well conclude that this was not a very comfortable time for traditionalists anywhere in Oxford. It was a time when they were to be found grumbling generally, whichever their College and whoever its head. Certainly no one will be able to lay at Christopher's door any diminished regard for certain traditional values, for serious purposes in higher education, and for the highest academic standards. I doubt if they will be able to pad out their work with droll anecdotes about the Master, for Christopher will not, I think, prove to have been the kind of College head about whom such stories multiply. But they will find memories of a Master who was unusually accessible and who was held in affectionate regard in every part of the College community. They will sense that he was not only a great scholar but also a man big enough for the difficult office to which his colleagues elected him. Bridget Hill will also leave vivid memories behind her in Balliol and I wish that I had the pen to say more of the part that she has played both in the success of Christopher's Mastership and in her own right, since I do not trust those future chroniclers to do it adequately. But I could not do justice to Christopher's and Bridget's quite special combination of interdependence and independence or to what it has added to both of them, and to Balliol in their time. I know though that when they have left Balliol I for one will feel a lot of nostalgia for their *ancien régime*—of which I am sure Christopher would heartily disapprove.

Unbelief in Seventeenth-Century England

G. E. AYLMER

'Sensible men are all of the same religion.' 'And pray,
what is that?' inquired the Prince. 'Sensible men
never tell.' (Benjamin Disraeli, *Endymion*, bk. i, ch. 81.)

How can he [the priest or minister] tell . . . what im-
pious atheisticall thoughts I may have about me when
I am approaching to the very table? (John Selden,
Table-Talk, s.v. 'Sacrament'.)

TRACKING down unbelievers has long been a pastime among
historians of sixteenth- and seventeenth-century England. And
few practitioners have shown more skill or persistence in this
than Christopher Hill. But were there in fact any atheists, and
how are we to set about establishing this?

From the 1580s onwards, there were numerous attacks on
atheism and on alleged, but normally unnamed unbelievers.
Indeed until the time of Hobbes and Spinoza (the 1650s or
1660s) they are seldom if ever identified. Even in the late
seventeenth and early eighteenth centuries, when there were
certainly a few avowed deists, those who explicitly denied the
existence of God are hard to find. Of course, openly expressed
disbelief in Christianity carried heavy penalties, in theory the
severest until the later seventeenth century; and the punishments remained severe, at least in theory, even after the repeal
of *De Haeretico Comburendo* in 1677 and the replacement of the
censorship by a new Blasphemy Act in the 1690s. Apart from
Christopher Marlowe, for whom the evidence appears fairly
strong, and perhaps Robert Greene, it is very hard to pin down

* I am extremely grateful to Messrs. Conrad Russell, Quentin Skinner, and
Keith Thomas for having read an earlier draft of this essay, and for having made
many helpful criticisms and suggestions. They are in no way responsible for such
errors and misjudgements as remain.

a single Elizabethan unbeliever—as opposed to numerous popular scoffers and blasphemers, and various types of religious deviant.[1] In the seventeenth century both Lord Herbert of Cherbury and Hobbes himself claimed to be Christians. Unless we include Socinians (or Unitarians) as deists, even if 'Christian' ones, there are no undisputed English deists until the 1680s–1720s, with Blount, Toland, Gildon, Collins, Woolston, and Tindal.[2] Yet before the end of their careers, we are well into the lifetime of the greatest of all pre-twentieth-century British sceptics, from whose devastating blows the intellectual basis of religious belief has never fully recovered; David Hume's earlier religious writings were published between 1748 and 1757, and his last—posthumously—in 1779.[3]

Were the divines and others who wrote in such detail and with such dedication to refute atheism from the time of Elizabeth I to that of Charles II doing so in response to avowed and vocal unbelievers, or to an assumed but silent body of such people, or merely to persuade themselves and their fellow-Christians that the case for the truth of their religion was irrefutable? If the first explanation is correct, why are no authentic unbelievers, or at least so very, very few, identifiable? If the second, did such mute unbelievers exist? If the third,[4] why was this all necessary, and what does it tell us about

[1] On Marlowe, I am persuaded by F. Brie, 'Deismus und Atheismus in der englischen Renaissance', *Anglia: Zeitschrift für englische Philologie*, new ser. 36 (1924), 54–98, 105–68; and P. H. Kocher, *Christopher Marlowe: A Study of his Thought, Learning, and Character* (Chapel Hill, 1946). On Ralegh, however, I have followed P. Lefranc, *Sir Walter Ralegh, Écrivain: L'œuvre et les idées* (Paris, 1968), in seeing him more as an intermittent patron of heterodox ideas than as an unbeliever himself, despite the eloquence of E. A. Strathmann, *Sir Walter Ralegh: A Study in Elizabethan Skepticism* (N.Y., 1951).

[2] See Edward Lord Herbert of Cherbury, *De Veritate*, transl. and introd. M. H. Carré (Bristol, 1937); *Lord Herbert of Cherbury's De Religio Laici*, ed. and trans. H. R. Hutchinson (New Haven, 1944). On Hobbes the literature is vast, but see particularly for a sane approach S. I. Mintz, *The Hunting of Leviathan: Seventeenth-Century Reactions to the Materialism and Moral Philosophy of Thomas Hobbes* (Cambridge, 1962) and Q. Skinner, review art. in *HJ* vii (1964), 321–33. For other authors see *DNB* and works cited below. David Berman, 'Anthony Collins and the Question of Atheism in the Early Part of the Eighteenth Century', *Proceedings of the Royal Irish Academy*, vol. 75, Section C, No. 5 (Dublin, 1975), 85–102, argues persuasively against James O'Higgins, *Anthony Collins, the man and his works* (The Hague, 1970), that Collins was in fact an atheist, not a deist.

[3] For a convenient selection, see *Hume on Religion*, ed. R. Wollheim (1963).

[4] For the most cogent expression of this view, see D. C. Allen, *Doubt's Boundless Sea: Skepticism and Faith in the Renaissance* (Baltimore, 1964).

religion in England at that time? One obvious difficulty is that
'atheism' and 'atheist' were constantly used as terms of abuse,
to be hurled against religious opponents, by Protestants and
Catholics alike. Moreover deviation from theological orthodoxy, notably in the directions of either unitarianism or
pantheism, could likewise often lead to accusations of 'atheism'.
Clearly, if these were the sole meanings attached to the words,
no more would need to be said about actual, substantive
unbelief. But such was by no means the case. To give one
example, in December 1591 the antiquarian William Lambarde
wrote to his friend Sir William Leveson about the choice of
suitable militia commissioners for the county of Kent:

> For, as touching religion, they ought to be, not only no papistes, but
> no Libertines, or Atheists, whoe are (next to the papistes) the most
> daungerous; by cause as the Romanistes desyre a chaunge, so theise
> Epicureans care not for the present estate, persuading theimselves
> that by that even hand which they beare, all mutations (I meane
> touching religion) will beare with theim.[1]

Despite the widespread tendency, which indeed appears later in
this same letter, to equate one's religious enemies with unbelievers, Lambarde's concern is suggestive—at least of what
some intelligent and informed contemporaries believed to be
the case, whether or not it was so.

On the Continent as in England, there was controversy as to
which was worse: no religion, or the wrong one. Whereas
Francis Bacon, in his essay, 'Of Superstition', seems to argue
that totally mistaken and perverted beliefs may indeed be
worse than none—in that atheism 'makes men weary of themselves', whereas 'Superstition hath been the confusion of many
States'—the commoner view was that expressed in the title of
Nicholas Breton's character-sketch 'An Atheist, or Most Bad
Man'.[2] And even so heterodox and suspect a work as Jean
Bodin's *Heptaplomeres* (which was not published until the
nineteenth century) condemned atheism as worse than super-

---

[1] Staffs. RO, MS. D. 593/s/4/14/16, Leveson Correspondence. I am grateful to
the County Archivist for supplying me with a copy of this letter, which is indexed
by the National Register of Archives.

[2] Bacon, *Essays* (1612 edn.), no. xvii, 'Of Superstition'; Breton, *The Good and
the Badde* (1616), quoted in D. Stauffer, *English Biography before 1700* (Cambridge,
Mass., 1930), 270.

stition, or pagan beliefs, and excluded atheists from the scope of religious toleration on the grounds of complete unbelievers having no respect for the law.[1] There were some, however, who argued for toleration of religious enemies precisely on the grounds that excessive persecution might drive some men to desperation, and so to unbelief. The opposite view, dominant in the sixteenth century, and still widely held in the seventeenth, was that toleration of a diversity of opinions and beliefs would, or might, lead to atheism. And even on the anti-persecution side of the argument, a recent authority on *Toleration and the Reformation* finds only the Dutchman Dirk Coornhert (1522–90) and the Englishman (and New Englander) Roger Williams (1604–83) to have been in favour of extending toleration to unbelievers.[2] To put the problem in another way, we might look for three main types of atheist or unbeliever:

1. the popular scoffer and blasphemer, of whom Keith Thomas and Christopher Hill himself have cited several instances.[3] Anti-clericalism and anti-sacramentalism would seem to have been the commonest mainsprings for such impulses. But what proportion of them were detected and brought to justice, either in the church courts or elsewhere, and what was the nature of their 'unbelief'? The very fact that even in this century G. K. Chesterton could, however misguidedly, describe Thomas Hardy as 'a sort of village atheist, brooding and blaspheming over the village idiot',[4] tells us something about the presumed traditions of English rural life.

2. the unquestionably rare but genuine philosophic doubter, unbeliever, or materialist who even dared to convey his sentiments to others in however disguised a manner. And here it would be necessary to distinguish between those who disbelieved in Christianity and those who rejected God altogether: a line seldom drawn by contemporaries before the late

[1] J. Lecler, *Toleration and the Reformation*, ii, trans. T. L. Westow (1960), bk. vi, 178–84.

[2] Ibid. 48, 52–3, 82, 106, 137, 169; and for Coornhert and Williams, bk. vii, 285, bk. viii, 471, 486. Lecler's testimony is particularly impressive on this score in that his magisterial survey was published with the imprimatur of the Roman Catholic Church.

[3] K. Thomas, *Religion and the Decline of Magic* (1971): see index entries 'Atheism' and 'Religious Scepticism'; C. Hill, *The World Turned Upside Down* (1972) and his *Irreligion in the 'Puritan' Revolution* (Barnett Shine Foundation Lecture, 1974).

[4] *The Victorian Age in Literature* (1913), ch. 2.

seventeenth century, save with reference to Jews, Mahometans, and Pagans. As we shall see, subsequent acceptance of the terms 'Deist' and 'Deism', if it complicated the contemporary debate, may serve to simplify our search for total unbelievers. On the Continent, as in England, well-authenticated individual instances and even quite widespread popular scoffing—or 'peasant materialism'—do not really constitute evidence of a general trend, or demonstrate the extent of intellectual unbelief. This remains true despite the terms of the debate being in part common to much of Catholic as well as Protestant Europe.[1]

3. the silent sceptic or cynic, who doubted or disbelieved but kept quiet. It is tempting to ascribe this position to such outward conformists as Hobbes, Charles II (until his death-bed), the first Marquis of Halifax, and others. But this description fits scarcely anyone before the 1650s, unless *politiques* such as Elizabeth I or Henri IV are to be included. Moreover the terms 'sceptic' and 'scepticism' must be used with particular care. For there was also a very strong current of specifically Christian scepticism prevalent in the sixteenth and seventeenth centuries, whose adherents combined extreme disbelief about our knowledge of the external world through the evidence of the senses or through our own mental processes with a complete acceptance of Faith, that is of religious doctrine, received through Revelation as mediated either via the Church (for Catholics) or through Scripture (for Protestants). This radical empiricism and 'fideism' can be seen, with varying degrees of emphasis, in Montaigne, Charron, La Mothe Le Vayer, and their English disciples who may be said to have included Dryden and Berkeley.[2] Even Descartes may be placed in this tradition.

[1] See M. Dommanget, *Le Curé Meslier, athée, communiste et révolutionnaire sous Louis XIV* (Paris, 1965); *Mathias Knutzen: ein deutscher Atheist und revolutionärer Demokrat des 17 Jahrhunderts*, ed. W. Pfoh (Berlin, 1965); C. Ginzburg, *Il Formaggio e i vermi: il Cosmo di un mugnaio del '500* (Turin, 1976; knowledge of which I owe to the review by P. Burke in *TLS* 9 July 1976), 844. I cannot accept what appears to be the argument of L. Febvre's *Le Problème de l'incroyance au xvie siècle, La Religion de Rabelais* (Paris, 1942), namely that true unbelief was not possible in the pre-scientific mental world of the sixteenth century. This is not necessarily to deny that the creator of Gargantua and Pantagruel was a good Christian, if an unusual one.

[2] The secondary literature is extensive. See L. I. Bredvold, *The Intellectual Milieu of John Dryden* (Ann Arbor, 1934); M. L. Wiley, *The Subtle Knot: Creative Scepticism in 17th Century England* (1952). Bredvold is both amplified and in some respects

While Thomist-trained Catholics and Augustinian-Calvinist Protestants might well disapprove of sceptical fideism because it discarded one of the two great weapons of Christian apologetics (that is, Reason, as opposed to Revelation), it seems unlikely that they would genuinely have confused a fideist with an unbeliever. Yet we must never forget that the seventeenth century was innocent of the name 'agnostic' and the very concept of agnosticism.[1]

Some anti-atheist Christian apologists certainly did distinguish between the second and third types, between 'speculative' atheists who did not believe in the existence of God, and 'practical' or 'careless' ones, who behaved as if they did not—or rather as if they disbelieved in an after-life. Only the very hardest cases, perhaps Christopher Marlowe, combined the attributes of both. One at least among the anti-atheistical writers of the century, Martin Fotherby (?1549–1620), Dean of Canterbury and finally Bishop of Salisbury, does indeed explain his motives. Part of his argument is that very few people, either in the past or in his own time, have been unbelievers in the positive sense.

But then . . . To what end, this whole worke serveth, which is written against Atheists, if they be few, or none such? . . . Yet there be very many, that beleeue it weakely: and, that being overcome by sodaine passions and temptations, do oftentimes doubt, and distrust; whether there be any God? . . . And few men can escape the very same temptations. Therefore, of this sort of Atheists, there is as great a plenty, as of the first sort, a scarcity. Nay, there is almost no man, but at some time or other, he falleth within the compasse of this doubting.

None the less, in his Preface to the Reader, Fotherby emphasized that his primary purpose was to convince unbelievers rather than to confirm believers.[2]

corrected by P. Harth in his *Contexts of Dryden's Thought* (Chicago, 1968), but on the other side see W. Empson, 'A Deist Tract by Dryden', *Essays in Criticism*, 25 (1975), 74–100, the tract in question being published in 1693 but first ascribed to the poet in 1745. For France see A. M. Boase, *The Fortunes of Montaigne: A History of the Essays in France, 1580–1669* (1935); R. Pintard, *Le Libertinage érudit dans la première moitié du xviie siècle* (Paris, 1943); J. S. Spink, *French Free Thought from Gassendi to Voltaire* (1960); M. Dreano, *La Religion de Montaigne* (Paris, 1969).

[1] Ascribed by *OED* to T. H. Huxley in 1869–70.
[2] Martin Fotherby, *Atheomastix: Clearing foure Truthes, Against Atheists and Infidels* (1622), 106–7 and Preface, sigs. B2–4.

If we turn from such pillars of orthodoxy to the greatest speculative intellect of Jacobean England, even Francis Bacon in his essay 'Of Atheism'[1] assumed that its causes must be extrinsic. These external pre-conditions he named as four: religious divisions (or inter-sectarian conflicts); anti-clericalism (though this may seem likely to be as old as organized institutional religion); profane scoffing (although at a fashionable level this is more often associated with the later than with the early seventeenth century);[2] finally, what he calls learned times with peace and prosperity (the corollary of which would seem to be that it takes a bit of adversity to keep most people religious). The intrinsic causes of unbelief, on the other hand— before they could be more or less openly articulated by Hume and others in the eighteenth century—have to be gleaned from the anti-atheistical writers. It is to their arguments, in support of Christian belief, that we must now turn, in order to assess the supposed grounds for unbelief.

Many arguments for the existence of God go back to the Christian philosophers of the Dark and Middle Ages—from Augustine to Thomas Aquinas—if not indeed to the Ancient Greeks. Except for nuances and shifts of emphasis, it is doubtful whether much has been added since, and it would be wrong to look for originality in English writers of the sixteenth to eighteenth centuries, save in so far as they were responding to changing circumstances: the scientific revolution and the new philosophy which accompanied it. Most of the standard arguments for the existence of God are to be found in most of the works to be discussed, though not all are present in all of them. These include:

1. the argument from beginnings, origins, causes, and ends;
2. the argument from the design of the universe and its contents, and from purpose or function;
3. the argument from morality, both from the existence, and for the preservation, of moral principles;
4. the argument from general human instinct, from what we may call 'common fame', or general consensus.

Some of these may be more vulnerable than others; as Locke

---

[1] Essay no. xvi of the 1612 edn., 'Of Atheisme'.
[2] See J. Redwood, *Reason, Ridicule and Religion: The Age of Enlightenment in England 1660–1750* (1976).

was to see a little later, it may be impolitic to ground belief in the existence of God on its being a universal human instinct, for this, unlike nos. 1–3, is potentially falsifiable. But for the Christian this, of course, is not enough; he must in addition demonstrate:

5. the authenticity of divine revelation, as manifest in Scripture and the teachings of the Church;

and here the difficulties begin, not least arising from the differences among different Christian apologists. For the sceptical fideist, no. 5 involves an act of faith, an absolute, unquestioning surrender to God's grace, whereas for the Christian rationalist it is necessary to argue that, if not the entire contents of the Old and New Testaments, at least the Four Gospels and the Acts of the Apostles are well documented and historically verifiable. But even this is not the end of it, because, most notably in the era of the Reformation and Counter-Reformation, some wished to ground the case for this primarily upon the individual believer's reading and understanding of the Bible, while others based it upon the received teaching of the Church—and, if the latter, which was the true church and when? On the other hand the interactions between arguments 1, 2, and 3 produced in a Christian context what has come to be known as 'theodicy', a continuing preoccupation with how to reconcile the omnipotence of God with his mercy and love. The authenticity of Scripture was in turn often supported by the occurrence, at any rate in the era of Christ and his Apostles, of well-authenticated miracles, while the existence of ghosts, spirits, witches, and other manifestations of what we should call 'the supernatural' (including the activities of the Devil) were commonly adduced as supporting evidence. Within theodicy, the seventeenth century saw a definite shifting of ground as to whether or not belief in the literal, physical, and unending torments of Hell was a necessary condition of true belief. As D. P. Walker has convincingly shown, Hell and the Devil gave grudging ground.[1] But this shift of emphasis should be seen in a wider dialectical context: the growing intra-Christian debate between adherents of 'minimalist' and

---

[1] D. P. Walker, *The Decline of Hell: 17th-century Discussions of Eternal Torment* (1964).

'maximalist' positions in defence of religious faith. This led to the denunciation of an Anglican archbishop as a Socinian and the attacks on another prelate as a deist if not worse.[1] Although all such divisions are artificial and arbitrary, the anti-atheistical writers and defenders of Christian belief can be grouped by date in a way which is more than merely convenient. As the denominational demarcation lines took shape out of the rage and havoc of the sixteenth-century religious conflicts, the genre re-emerges in the 1580s. On the Catholic side it appears in the work of the English Jesuit, Robert Parsons, translated somewhat paradoxically by the strongly Calvinist Canon of York, Edmund Bunny,[2] and on the Protestant side— at, it should be said, a far inferior intellectual level—in that of the French Huguenot leader, Philip du Plessis Mornay, the translation here being begun by no less a luminary of the Elizabethan renaissance than Sir Philip Sidney.[3] Among the most popular, though hardly the most cogent, of the works which followed these pathfinders was *Gods Arrow Against Atheists*, by the Calvinist defender of the Church of England, Henry Smith, which went into eleven editions or reprints between 1593 and 1640. 'Silver-tongued' Smith's forte was as a preacher rather than as a writer, at least where logic was involved. We must charitably assume that he did not know when he was weakening his own case by begging the question or by circularity of reasoning:

Another argument I frame thus: that Religion which proceeds undoubtedly from God, is the true Religion: But the Christian Religion proceedeth undoubtedly from God: Ergo, etc. That it proceedeth undoubtedly from God, I prove thus. Either it must proceede from God, or from the Divell, or from men: But it is too holie to proceed either from men or divels, for it overthroweth the workes and kingdome of the one, and forbiddeth the revenging

[1] John Tillotson (1630–94), archbishop 1691; Benjamin Hoadly (1676–1761), bishop successively of Bangor, Hereford, Salisbury, and Winchester, hence the 'Bangorian controversy' of 1717–20.
[2] *The First Booke of the Christian Exercise* . . . (1582); *a booke of Christian Exercise* . . . *Perused* . . . *By Edmund Bunny* (1585); *The Second Part of the Booke of Christian Exercise* (1591); *A Christian Directorie* . . . *corrected by the author* (Louvain, 1598).
[3] Philip of Mornay Lord of Plessie Marlie (*sic*), *A Woorke concerning the trewnesse of the Christian Religion, written in French: Against Atheists, Epicures, Paynims, Iewes, Mahumetists, and other Infidels* (1587). Three more edns. by 1617.

spirit of the other (commaunding men to loue their enemies, to doe good to them that hate them and persecute them) . . .[1]

Perhaps Smith's heart was more in his refutation of Papists, Separatists (under the designation of 'Brownists' and 'Barrowists'), and Mahometans. But, in the context of such feeble apologetics, it is easy to understand how dangerous speculation and heterodoxy could flourish in intellectual circles—and such men as Ralegh, Hariot, Dee, or the 17th Earl of Oxford be accused of atheism. Just as Smith and other apologists for the Church of England saw deviants to Left and Right—Separatists and Anabaptists, and Roman Catholics—along with unbelievers in the serried ranks of Antichrist, so the adherents of Browne, Barrow, and Greenwood reciprocated, denouncing the 'mixed Assemblies' of Anglican parish churches for 'profaneness, ignorance, Atheisme and Machevelisme', whereas a true church should exclude all the profane, that is 'Atheists, men without the knowledge or fear of God, together with the Papists, heretics, and all other infidells'.[2] Again, Bacon's first extrinsic cause of unbelief—religious divisions—is writ so large as to be almost self-evident.

Meanwhile, despite the researches of Thomas, Hill, and others, the extent of 'grass-roots' unbelief, going beyond mere heterodoxy, eccentricity, or blasphemous scoffing, remains obscure. In 1587 Augustine Draper of Leigh in Essex was indicted for disbelief in the immortality of the soul and sentenced to repeated conferences in the parish church with three divines until he was persuaded otherwise; but when we also read that he was further to be persuaded that transubstantiation was false, and that there were lawful ministers (clergy), who could legitimately be salaried, we begin to suspect that Draper, like many presumably of his contemporaries, had simply got muddled and entangled in the conflicts and controversies of his time.[3] Or take the case of John Minet, alias Mynett, lay reader in the parish church of East Drayton, Notts., against whom the

---

[1] Henry Smith, *Gods Arrow* (1604 edn.), 45.

[2] From *An Apologie or Defence of . . . Brownists* (1604) and Henry Barrow, *A Collection of . . . Articles* (n.d.), quoting John Greenwood, who like Barrow was executed in 1593. I owe these citations to E. S. Morgan, *Visible Saints* (N.Y., 1963), 35–6.

[3] W. Hale, *A Series of Precedents and Proceedings in Criminal Causes . . . from . . . 1475 to 1640* (1847), 193–4.

charges—of atheism, sorcery, and brawling in church—at first indeed look circumstantial:

first we present the said John Minet as ane Athiest, hethen, or Infidell who in the contempt of god and of his blessed word, hath openlie and manifestlie reported that ther is no god, no devill, no heaven, no hell, no lyf after this lyf, no iudgment to come, wherof he beinge perswaded as it seameth, he therupon reioyceth in his sinnes and glorieth in his wickednes, sayinge that he cannot rest for covetousnes, that he cannot sleep for deuisinge and Ingageinge with him self how he may ioyne house to house[,] land to land, and how he may deceiue his neighbour.

But Minet's answer suggests that he had spoken in the heat of the moment in a dispute with one of his tenants about a deduction from the rent: 'yet notwithstanding he thinketh that he spoke the wordes . . . yet unadvisedly for the which he asketh god forgeavnes.' Maybe he could hear and smell the faggots crackling about him, for perhaps appropriately he admitted, amongst other 'false and erronius doctrine' that when allowed to read in another chapel, he 'did openlie warne the people to kepe holiday upon midsomer day, and as for bonefires he told them they might vse them or refuse them at ther pleasure'. Minet received the relatively mild sentence of performing (public) penance in three local churches, on pain of forfeiting his bond.[1] Once more we must allow for the role of sheer muddle and misunderstanding in history.[2]

That even an educated layman of the upper class might find the subject a difficult one to handle adequately can be seen in the case of Sir George More of Loseley, M.P. and sheriff, who was to be quite an important office-holder under James I and Charles I, when he entered the lists as an atheomastix in 1598. He was reduced to arguing that the fool who denied the existence of God was not really a man, and adduced the existence of the soul as proof of the existence of God, though he could combine such philosophical *naïveté* with shrewd common-sense

---

[1] Borthwick Inst. of Hist. Res., York, High Commission, C.P. 1580/90; H.C., Act Book 11, 1585–91, fols. 223ᵛ, 230ᵛ, 234ᵛ, 251ᵛ. I am grateful to Dr. W. J. Sheils for his help, especially with the Act Book entries.

[2] The danger of 'over-explaining' the phenomena of the past, evident in the writings of Christopher Hill as of other distinguished present-day historians, had been pointed out with diffidence by the present writer and others long before the recent criticisms of Professor Hexter.

observations, noting that it was 'hard in poverty not to sinne', yet at the same time for him 'the greatest men [were] the greatest sinners.' He got into particular difficulties with the doctrines of divine providence and of the after-life.[1] By contrast, the systematizing theologian appears again in John Dove, D.D. whose title does not err on the side of modesty: *Atheism Defined and confuted by undeniable Arguments; Drawne from Scripture and Reason*, which also went through several editions between 1605 and 1656. He reserved a special condemnation for those 'Englishmen Italianat' who followed the insidious lead of Machiavelli in professing religion for political advantage, while secretly not believing; he argued that (genuinely Christian) princes should err on the side of too little toleration rather than too much. Apart from the fact that his chapter order tends to confuse scriptural and natural arguments for God's existence, Dove might have been found more persuasive by the sincere intellectual doubter than most of those so far discussed.

The two last in this sequence of early seventeenth-century apologists were Bishop Fotherby, whose work, if he had lived to complete it, might well have been superior to that of Dove or Smith, and Thomas Jackson, future President of Corpus Christi College, Oxford, and High-Church Dean of Peterborough. In an earlier book Jackson had already seized the initiative and counter-attacked by arguing that complete atheists showed greater credulity than religious believers.[2] His most substantial atheomastical work is distinguished by an unusually strict definition of atheists, limiting the term to those who deny the existence of God; his tone keeps a fine balance between the sympathetic and the patronizing: 'The best method, in my Opinion, to prevent Atheism, or to cure an Atheist, woulde be to hold the Meane betwixt the contemplative Philosopher, and the practicall Physitian . . . Atheisme in graine is but a spirituall madnesse.'[3] This clinical view of the matter was of course shared by the greatest English psychologist

---

[1] Sir George More, *A Demonstration of God in his Workes Against all such as eyther in word or life deny there is a God* (1598, but Pref. dated Jan. 1596/7). Contrast chs. 1–4 with ch. 5, 70–82, and on providence and after-life, chs. 6 and 7. For More see *DNB*; the Loseley MSS. are now in the Folger Library.

[2] *The Eternall Truth of Scriptures and Christian Belief* . . . (1st edn. 1613) in *A Collection of the Works of Thomas Jackson* (1653).

[3] *A Treatise containing the Originall of Unbeliefe* (1625), esp. 1–2, 9–10.

C

of the time, Robert Burton, though admittedly the way had
been shown by his Elizabethan predecessor Timothy Bright.[1]
For 'Democritus Junior', the anatomist, 'Atheism, Idolatry,
Heresy, Hypocrisy, though they have one common root, that is
indulgence to corrupt affection, yet their growth is different,
they have divers symptoms, occasions, and must have several
cures and remedies'.[2] It is ironical that some materialist
psychologists of the twentieth century have inverted this view
and seen religious enthusiasm as an outcome of mental stress:
if you cannot persuade them, have them certified!

While earlier works continued to go into new editions, there
seems to have been a pause in the production of new treatises
against atheism in the later 1620s and 1630s. Perhaps everything that could be said had been, at least until changed
circumstances required fresh arguments. The puritan moralist,
and future Cromwellian church official, Richard Younge of
Roxwell, Essex, related atheism—together with some other
major sins and vices—to drunkenness, which he anatomized
over some 800 pages. Like Dove, he assumed that the typical
atheist would profess belief in God with his tongue while
denying him in his mind.[3]

Perhaps predictably, the upheavals of the 1640s saw a
recurrence of the tendency, inherited from the sixteenth century,
to denounce religious opponents as no better than atheists. In
November 1642 a pro-parliamentarian pamphleteer defended
Machiavelli at the expense of Strafford and Laud, thereby
inaugurating that process of rehabilitation which the late Felix
Raab so admirably delineated and which Professor John Pocock
has now analysed in greater depth.[4] The mildly xenophobic
anonymous author of *A Dispute betwixt an Atheist and a Christian:
the Atheist being a Flemming, the Christian an Englishman* seems to
formulate the concept of a deist, but still lacks the word or an
equivalent; nor does he simply mean Socinians or other anti-

---

[1] T. Bright, *A Treatise of Melancholie* (1586; repr. ed. H. Craig, N.Y., 1940).

[2] Robert Burton, *The Anatomy of Melancholy* (1st edn. 1621; ed. F. Dell and
P. Jordan-Smith, N.Y., 1955), 935. The word 'Deist' is also used by Burton
(p. 929), but he does not develop the concept further.

[3] 'R. Junius' [Richard Younge], *The Drunkard's Character* (1638), esp. 559.

[4] *The Atheisticall Polititian Or a Briefe Discourse concerning Nicolo Machiavell*
(1642). See F. Raab, *The English Face of Machiavelli* (1964) and J. G. A. Pocock,
The Machiavellian Moment (Princeton, 1975).

Trinitarians, or he would surely have said so: 'I perceive then that you are an Atheist: but a refined one, one of the new stamp: you believe in God, but not in Christ his son, nor in the holy Ghost: but according to our opinion, he that denyes the Son and holy Ghost; denyes the Father, and therefore is an Atheist.'[1] For his ability to detect total subversion in even the mildest forms of deviance, pride of place among the heresio-mastices of the revolutionary decades must be given to the Presbyterian divine Thomas Edwards. His *Gangraena* (1646) is a comprehensive catalogue of popular heresies and a violent onslaught on their revolutionary tendencies. It was not *Gangraena*'s purpose to 'explain' atheism or any of the other evils which Edwards saw about him. But he provides the first sustained testimony to the heterodoxy of the future Leveller leader William Walwyn, which may fairly be taken in con-junction with the attack made by Congregationalist and Baptist ex-allies of the popular cause three years later, in *Walwin's Wiles*.[2] Not that we should emulate Edwards or other cham-pions of orthodoxy and classify Walwyn as an atheist because he was a neo-Montaignian sceptic and Christian humanist, nor Richard Overton as one because he was, at least probably for a time, an adherent of the very old heresy of 'mortalism' or 'soul-sleeping'.[3] Another moderate parliamentarian, and like Younge a future Cromwellian office-holder, Nathaniel Bacon republished in the year of regicide his account of what came to be the classic 'death-bed repentance' story against atheists, that of a Venetian lawyer named Francis Spira who died in 1548.[4] Neither on this occasion, nor when the theme was revived with the so-called 'Second Spira's' story in the 1690s,[5] do the

[1] Published by order, 17 Aug. 1646, 13.
[2] For the 1649 pamphlets see *Leveller Tracts, 1647–1653*, ed. W. Haller and G. Davies (N.Y., 1944); some of the responses to *Gangraena* by Walwyn and others are in *Tracts on Liberty, 1638–1647*, ed. W. Haller (N.Y., 1934).
[3] Assuming Richard Overton, the Leveller, to be the author of *Man's Mortallitie* (1643; 1644), republished as *Man Wholly Mortal* (1655; 1675).
[4] Nathaniel Bacon, *A Relation of the Fearful Estate of Francis Spira* (1649, but dated at the end 2 Dec. 1637, with the imprimatur of the Bishop of London's chaplain).
[5] See J. S., A Minister of the Church of England, a frequent visitor of him during his whole Sickness, *The Second Spira: Being a fearful Example of an Atheist, who Had Apostatised from the Christian Religion, and dyed in despair at Westminster Decemb 8. 1692* (1693); H.L. A Layman, Mr N's particular Acquaintance and frequent visitor during his Sickness, *The Second Spira: Being a Fearful Example of F.N. An Atheist Part the Second* (1693); anon., *A Conference Betwixt a Modern Atheist, and his*

defenders of religious orthodoxy appear at their best or most persuasive on the theme of reconversion faced with the terrors of eternal torment, though by the latter occasion they had a more desperate need for ammunition in the face of an advancing enemy.

Although Lord Herbert of Cherbury, the principal editions of whose works did not appear till the 1640s, has often been accounted the 'father of English deism', undoubtedly the seminal event of these years was the earliest appearance in English of Hobbes's major writings. However genuine and sincere his and his friends' denials, the champions of orthodoxy chose to treat him as an actual or virtual atheist. And the new series of defences of religious belief and attacks on atheism which mark the 1650s to 70s are almost all in some measure responses to Hobbes, though only certain of them are primarily, let alone exclusively, that. And, since 'sorrows come not single spies . . .', it is fitting that another phantom from the intellectual underworld should have broken surface again about the same time. In 1652 the elderly German-born parliamentarian official Georg Rudolf Weckherlin wrote to his daughter Elizabeth Trumbull, mother of a future Secretary of State: 'The damnable Booke is printed in English (and many other wicked divillish pamphletts) whereby Moses, Christ and Mahomet, are set together as, I have horror to thinke it: . . .' There seems in fact to be no firm evidence that the famous, or notorious *de Tribus Impostoribus*, fathered on every great heresiarch from the Emperor Frederick II to Voltaire, was in fact published then, nor indeed indisputably until a century later (an edition with a 1598 imprint has usually been considered fraudulent); but it may be symptomatic of the times that the worthy Weckherlin thought that it had been.[1]

Freind, By the Methodizer of the Second Spira (1693); Richard Sault, *The Second Spira* (Boston, 1693). The only F. N. who remotely fits is Francis Newport, third son of the 2nd Baron Newport, later Earl of Bradford, and grandson of the 4th Earl of Bedford; but unfortunately his burial date is given as 25 November (*Westminster Abbey Regrs.*, ed. J. L. Chester (Harleian Soc., 1876), 231). The publicity given to the edifying end made by John Wilmot, 2nd Earl of Rochester, in 1680 is well known.

[1] Downshire Papers, Trumbull MSS., Weckherlin's Letters, fol. 148ᵛ (Lib. of Congress microfilm). For the story of *The Three Imposters*, see secondary works already cited, and J. M. Robertson, *A Short History of Free Thought* (3rd edn. 1914–15), esp. i. 323–4. Matthew Griffith, *Bethel: or, a forme for families* (1633), 310, lends support to its having been published around 1600.

Fittingly too a new series of more coherent and sophisticated anti-atheistical treatises began to appear from 1652 onwards.[1] With the royalist physician Walter Charleton we seem to move into a new era. Whereas Democritus, Epicurus, and Lucretius had always been the principal materialist philosophers of the ancient world whose possible 'atheism' needed to be either refuted or reinterpreted, the growing influence of the new science now posed new challenges. Religious apologists, unless they were simply to neglect such developments altogether, had to decide whether or not the revived corpuscular (or 'particle') theory of matter was, *ipso facto*, incompatible with Christian belief.[2] Only less urgent were the new developments in astronomy, mechanics, and medicine. Despite taking his stand avowedly in the scholastic tradition, Charleton shows a sophisticated, indeed intellectually 'progressive', awareness of these issues. In his preliminary pages he refers to Mersenne, Hobbes, Descartes, and Gassendi, and in his main text goes out of his way to praise William Harvey as well as Descartes, for their indeterminism or upholding of free will: 'this indeliberate Syndrome or Combination of Causes, is always uncertain and various'. He sets out to 'rescue' atomism, alias corpuscularism, from the materialists of the classical past; by contrast, Copernicus, Kepler, and Galileo are conspicuous by their absence. Either Charleton was unaware of their work, or—as seems more likely—did not consider that it posed a challenge of the same urgency as that of the scientists and philosophers whom he did discuss.[3] Whatever its stylistic qualities, with the first major foray into atheomasticism by one of the Cambridge Platonists, we return to an earlier intellectual tradition. Although Henry More too expresses admiration for Descartes in his Preface, and

[1] Technically the Cambridge Platonist John Smith (1618–52) preceded the authors discussed in the following paragraphs. But his ten discourses, although delivered between his election as a fellow of Queens' College, Cambridge, in 1644 and his final illness (*c.* 1650), were not published until 1660. See *Select Discourses of John Smith*, ed. H. G. Williams (4th edn. Cambridge, 1859), especially John Worthington's Preface to the 1660 edn.

[2] See T. F. Mayo, *Epicurus in England (1650–1725)* ([Dallas], 1934) and R. H. Kargon, *Atomism in England from Hariot to Newton* (Oxford, 1966) in addition to other works already cited.

[3] Walter Charleton, *The Darknes of Atheism Dispelled by the Light of Nature* (1652), 'Preparatory Advertisement to the Reader', and 40, 131, 274, 295. Besides *DNB*, see L. Sharp, 'Walter Charleton's Early Life', *Annals of Science*, 30 (1973), 311–40.

although he provides an accomplished résumé of the traditional arguments, especially that from design, he then goes on to rest his case on miracles, charms, portents, apparitions, witches, and other supernatural activities by spirits. Like the French philosopher of the previous century whom he admires so much, Jean Bodin, More displays an extraordinary mixture of credulity and acute analysis. For, embedded in this farrago is a splendid naturalistic explanation of witchcraft accusations, substantially anticipating the approach of Keith Thomas and Alan Macfarlane in our own time. None the less, More concludes his *Antidote against Atheisme* with the following admonition: 'For assuredly that Saying was nothing so true in Politicks, No Bishop, no King; as this is in Metaphysicks, No Spirit, no God.'[1] The next year a broadly similar but inferior performance by the one-time Oxford don, William Towers, is notable mainly for its introduction of the term 'deist' in its modern sense, although little was to be made of it until the following decades.[2] While it may be no coincidence that this word, 'syndrome', and 'anthropologie'[3] all reappear about the same time, we must not make the men of the 1650s more 'modern' than they were. For Thomas Blount in his *Glossographia* merely defines atheism as 'the damnable doctrine and opinion of the Atheists, infidelity, the denying of, or not believing in God' and an atheist as 'he that beleeues there is no God or rule of Religion, and that the soul dies with the body'.[4]

The doughtiest, most prolific, and longest-lived of all seventeenth-century apologists now entered the lists. Richard Baxter's *Unreasonableness of Infidelity* (1655), dedicated to the leading Cromwellian Lord Broghill (the future Earl of Orrery, and brother of Robert Boyle, the 'skeptical chymist'), while by no means brief is philosophically somewhat sparse compared

---

[1] Henry More, *An Antidote against Atheism Or An Appeal to the Natural Faculties of the Minde of Man, whether there be not a God* (1653), 146, 164. Books i and ii are reprinted in *The Cambridge Platonist*, ed. C. A. Patrides (1969), 213–87. As Dr. Patrides remarks (xxv, 32), the omission of Book iii is intellectually flattering to More, despite the witchcraft argument in ch. xi.

[2] William Towers, *Atheismus Vapulans, or A Treatise against Atheisme Rationally Confuting the Atheisme of these Times* (1654), 179.

[3] Anon., *Anthropologie Abstracted: or the Idea of Humane Nature Reflected in briefe Philosophicall, and Anatomicall Collections* (1655).

[4] T[homas] B[lount], *Glossographia: Or A Dictionary Interpreting all such Hard Words* (1656).

with Charleton or More. In the face of Hobbes's *Leviathan* and other temptations from Satan, Baxter seeks to make good 'the two principles of our faith, *viz.* that God is True, and that Scripture is his Word'. Perhaps predictably he shows himself more at home with the case for specifically Christian beliefs, based upon revelation, than with the philosophical arguments for God's existence.[1] At the end of his long life Baxter returned to these preoccupations, now resting the case for Christian belief more positively on the reality of spirits, ghosts, witches, etc. Or rather, basing his campaign for the reconversion of 'Atheists, Sadduces [*sic*] and Infidels' on this reality. For the first major item in his collection, he reverted to a *cause célèbre* of the 1650s: the case of Lieutenant-Colonel Henry Bowen, the ancestor of the twentieth-century novelist Elizabeth Bowen.[2] Meanwhile, in the later 1650s Dr. Charleton returned to the fray with his treatise on *The Immortality of the Human Soul*, in the form of a dialogue between Lucretius, Athanasius, and Isodicastes. Narrower than his *Antidote*, this work is more specifically anti-Hobbist and pro-Cartesian, exhibiting in a somewhat extreme form what Gilbert Ryle called the concept of 'the ghost in the machine', in that he seeks to make the human intellect as well as the soul immaterial.[3]

A more balanced temperament, if combined with a basically conservative outlook, is reflected in John Evelyn's letter to his friend and legal adviser, Edward Thurland. He had sent the diarist a draft manuscript treatise on prayer, which included a defence of the existence of God against doubters. Replying, Evelyn recommends, besides various classical and medieval authors, Du Plessis Mornay, Lancelot Andrewes, Grotius, Hammond, More, and Charleton, who 'have all treated on this subject, but in so different a manner, and with so much confusion and prolixity, some few of them excepted, that it will greatly add to the worth and lustre of your piece, who have comprehended so much in so little and to so excellent purpose'. Whether because Evelyn was much more critical of what his friend had written on prayer itself, or because

[1] Richard Baxter, *The Vnreasonableness of Infidelity* (1655), Preface, sig. d2.
[2] See below, p. 41, n. 1.
[3] [Walter Charleton], *The Immortality of the Human Soul, Demonstrated by the Light of Nature . . . In Two Dialogues* (1657).

Thurland's heart was in his legal career, the treatise was never printed, so its cogency cannot be assessed.[1]

The case of Henry Bowen is peculiarly instructive. Rising in the parliamentarian forces to be lieutenant-colonel of Thomas Rainsborough's regiment of foot, he was in the van when the New Model stormed its way into Bristol in September 1645, having been in Oliver Cromwell's words 'two hours at push of pike, standing upon the palisadoes, but could not enter'. Ironically in view of what was to come, the making of the breach and consequent fall of the city Cromwell saw as such an indisputable manifestation of divine providence that only 'a very Atheist' could, or would wish to, deny it. Not long after this, Bowen became second-in-command of Cromwell's own infantry regiment, and seems to have crossed over to Ireland with the main English army in 1649. But in 1652 he was said to have 'become a professed Athiest' and was 'shortly to come to his trial for the same'. In the absence of any court-martial records for the army in Ireland during the 1650s, one cannot be certain; but it seems likely that he was allowed to resign his commission but was not proceeded against further. Meanwhile he acquired an estate in County Cork, and then in 1655 was alleged to have haunted his own house in the Gower peninsula, Glamorgan, where his unfortunate wife was still living. Even among ghost stories, Bowen's is a remarkable one. For the noisy and violent apparition alleged to have persecuted Mrs. Bowen was connected with a living and not a dead person; and that individual was regarded—not just by one contemporary—as 'an absolute Atheist' and 'a Blasphemer . . . unworthy to live'. Yet when we come to examine the positive allegations of unbelief made against him, Bowen turns out to be—in twentieth-century terminology—somewhat between a deist and an agnostic, emphatically not a doctrinaire materialist: 'denying Heaven or Hell, God or Devil, acknowledging only a Power, as the antient Heathens did fate . . . all his Religion, if I may call it so, being comprised in the acknowledging a Power, which we, as he saith, may call God.' And from another witness, shortly before Bowen's death in 1658: 'Not long since, in Discourse with Baronet

---

[1] *Diary and Correspondence of John Evelyn*, ed. W. Bray (rev. edn. 1854), iii. 87–90, 20 Jan. 1657. *DNB s.n.* 'Edward Thurland (1606–83)', says it was never published.

Ingolsby and Mr Gilbert, Minister of Limerick ... he said, he would give Ten Thousand Pounds to know the Truth about God'—which may be naïve but is scarcely atheistical. Finally his will, made very soon after this, is compatible in its wording with deism or indeed with (non-Christian) theism: 'Whereas the lives of all Creaters are in the dispose of the Eternall god and maker of all into whose hand I Committ my Spritt . . .'[1]

Historians of thought have been readier to explain the greater prevalence of unbelief after the Restoration than to demonstrate its extent. The most recent author to discuss the changed intellectual and religious climate ascribes the defensive tone of Christian apologetics primarily to ridicule.[2] Unhappily this may be to overestimate the role of humour in history. Alternatively, despite the fact that most of the major scientists and mathematicians were believers (even if often, as with Newton, heterodox ones), the scientific revolution may have created a new climate, regardless of its protagonists' intentions. How a presumed increase in unbelief should be related to the events of 1640–60 is a question which a contribution to this volume can hardly evade, but one which is certainly easier posed than answered. That extremes of heterodoxy flourished among the Ranters and other sects, is not in dispute; whether the outcome was a net increase in unbelief seems to me more debatable. In so far as unresolved religious conflicts, the see-saw of persecution and proscription, the ineffectuality of forcing conformity upon deviants, were all writ large in the religious history of the country from the 1630s to the 1680s, it may appear self-evident that orthodoxy would be increasingly discredited. This is on the assumption that Bacon was correct in supposing conflict more dangerous to religious belief than the settled calm of an unchallenged orthodoxy. In the parish register of Eckington,

---

[1] E. Bowen, *Bowen's Court* (1942; 1964), chs. 2–3, tells the story with a skill and beauty which I cannot hope to emulate. None the less there is a little more to it. See R. Baxter, *The Certainty of the Worlds of Spirits* (1691), sigs. A3ᵛ–A4; for Col. Bowen's story told in letters dated from the 1650s, 20–36; *A Contemporary History of Affairs in Ireland, from 1641 to 1652*, ed. J. T. Gilbert (Dublin, 1879–80), iii. 372–3; *Writings and Speeches of Oliver Cromwell*, ed. W. C. Abbott (Cambridge, Mass., 1937–47), i. 376; C. H. Firth and G. Davies, *Regimental History of Cromwell's Army* (Oxford, 1940), 419, 625; Bowen, *Bowen's Court* (1964 edn.), 76. The letter cited by Gilbert is quite independent of those printed by Baxter.

[2] Redwood, *Reason, Ridicule and Religion*.

Derbyshire, at the year 1686–7, there appears the following quatrain:

> Our Grandfathers were Papists,
> Our Fathers Oliverians,
> We their Sons are Athiests
> Sure our Sons will be queer ones.[1]

Meanwhile, if many apologists continued in a well-worn groove, others—a few from the 1660s–70s and many more from the 1690s on—showed a greater readiness to face, and attempt the rebuttal of, the intrinsic arguments against belief. These have become so commonplace since the eighteenth century that it requires a real effort of the historical imagination to take the force of their first open admission into the debate: the rejection of gratuitous improbabilities contrary to the normal laws of nature; the impossibility of our knowing, either empirically or deductively, the nature of God, or of our having proof of the existence of incorporeal substances or spirits, or of an after-life; the implausibilities involved in the alleged occurrence of miracles and in the divine inspiration and literal truth of the Bible; the likenesses and differences of different religions considered comparatively and in their historical context. The deployment of these intellectual difficulties was to culminate in Hume's arguments against belief; they led also to the fashion for 'Natural Religion', where an Anglican or Presbyterian Christianity became so diluted as to shade off into a kind of Christian deism. But it would be a mistake to think of all this suddenly happening at once in 1660.

Although most of his arguments are familiar enough, Edward Stillingfleet, the future Bishop of Worcester, in his *Origines Sacrae* (1662) showed a sensitive awareness of historical change:

But as the tempers and geniuses of ages and times alter, so do the arms and weapons which Atheists employ against religion. The most popular pretences of the Atheists of our age, have been the irreconcilableness of the account of times in Scripture with that of the learned and ancient heathen nations; the inconsistency of the belief of the Scriptures with the principles of reason; and the account

---

[1] Derbyshire RO, Matlock, D750A/PI23, cited in R. L. Hine, *Confessions of an Un-Common Attorney* (1945), 76. I am grateful to Miss Joan Sinar, the County Archivist, for confirming this reference and giving me the exact wording.

which may be given of the origin of things from principles of philosophy without the Scriptures. These three therefore I have particularly set myself against . . .

Besides the 'atomistic' materialists of classical antiquity, his main targets were Hobbes and—unlike Charleton and others—also Descartes.[1]

To remind us that the frontiers of intellectual debate are seldom clear-cut and unilinear, in 1668 Joseph Glanvill, most often remembered as a believer in the reality of witchcraft, felt obliged to defend himself against charges of atheism, besides attacking it in others.[2] Next on the scene was Sir Charles Wolseley, Bart., who had been one of the youngest of Cromwell's councillors (1653–9). Not a professionally trained philosopher or theologian, Wolseley does at least deal candidly with one of the harshest arguments against belief: that all religion has originated and been maintained by a combination of fear and fraud. Perhaps because it was easier reading than many such treatises, perhaps because of the author's reputation, his went into three editions in six years. His formulation of the 'common fame' argument for belief involves a nice analogy with politics: 'If there be some Torys and Moss-Troopers, and such who will come under no Government; were it reasonable therefore to say, that Government is not such a thing as the World have agreed in, and an Institution Universally founded in Natural Light?'[3]

Besides the continuing stream of anti-atheistical, and latterly anti-deistical works, of which Ralph Cudworth's *True Intellectual System of the Universe*[4] may be the weightiest but is certainly not the most readable, we must also consider the actual position of unbelievers. In 1666 the House of Commons concerned itself with Hobbes's *Leviathan* and other supposedly dangerous books —as if the existing laws and the censorship were not enough.[5]

---

[1] Edward Stillingfleet, *Origines Sacrae* (1662), Preface to the Reader; the 1677 edn. has added to it, *Letter to a Deist in Answer to Scholarly Objections against the Truth and Authority of the Scriptures*, dated 11 June 1675.

[2] *Plus Ultra* (1668), Preface and 137, 139, 144; *A Blow at Modern Sadducism* (1668), 154 (I owe this reference to Mr. Thomas).

[3] *The Unreasonableness of Atheism Made Manifest* (1669; 3rd edn. 1675), 70.

[4] Published in 1678, but probably written by 1671.

[5] *The Diary of John Milward*, ed. C. Robbins (Cambridge, 1938), 24–5, and refs. given in Mintz, *Hunting of Leviathan*. See also Mintz, 'Hobbes on the Law of Heresy:

In the following decade the Bishops solicited the King to help suppress atheism, 'without the amendment or punishment of which nothing can avail to the preservation of a Church which God has threatened for such sins unrepented and unpunished, to destroy'.[1] Churchmen might debate whether limited toleration or rigorous conformity, and if necessary persecution, were the more conducive to the diffusion and strengthening of true belief.[2] It is by no means clear what effects the statutory changes of the period had on either the spoken or the printed word. In 1675, when *de haeretico comburendo* was still theoretically in force, a Guildford man called Taylor was tried and sentenced (but to fine and imprisonment, and public penance, not death) by King's Bench for blasphemy more akin to profane scoffing than to sustained disbelief.[3] Despite the limited toleration inaugurated in 1689, the Blasphemy Act of 1697 might seem to have more than outweighed—for the sceptic or unbeliever—the lapsing of the censorship laws earlier in the 1690s.[4] In Scotland a young man of eighteen was hanged for blasphemy in the year of the new act.[5] Whether the forces of orthodoxy gained more from the endowment of the 'Boyle Lectures' in 1691 and the annual series launched by Bentley the next year, than the opponents of

a New MS.', *Journ. of the Hist. of Ideas*, xxix (1968), 409–14. This was shortly followed by the slightly pathetic case of the Cambridge 'Hobbist' Daniel Scargill, who recanted after being proceeded against in 1669; see D. Krook, 'The Recantation of Daniel Scargill', *Notes and Queries*, 198 (1953), 159–60; C. L. S. Linnell, 'Daniel Scargill. "A Penitent 'Hobbist' " ', *Church Qtly. Rev.* 156 (1955), 256–65; and J. L. Axtell, 'The Mechanics of Opposition: Restoration Cambridge v. Daniel Scargill', *BIHR* 38 (1965), 102–11. Pepys had to pay three times the original price for *Leviathan*, 'it being a book the bishops will not let be printed again'; *Diary*, 3 Sept. 1668.

    [1] *CSPD, 1673–5*, 548–9, the Archbishop and seven other Bishops to the King, Jan. 1675.
    [2] For example [S. Parker], *A Discourse of Ecclesiastical Politie* (1670), esp. ch. v; [Herbert Croft] *The Naked Truth . . . By an Humble Moderator* (1675), ed. H. H. Henson (1919).
    [3] Joseph Keble, *Reports in the Court of King's Bench*, iii (1685), 607, 621; see also W. Nelson, *The Rights of the Clergy of Great Britain* (1709), 117. Another bill was apparently introduced in 1677–8, but not proceeded with; *HMC, Portland*, ii. 46.
    [4] The most satisfactory account of the legal position still appears to be C. Kenny, 'The Evolution of the Law of Blasphemy', *Cambridge Law Journ.* i (1922), 127–42; see also G. D. Nokes, *History of the Crime of Blasphemy* (1928); *S. of R.*, v. 850, and vii. 409, for the Acts of 1677 (29 Car. II, c. 9) and 1697 (9 Guil. III, c. 35).
    [5] In January 1697; see T. B. Macaulay, *History of England*, ch. xxii (Everyman edn. 1906), iii. 508–10; *DNB s.n.* 'Thomas Aikenhead'.

Christianity did from so much free publicity was debated at the time—and remains arguable either way.[1]

The identification of atheism with loose-living and a totally amoral attitude continued to find expression, sometimes in surprising places. 'Atheist' continued to be used as a colloquial term of abuse or disapprobation; as when Clarendon so described Sir George Savile, the future Marquis of Halifax, in 1665.[2] Andrew Marvell, himself accused of being 'Atheistical', reported a Doctor Stubbs 'physician atheist found dead I mean drowned . . . suppost drunk. *es magne Deus*'.[3] About this time Mrs. Aphra Behn's friend or lover, and benefactor, John Hoyle, was described as 'an atheist, a sodomite professed, a corrupter of youth, and a blasphemer of Christ'—the Marlowe syndrome perhaps?[4] More serious, John Locke specifically excepted atheists from the scope of religious toleration, because:

Promises, covenants, and oaths, which are the bonds of human society, can have no hold upon an atheist. The taking away of God, though but even in thought, dissolves all; besides also, those that by their atheism undermine and destroy all religion, can have no pretence of religion whereupon to challenge the privilege of a toleration.[5]

That this was by no means simply the opinion of an 'arm-chair' philosopher, may be seen from a Lancashire court case reported by William Stout in 1699. One John Horsfall was accused

[1] Many of the 'Boyle Lectures', delivered as sermons, from 1691 to 1732, are conveniently collected in *A Defence of Natural and Revealed Religion*, ed. S. Letsome and J. Nicholl (1739). M. C. Jacob, in her cogent and learned study, *The Newtonians and the English Revolution 1689–1720* (Hassocks, 1976), argues that the latitudinarian churchmen took over the new science and used it as a weapon against both unbelief and the wrong sorts of religious enthusiasm.

[2] Quoted by B. Greenslade in *TLS*, 30 May 1975, 599, presumably from *The Continuation of the Life of Edward Earl of Clarendon . . . Written by himself* (Oxford, 1759), 297.

[3] *The Poems and Letters of Andrew Marvell*, ed. H. M. Margoliouth (2nd edn. Oxford, 1952), ii. 325. I am grateful to Dr. Caroline Robbins for this reference and for other information on Marvell (her unpublished typescript, 'Andrew Marvell', ii. 46–7, 72–3); see also *DNB s.n.* 'Henry Stubbe'; P. M. Holt, *A Seventeenth-Century Defender of Islam Henry Stubbe (1632–76) and his Book* (Dr. Williams's Lib., 1972).

[4] *Selected Writings of the Ingenious Mrs Aphra Behn*, ed. R. Phelps (N.Y., 1950), 8.

[5] *A Letter Concerning Toleration*, ed. J. W. Gough (Oxford, 1946), 156. Note the wry comment in R. I. Aaron, *John Locke* (3rd edn. Oxford, 1971), 295, n. 1. And compare with Locke's *An Essay Concerning Human Understanding*, I. iv and IV. x.

of counterfeiting stamped paper (to evade tax), and the principal witness against him was his cousin Henry, but

The above said Henry Horsfall was a lewd, athestical man, and although it was beleived he made a full and true confession of what he knew of counterfeating and making stamps, yet upon prosecuting the accused the jury would not convict any upon his evidence, and gave for their reason that he was a professed athist and not to be credited.[1]

Setting aside the voluminous controversial writings for and against deism and 'free-thinking', dating from the 1690s to the 1720s, the extent to which orthodoxy had had to give ground is nowhere better illustrated than in the fact that by 1720 Bernard Mandeville could actually publish a total denial of Locke's thesis: 'it ought not to appear more strange to us, that an Atheist should be a quiet moral man, than that a Christian should lead a very wicked life.'[2]

In so far as one can speak of a debate when one side is disabled from free expression of its viewpoint, the arguments between Christianity and unbelief in the seventeenth century seem to resemble a joust where two knights in armour lumber towards each other, and each—unable to see his opponent— completely misses his target. Or, to vary the metaphor, it reminds one of a *dialogue des sourds*. This was not due only to the legal and other inhibitions on the open expression of unbelief, but to the ambivalent, two-edged nature of scepticism and— above all—to the absence throughout of any concept corresponding to 'agnosticism', and before the 1670s–80s of any clear distinction between atheism and deism. In one sense the task of the religious apologists should have been made easier as they were thrown increasingly on to the intellectual defensive; for it is certainly no more possible to prove that God does not exist than it is to prove that he does. By the early eighteenth century the question was being put, and answers to it attempted, very differently from a hundred years earlier. Yet this should not conceal the fact that the question was essentially the same, and that it is one which—by definition—permits of no answer.

[1] *The Autobiography of William Stout of Lancaster 1665–1752*, ed. J. D. Marshall (Chetham Soc., 1967), 127–8, 262, n. 154.
[2] In his *Free Thoughts on Religion* (1720), 4 (quoted in Wiley, *The Subtle Knot*, 248).

The Alehouse and the Alternative Society

PETER CLARK

'ALEHOUSES', cried Christopher Hudson at Preston in 1631, 'are nests of Satan where the owls of impiety lurk and where all evil is hatched, and the bellows of intemperance and incontinence blown up.' Similar complaints echoed through town and countryside for much of the sixteenth and early seventeenth centuries. Puritan preachers were especially vociferous against alehouses. William Vaughan made a typical attack in 1611, declaring: 'here breed conspiracies, combinations, common conjurations, detractions, defamations.' The threat posed by the alehouse was constantly growing, for, as Richard Rawlidge declared in the 1620s, while alehouses were previously few in number, 'now every street [is] replenished' with them.[1] Magistrates joined in the attack. At Northampton the Puritan corporation denounced the many alehouses frequented by the poor through which 'the horrible and loathsome sin of drunkenness does daily increase to the dishonour of God [and] the impoverishing of this town and commonwealth.' In Kent the county justice William Lambarde also had harsh words for the disorder spawned by alehouses: 'your children and servants be corrupted in manners, bastards be multiplied in parishes, thieves and rogues do swarm in the highways, the lawful pastimes of the land be abandoned, and dicing, cards, and bowling be set up in place.'[2] Alehouses also figure prominently in Elizabethan and Jacobean plays and literary pamphlets, though here the

* I am grateful to Dr. P. Corfield and the editors for their comments on an early draft of this paper.

[1] Quoted in R. C. Richardson, *Puritanism in North-West England* (Manchester, 1972), 52; William Vaughan, *The Spirit of Detraction* (1611), 129; Richard Rawlidge, *A Monster late Fovnd ovt and Discovered* (Amsterdam, 1628), 8.

[2] *The Records of the Borough of Northampton*, ed. J. C. Cox (1898), ii. 304–5; *William Lambarde and Local Government. His 'Ephemeris' and Twenty-Nine Charges*, ed. C. Read (Ithaca, N.Y., 1962), 73.

treatment is rather less hostile. In Jonson and Dekker, for example, the alehouse appears as the trysting-place of an underworld populated by gulls and vagabonds, robbers and whores, a world which though parasitical is also a mirror image of the moral sham, the trickery and hypocrisy of respectable society.[1]

In sum there was a broad consensus of opinion among the middling and (to some extent) the upper ranks of society in Tudor and early Stuart England: that alehouses were a new and increasingly dangerous force in popular society; that they were run by the poor for the poor, victualling and harbouring the destitute and vagrant, breeding crime, disorder, and drunkenness, fostering promiscuity and other breaches of orthodox morality; and that they served as the stronghold of popular opposition to the established religious and political order. In other words the alehouse was perceived as the command post of men who sought to turn the traditional world upside down and create their own alternative society.

I

In the following pages we shall investigate whether the portrait of the alehouse drawn by its critics accords with social and political reality. If the sixteenth and early seventeenth centuries did indeed see the rise of the alehouse as a major popular institution we must also examine some of the principal factors behind the phenomenon.

First of all, however, we need to define what we mean by the 'alehouse'. Terms for victualling establishments were not always precise, but we can construct a kind of victualling hierarchy for the sixteenth and seventeenth centuries. At the top was the inn, a large establishment with a multitude of guest-rooms, extensive stables, and warehouses. Frequently standing in the main street of town or village, it offered ale, beer, and usually wine, together with quite elaborate food and lodging for the traveller. Increasingly important as a meeting-place for town merchants, county justices, and landowners, it was strongly identified with the social and political élite. Though the number of inns rose during our period the total

[1] Cf. N. Berlin, *The Base String. The Underworld in Elizabethan Drama* (Cranbury, N.J., 1968), 22 and *passim*.

was never high: in 1577 a survey of 27 counties listed about 2,000 inns with the great majority located in larger towns.[1] By virtue of selling wine some inns were technically taverns, but the 1577 survey further listed about 300 taverns in a separate category. The tavern also was a fairly select establishment with a licence to sell wine regulated by legislation in 1553, but without the extensive accommodation of the inn. In London the tavern often had several drinking rooms, furnished with panelling, plate, and paintings; some were housed in city mansions (one in the house of a former Lord Mayor). In the provinces they were rather less splendid, but most of them could still claim superiority to the alehouse. As John Earle put it: a tavern 'is a degree or (if you will) a pair of stairs above an alehouse, where men are drunk with more credit and apology'.[2]

At the bottom of the victualling hierarchy was the alehouse or tippling house, a much more basic establishment. Essentially it sold ale and beer with the occasional rough spirits (aquavita), cider or perry, which customers either took home or, more commonly, drank on the premises.[3] It also offered food and one or two beds for the foot traveller or lodger. Most alehouses were kept in ordinary houses, in a back room (sometimes behind a curtain) or in a cellar; there are frequent references to them being located in back-alleys.[4] As we shall see, alehouse-keepers and their customers tended to be drawn from the poorer classes. Despite the beginning of statutory regulation of alehouses from the 1550s, licensing was often lax and unlicensed houses common—at least into the early seventeenth century. At Buckingham in 1600 and Caernarvon in 1634 as many as half the alehouses were kept without a licence.[5]

So far as one can judge, alehouses only became widespread in

[1] A. Everitt, 'The English Urban Inn, 1560–1760' in *Perspectives in English Urban History*, ed. A. Everitt (1973), 93–119; *The Description of England by William Harrison*, ed. G. Edelen (Ithaca, N.Y., 1968), 399.

[2] Everitt, 'English Urban Inn', 93; City of London RO (hereafter CLRO), Repertories 38, fol. 38; 30, fol. 330; PRO, E 317/Middlesex 81 (I owe this reference to Dr. M. Power); J. Earle, *Micro-cosmographie* (1628), fol. 30ᵛ.

[3] East Sussex RO, QR/E 10/70; Kent AO, QM/SB 707; Bodl., University Chancellor's Court, Deposition Book 1619–27 (unfol.).

[4] Bodl., MS. Oxon dioc. c. 26, fol. 93; *Calendar of Chester City Council Minutes, 1603–1642*, ed. M. J. Groombridge (Lancs. and Ches. Rec. Soc., 1956), 20–1; Dover records, Town Minute Book (James I etc.), fol. 169.

[5] Bucks. RO, Buckingham Qtr. Sessn. Bk. 2; J. B. H. Jones, 'Puritanism and Moral Legislation before the Civil War' (M.A. thesis, Univ. of Wales, 1954), 62.

the sixteenth century. The medieval evidence, patchy though it is, would indicate that alehouses as such were relatively few in number; most victuallers we do find sold drink out of their houses, on an 'off-licence' basis. Only in the larger towns such as Bristol or London do alehouses appear on any scale and there the magistrates regularly sought to close them down.[1] By the early decades of the sixteenth century the situation was rapidly changing, with town councils in particular worried by what appeared to be an inundation of alehouses. The Coventry magistrates noted in 1544 that the number of alehouse-keepers (and brewers) had grown so much that 'a great part of the inhabitants of this city be now become brewers and tipplers'.[2] By 1577 there were at least 14,000 houses in 27 counties. Allowing for the counties and unlicensed houses omitted from the survey, there may have been as many as 18,000 or 19,000 alehouses functioning in the whole country at this time; by the 1630s the total figure was probably in excess of 30,000 and by the 1680s was certainly well over 40,000.[3] Even taking into account the upward population trend during our period, there was clearly a substantial rise in the general incidence of alehouses.

The growth rate was especially high in towns. In 1618 London magistrates spoke of 'the multitude of alehouses and victualling houses within this city increasing daily'. According to one account there were upwards of 3,000 tippling houses in the capital by the 1620s, many of them in the poorer suburbs.[4] In the Finsbury division of Middlesex the number of licensed houses alone rose between 1630 and 1632 from 118 to 167. In the provinces Canterbury nearly doubled its number of alehouses between 1577 and 1596, while at Taunton the figure rose by a third in the years 1587 to 1618.[5] Data for the country-

---

[1] R. V. Lennard, *Rural England 1086–1135* (Oxford, 1959), 405; R. H. Hilton, *The English Peasantry in the Later Middle Ages* (Oxford, 1975), 104–5; H. A. Monckton, *A History of the English Public House* (1969), 25, 27; *The Little Red Book of Bristol*, ed. F. B. Bickley (1900), ii. 38; *Liber Albus: The White Book of the City of London*, ed. H. T. Riley (1861), 312–13.

[2] *The Coventry Leet Book*, ed. M. D. Harris, iii (Early Engl. Text Soc. or. ser., 1909), 770–2, 786; Canterbury Cathedral Lib. (hereafter CCL), AC 2, fol. 36ᵛ.

[3] Everitt, 'English Urban Inn', 93; *CSPD, 1635–6*, 429 (figure adjusted to allow for London alehouses); BL, Stowe MS. 314, fols. 8ᵛ–9.

[4] CLRO, Journals 30, fol. 293; Rawlidge, *A Monster*, iii.

[5] PRO, SP 16/226/77; *Crisis and Order in English Towns 1500–1700*, ed. P. Clark

side suggest a lower rate of growth; however, woods, hills, and heathlands attracted a host of poor victualling houses.[1]

How do we explain this surge in the number of alehouses during the sixteenth and early seventeenth centuries? Inevitably the answer is complex, but several major points can be noted here. One factor was taste. As with the wine trade at the top end of the market, changes in consumer taste had a considerable influence on the pattern and organization of the popular drink trade in our period. Particularly crucial was the swing away from the favourite medieval tipple, ale (made with fermented malt, water, and spices), to beer (basically fermented malt, water, and hops). Hops had been known to continental brewers since at least the eleventh century, but only started to be used in England on any scale from the late fifteenth century.[2] In spite of official opposition, beer-brewing became steadily more common during the early Tudor period, particularly in the south and east, where the beer-brewers were often Dutch or Flemish immigrants.[3] Beer was a much more attractive drink than ale: it was brighter, stronger, and less prone to deteriorate, while its price was about the same. By 1600 beer was also becoming popular in the North and West, and thereafter ale was increasingly confined to the more backward rural areas.[4]

The introduction of hops caused major changes in the drink trade. Ale had never been a good commercial product. It had a short life and was vulnerable to sudden atmospheric changes; nor did it travel well. Its main advantage was that it was relatively easy to brew. Consequently, ale-brewing was primarily a small-scale, domestic industry with many people

and P. Slack (1972), 140; H. B. Sheppard, 'Courts Leet and the court leet of . . . Taunton', *Somerset Arch. and Nat. Hist. Soc.* lv (1909), 44.

[1] *Quarter Sessions Records . . . 1607–1625*, ed. E. H. Bates (Somerset Rec. Soc., 1907), 3, 8; *Worcestershire County Records*, ed. J. W. Willis Bund (Worcester, 1900), i. 78, 314–15; East Sussex RO, QR/E 9/94.

[2] R. Davis, 'The English Wine Trade in the Eighteenth and Nineteenth Centuries', *Annales Cisalpines d'Histoire Sociale*, iii (1972), 87–103; R. F. Bretherton, 'Country Inns and Alehouses' in *Englishmen at Rest and Play*, ed. R. Lennard (Oxford, 1931), 168–9.

[3] P. Mathias, *The Brewing Industry in England 1700–1830* (Cambridge, 1959), 3–5; A. B. Rosen, 'Economic and Social Aspects of the History of Winchester 1520–1670' (D.Phil. thesis, Oxford Univ., 1975), 29–31.

[4] *West Riding Sessions Rolls 1597/8–1602*, ed. J. Lister (Yorks. Arch. Soc. rec. ser., 1888), 59–60, 81; *York Civic Records*, ed. A. Raine (Yorks. Arch. Soc., rec. ser., 1939–53), viii. 120.

brewing for their own households and selling any surplus to a few neighbours. In comparison beer was more stable and kept longer, while one could brew twice as much drink from a bushel of malt with the addition of hops. At the same time, beer-brewing tended to be a more lengthy and complicated process than ale-making and probably required greater capital expenditure.[1] Thus the spread of beer-brewing was accompanied by growing commercialization in the drink trade. Domestic brewing by ordinary folk tended to decline and the house-holder bought supplies from the alehouse-keeper. In Yorkshire in the 1630s it was reported that the county's many clothiers 'have their drink from the alehouse-keepers and scarce one brews his own'. In turn a growing proportion of alehouse-keepers came to rely on the brewer for their drink. The trend was most evident in the south, particularly in or near towns. Elsewhere brewing by alehouse-keepers was more common, though it declined during the seventeenth century owing to official discouragement and the growing power of major brewers.[2]

This is not to say that we can explain the growing number and importance of alehouses simply in terms of changes in consumer taste and brewing technology and organization. Other factors almost certainly played their part. In the first place there was the increase in poverty. It was no coincidence that the first major attack on the growing number of alehouses occurred in the 1540s and 1550s, a time of widespread economic and social disorder. As we shall see, the upsurge of poverty during this period, owing to the failure of economic develop-ment to keep pace with population expansion, created a power-ful demand for the services offered by the alehouse. On the supply side, widespread poverty also forced numerous people to set up alehouses in order to subsist. In addition the rise of the alehouse was closely related to growing migration and urbaniza-tion; many poor victuallers and their customers were recruited from the great mass of migrants who flocked into towns at this time.[3] Also vital were changes in the fabric of local society and

[1] H. A. Monckton, *A History of English Ale and Beer* (1966), 11 and *passim*; Richard Bradley, *The Riches of a Hop-Garden* (1729), 25–6.

[2] *West Riding Sessions Records*, ed. J. Lister (Yorks. Arch. Soc. rec. ser., 1915), xxxvi–xxxvii; Essex RO, Q/SR 201/91; Mathias, *Brewing Industry*, 6.

[3] For the development of similar drinking establishments in Third World

the role of the parish church. While the parish and church officers acquired a new administrative importance during the sixteenth century, the same period also saw the erosion of the traditional sense of the community focused on the local church, and the need for a new popular centre such as the alehouse. Many of these points will need to be discussed again in more detail as we examine the various charges levelled against the alehouse as the bastion of the alternative society.

II

Puritan and other complaints that alehouses were run by the poor for the poor were certainly near the mark. The Norfolk justices reported in 1577 that those people exercising the trade there 'are commonly the poorest in every parish', while at Chester in the 1630s the alehouse-keepers described themselves as of the 'poorer sort'. Generally speaking, many alehouse-keepers followed the poorer occupations such as tailoring, shoe-making, or husbandry.[1] Again there was always a substantial number of impotent poor, the sick and the elderly, such as Alice Underhill of East Grinstead, 'now aged, lame' and a widow. Widows, among the poorest members of the local community, were often alehouse-keepers: at Bideford in 1660 about a quarter of those licensed were widows. The average household size of victuallers, like that of other poor people, was small and quite often they were recent arrivals in village or town.[2]

For the poor the drink trade undoubtedly offered a vital source of extra or alternative income to help them face rising food prices. The capital investment in setting up an alehouse was minimal: a few alepots and a bench for the back room or cellar-turned-bar. The ale or beer, if it was bought from a brewer, could often be obtained on credit, sometimes on a

societies currently undergoing comparable change: *Social Change in Modern Africa*, ed. A. Southall (1961), 213–16, 227.

[1] PRO, SP 12/116/10; BL, Harley MS. 2104, fol. 148 and *passim*; Kent AO, Sa/ZB 3/14.

[2] East Sussex RO, QR/E 1/31; A. G. Duncan, 'Bideford under the Restored Monarchy', *Trans. Devon Assoc.* xlvii (1915), 316; CCL, E/Q/1; Rawlidge, *A Monster*, sig. E 1; *Chester City Minutes*, 132.

sale-or-return basis.[1] Licensing, as we have said, was frequently ineffective, at least until the early seventeenth century, and consumer demand was strong.

While the alehouse was never the exclusive preserve of the poor, there can be little question that the great majority of its regular customers came from the lower orders—small craftsmen, journeymen, husbandmen, and labourers. A list of customers who frequented Samuel Wood's unlicensed house at New Romney in 1606 included an itinerant baker, a Fulham butcher, unemployed and looking for 'work in haying', a Dover rippier called 'Jack the Pouch', and several local servants and journeymen engaged in poorer crafts like shoemaking.[2] What did the alehouse offer these people? Both beer and ale were a relatively safe tipple, compared say to water which was increasingly suspect, particularly in towns, as a result of deteriorating sanitation caused by population increase.[3] Ale and beer were also a fairly cheap source of nutriment, their prices moving more sluggishly than the leaps and bounds of bread prices. No less important, when social misery became overwhelming for the lower orders in the late sixteenth century, alcoholic beverages had an obvious narcotic value. As one writer observed, the poor man 'quite forgets hunger and thinks on it no longer' with 'a pot of good ale'. That other narcotic, tobacco, was also being smoked and sold in alehouses by the early years of the seventeenth century.[4]

The alehouse provided another basic service for the poor through the provision of food. Cakes, buns, and cheese were the staple fare, though occasionally there was something tastier like the 'pies, pasties and . . . spiced bread' baked by a Leicester victualler; quite often customers brought their own meat to be cooked. Here the alehouse catered not only for the tramping poor in need of sustenance, but also perhaps for poor artisans and day-labourers from the locality, some of whom were now paid just a bare money wage out of which they had to find their

---

[1] Kent AO, PRC 10/24, fol. 321; Bodl., Univ. Chancellor's Court, Depos. Bk. 1604–19, fol. 326ᵛ and *passim*.

[2] Kent AO, NR/JQf 1/2; also QM/SB 49.

[3] D. Hartley, *Water in England* (1964), 194 and *passim*.

[4] J. C. Drummond and A. Wilbraham, *The Englishman's Food* (1939), 137–8; *The Ex-ale-tation of Ale* (1646), 3; K. Thomas, *Religion and the Decline of Magic* (1971), 19–20; Essex RO, Q\SR 235/46–7.

own food; in the past they had usually received part of their wages in kind, in the form of food (and drink) consumed in their employers' households.[1] Equally important, the alehouse also provisioned those many poorer folk who were no longer able, because of declining real wages, to purchase the relatively large units of bread and other food sold at the baker's or the market. In 1615, for instance, one Essex alehouse-keeper retailed brown bread 'to a great number of the very poor people' using 'such weight and measure' as no other trader did.[2]

To some extent, demand for alehouse accommodation also reflected the particular problems of the poor for much of our period. Recent work has indicated that the century or so before the Civil War saw a marked increase in the incidence of physical mobility, as the poor went on the road in search of work. In the late Middle Ages migration had been mainly localized and small-scale, sustained by kinship connections and the hospitality of landowners, clergy, and almshouses. By the late sixteenth century, however, traditional hospitality was in decline, while migration often involved travelling outside the bounds of the extended kinship network. Some migrants slept in barns or ditches, but many others, particularly in bad weather, stayed in alehouses. The accommodation was rudimentary. Evans ap Rice of West Ham was charged in 1584 with 'lodging strange men and women together in one chamber and lodging strange men in his bed with him and his wife'. On other occasions travellers slept on tables or ale-benches.[3] Some of the guests stayed for more than the night. In towns, the most common destination of long-distance migrants at this time, the alehouse regularly functioned as a lodging- or doss-house offering outsiders a foothold in the community until they had found themselves a job or place to live. In 1600, for example,

---

[1] R. F. B. Hodgkinson, 'Extracts from the Act Books . . . Nottingham', *Trans. Thoroton Soc.* xxx (1926), 55; Leics. RO, Leicester Hall Papers, II/18/5/39–40; *Tudor Royal Proclamations*, ed. P. L. Hughes and J. F. Larkin (1969), iii. 18–19 and *passim*.

[2] Essex RO, Q/SR 209/108; also Q/SBa 2/76 and *Poverty in Early-Stuart Salisbury*, ed. P. Slack (Wilts. Rec. Soc., 1975), 111.

[3] Clark and Slack, *Crisis and Order*, 138–40; P. Slack, 'Vagrants and Vagrancy in England, 1598–1664', *EcHR* 2nd ser., xxvii (1974), 360–79; W. H. Hale, *A Series of Precedents and Proceedings in Criminal Causes* (1847), 180; Kent AO, QM/SB 373.

the Norwich magistrates ordered a search to be made 'for such
as make stay in alehouses . . . until they may have opportunity
to be inmates'.[1]

The alehouse also provided economic services for the poor.
Alehouse-keepers frequently acted as pawnbrokers and also
allowed credit—crucial to tide the poor family over the worst
weeks of a bad harvest year. For the newcomer to a community
the victualler and his customers afforded information about
local economic conditions, wage-rates, and places of work. Jobs
could even be fixed up in alehouses as when Prunell Cowling,
who had just come from the Isle of Wight to Southampton and
was staying at the Three Mariners, was approached there by
one French Nicholas and asked 'if she would go to service and
she said yes'. The many poor newcomers to towns often found
temporary jobs in the alehouse itself, as tapster or maid.[2]

Of course the victualling and economic functions of the alehouse were not geared exclusively to the desperate needs of the
poor. In addition to tramping labourers, the alehouse lodged
and entertained many petty traders—tinkers, chapmen, and
broggers riding the coat-tails of the general expansion of inland
trade from the late sixteenth century. These lesser members of
Professor Everitt's 'wayfaring community' not only stayed in
alehouses but made bargains and sold wares there.[3] Again in
better times alehouses might afford the craftsman or small-
holder one of the few local opportunities for conspicuous
consumption and convivial entertainment—drinking, smoking,
and perhaps singing or dancing. Indeed they were an obvious
focus for that high leisure preference found in most under-
developed agrarian economies.[4] None the less, the meagre,
often sordid facilities of most tippling houses were a constant

[1] Norfolk and Norwich RO, Norwich Assembly Book 5, fol. 244.

[2] *Quarter Sessions Records*, ed. J. C. Atkinson, i (North Riding Rec. Soc., 1884),
252; Bodl., MS. Oxon dioc. d. 15, fol. 178ᵛ; *Books of Examinations and Depositions
1570–94*, ed. E. R. Aubrey and G. H. Hamilton (Southampton Rec. Soc., 1914), 73;
Minutes of the Norwich Court of Mayoralty 1632–1635, ed. W. L. Sachse (Norfolk Rec.
Soc., 1967), 156–8.

[3] Essex RO, Q/SR 306/99; 170/61–3; *The Minute Book of Bedford Corporation
1647–64*, ed. G. Parsloe (Beds. Hist. Rec. Soc., 1949), 110; A. Everitt, *Change in the
Provinces: the Seventeenth Century* (Leicester, 1972), 39–40; *Hertfordshire County Records:
Sessions Rolls 1581–1698* (Hertford, 1905), 35.

[4] Gloucester City Lib., GDR 109 (*Keak* v. *Jelf*); D. C. Coleman, 'Labour in
the English Economy of the Seventeenth Century', *EcHR* 2nd ser., viii (1955–56),
esp. 291.

reminder that the alehouse's role was dominated for much of our period by the very basic needs of the poor and destitute.

III

This brings us to another complaint against the alehouse, that it was not only the sanctuary of the poor but also a constant danger to public order. Undoubtedly not all the employment arranged in alehouses was strictly legal. Petty crime was often planned or initiated there. An assault, for example, by five footpads on a gentleman outside Southampton in 1576 seems to have been organized in a city alehouse, and numerous other cases involving alehouses are also known. Poaching expeditions regularly sallied forth from tippling houses.[1] Petty crime was sometimes encouraged by alehouse-keepers. Thus Nicholas Gill, a teenager on the tramp who stayed at the White Hart on the outskirts of Canterbury in 1602, claimed that the host 'knowing him to want money told him that if he would go abroad and find out anything that was worth money and bring the same unto him, he would give him money.' Gill went out, stole four sheep, and was arrested.[2] Not surprisingly, we commonly find victuallers indicted for receiving stolen property.[3]

However, it would be wrong to over-stress the connection between the alehouse and crime. Despite allegations by Thomas Harman, Thomas Dekker, and others that tippling houses were often the full-time headquarters for professional gangs of criminals, almost all our evidence would indicate that the criminal activity centred on alehouses was amateur, small-scale, and sporadic. Only occasionally do we hear of anything more serious, as in William Fleetwood's account of how one Wotton, a decayed merchant keeping an alehouse near Billingsgate, 'procured all the cutpurses about this city to repair to his house [and] there was a school-house set up to learn young boys to cut purses'.[4]

---

[1] *Southampton Court Leet Records 1550–77*, ed. F. J. C. and D. M. Hearnshaw (Southampton Rec. Soc., 1905), 137; Kent AO, QM/SB 456; *Worcestershire County Records*, 78.

[2] Kent AO, QM/SB 485.

[3] *Hertfordshire County Records*, 59; PRO, Assizes 35/67/4/39B; Kent AO, QM/SB 993.

[4] *The Elizabethan Underworld*, ed. A. V. Judges (1930), xxxix. 65, 367.

In the same fashion, pamphlet accounts of the many horrible murders and other acts of violence perpetrated in alehouses were exaggerated, coloured by a concern to shock and condemn. Some violence did of course occur. Edmund Tibbottes of Rowington in Warwickshire lost his licence for suffering 'one Robert Pettitt to be drunk lately in his house, who in the time of his drunkenness there did lately kill one William Benyon'. But, generally speaking, violence of this sort was comparatively unusual. More common were minor disorder and hooliganism. At Malpas in 1615 there suddenly erupted a great tumult in the house of an ale-seller which started as a brawl between two drinkers and ended with 'most of the town . . . disquieted'.[1]

In many cases this kind of disorder in and around the alehouse was caused by drunkenness. At Bayton in Worcestershire, for example, the drunken villagers who reeled out of two unlicensed alehouses were said to 'roll men's timber in the night time into the highways . . . pull up men's pales and stiles and rails', and cause general havoc. On other occasions drunken servants returned home to assault their masters. A medley of commentators argued that drunkenness was escalating in the period. If we are to believe Thomas Young, before the late sixteenth century 'drunkenness was held in the highest degree of hatred that might be amongst us . . . but now [in 1617] it is grown for a custom and the fashion of our age'. Predictably the alehouse was often blamed.[2] Though reliable quantitative evidence is lacking, there may well be some truth in these claims. One reason for the possible growth in drunkenness may have been the rising consumption of beer, more potent than the old ale. Another factor, indicated by William Harrison, may have been the vulnerability of poorer men to the effects of alcohol because of their 'hard and pinching diet'.[3] In addition, research on present-day developing societies has suggested that drunkenness is often associated with the disruption of traditional

---

[1] *Warwick County Records*, ed. S. C. Ratcliff and H. C. Johnson (Warwick, 1935–64), ii. 49; *Quarter Sessions Records . . . for the County Palatine of Chester 1559–1760*, ed. J. H. E. Bennett and J. C. Dewhurst (Lancs. and Ches. Rec. Soc., 1940), 74.

[2] *Worcestershire County Records*, 345; *HMC*, v. 587; Thomas Young, *Englands Bane* (1617), sig. D1ᵛ; see also Robert Harris, 'The Drunkards Cup' (1619) in *Works of Robert Harris* (1654), 304.

[3] Bretherton, 'Country Inns', 169; Edelen, *Description of England*, 132.

communal sanctions as a result of economic and social change. In Tudor and early Stuart England one might argue that increased drunkenness reflected similar developments, with widespread poverty and other pressures helping to cause a shift away from conventional drinking at home towards alehouse drinking, often just with other males, frequently (as in the case of the tramping poor) with complete strangers.[1]

IV

If Puritan preachers and other commentators over-drew the threat to public order posed by the alehouse, how much credence should we give to their further charges, that it was a hot-bed of promiscuity and a corrupter of conventional family life? Prostitution was certainly common in alehouses during the Tudor and early Stuart period. Thus of the twelve unlicensed victuallers presented at Chelmsford in 1567, three or four were further charged with keeping brothels; most were apparently small-scale affairs like the house kept by the aged Mother Bowden with her daughter as the sole whore. Alehouse brothels were rather more organized in the metropolis. According to one report in 1627 the suburbs of Bloomsbury, Petticoat Lane, Wapping, and Radcliffe were swarming with 'many immodest, lascivious, and shameless women generally reputed for notorious common and professed whores, who are entertained into victualling or other houses . . . for base and filthy lucre', sitting at their doors 'exposing and offering themselves to passers by'.[2] Of course prostitution was hardly a new phenomenon in the sixteenth century but the many alehouse brothels clearly did a good trade, catering for the innumerable labourers now on the road, away from their families. Likewise, at least some of the prostitutes were drawn from the same social class, especially in towns, where the influx of poor women led to a surplus over men and a probable loosening of the constraints on female sexuality.[3]

[1] Cf. C. MacAndrew and R. B. Edgerton, *Drunken Comportment. A Social Explanation* (1970), 17 and *passim*; *Society, Culture and Drinking Patterns*, ed. D. J. Pittman and C. R. Snyder (1962), 57–8.

[2] Essex RO, Q/SR 24/20; *Middlesex County Records*, ed. J. C. Jeaffreson (1886–8), iii. 13.

[3] P. Clark and P. Slack, *English Towns in Transition 1500–1700* (1976), 87–8; R. Thompson, *Women in Stuart England and America* (1974), 31–5, 240–1.

At the same time, the alehouse was more than just a venue for commercial sex. Many poorer couples on the tramp struck up casual liaisons there, aided no doubt by the cramped accommodation already noted. Even for the local poor the alehouse served as a rendezvous away from the overcrowded living conditions and prying eyes at home. When Joan Lowe fell in love with a Salisbury apprentice boy they 'met at several alehouses in the city . . . privately' and made love together.[1] Sometimes these liaisons among the poor led to common-law unions; not infrequently they were confirmed by clandestine marriages (often bigamous). On numerous occasions these took place in alehouses. To take one example, in 1621 a Gloucestershire couple went to an alehouse in Minsterworth where they found the local curate. After haggling over the fee he agreed to marry them there: 'having neither book nor candle, the said Mr Jones took [them] by the hands and joined their hands together'.[2] Again, if the liaison led to a pregnancy the unfortunate girl was often packed off to an alehouse, usually in a distant town or village, to be delivered. Some houses were notorious for their association with sexual permissiveness: at one tippling house in Oxfordshire in 1623 the host, his wife, and two helpers had all been charged with various sexual offences in recent years. Not surprisingly, respectable married women tended to stay away from such establishments.[3]

The role of the alehouse as a centre for extra-marital sex, so loudly denounced by respectable society, was once more clearly related to those critical developments in our period already stressed—the growth of poverty, migration, and urbanization. But it would be wrong to see the alehouse merely responding to social and economic forces. If the alehouse appeared such a major threat to the established social order it was also because it came to serve as a focus for traditional values, which were often in conflict with those Puritan concerns and social attitudes now steadily gaining ground among the middling and upper orders of local society. Such traditional values not only rejected or

[1] Essex RO, Q/SR 80/26; Salisbury Dioc. RO, Dean's Court Dep. Book 18, fols. 13 et seq.; Gloucester City Lib., GDR 168 (*Office* v. *Peckes*).

[2] *Quarter Sessions . . . Chester*, 40; Gloucester City Lib., GDR 148 (*Powell* v. *Rastall*); also Bodl., MS. Oxon dioc. d. 16, fol. 187.

[3] CCL, X.2.10, fol. 86; East Sussex RO, QR/E 26/4–5; Bodl., Univ. Chancellor's Court Dep. Bk. 1619–27 (unfol.).

discounted the more restrictive Puritan emphasis on social discipline and family morality, but also stressed the continuing role of the community in popular society.

V

In order to explain the growing importance of the alehouse as a focus for traditional communal values and activities we need to say a few words about the medieval background. Everything would indicate that in the late Middle Ages it was the parish church and the churchyard which provided the principal centre for communal life. It was there that fraternities met, that religious and civic processions assembled, local plays and pageants were performed, villagers participated in folk games, and most inhabitants celebrated at feasts and church-ales.[1] With the Reformation this communal function of the local church came under criticism and attack, particularly in the south and east where Protestant and later Puritan activists sought to purge the English church of what they saw as pagan and Romanist excrescences. Church-ales were bitterly denounced and frequently suppressed; May games and other communal activities centred on the church were likewise discouraged. Even in the highland zone the early seventeenth century saw the church begin to lose its position as the hub of communal life as the result of concerted action by godly ministers and Puritan justices.[2] The royal *Book of Sports* (first published in 1618 and reissued in 1633) and Archbishop Laud's notorious intervention in support of the Somerset church-ales did little to reverse the trend.[3] The parish church came to be one of the principal instruments by which the leading members of local society sought to regulate and control the behaviour of ordinary inhabitants. This development was underscored by the progressive economic and social polarization within local society, in both town and countryside.

[1] For a recent account see C. Phythian-Adams, *Local History and Folklore: a new framework* (1975), 17–18; R. V. French, *Nineteen Centuries of Drink in England* (1884), 116–18.
[2] C. Hill, *Society and Puritanism in Pre-Revolutionary England* (1964), 169; T. G. Barnes, 'County Politics and a Puritan *Cause Célèbre*: Somerset Churchales 1633', *TRHS* 5th ser., ix (1959), 108–10.
[3] Hill, *Society and Puritanism*, 194–7; Barnes, 'Somerset Churchales', 110–11.

In this situation the alehouse provided the obvious alternative forum for communal activity. William Simpson of Springfield in Essex, for instance, was said to allow 'common resorting
of minstrels to his house where the youths of the parish do resort
together on the Sundays and holidays', while further north
'above the number of one hundred persons were assembled
together' at Cuthbert Cowston's alehouse at Normanby 'with
pipes and drums and dancing' during divine service.[1] It was at
the alehouse or in its yard that traditional games and rituals
were now regularly performed. Morris dancers sometimes used
the alehouse as their base, as when a band of them came to
Canterbury in 1589 and 'put on the bells and furniture for the
morris dance' at the George. Football games we know were
played outside the tippling house and bulls were baited from
one alehouse to the next.[2] While the old calendar of folk ritual
increasingly lost its connection with the church there is evidence
that at least some of the observances of the folk year, particularly of the so-called ritual half from Christmas to Midsummer,
continued to be kept in the alehouse with a medley of games and
celebrations. Thus we find examples of mummers in the alehouse at New Year; of dancing at Candlemas; of football and
other jollifications at Shrovetide and on Mid-Lent Sunday; of a
garland and fiddlers at Easter and Ascension Thursday; and of
large-scale feasting and dancing in alehouses on May Day, and
at Whitsuntide and Midsummer.[3]

Again in the case of those *rites de passage* which were still
formally controlled by the Church the alehouse often played an
important role. We noted earlier how clandestine weddings
could occur in tippling houses, but it is important to remember
that even where marriages were solemnized in church the
wedding ceremony was only part of the ritual process of getting
married. Equally important were the dowry negotiations, the
betrothal ritual and post-nuptial feast, all of which frequently

[1] Essex RO, Q/SR 41/30; *Quarter Sessions Records* (N. Riding), ed. Atkinson, 50.
[2] CCL, JQ 1589; Bodl., MS. Oxon dioc. c. 23, fol. 140; Essex RO, Q/SR 5/36;
Quarter Sessions . . . Chester, 166.
[3] Phythian-Adams, *Local History and Folklore*, 22–4; HMC, *Var. Collns.*, i. 130;
W. Addison, *Essex Heyday* (1949), 90–1; Bodl., MS. Oxon dioc. c. 23, fol. 140;
Kent AO, QM/SB 937; Essex RO, Q/SR 5/36; CCL, X.4.1, pt. ii, fols. 51ᵛ, 83
et seq.; F. W. Hackwood, *Inns, Ales and Drinking Customs of Old England* (1909),
116.

took place in alehouses.[1] Likewise christenings and churchings, the ritual purgation of women after childbirth, were also accompanied by heavy feasting at the local tippling house, celebrations which probably overshadowed the church service. As one writer observed: 'at the next churching or christening [the alehouse-keeper] is sure to be rid of two or three dozen of cakes and ale by gossiping neighbours'. Funeral wakes also tended to adjourn, after the burial, to convivial refreshment at a victualling establishment.[2]

At the same time we must be wary of viewing the alehouse as the direct, lineal successor to the parish church in local communal life. The communal activity now centred on the alehouse was less socially comprehensive than in the past, often lacking the presence of more substantial inhabitants; while even in small villages communal life was usually fragmented among two or more alehouses. Moreover, there are already signs of commercialization fostered by alehouse-keepers, and with this went important changes in the format of communal activities. Thus outside games and rituals were increasingly dominated by the young and were probably of declining importance. Instead there was an efflorescence of indoor games better suited to the confines of the small alehouse. Card games became more popular along with the older dice and tables (backgammon). Other indoor games regularly played in alehouses included shove-groat, slide-thrist, tyck-tack, guile-bones or ten-bones, rifling, skittles, and nine-holes. Outdoor games like bowls were brought within the precinct of the alehouse by the construction of bowling-alleys.[3]

In many cases these indoor games involved gambling, previously mainly an upper-class phenomenon. At John Border's house at Aston in Staffordshire a number of local men played

---

[1] Gloucester City Lib., GDR 114 (*Clarke* v. *Lane*); Bodl., MS. Oxon dioc. c. 23, fol. 37; *Depositions and other Ecclesiastical Proceedings from the Courts of Durham* (Surtees Soc., 1845), 254–5.

[2] *HMC*, x, appx. iv, 311; Hale, *Precedents*, 216; Hackwood, *Inns*; 'A Description of the State, Civil and Ecclesiastical, of the County of Lancaster . . .', ed. F. R. Raines, *Chetham Miscellany*, v (Chetham Soc., 1875), 6; *The Acts of the High Commission Court*, ed. W. H. D. Longstaffe (Surtees Soc., 1858), 124–5.

[3] Essex RO, Q/SR 143/24; Kent AO, PRC 39/44, fol. 209; QM/SB 900, 1129; CCL, Hales MSS., Misc.; *Southampton Leet Records*, 120; *HMC* xv, appx. x, 56; *Quarter Sessions Records*, ed. Atkinson, 49; F. G. Emmison, *Elizabethan Life: Disorder* (Chelmsford, 1970), 221.

for money at tables and cards with a stake of 8 shillings a game (probably unusually high). Sometimes the victualler sponsored the gambling. In John Collyn's house at Barling, Essex, Collyn's own son acted as banker, while at Canterbury the victualler Ingram Ellis lent 'to divers of the players money to bear play . . . [winning] the said money from them again'.[1] Gambling always seems to flourish amid adversity and it is likely that many labourers saw it as one of the few chances to improve their meagre earnings in the bleak conditions of the late sixteenth and early seventeenth centuries.

Just as the old communal games acquired a new orientation in the world of the alehouse, so traditional neighbourliness was transmuted into new-style drinking camaraderie. Simple pledges were steadily replaced by elaborate toasting rituals, what William Prynne with typical vehemence called 'this idle, foolish, heathenish and hellish ceremony of beginning, second-ing and pledging healths'. Other conventions included kneeling during the toasts and the adoption of titles by the various drinkers.[2] Many of these customs, one suspects, had filtered down from upper-class practices. The new communal world based at the alehouse never had the same degree of cohesion and unity found in the old traditional community centred on the church.

VI

All this would seem to justify at least some of the middling and upper-class concern with the alehouse as an increasingly com-mon institution of the poor, and as a centre for disorder, immor-ality, and old-style communal activity. None the less, there is still the vital question: how far alehouses represented a real threat to the ecclesiastical and political order of sixteenth- and early seventeenth-century England. Were they really the general headquarters of revolution as some opponents claimed?

During the early years of the Reformation the alehouse fre-quently echoed to the denunciation of the old Catholic order.

[1] *Staffordshire Quarter Sessions Rolls 1581–89*, ed. S. A. H. Burne (William Salt Arch. Soc., 1931), 265; Emmison, *Disorder*, 224; CCL, JQ 1592.

[2] William Prynne, *Healthes: Sicknesse* (1628), sig. B3ᵛ; Harris, 'Drunkards Cup', sig. B3ᵛ; Thomas Nash, *Pierce Penilesse His Supplication* (1592), fol. 23ᵛ; Essex RO, Q/SR 199/144–5; Hale, *Precedents*, 196, 220.

With the restoration of the mass under Mary at least one Protestant group met at a London alehouse, and the Dean of St. Paul's was obliged to complain of the 'wranglers and talkers of holy scripture and of the holy mysteries thereof openly in taverns and common victualling houses'.[1] But in the later sixteenth century, after the Elizabethan settlement, the connection between the alehouse and religious radicalism peters out and only one or two separatist groups are known to have had contact with alehouses before the Civil War.[2] Much more often the alehouse figures as a centre for religious conservatism. One Christopher Clark, who lodged at a Kentish alehouse in the 1570s, was reported to rail there 'upon the ministers and their wives' and trusts 'to shoot a sheaf of arrows' amongst them. Richard Brock, an ale-seller of Bunbury in Cheshire, went further and kept popish relics in his house, which he 'openly sets up before such as come to drink'.[3]

The alehouse also provided a focus for lower-class irreligion and ignorance. The latter was probably a growing phenomenon by the late sixteenth century with the decay of popular Catholicism and the upsurge of poverty—many of the destitute, particularly vagrants, rarely went to church. In one southern county it has been estimated that as many as a fifth of the Elizabethan inhabitants never regularly attended church; the proportion may have been even higher in the larger towns and the woodland areas of the kingdom. As we know, many poorer people drifted instead to the alehouse and its rival entertainments. According to Thomas Young, the inhabitants of the New Forest and Windsor Forest 'go ten times to an alehouse, before they go once to a church'. In towns there were constant complaints of alehouses keeping poor parishioners from worship, while alehouse-keepers themselves were often flagrant, long-service absentees.[4] Given the continuing undercurrent of magic

---

[1] J. E. Oxley, *The Reformation in Essex* (Manchester, 1965), 143–4; D. M. Loades, 'The Enforcement of Reaction, 1553–58', *Journ. of Eccl. Hist.* xvi (1965), 59; CLRO, Repertories 13(i), fol. 193.

[2] *CSPD, 1635–36*, 98; also PRO, SP 16/520/85.

[3] CCL, Y.4.13, fol. 38ᵛ; *Quarter Sessions . . . Chester*, 94.

[4] P. Clark, *English Provincial Society from the Reformation to the Revolution: Religion, Politics and Society in Kent 1500–1640* (Hassocks, 1977), 156–7; Thomas, *Religion and the Decline of Magic*, 160–1; Young, *Englands Bane*, sig. E4ᵛ, F 1; CCL, X.6.10, fol. 16ᵛ; Dover, Town Minute Book (James I etc.), fol. 46ᵛ; *Worcestershire County Records*, 222.

in popular belief at this time, it is hardly surprising that ale-houses also harboured fortune-tellers and witches.[1]

On the other hand, we have found only a few cases of the alehouse playing a positive role as the centre of concerted opposition to the established ecclesiastical order. One instance was at Rye in the 1630s, where a libel spread through the town against those Puritan leaders who 'go to church carefully to hear prayer and to hear sermons' was 'begun in Ryme's house, an alehouse'. Another was the campaign organized against the Puritan minister of Eccleshall about 1600 by Thomas Jackson, a local alehouse-keeper. It was said that Jackson not only kept open house during service-time, but denounced the preacher in church, and arranged for several minstrels to lead a band of a hundred or more local youths to attack the minister's hay. But these were the colourful exceptions to prove the rule.[2]

The alehouse's contribution to political resistance to the ruling class also tended to be small. Alehouses, it is true, some-times served as places where riots were planned or organized. Thus the agitation against the enclosure of Knavesmire at York in the 1530s had one of its preliminary meetings in an ale-house by Micklegate, and rioters also gathered in a Goudhurst alehouse during the Wealden disturbances of 1595. At Maldon the previous year popular action against the corrupt town government was 'prattled in alehouses' and led by an alehouse-keeper, Thomas Spickerwell.[3] In general, however, popular protest in alehouses was mostly confined to the desperate seditious outbursts of individual labourers, outbursts which seem almost invariably to have fallen on deaf ears. There is no evidence that the various abortive artisan combinations of the seventeenth century ever met in alehouses.[4]

The relative failure of the alehouse as a medium for mobiliz-ing popular radicalism, whether religious or political, was finally exposed in the Revolution. Admittedly, a few of the more

[1] *HMC*, xiii, appx. iv, 346; *Acts of the High Commission Court*, 34–42; Kent AO, Fa/JQs 91.
[2] *Reports of cases in the Courts of Star Chamber and High Commission*, ed. S. R. Gardiner (Camden Soc., 1886), 149–52; *Staffordshire Quarter Sessions Rolls 1598–1602*, ed. S. A. H. Burne (William Salt Arch. Soc., 1936), 132–3.
[3] *York Civic Records*, iv. 2 et seq.; Staffs. RO, D.593/S/4/36/10 (exam. Robt. Copping); Essex RO, D/B3/3/397/18; W. J. Petchey, 'The Borough of Maldon, Essex 1500–1688' (Ph.D. thesis, Leicester Univ., 1972), 248–9.
[4] PRO, SP 14/107/31; Dover, Town Minute Book (James I etc.), fol. 141.

extreme sects like the Ranters may have met in alehouses in the 1650s. Likewise, at the start of the political crisis with the meeting of the Long Parliament alehouses were alive with the latest political gossip; in December 1641 it was reported that 'every tinker and tapster called for justice' against the king.[1] But it would be dangerous to give too much credence to Henry Wilkinson's claim in 1646 that 'alehouses generally are the Devil's castles, the meeting places of malignants and sectaries'. Just as the Puritan campaign against the royalist oligarchy in London in 1641 was organized in taverns, so the Levellers seem to have chosen similar select establishments for their meetings— not alehouses.[2] In the 1650s alehouses were haunted more by cavalier agents and disenchanted republicans plotting the restoration of the king than by committed radicals. During the royalist rising in the West in 1655 numerous plotters lodged in alehouses about Shrewsbury, while anti-Cromwellian tracts were probably stored in similar establishments in London.[3]

VII

How do we explain the failure of alehouses to live up to their reputation as the command centres of popular revolution? Part of the answer is structural, relating to the alehouse, its host, and customers. Though the alehouse certainly offered the poorer orders a wide range of services (victualling, economic, social, and communal), only rarely do we have a sense that it exercised a positive independent function in popular society rather than simply responding to large-scale economic and other change. As we have seen, there is little evidence to support allegations that the alehouse was the nexus of a tightly knit popular subculture. To some extent this reflects the fact that the fully fledged alehouse was a relatively new institution in our

[1] C. Hill, *The World Turned Upside Down* (1972), 198–201; *Depositions from the Castle of York* (Surtees Soc., 1861), 3; B. Manning, *The English People and the English Revolution, 1640–1649* (1976), 84.

[2] Henry Wilkinson, *Miranda, Stupenda* (1646), 26; V. Pearl, *London and the Outbreak of the Puritan Revolution* (1961), 233–4; *The Clarke Papers*, ii, ed. C. H. Firth (Camden Soc., 1894), 256; *The Leveller Tracts 1647–1653*, ed. W. Haller and G. Davies (N.Y., 1944), 100. The 'Whalebone' where the Leveller leaders met was almost certainly a tavern (I am indebted to Prof. Aylmer for his advice on this point).

[3] Thurloe, iii. 211, 254–5; vi. 315.

period, but other variables were also involved. One was the ambiguous position of the alehouse-keeper. As we know, he had close ties with his customers; he was frequently poor, quite often a newcomer; to make a reasonable living he had to defer to popular opinion. And yet he was never simply the people's man. To secure an alehouse or (if he were unlicensed) to avoid suppression, he needed at least the toleration of local land-owners or parish big-wigs—especially when licensing controls were strengthened. He might also need official protection if his premises were threatened by drunken revellers. Moreover, the alehouse-keeper, though poor, was normally a man with an eye for the main chance. Like other small middlemen he was repeatedly accused of market offences, as at Southampton in 1574 when many of the town's victuallers were presented as 'common forestallers and regrators and engrossers of the market'. Alehouse-keepers were also notorious for giving short measure and dispensing adulterated drink.[1] Thus in practice there was a division of interest between the victualler and his customers which the authorities took care to exploit. During the rebellion of the Northern Earls in 1569 the Council of the North adjured all alehouse-keepers to report suspicious visitors or sinister news to the authorities.[2]

The clientele of the alehouse was also rather a heterogeneous body. As we have seen, many of its customers were tramping poor, men of questionable status, at best tolerated, quite often disliked, by local residents. No less significant, the political awareness of these marginal people was minimal, mostly limited to the pathetic shout of sedition. It is true that the alehouse had some kind of communal function for local inhabitants and on occasion there might be concerted disorder centred around it. But recent work on the small community has shown how narrow its perspective usually was—mainly focused on the locality and its neighbourhood. Communal action and protest tended to be negative and defensive—primarily concerned with protecting local custom and interests against outsiders.[3]

The radical potential of the alehouse, such as it was, was

[1] Bucks. RO, D/A/c 23, fol. 49ᵛ; *Southampton Leet Records*, 104; *Worcestershire County Records*, 647.
[2] *York Civic Records*, vi. 160.
[3] Clark and Slack, *Crisis and Order*, 152; P. Clark, 'Popular Protest and Disturbance in Kent, 1558–1640', *EcHR* 2nd ser., xxix (1976), 378.

further restricted by external developments. The period from the mid-sixteenth century saw the steady expansion of administrative control over alehouses. A flurry of local ordinances appeared in the 1540s, regulating and suppressing disorderly or superfluous alehouses, and many of these were put on a national footing by the introduction of statutory licensing in 1552. Over the next hundred-odd years Parliament enacted a succession of measures seeking to tighten sanctions against alehouses and the disorders which occurred there. Local action during Elizabeth's reign tended to be patchy and sporadic, with concerted campaigns limited to periods of economic crisis when magistrates feared that the drink trade would consume too much corn for brewing and that alehouses might serve as flash-points for social and political discontent. However, by the turn of the century there is evidence of a mounting local attack on alehouses aided by the improved efficiency of provincial administration.[1] At first the attack was hampered by royal efforts to use alehouse licensing as a source of revenue, but with the collapse of the alehouse patent in 1621 the campaign really got under way, in both town and countryside. Licensed victuallers were now required to find substantial sureties and unlicensed tipplers were firmly suppressed, with persistent offenders going to gaol.[2] Of major significance was the growing power over victuallers wielded by petty sessions—less open to corruption than individual justices and with a closer ear to the ground than quarter sessions. All these moves were given further impetus by the Book of Orders and the general consolidation of county government during the 1630s.[3] While the Civil War may have caused some relaxation of control at the local level, by 1650 Puritan magistrates and preachers had allied together in many areas to suppress tippling houses. In some counties surveillance

[1] CCL, AC 2, fol. 36ᵛ; Clark and Slack, *Crisis and Order*, 19; Bretherton, 'Country Inns', 149–50; Colchester, Assembly Book 1576–99, fol. 149 et seq.; Rawlidge, *A Monster*, sig. F1 et seq.

[2] *Records of the Borough of Leicester 1603–1688*, ed. H. Stocks (Cambridge, 1923), 174–5, 192–3; J. R. Kent, 'Attitudes of members of the house of commons to the regulation of personal conduct in late Elizabethan and early Stuart England', *BIHR* xlvi (1973), 58–60; East Sussex RO, QR/E 24, 26, 27; E 32/101; F. G. Emmison, *Early Essex Town Meetings* (1970), 1, 7, 81, 109.

[3] Clark, *English Provincial Society*, 311, 350–2; T. G. Barnes, *Somerset 1625–1640* (1961), 173–4, 176; A. Fletcher, *A County Community in Peace and War: Sussex 1600–60* (1975), 154.

was also strengthened by local justices working in close co-operation with committees of parish worthies.[1]

Needless to say, there was a good deal of administrative huffing and puffing when the Major-Generals confronted the problem of the alehouse in the mid-1650s. In Lincolnshire we hear of the suppression of 'forty, fifty, and three-score alehouses in some corporations'; in East Anglia comprehensive regulations were issued by quarter sessions for the licensing and control of alehouses doubtless at the instigation of Deputy Major-General Haynes.[2] But as in other fields the Major-Generals exaggerated their own impact. Many of the regulations they issued were merely revamped versions of measures already in force before the Civil War. Purges of alehouses were only really effective if they were followed up by strict local control; and for this the Major-Generals were dependent on the ordinary county administration. Their only significant contribution to the long-term regulation of alehouses was the establishment in the provinces of special licensing meetings of petty sessions. By the 1670s these so-called brewster sessions had been adopted in most counties. The county governments of Restoration England continued the administrative advance in other ways too, and by 1700 the alehouse was firmly under control in all but the largest urban centres.[3]

This mounting official control over the alehouse was underlined by another development—the growing power of larger brewers in the drink trade. By the start of the seventeenth century we find the leading brewers in many towns banding together as trade companies under civic auspices in order to curb competition from petty brewers and brewing victuallers. The trend was accelerated by the Crown's scheme in the 1630s

[1] J. P. Cooper, 'Social and Economic Policies under the Commonwealth' in *The Interregnum*, ed. G. E. Aylmer (1972), 126; K. E. Wrightson, 'The Puritan Reformation of Manners with special reference to the counties of Lancashire and Essex 1640–1660' (Ph.D. thesis, Cambridge Univ., 1973), 142 et seq.; J. S. Morrill, *Cheshire 1630–1660* (Oxford, 1974), 239–41.

[2] *The Publick Intelligencer* (28 Jan.–4 Feb. 1656); *Norfolk Quarter Sessions Order Book 1650–1657*, ed. D. E. H. James (Norfolk Rec. Soc., 1955), 16, 86; Essex RO, Q/SO 1, fol. 120.

[3] Essex RO, Q/SR 423/22 et seq.; J. A. Chartres, 'The Place of Inns in the Commercial Life of London and Western England 1660–1760' (D.Phil. thesis, Oxford Univ., 1973), 53 et seq. Special licensing sessions had been active in London since at least 1613 (CLRO, Repertories 32(ii), fol. 216).

to restrict brewing to those licensed by royal patentees. It was also encouraged by local magistrates, anxious to regulate the drink trade: in Essex in 1637 there was a plan to confine brewing in the county to fifty-six common brewers, while at Winchester during the 1650s the corporation established a municipal monopoly with just two brewers. Elsewhere we find informal combinations operating and the start of brewing dynasties.[1] Along with this growing domination of production, the larger brewers were also expanding their influence over the alehouse. Already by the 1620s the tied house had probably appeared in a number of centres with the alehouse-keeper the tenant of a local brewer (though tied houses only became widespread in the following century). More important in our period was the increase in informal influence exercised by brewers—through loans, credit, agreement to act as sureties, and a friendly word to the justices when licences were renewed.[2] With larger brewers often hand-in-glove with local magistrates, administrative controls over victuallers now had considerable bite: offending tipplers faced not only the loss of their licence, but, even more important, the cessation of credit and supplies.

By the late seventeenth century the problem of the alehouse appeared increasingly under control. Numbers had probably started to stabilize, at least outside the largest urban centres, and there was a marked reduction in the output of polemic against the alehouse and its threat to respectable society. No doubt all this stemmed in part from the success and effectiveness of the growing formal and informal regulation just described. But it also reflected the diminution of some of those acute pressures which had contributed to the development of the alehouse as an important popular centre before the Revolution. By 1700 the condition of the poor was less critical and may even have started to improve; large-scale subsistence migration was on the wane and the rate of urban growth, outside the major centres, was tending to slacken. There was

[1] Gloucester City Lib., City MS. 1697/1888; BL, Harley MS. 2104, fols. 172 et seq.; Wrightson, 'The Puritan Reformation of Manners', 92; Rosen, 'History of Winchester', 272; PRO, SP 18/179/16; R. Fitch, 'Notices of Norwich Brewers' Marks and Trade Regulations', *Norfolk Archaeol.* v (1859), 315–16, 328–9.

[2] Rawlidge, *A Monster*, 15–16; PRO, E 134/22 James I/Hilary 17. For eighteenth-century tied houses see Mathias, *Brewing Industry*, 117–38; East Sussex RO, QR E 33/3–6, 8, 11, 12; Essex RO, Q/SR 103/261.

even a limited, self-conscious move by the landed classes to reassert the traditional values of communal life, to bring communal activities and games back within the ambit of church and manor.[1]

In conclusion we can say that the century or so before the Civil War witnessed the new importance of the alehouse as a vital and widespread institution in the popular landscape, an importance created by a complex of factors, many of them associated with a developing and urbanizing society. In a number of respects the alehouse seemed to threaten the general order and conventions of established society. Yet the alehouse was never quite the radical levelling centre that preachers and magistrates portrayed. If it had been, the course of the English Revolution might have been rather different.

[1] The Moral Reform Movement from the 1690s probably had only limited success in its campaign against alehouses; T. C. Curtis and W. A. Speck, 'The Societies for the Reformation of Manners', *Literature and History*, iii (1976), 46–51; Clark and Slack, *English Towns*, 124–5; R. W. Malcolmson, *Popular Recreations in English Society 1700–1850* (Cambridge, 1973), 13. For a somewhat different view see E. P. Thompson, 'Patrician Society, Plebeian Culture', *Journ. of Soc. Hist.* vii (1974), 393–4.

Science and Religion at Oxford
before the Civil War

NICHOLAS TYACKE

WHY did the 'new philosophy', as contemporaries called it, make such rapid strides in seventeenth-century England? Or, rephrasing the question, what underlying explanation can be offered for such phenomena of the period as William Harvey, Robert Boyle, and the Royal Society? Historians of science, in addressing themselves to this problem, have canvassed various aspects of the environment, religious, institutional, and economic. Puritanism especially has been seen as integral to the triumph of the new scientific values. At the same time the importance of institutionalization is widely recognized; Gresham College in London, with its chairs of astronomy and geometry, and the similar Savilian professorships at Oxford came into existence respectively in 1597 and 1619. The mercantile setting of Gresham College has also been stressed, as well as the college's involvement with navigational instruction and its different clientele compared to the universities. Christopher Hill has been an outstanding contributor to the recent debate.[1]

Difficulties of definition, however, have arisen, because

* An earlier version of this essay was read to a Monday seminar at the Institute of Historical Research, and I am especially grateful to Professor P. M. Rattansi and Mr. B. D. Greenslade for their comments. Inspiration to break what is for me new historical ground has come mainly from my wife, Sarah Tyacke. Mr. J. P. Cooper, Dr. Roger Highfield, Professor T. W. Moody, Dr. J. A. North, and Mr. Keith Thomas have also kindly helped in various ways, and I am particularly indebted to the following librarians and archivists: at Dublin Mr. W. O'Sullivan of Trinity College, at Oxford Dr. D. G. Cooper of Corpus Christi College, Mr. Charles Morgenstern of St. John's College, Miss Helen Powell of The Queen's College, Mr. David Vaisey of the Bodleian Library, and Mr. H. J. R. Wing of Christ Church, and at Mercers' Hall, London, Miss Jean Imray.

[1] C. Hill, *Intellectual Origins of the English Revolution* (Oxford, 1965), esp. 14–84, 301–14, and in *The Intellectual Revolution of the Seventeenth Century*, ed. C. Webster (1974), 243–53, 280–3.

Puritanism is an elastic term. Science too as a concept presents problems, but from 1600 onwards, with the publication of *De Magnete*, we can talk of a 'Gilbert tradition' in England, its hallmarks 'a weakening of confidence in the ancients, a growing appreciation of the importance of experiment and direct observation, and the spirit of independent thought'. This was accompanied by an increasingly sophisticated mathematics and an improved instrumentation.[1] Disagreement about religious identity can moreover be sidestepped by examining the fate of science in a context generally agreed to have been hostile towards Puritanism. Here a crucial case study is Oxford University, which from 1630 came under the direct Arminian control of William Laud as Chancellor.[2] For if a positive correlation exists between Puritanism and science we would expect the eclipse of one adversely to affect the other, and the rise to power of Arminianism in the late 1620s to be accompanied by scientific decline or at least stagnation. Therefore this essay concentrates on the Oxford quarter-century which runs from the endowment of new teaching posts in astronomy, geometry, and anatomy, as well as a botanical garden, during the years 1619–24, to the period of the Civil War.

Philosophic reform had its Oxford advocates even before the 1620s, as can be illustrated by two plays performed at Christ Church in February 1618. Both plays are comedies but they also carry reformist messages. *Technogamia*, written by Barten Holyday, concerns the fate of Astronomia and Geometres at the hands of the villains Magus and his wife Astrologia, ending with Magus and Astrologia being exiled from 'the commonwealth of the sciences'. Such treatment is a far cry from the Elizabethan John Dee, who happily mixed magic with science, and it anticipates the debarring by Sir Henry Savile of his astronomy professor from 'professing the doctrine of nativities and all judicial astrology without exception'.[3] The second play,

---

[1] R. F. Jones, *Ancients and Moderns* (Berkeley, 1965), 84; E. G. R. Taylor, *The Mathematical Practitioners of Tudor and Stuart England* (Cambridge, 1970), 49–83 and *passim*; D. W. Waters, *The Art of Navigation in England in Elizabethan and Early Stuart Times* (1958), pt. ii.

[2] The disastrous consequences for Puritanism stemming from the Arminianization of the Church of England are discussed in my essay, 'Puritanism, Arminianism and Counter-Revolution' in *The Origins of the English Civil War*, ed. C. Russell (1973), 119–43.

[3] Barten Holyday, *Technogamia*, ed. M. J. C. Cavanaugh (Washington, D.C.,

Robert Burton's *Philosophaster*, is an attack on 'pseudo' philosophy. The heroes are Polumathes and Philobiblos, two wandering scholars, while the false philosophers include an Aristotelian logician and are generally identified as those able 'to explain a syllogism'. The only explicit Oxford reference is to the Bodleian Library 'wherein many dead are found, unhappily held by chains'.[1] Burton like Holyday was a Student of Christ Church. Also in 1618 Michael Barkley, on graduation, presented the Christ Church Library with a set of globes, celestial and terrestrial, 'in gratiam studiosorum mathematicae'.[2] That some Christ Church tutors were teaching mathematics at this date is less surprising when we recall that Edmund Gunter, a future Gresham Professor of Astronomy, had only recently left the college after a residence of fifteen years. Gunter's *Description and Use of the Sector* had circulated in Latin manuscript since 1607, and when an English version was finally published in 1623 one of those who received a presentation copy was Robert Burton.[3]

As regards astronomical theory, Holyday was a conservative who denied both the diurnal rotation of the earth on its axis and its annual rotation about the sun. Burton was more adventurous; in the 1628 edition of his *Anatomy of Melancholy* he says that diurnal rotation is 'most probable' and remarks on his use of an eight-foot telescope to observe the satellites of Jupiter.[4] He was outshone, however, by Brian Twyne, a Fellow of Corpus Christi College, who as early as 1613 drew attention to the telescopic discoveries of Galileo, in a volume of verses published by the University. Twyne's copy of the 1610 Venice edition of Galileo's *Siderius Nuncius* is still extant, as are some of his

1942), 104–5; P. J. French, *John Dee: the World of an Elizabethan Magus* (1972), esp. 89–125; *Oxford University Statutes*, trans. G. R. M. Ward (1845–51), i. 274.

[1] Robert Burton, *Philosophaster*, ed. and trans. P. Jordan-Smith (Stanford, 1931), 53, 211.

[2] Christ Church, Oxford, Donors' Book, fol. 55. A pair of globes was also donated to Trinity College, in the mid 1620s, by Devorox Frogg; Trinity College, Oxford, Benefactors' Book, no. 28. For earlier globes see E. Craster, 'Elizabethan Globes at Oxford', *Geographical Journ.* cxvii (1951), 24–6.

[3] Edmund Gunter, *The Description and Use of the Sector* (1623), 143. The copy of Gunter's *Description* owned by Burton, and now in Christ Church Library, is inscribed 'ex dono authoris'.

[4] Barten Holyday, *A Survey of the World* (Oxford, 1661), 1–2, 8; Robert Burton, *The Anatomy of Melancholy* (Oxford, 1628), 239–40.

astronomical notebooks.[1] He owed his scientific interests to Thomas Allen of Gloucester Hall, who was to be described at his death in 1632 as 'omnium sui aevi mathematicorum . . . ipsam animam atque solem'.[2] In religion Holyday and Burton were orthodox Calvinists, like most Church of England clergy at this time. Twyne by contrast was a member of the earliest Oxford group conversant with Dutch Arminianism, and probably belonged to that theological school.[3] His scientific mentor Allen inclined to Catholicism.[4]

By 1620 individual scientific enthusiasm of the kind fostered by Allen was gaining a more permanent Oxford base, thanks to the book-acquisition policy of the Bodleian Library. The printed catalogue of that year reveals a considerable holding of recent scientific works, some of them in English. For example, eight separate items by Kepler are listed, while English books include Aaron Rathborne's *Surveyor* and the translation by Edward Wright of Napier's *Logarithmes*, both of 1616, as well as Mark Ridley's *Treatise of Magneticall Bodies and Motions* of 1613. But books on the shelves are one thing, readers are another. Here the new Savilian professorships were of prime importance in providing a regular scientific focus. Attendance at lectures in geometry became compulsory from 1620 for all students in their third to fifth years at university, and astronomy lectures were similarly obligatory on all sixth- and seventh-year students. Both professors were expected to lecture twice weekly in term time.[5]

Explaining the reasons for his munificence to the University, Savile wrote of his desire 'to redeem so far as in me lies, almost from destruction, sciences of the noblest kind'. His subsequent references to surveying, mechanics, and navigation suggest a more practical concern. Indeed as early as 1592, in an Oxford

---

[1] *Justa Funebria Ptolemaei Oxoniensis* (Oxford, 1613), 115; R. F. Ovenell, 'The Library of Brian Twyne', *Oxford Bibliog. Soc.* new ser. iv (1952), 24; M. H. Curtis, *Oxford and Cambridge in Transition, 1558–1642* (Oxford, 1959), 120–1.

[2] Anthony Wood, *Athenae Oxonienses*, ed. P. Bliss (1813–20), ii. 543; [William Burton and George Bathurst], *In Thomae Alleni . . . exequiarum . . . Orationes Binae* (1632), 6.

[3] Barten Holyday, *Of the Nature of Faith* (1654), 16–17; Robert Burton, *Anatomy* (Oxford, 1628), 641. I discuss the evidence for Twyne's Arminianism in my forthcoming book, *The Rise of English Arminianism*.

[4] Anthony Wood, *History and Antiquities of the University of Oxford*, ed. J. Gutch (Oxford, 1792–6), ii. 232. I am grateful to Dr. A. Davidson for this reference.

[5] Thomas James, *Catalogus Universalis Librorum in Bibliotheca Bodleiana* (Oxford, 1620), 278–9, 414, 424, 533; Ward, *Statutes*, 275–6.

oration delivered before Queen Elizabeth, Savile had argued for the compatibility of philosophy with a life of active soldiering and quoted Plato on the use of mathematics in warfare.[1] Savile in his own life had successfully combined action with scholarship, service to the state with the editing of classical and patristic texts, and his educational ideal would appear to have approximated to that of the virtuoso. Yet England's need for military preparedness was probably also in his mind, a matter made all the more urgent by the outbreak of the Thirty Years War in 1618.[2]

The first Savilian professors were handpicked by the founder. Henry Briggs, appointed from Gresham College to the geometry chair, is mainly remembered for his work on logarithms. His religious position at this date is best described as Puritan; in 1589, as a young Fellow of St. John's College, Cambridge, he had supported the cause of Puritan nonconformity and his surviving letters from the second decade of the seventeenth century seem to place him firmly in the Puritan camp. Thus he wrote in 1610 of difficulties experienced in getting a religious book printed in England without the 'index expurgatorius, if anything in it do sound suspiciously'. But as the modern historian of Gresham College, Dr. Ian Adamson, has written of Briggs, 'it is perhaps more accurate to describe him as a Puritan and scientist than a Puritan scientist'.[3] Savile's other appointment, to his chair of astronomy, was John Bainbridge. In 1619 Bainbridge had published his account of the comet of the previous year, opening with the remark that 'I hope there bee none so farre more precize than wise, as to thinke it unlawfull to looke on this celestiall signe with other then vulgar

[1] Ward, *Statutes*, 272–4; Henry Savile, *Oratio Coram Regina Elizabetha Oxoniae Habita* (Oxford, 1658), 6. On this same occasion Savile argued for the abolition of astrology, ibid. 8–9.

[2] W. E. Houghton, 'The English Virtuoso in the Seventeenth Century', *Journ. Hist. Ideas*, iii (1942), 51–73, 190–219; Curtis, *Oxford and Cambridge*, 126–9, 258–60, 263–5. Discussing Roman warfare, Savile wrote that 'no state may looke to stand without notable molestation and danger of ruine, much lesse to enlarge, which in any kind of service, on foote, or on horsebacke, or by sea is quite defective and utterly disfurnished', *Annotations upon . . . Tacitus* (Oxford, 1591), 71.

[3] H. C. Porter, *Reformation and Reaction in Tudor Cambridge* (Cambridge, 1958), 188; James Ussher, *Works*, ed. C. R. Elrington (Dublin, 1847–64), xv. 62; I. Adamson, 'The Foundation and Early History of Gresham College London, 1596–1704' (Ph.D. thesis, Cambridge Univ., 1976), 133. I am grateful to Dr. Adamson for permission to read his thesis.

and pore-blinde eyes: (which were still to maintaine ignorance mother of devotion)'. Later in the same work, discussing the origins of comets, he refers to those 'who have beene scrupulous to conceit any creation since that first saboth'. Such references to preciseness and scrupulosity seem to have Puritans in mind. At the same time Bainbridge's epistolary style is much more secular than that of Briggs.[1]

According to the Savilian statutes the Professor of Geometry was to expound three set books: Euclid's *Elements*, the *Conics* of Apollonius, and all of Archimedes. In addition he was required to provide classes in surveying and arithmetic, and given the interests of Briggs it is likely that the latter included instruction in the use of logarithms. Certainly Bainbridge assumed knowledge of logarithms when lecturing.[2] The prescribed text in astronomy was Ptolemy's *Almagest*. But there was no archaism involved here for, as F. R. Johnson has pointed out, 'a mastery of the mathematics of the *Almagest* was, until the time of Newton, the necessary foundation of mathematical astronomy for Copernicans as well as for the adherents of the old cosmology'. Furthermore it is clear from his surviving lecture notes that Bainbridge took seriously the Savilian injunction to include in his exposition 'the discoveries . . . of modern writers'. Thus in his inaugural lecture of 9 January 1621 Bainbridge referred to recent telescopic findings concerning the three-bodied appearance of Saturn, the satellites of Jupiter, sun-spots, the phases of Venus, and the mountainous surface of the moon. Similarly in January 1625 he discussed the work of Galileo, Kepler, and Scheiner. Bainbridge also, on 11 May 1621, commenced a series of solar and lunar eclipse observations at Oxford, part of which was communicated to Pierre Gassendi in the 1630s.[3]

Two distinguished products of this new scientific teaching were Henry Gellibrand of Trinity College, who in 1627 succeeded Gunter as Gresham Professor of Astronomy, and John

[1] John Bainbridge, *An Astronomicall Description of the Late Comet* (1619), 1, 24; Ussher, *Works*, xv. 62–4, 89–90, 213, 351–3, 394, 447–8.

[2] Ward, *Statutes*, 272–4; Trinity College Dublin, MS. 386(5), fol. 67. I was alerted to the existence of the Bainbridge papers at Dublin by R. G. Frank, 'Science, Medicine and the Universities of Early Modern England: Background and Sources', *History of Science*, xi (1973), 203 and n. 25.

[3] Ward, *Statutes*, 273; F. R. Johnson, *Astronomical Thought in Renaissance England* (Baltimore, 1937), 270; Trinity College Dublin, MS. 382, fols. 27, 27ᵛ, 122–4; ibid., MS. 386(4), 13–14; Pierre Gassendi, *Opera Omnia* (Lyons, 1658), vi. 424–5.

Greaves of Merton College, who in 1630 became Gresham Professor of Geometry. The academic references supplied for them by Bainbridge make instructive reading. Gellibrand, he writes, 'was for some yeares a frequent and attentive auditor at my lectures, and hath had many private conferences with me in astronomicall matters, whereby he hath shewed his singular affection to those studies, and his good proficiency in the same'. That Bainbridge did not exaggerate the abilities of Gellibrand is borne out by his later career; as Gresham professor he was, for example, to complete the *Trigonometria Britannica*, which Briggs had left unfinished at the time of his death. Concerning Greaves, Bainbridge wrote that, in addition to attending astronomy lectures he 'hath by many private conferences given me occasion to take notice of his singular skill in the mathematicks, especially in the geometry of Euclide'. During the 1630s Greaves was to make an astronomical expedition to Alexandria, 'a thing that hath beene much desired by the astronomers of this age, but never undertaken by any'. Gellibrand was clearly one of the 'hotter sort' of Protestants, sponsoring in 1630 an almanack with a calendar of saints based on Foxe's *Book of Martyrs*.[1] Greaves, by contrast, became a protégé of Laud and fled to Oxford at the outbreak of the Civil War.

In addition to the specialist labours of Briggs and Bainbridge, a more general Oxford current of philosophic reform continued to flow. Evidence for this comes from a series of books published at Oxford, and therefore licensed by the Vice-Chancellor. Thus in 1621 there appeared the first edition of Burton's *Anatomy of Melancholy*, a book with important implications for the cult of virtuosity. 'What more pleasing studies can there be', Burton asked, 'then the mathematickes, theorick or practick part?' Or, as he elaborated in a later edition, 'what [is] so intricate or pleasing withall as to peruse Napier's *Logarithmes*, or those tables of artificiall sines and tangents not long since set out by mine old collegiat, good friend and late fellow Student of Christ Church in Oxford, Mr. Edmund Gunter . . . or those elaborate conclusions of his *Sector, Quadrant and Crosse-Staffe*?' Burton was here prescribing mathematics as a cure for

---

[1] Mercers' Hall, London, Gresham Repertory, ii. 3, 23; PRO, S.P. 16/381/75: John Greaves to Peter Turner, 10 Feb. 1637. This letter has previously been dated incorrectly to 1638; William Prynne, *Canterburies Doome* (1648), 182.

melancholy, and it is interesting that Robert Boyle later recommended their study in similar terms.[1] But Burton also advocated
scientific 'experiments'. Like Boyle too he believed in the practical application of knowledge, his special concerns being inland
navigation, fen drainage, and 'industry [which] is a lodestone
to drawe all good things'.[2]

The year following the first appearance of Burton's *Anatomy*
saw the Oxford publication of *Philosophia Libera* by Nathanael
Carpenter. Highly critical of Aristotelian philosophy, the book
invites comparison with a similar manifesto published in 1624
by the Catholic Gassendi.[3] Carpenter, a Fellow of Exeter
College, begins by enunciating the principle 'in nullius iuratus
verba', and then proceeds to a series of anti-Aristotelian
propositions. Like Burton he accepted the daily rotation of the
earth, but rejected the idea of a sun-centred universe. In 1625
Carpenter incorporated the astronomical ideas of *Philosophia
Libera* in his *Geography Delineated*, which was also produced by
the Oxford press.[4] More important, however, than either
Burton or Carpenter, as regards breadth of appeal, was George
Hakewill, whose *Apologie of the Power and Providence of God in the
Government of the World* was published at Oxford in 1627.
Dedicated to the University, the book attacked the then
widely held belief in the historical decay of intellectual and all
other natural powers. On the contrary, says Hakewill, 'not any
one man, or nation, or age, but rather mankinde is it which in
latitude of capacity answeres to the universality of things to be
knowne'. As part of his argument Hakewill instances recent
scientific achievements, such as the invention of logarithms,
although his book was chiefly significant as a solvent of traditional attitudes. Some idea of its effect is conveyed by the
testimonials of various Oxford contemporaries, which preface
the 1635 edition; while scientists like Allen and Briggs claim
always to have believed the truth of Hakewill's argument that

[1] Robert Burton, *Anatomy* (Oxford, 1621), 352 and (Oxford, 1628), 264;
R. E. W. Maddison, *The Life of the Honourable Robert Boyle* (1969), 17–18.

[2] Burton, *Anatomy* (1621), 51–8, and (Oxford, 1632), 280–1; Jones, *Ancients
and Moderns*, 202–4.

[3] Pierre Gassendi, *Exercitationum Paradoxicarum Adversus Aristoteleos* (Grenoble,
1624).

[4] Nathanael Carpenter, *Philosophia Libera* (Oxford, 1622), 'Ad Florentissimam
Oxoniensis Academiae Iuventutem Praefatio' and *passim*; id., *Geography Delineated*
(Oxford, 1625), bk. i. 75–97.

nature remains unimpaired over the centuries, others such as Degory Wheare, Camden Professor of History, and Samuel Fell, Lady Margaret Professor of Divinity, admit to having been converted by him.[1] For the non-specialist the book opened up the prospect of new mental worlds to conquer.

Carpenter and Hakewill, like Burton, were Calvinists in their theology.[2] As such they were in accord with the Church of England norm under James I, yet during the 1620s dramatic changes were overtaking official English religious teaching. The crisis centred on the writings of Richard Montagu, who in 1624 publicly denied the credal Calvinism of the English Church. Montagu turned out to have powerful episcopal backers, and within little more than a year of the accession of Charles I Calvinist doctrine was outlawed by royal proclamation.[3] The resulting sense of shock is well illustrated by an entry for 1626 in the diary of Thomas Crosfield, a Fellow of Queen's College, Oxford. 'Nota', he wrote, 'quod statim post inauguratio-nem Regis Caroli, non sine periculo inter orthodoxos, serpebat Pelagianismi cancer a Montagu pestis doctrinae corporis.'[4] A less derogatory and more accurate term than Pelagian to describe the religious views favoured by Charles I is Arminian. The full impact of the Arminian revolution on Oxford was nevertheless delayed some two years thanks to the influence of the University Chancellor, the third Earl of Pembroke, who favoured the Calvinist party. But in 1628 Charles I reiterated his earlier ruling against Calvinism, and explicitly included the doctrinal teaching of the universities within his prohibition. Henceforth predestinarian teaching was effectively banned in Oxford as elsewhere, and the term Puritan was now redefined by Arminians to include Calvinism. One of the leading archi-tects of the new Arminian policy was, of course, Laud, who in

[1] George Hakewill, *An Apologie* (Oxford, 1627), sigs. b3, Ooo 2ᵛ, and (Oxford, 1635), sigs. c1ʳ⁻ᵛ, c2.

[2] Nathanael Carpenter, *Achitophel, or the Picture of a Wicked Politician* (1629), 13–14, 30–4; George Hakewill, *An Answere to . . . Dr. Carier* (1616), 284–92.

[3] This proclamation 'for the establishing of the peace and quiet of the Church of England' was issued on 14 June 1626 and is reprinted in J. P. Kenyon, *The Stuart Constitution* (Cambridge, 1966), 154–5. For the official and anti-Calvinist interpretation put upon it, see Bishop Neile's letter to the Vice-Chancellor of Cambridge University, dated 16 June 1626; Cambridge Univ. Archives, Royal Letters of Charles I, no. 6.

[4] The Queen's College, Oxford, MS. 390, fol. 19.

1630 succeeded Pembroke as Chancellor of Oxford. What, however, is most striking in the scientific context is the *irrelevance* of these religious changes. Far from withering on the bough the scientific movement at Oxford continued to flourish.

Thus in October 1626 Bainbridge can be found writing to Archbishop Ussher, who was interested in astronomy from the point of view of chronology. His letter shows no interest in recent religious changes, despite Ussher being a declared opponent of Arminianism. Instead Bainbridge reports that he has begun a study of Arabic, in order to read mathematical works in that language, and says he is also 'very busy in the fabric of a large instrument for observations, that I may, mea fide, both teach and write; and here again I humbly entreat you to take in your consideration my petition at Oxford, that you would, as occasion shall be offered, commend to the munificence of some noble benefactors this excellent and rare part of astronomy, (ὕλη ἀστρονομική), which would certainly commend them to posterity; in the mean time I would not fail to publish their fame unto the learned world.' As well as continuing his series of eclipse observations, it is probable that Bainbridge hoped to witness the predicted transit of Venus across the face of the sun in December 1631. Certainly he discussed the subject in 1630, describing the technique of projecting the solar disc through a telescope and on to a white screen in a darkened room. Unfortunately and, owing to an error in Kepler's tables, unexpectedly, the transit occurred during the European night and was consequently invisible.[1]

But by 1631 Bainbridge was embarked on a far more ambitious project, namely the organization of an astronomical expedition to South America. As before he was on the look-out for a patron, and he found him in Sir Thomas Roe, the distinguished explorer and diplomat. Again the appeal for financial support is couched in terms of the enduring fame that will accrue to the benefactor, whose name, says Bainbridge, 'shall bee resplendent ... when all other the most precious jewels that ever were brought from either India shall bee consumed and forgotten'.[2] The proposal was to employ the services of a sea

---

[1] Ussher, *Works*, xiii. 351, xv. 352; Bodl., Smith MS. 92, p. 23; B. H. Woolf, *The Transits of Venus* (Princeton, 1959), 10–12.

[2] Trinity College Dublin, MS. 386(1), fols. 43, 43ᵛ.

captain, Roger Fry, who was already bound on a colonizing venture to Guiana. We can show from his own notebook that Fry was at Merton College in December 1626 and December 1627, measuring star altitudes, although there appears to be no trace of him in either the University or College records. Fry also notes a number of sun-spot observations which he made in June and July 1630, using the same method as recommended by Bainbridge in order to observe the transit of Venus.[1] For the Guiana expedition of the following year Bainbridge furnished Fry with a set of detailed astronomical instructions, and clearly one of the objectives was to obtain simultaneous eclipse observations with a view to an improved cartography. More generally Bainbridge hoped that accurate recordings from 'under the aequator or neer thereabouts' would 'clear many doubts in the moste principall poynts of astronomy and bee of singular use in geographye and navigation'.[2] In the event the expedition was attacked by the Portuguese, and Fry was taken as a prisoner to Brazil. But undeterred he proceeded to make a series of astronomical observations at São Luis do Maranhão on the Brazilian coast, and sent the first results back to Oxford in May 1633.[3] Bainbridge, with understandable excitement, announced the news in his lectures, speaking of 'Marenhamiae urbis Brasiliae . . . in quo loco multas observationes caelestes nuper fecit Anglus quidam astronomiae scientissimus'. In particular he cited his and Fry's observations of a solar eclipse which had occurred on 29 March 1633; this indicated that the longitudinal position of São Luis do Maranhão was just under 45° west of Oxford.[4]

At the same time as the Guiana expedition Bainbridge also planned to send a qualified astronomer to Alexandria, in order to check the results of the ancient Greeks.[5] The choice ultimately fell on his former pupil John Greaves, although the latter did not set out until 1637. Finance as ever was a problem,

---

[1] Ibid., MS. 443, fols. 23ᵛ, 25ᵛ, 28ᵛ, 40.

[2] Ibid., MS. 386(1), fols. 43–44ᵛ.

[3] Roger Fry to Bainbridge, 10 May 1633. Ibid., MS. 382, fols. 105, 105ᵛ. The subsequent fate of Fry is at present unknown, but J. A. Williamson is clearly mistaken when he writes that Fry was killed by the Portuguese in 1631; *English Colonies in Guiana and on the Amazon, 1604–1688* (Oxford, 1923), 139.

[4] Trinity College Dublin, MS. 386(5), fols. 48, 101ᵛ.

[5] William Hakewill to Bainbridge, 5 April 1631. Ibid., MS. 382, fol. 98.

but one of those soliciting funds on behalf of Greaves was Lord
Treasurer Juxon, who had succeeded Laud as President of
St. John's College, Oxford, and then as Arminian Bishop of
London. 'This worke', wrote Juxon of the proposed Alexandria
expedition, 'I find by the best astronomers, especially by Ticho
Brache [*sic*] and Kepler, hath bynn much desired as tending to
the advancement of that science, and I hope it wil be an honour
to that nation and prove ours if we first observe it.' He went on
to suggest that Greaves's employers should assist 'the advancement of learning' by subsidizing his purchase of astronomical
instruments.[1] Like Fry, Greaves also hoped to contribute
towards solving the problem of longitude on land, by the
method of simultaneous eclipse observations. Writing from Constantinople in August 1638, Greaves outlined his preparations:
'the eclipse of the moon in December next will be observed
(if it please God) at Bagdad, Constantinople, Smyrna and
Alexandria, all which places I have furnished with convenient
instruments, and given them instructions according to Tycho
Brahe's how they should observe.' From Constantinople
Greaves sailed to Alexandria, which was his main astronomical
goal, and spent six months there making observations chiefly
of the fixed stars.[2]

Medical studies at Oxford were undeniably slower to take
off than the mathematical sciences. This was partly due to the
fact that the new Tomlins Lectureship in Anatomy was held in
plurality by the Regius Professor of Medicine, Thomas Clayton,
much of whose time was taken up with transforming Broadgates Hall into Pembroke College. Nevertheless statutory
provision was made in 1624 for regular dissections to be performed by a surgeon under the direction of the Regius Professor,[3] and one of Clayton's pupils was Edward Dawson who in
1633 publicly maintained the probability of the circulation of
the blood, at the annual Oxford Act. Dawson's thesis, which I
discovered in 1963, has been described as 'an exceptional
concession to contemporary issues, in a period of Galenic

[1] Bishop Juxon to the Gresham Committee, 30 April 1637. PRO, T. 56/13, fol.
2ᵛ. I owe this reference to the kindness of Mr. T. A. Mason.
[2] John Greaves, *Miscellaneous Works* (1737), ii. 437–8, 443–4. According to
David Gregory, writing in 1697, Greaves's observations were not superseded until
those made by Halley and Hevelius. Bodl., Smith MS. 93, pp. 165–7.
[3] Ward, *Statutes*, 289–90.

supremacy'.[1] Yet it can also be seen as exemplifying the best of Oxford medical science at that time. Dawson was clearly considered an outstanding student, being chosen for instance in July 1621, while a member of Broadgates Hall, to make a speech at the foundation of the Oxford botanical garden.[2] Another Oxford exemplar is George Joyliffe of Pembroke College, who in the 1640s 'exercising himself much in anatomy with the help of Dr. Clayton, Master of his College and the King's Professor of Physic, . . . made some discovery of that fourth sort of vessels plainly differing from veins, arteries, and nerves, now called the lympheducts'.[3] Moreover close links existed between medical and mathematical practitioners. Thus Bainbridge in addition to being Savilian Professor of Astronomy was a licentiate of the College of Physicians and practised medicine, while Clayton in 1622 addressed some verses jointly to Bainbridge and Briggs, 'doctissimos professores mathematicos'. In 1640 both Bainbridge and Clayton contributed letters of recommendation to *Theatrum Botanicum* by John Parkinson, at the same time taking the opportunity to advertise the Oxford botanical garden which was now at long last nearing completion.[4] The following year John Greaves, who was to succeed Bainbridge as Savilian Professor in 1643, supplied a prefatory poem for George Ent's *Apologia pro Circulatione Sanguinis*.[5] It is further worth remembering that there existed an experimental tradition among members of the College of Physicians well before Harvey's discovery of circulation, but a tradition of experiment in magnetism not anatomy, outstanding names being Gilbert and Ridley. We would therefore expect medicine to lag somewhat behind other sciences at Oxford, as elsewhere in England. Later, during the Civil War, Harvey was to come in person to Oxford and head a group working on embryology.[6]

---

[1] C. Webster, *The Great Instauration: Science, Medicine and Reform, 1626–60* (1975), 125, 139.

[2] R. W. T. Günther, *Oxford Gardens* (Oxford, 1912), 2.

[3] Wood, *Athenae*, iii. 351.

[4] W. Munk, *Roll of the Royal College of Physicians* (1878), i. 175–6; Bodl., Rawlinson MS. letters 41, fols. 3–36; *Ultima Linea Savilii* (Oxford, 1622), sig. F2ʳ⁻ᵛ; John Parkinson, *Theatrum Botanicum* (1640), sig. a.

[5] George Ent, *Apologia pro Circulatione Sanguinis* (1641), sig. A4ᵛ.

[6] R. G. Frank, 'John Aubrey, F.R.S., John Lydall, and Science at Commonwealth Oxford', *Notes and Records of the Royal Society*, 27 (1972–3), 195.

Meanwhile in the mid 1630s Archbishop Laud had begun to take a direct interest in the advancement of Oxford science. As part of his building programme at St. John's College, he projected a mathematical library which was designed to reinforce the Savilian lectures at collegiate level. He envisaged a special collection of 'mathematical books and instruments', and expressed the wish in October 1635 that 'the younger Fellows and students' of St. John's would 'give themselves more to those [mathematical] studies'. Some two and a half years later, in May 1638, he wrote to the President and Fellows of the College 'I am glad to hear from you that my mathematical library is in such forwardness.'[1] By now donations were beginning to arrive; for example William Oughtred's *Circles of Proportion and the Horizontall Instrument*, both the book and the brass instrument, were presented this year by George Barkham, son of a member of Laud's household.[2] At about the same time the library acquired a pair of globes and a quadrant, and John Speed, son of the map-maker, gave a pair of human skeletons.[3] In 1634 Laud had also purchased a number of books probably with the intention of giving them to the St. John's mathematical library. These books included Napier's *Logarithmes*, in the English translation by Edward Wright, Harriot's *Ars Analytica Praxis*, and atlases by Bertius, Mercator, and Ortelius.

The foundation by Laud of an Arabic lectureship in 1636 also had a related scientific purpose. For it was hoped that the Muslim world would yield a rich harvest of mathematical manuscripts. The first holder of the post, Edward Pococke, accompanied John Greaves to the Middle East in 1637, and his Oxford duties were undertaken temporarily by Greaves's brother Thomas, who began his course, on 19 July 1637, with an oration entitled *De Linguae Arabicae Utilitate et Praestantia*.

[1] William Laud, *Works*, ed. W. Scott and J. Bliss (Oxford, 1847–60), vii. 192, 434. Unless otherwise stated, information concerning items in the St. John's College Library is derived from inscriptions in the extant books.

[2] St. John's College, Oxford, MS. 37, fols. 163–4. The book and instrument are at present divided between the St. John's College Library and the Oxford Museum of the History of Science; it is to be hoped that they will one day be reunited.

[3] W. C. Costin, *The History of St. John's College Oxford, 1598–1860* (Oxford Hist. Soc., 1958), 76; St. John's College, Oxford, Computus Annuus, 1640–41, fol. 38; Wood, *Athenae*, ii. 660 (I owe this reference to Mr. J. F. Fuggles).

'Utilitas' for Thomas Greaves comprehended algebra, arith-metic, and astronomy. Such subjects, together with the grow-ing importance of the Arabic language for trade, had been stressed by Pococke's teacher William Bedwell as early as 1612, when dedicating his edition of the Arabic version of St. John's Epistles to the Arminian Lancelot Andrewes. Pococke too, as former chaplain to the Turkey merchants at Aleppo, would be aware of the significance of the Levant in these years for English commerce.[1] The idea of utility also occurs in such a seemingly unlikely place as the imprimatur affixed in 1634 to Captain Luke Foxe's account of his search for a North-West Passage. The licence by Samuel Baker, chaplain to Bishop Juxon, runs 'resensui librum hunc . . . in quo nihil reperio quo minus cum utilitate publica imprimatur'.[2]

The book-acquisition policy of the Bodleian Library continued to favour the growth of science at Oxford, as can be seen from the supplementary catalogue published in 1635. New arrivals included Harvey's *De Motu Cordis et Sanguinis* of 1628 and Gassendi's *Mercurius in Sole Visus et Venus Invisa* of 1632, as well as ten further works by Kepler. Examples of recent English scientific works listed are Richard Norwood's *Trigonometrie* of 1631 and Oughtred's *Circles of Proportion and the Horizontall Instrument* of 1632.[3] Similarly colleges like Merton and Christ Church maintained their scientific interests. In 1632 at Merton, the college to which the Savilian professorships were attached, John Greaves and Hugh Cressy respectively answered in the affirmative the thesis questions 'An mathesis sit scientiarum praestantissima?' and 'An scepticorum dubitantia praeferenda sit peripateticorum thesibus?' Greaves was already Gresham Professor of Geometry and kept in touch with his 'friends at Merton College' even when in the Middle East during the late 1630s. Cressy had delivered an oration at the funeral of

[1] Thomas Greaves, *De Linguae Arabicae* (Oxford, 1639), 9, 12; William Bedwell, *D. Johannis Apostoli et Evangelistae Epistolae Catholicae Omnes Arabicae* (Leyden, 1612), sig. A2; *DNB s.n.* Pococke, Edward; R. Davis, 'England and the Mediter-ranean, 1570–1670' in *Essays in the Economic and Social History of Tudor and Stuart England*, ed. F. J. Fisher (Cambridge, 1961).

[2] *The Voyages of Captain Luke Foxe of Hull, and Captain Thomas James of Bristol*, ed. M. Christy (Hakluyt Soc., 1894), ii. 445.

[3] John Rous, *Appendix ad Catalogum Librorum in Bibliotheca Bodleiana* (Oxford, 1635), 78, 89, 105–6, 135.

Henry Briggs in 1630 and subsequently became chaplain to the Earl of Strafford, ending his days as a Benedictine monk.[1] At Christ Church Burton was now Librarian and remained abreast of astronomical developments, possessing not only Gassendi's account of the transit of Mercury across the face of the sun in November 1631 but also the related commentaries by Hortensius and Schickard. He also owned a set of 'surveighing books and instruments', 'two crosse staves', and a collection of 'Englishe bookes of husbandry', whose authors included Gabriel Plattes the agricultural improver.[2]

Whether Burton gave formal instruction in scientific subjects is unclear,[3] although John Gregory, chaplain of Christ Church at this time, apparently did, to judge from his posthumously published 'Description and Use of the Terrestrial Globe . . . [and] of Maps and Charts Universal and Particular'. This certainly reads as if originally delivered in lecture form. It also draws on recently published scientific material. Thus Gregory cites Gellibrand's work on magnetic variation, published in 1635, and illustrates a discussion of longitude with the simultaneous observation of a lunar eclipse on 29 October 1631, by Gellibrand at London and Captain Thomas James at Charlton south of Hudson Bay. He refers as well to the 'use of the celestial and terrestrial spheres by the supposition of Copernicus per terram mobilem'. Gregory subsequently became domestic chaplain to Bishop Duppa, dying near Oxford in 1646 his circumstances financially reduced.[4] His departure from Christ Church in about 1639 was marked by the return of Robert Payne, who had migrated in 1624 to Pembroke College as one of the original Fellows. Payne had then left Oxford for service with the Earl of Newcastle, assisting him in his laboratory experiments and in 1636 translating into English Galileo's *Della Scienza Mecanica*.[5] As Canon of Christ

[1] Merton College, Oxford, Register, ii. 310; Bodl., Smith MS. 93, pp. 137–8; Wood, *Athenae*, ii. 492; *DNB s.n.* Cressy, Hugh.

[2] W. Osler *et al.*, 'Robert Burton and the *Anatomy of Melancholy*', *Oxford Bibliog. Soc.* i (1927), 219–20, 230, 233–4, 240.

[3] Among those to whom Burton bequeathed mathematical instruments in August 1639 was the Earl of Downe, who had matriculated two months previously; ibid. 220.

[4] John Gregory, *Gregorii Posthuma* (1649), 272, 281, 289. My attention was drawn to John Gregory by Mr. A. J. Turner; *DNB s.n.* Gregory, John (1607–46).

[5] J. Jacquot, 'Sir Charles Cavendish and his Learned Friends', *Annals of*

Church he presented the college in 1642 with Galileo's *Systema Cosmicum* and a brass instrument by Gunter. In 1648 Payne was purged by the Parliamentary Visitors, along with the Savilian professors John Greaves and Peter Turner.[1]

At a more popular philosophic level during the 1630s new editions of Burton, Carpenter, and Hakewill were all produced by the Oxford press. Over the same period Copernican theory was becoming more widely accepted. We can tell from Bainbridge's lecture notes that he positively recommended the heliocentric hypothesis to his audience,[2] but in 1635 a particularly bold step was taken. Codification of the University Statutes had recently been completed, and it was now further decided to print the University syllabus in diagrammatic form. The resulting sheet, dedicated to Laud, shows the day and hour of each lecture, by means of a series of concentric circles with a sun in the middle; the moon, representing Monday, and a clock are so placed in relation to the sun as to indicate that the motif is Copernican.

The most likely author was Turner, who had succeeded Briggs as Savilian Professor of Geometry in 1630 and was a protégé of Laud. Turner had earlier devised a proctorial cycle which was similarly illustrated by a circular diagram, and he was instructed by Laud in 1634 to 'review' the draft of the new statutes. The Vice-Chancellor's accounts of 1635–6 record a payment to Turner of £40 for three journeys to London 'about the University Statutes'.[3] One result seems to have been the *Encyclopaedia seu Orbis Literarum*, as it was called, and in 1638 this Copernican diagram was bound up with an abridged version of the University Statutes intended for student use.[4] Therefore we can say, with pardonable exaggeration, that from

Science, 8 (1952), 21; B. D. Greenslade, 'The Falkland Circle: a Study in Tradition from Jonson to Halifax' (M.A. thesis, Univ. of London, 1955), 153–9. Mr. Greenslade has most generously made available to me his information concerning Payne.

[1] Christ Church, Oxford, Donors' Book, fol. 94; *The Register of the Visitors of the University of Oxford, 1647–58*, ed. M. Burrows (Camden Soc., 1881), lxxxii.

[2] Trinity College, Dublin, MS. 386(3), fol. 22ᵛ.

[3] F. Madan, *The Early Oxford Press, 1468–1640* (Oxford Hist. Soc., 1895), 145, 186–7; Wood, *Athenae*, iii. 307; Laud, v. 99; Oxford Univ. Archives, W.P.B. 21(4), 233.

[4] Madan, *Oxford Press*, 208–9. Samuel Boyes of Magdalen Hall, who had matriculated in 1637, paid 1s. 4d. for his copy of the *Statuta Selecta* in 1638; St. John's College Lib., Oxford.

the late 1630s every Oxford undergraduate carried a Copernican system in his pocket.

The sun at the centre of the 1635 *Encyclopaedia* may in addition be intended to represent King Charles I, since Copernican

Centre detail from *Encyclopaedia seu Orbis Literarum* (Oxford, 1635)
(*Reproduced by permission of the British Library*)

sun-king imagery can be found two years earlier in a collection of verses published by the University. Entitled *Solis Britannici Perigaeum*, the volume marked the occasion of Charles's journey to Scotland in 1633. Thomas Lockey, one of the contributors and a Student of Christ Church, had written that with the King 'ticed from his sphere . . . our shine with him' England 'wandered in shadow darke' and 'walk't in night'. Use of the terms wander and walk, together with a reference to Queen Henrietta Maria as the moon, indicate that Lockey was here extending the analogy of the king as sun to that of the state as planet earth in orbit around the sun. Silenced in 1651, Lockey returned to Oxford at the Restoration as Librarian of the Bodleian; the inventory taken at his death in 1679 notes, among items 'in the summer house', a 'telescope with some other mathematicall instruments'.[1] Of a piece with the increasing vogue for Copernicanism at Oxford during the chancellorship of Laud is the fact that in February 1640 John Wilkins's *Discourse Concerning a New Planet* was licensed by a chaplain of Juxon *and* by Accepted Frewen, Vice-Chancellor of Oxford University and as such deputy to Laud.[2] This book was the first full-scale English defence of Copernicanism and the author, who had recently left Magdalen Hall, both sought and got the official approval of his alma mater.

In some ways, however, the philosophic climax of this Laudian decade was the Oxford publication in 1640 of Francis Bacon's *Advancement and Proficience of Learning*. This was a translation by Gilbert Watts, Fellow of Lincoln College, from the 1623 Latin edition. Dedicating his efforts to King Charles and the Prince of Wales, Watts claimed that 'it is only the benigne aspect and irradiation of princes that inspires the globe of learning, and makes arts and sciences grow up and florish', and he described Bacon as 'the first that ever joynd rationall and experimentall philosophy in a regular correspondence'. The title-page is an adaptation of the one found in Bacon's *Novum Organum* of 1620 which shows the ship of human intellect sailing through the Pillars of Hercules. In the 1640 version the pillars are transformed into spires, the one labelled Oxonium and the other Cantabrigia, each resting on volumes by Bacon. Above float two spheres, the 'mundus visibilis' and the 'mundus intellectualis', joined by two hands: 'ratione et experientia foederantur'. The legend from Daniel 12: 4, 'multi pertransibunt et augebitur scientia', occurs in both versions.[3] Such a

---

[1] *Solis Britannici Perigaeum* (Oxford, 1633), sig. L1ᵛ; *DNB s.n.* Lockey, Thomas; Oxford Univ. Archives, Hyp. B. 15.

[2] E. Arber, *A Transcript of the Register of the Company of Stationers of London, 1554–1640* (1875–94), iv. 472.

[3] Francis Bacon, *Of the Advancement and Proficience of Learning* (Oxford, 1640), sigs. ¶2ᵛ, ¶ 3ᵛ.

prophecy had already begun to be realized literally in the astronomical expeditions organized from Oxford by Bainbridge during the 1630s and the phrase 'advancement of learning' was now part of the vocabulary of educated Englishmen. Bishop Juxon, as we have remarked, used the phrase in 1637 and so did Bainbridge in 1629.[1] But the novelty of Bacon lay primarily in his call for the systematic construction of a 'natural history' of observations and experiments, as the basis of a 'new philosophy'. This looks forward to the work of the Oxford philosophical 'clubb' in the early 1650s and ultimately to that of the Royal Society.[2]

Watts, the translator of Bacon, was presented by the King to an Essex living in 1642, which was subsequently sequestered by Parliament. Before his death in 1657 he had begun work on an elaborate edition of the works of Charles I.[3] Enthusiasm for the philosophy of Bacon was shared by many of the royalist gentry gathered in Oxford during the Civil War, men like Justinian Isham and Sir Christopher Hatton. By 1639 Isham had made an 'abridgement' of Bacon's ideas concerning scientific advance, and earned the compliment from William Rawley, former secretary to Bacon, that 'of our nation your self is the second, or third man, that I know of who hath addicted himself [to] or profitted by those studies'. At about the same time Hatton provided Samuel Hartlib, the pansophical reformer, with an unpublished Bacon manuscript.[4] Isham was a committed defender of the English Prayer Book, while Hatton was a patron of the Arminian Jeremy Taylor.[5] They were to become Fellows of the Royal Society in 1663. Thus it would seem that no particular religious or political group had a majority interest in Bacon.

Close scrutiny then of scientific developments at Oxford,

---

[1] Ussher, *Works*, xv. 447.

[2] H. W. Robinson, 'An Unpublished Letter of Dr. Seth Ward Relating to the Early Meetings of the Oxford Philosophical Society', *Notes and Records of the Royal Society*, 7 (1950), 69.

[3] Richard Newcourt, *Repertorium* (1708–10), ii. 668; *DNB s.n.* Watts, Gilbert; Corpus Christi College, Oxford, MS. 326.

[4] Northants RO, MS. I.C. 228; Sheffield Univ. Lib., Hartlib MSS. 44/2/1, 44/29.

[5] *The Correspondence of Bishop Brian Duppa and Sir Justinian Isham, 1650–60*, ed. G. Isham (Northants Rec. Soc., 1955), xxxix; F. Madan, *Oxford Books* (Oxford, 1912–31), ii. 165, 342–3.

in the decades before the Civil War, indicates a negative correlation between religion and science. Despite Arminianism, the upward movement of science continued unabated. At the same time we can detect the growth of new values. Concepts like advancement and utility emerged during these years, as did the ideal of the virtuoso. Clearly the institutional endowment of science played a central role. But in a wider context the fortunes of Oxford science reflected changes in the English economy. Oxford efforts to grapple with the problem of longitude, 'the major practical problem of the science of the day', paralleled the work in France of Nicolas Peiresc and in the United Provinces of Willem Blaeu.[1] For it was no accident that the countries moving into the commercial leadership of Europe were also those in the scientific vanguard. In England we must take account too of changes in land management and the accompanying rise of the estate surveyor. The religious background, however, remained pluralistic, embracing all manner of Protestants *and* Catholics. To this evolving pattern of seventeenth-century science, European as well as English, Laudian Oxford made a significant contribution.

[1] S. L. Chapin, 'The Astronomical Activities of Nicolas Claude Fabri de Peiresc', *Isis*, 48 (1957), 13–29; P. H. J. Baudet, *Notice sur la part prise par W. J. Blaeu . . . dans la determination des longitudes terrestres* (Utrecht, 1875).

The Art of Law and the Law of God
Sir Henry Finch (1558–1625)

WILFRID R. PREST

CHRISTOPHER HILL has made an important contribution to our understanding of the sociological links between Puritanism and the legal profession, a conjunction previously examined largely in terms of church and parliamentary politics.[1] More recently Professor Bouwsma further broadened the discussion by his assertion that lawyers throughout post-Reformation Europe showed a common tendency to uphold the claims of their profession to manage men's disputes according to its own institutionalized values, 'rather than in subordination to some larger definition of the ultimate purpose of existence'. Thus the lawyers were 'supreme secularisers'; although not necessarily indifferent to the claims of religion as individuals, Catholic and Protestant jurists shared a preference for 'a kind of piety that stressed the spiritual and inward quality of faith, contrasted it sharply with the world and its ways, and by emphasising the incongruity liberated secular life from direct religious control'.[2]

Bouwsma's thesis clearly merits and requires further investigation, for we know very little about the religious attitudes and beliefs of individual English common lawyers in this period (let alone their counterparts across the Channel). Apart from the fact that it falls within what Dr. Baker aptly terms the Dark Age of English legal history, historians have tended to

* Drafts of this essay were kindly read by Leland Carlson, Trish Crawford, Frank McGregor, and Keith Thomas, and heard by members of the seminars of Professors Joel Hurstfield and Tom Barnes. I have benefited considerably from their helpful comments, and those of colleagues and friends too numerous to mention here; the responsibility for remaining errors of fact and judgement is entirely my own.

[1] *Society and Puritanism in Pre-Revolutionary England* (1964), 162, 302–7, 330–42, 349–53, and *Intellectual Origins of the English Revolution* (Oxford, 1965), ch. 5.

[2] W. J. Bouwsma, 'Lawyers in Early Modern Culture', *Amer. Hist. Rev.* lxxviii (1973), 321–2.

regard the law and lawyers as intrinsically less rewarding subjects than the persons and concerns of politicians, clergymen, merchants, scholars, and soldiers.[1] While that general neglect cannot be explained solely by a lack of source material, there is the particular difficulty that few lawyers of this period left direct evidence of their religious views, so that an individual's beliefs can usually be inferred only at second hand from a wide range of miscellaneous sources.

Among the fortunate exceptions to this generalization, Sir Henry Finch, serjeant-at-law to James I, is best known today as the author of two legal texts, the law-French *Nomotexnia* (1613) and the posthumously published English version, *Law, or a Discourse thereof*... (1627), which sought to provide students with a comprehensive and systematic guide to the intimidating complexities of English law.[2] However, Christopher Hill reminds us that Finch also published *The Worldes Great Restauration, Or The Calling of the Jewes* (1621), a treatise collating Biblical references to the conversion of the Jews in the Last Days, and prophesying the imminent return of the scattered tribes of Israel to the Holy Land, where they would establish a Judaeo-Christian empire exercising sovereignty over the entire world.[3] This remarkable apocalyptic tract was in fact only the culmination of Finch's published religious writings, which are now largely forgotten and unidentified. Read in conjunction with the surviving (albeit sadly fragmentary) biographical evidence, they permit us to trace the development of Finch's visionary Zionism from seeds implanted during his student days at Christ's College, Cambridge, and illuminate the process by which a learned and zealous lay Puritan differentiated the demands of his worldly and spiritual professions.

After a brief account of Finch's family and education, we shall examine an early manuscript treatise which foreshadows the major preoccupations of his later writings, seeking both to methodize the common law according to the dialectical precepts of the influential French philosopher Peter Ramus, and to clarify its relationship to the Laws of Moses. Thereafter,

[1] J. H. Baker, 'The Dark Age of English Legal History', in *Legal History Studies 1972*, ed. D. Jenkins (Cardiff, 1975).
[2] Cf. W. S. Holdsworth, *A History of English Law*, v (1924), 399–401.
[3] Hill, *Society and Puritanism*, 203.

however, Finch's works divide into a legal and a religious stream, flowing along parallel but separate channels. In a group of three religious treatises, the first of which appeared in 1590 and provided the model for two subsequent versions published in the second decade of the seventeenth century, Finch applied Ramist techniques to the exposition of the doctrines of reformed Christianity. We shall attempt to relate the content and appearance of these three books to Finch's changing personal circumstances, particularly his identification with the radical Protestant cause in the 1580s and '90s, his subsequent withdrawal from public notice and his sudden elevation to Court office and favour in the middle years of James I.

Finch's growing preoccupation with the calling of the Jews is already evident in the last of these works. Following a brief discussion of Judaizing tendencies in post-Reformation England and of other influences which may help to explain the development of Finch's distinctive Zionist eschatology, we shall examine the significance of his final tract, *The Worldes Great Restauration* (1621), as a polemical critique of the Jacobean church and state. After an account of the official reaction to Finch's book, the essay concludes with an attempt to clarify some seeming paradoxes of Finch's career and writings by reference to the changing role of the legal profession in early modern English society.

The Law and the Word

Born in 1558, the third son of a Kentish squire and soldier, Henry Finch was the first (though by no means the last) of his name to achieve high rank in the legal profession.[1] Finchs from Kent had been members of Gray's Inn since the late fifteenth century, but Henry's closest hereditary connection with the law came via his mother, the heiress of Sir Thomas Moyle, Chancellor of the Court of Augmentations under Henry VIII. After the death in 1563 of Sir Thomas Finch, her first husband and Henry's father, Lady Katherine Finch married Nicholas St. Leger, a Puritan M.P. and lawyer from yet another prominent Kent family. St. Leger seems to have exercised consider-

---

[1] I am most grateful to the History of Parliament Trust for access to their unpublished file on Finch, which supersedes all previous accounts and from which biographical information is drawn except where noted below.

able influence over his stepson and subsidized his expenses at Christ's College, Cambridge, where he was admitted in 1572 under the tutorial supervision of the famous Puritan Laurence Chaderton.[1]

The example of 'that excellent and learned man' (to whom he later sent his own eldest son as pupil) doubtless encouraged Henry to learn Hebrew, an unusual undertaking for one not committed to the ministry. He also enthusiastically imbibed the Ramist dialectic of which his tutor was Cambridge's first public exponent. The first fruits of this discipleship took the form of an academic exercise presented to his stepfather in 1577. This hitherto neglected manuscript, 'Artificii Dialectici et Rhetorici in Q. Horatii Flaci carminium odas decem, analysis', is Finch's earliest surviving work and possibly the earliest known attempt of any English author to illustrate Ramist principles through the exposition of a body of texts.[2] The young graduate's stated resolution 'to follow in the steps of Peter Ramus and refute by my example those who wish logic and rhetoric, which no part of human life can do without . . . to be confined to argumentative conjecture and sophistical quibbles . . .' foreshadows his lifelong concern to put his learning to practical use and locates the precise source of that didactic, methodizing strain which characterizes all his later writings.[3]

After taking his B.A., Henry Finch was admitted in 1577 to Gray's Inn, where little is known of his early career (even the precise date of his call to the Bar being uncertain).[4] But the linguistic and philosophical skills acquired at Cambridge did not atrophy under the weight of legal studies. Indeed his next surviving manuscript sought to apply both to the common law itself.

'Nomotexnia, or the Common Law of England in such lawful method written as it may justly challenge the name of an art. With a Conference or Reformation of the same law by the law

---

[1] E. Searle, *Lordship and Community* (Toronto, 1974), 423; J. Peile, *Biographical Register of Christ's College, I: 1448–1665* (Cambridge, 1910), 122.

[2] W. S. Howell, *Logic and Rhetoric in England, 1500–1700* (Princeton, 1956), 179; H. C. Porter, *Reformation and Reaction in Tudor Cambridge* (Cambridge, 1958), 236–8; BL, Sloane MS. 2737, fols. 1ᵛ–2.

[3] Ibid., fol. 2ᵛ (I am indebted to Mrs. C. Young for help with this and other passages of translation).

[4] The 'Thomas' Finch called on 22 June 1585 is probably a mistake for Henry: Gray's Inn MS., Pension Order Book I, fol. 186.

of God' is undated, but the dedication to Sir Philip Sidney suggests that it was composed before the latter's death in 1586.[1] 'Nomotexnia', the first part of this treatise, is primarily descriptive and expository in intent, using standard Ramist techniques to reduce the complex bulk of the law to a neat and rational system. Its companion piece, the 'Conference or Reformation', develops a Puritan-Hebraist critique of various common-law doctrines and principles enunciated in 'Nomotexnia'. Here Finch aims first to demonstrate that 'our law, though in all circumstances and ceremonies not the same, yet in substance is so far from disagreeing' with God's law as set out in the Old Testament, 'that it may rather seem to be built and grounded upon it'; and second, to urge specific reforms so as to bring the law of England into fuller accord with the law of God.[2]

While Protestant reformers generally agreed that the ceremonial part of the Mosaic law had been abrogated by Christ, and that the moral law of the Decalogue continued in force as part of the law of nature, the precise status of the judicial or civil law of the Jews remained in dispute. Whereas the Thirty-nine Articles denied that the civil part of Moses' law 'ought of necessity to be received in any Commonwealth', Thomas Cartwright and William Perkins both held the judicial law to be still binding in substance.[3] Finch agreed, although his Biblicism was by no means naïvely fundamentalist:

the books of Moses are rather an epitome of [the Jews'] head and principal laws . . . than a perfect and absolute comprehension of all. Especially in matters concerning contracts and possessions. And therefore it were too ridiculous and absurd so far to urge the precise letters of these laws as though nothing were to be tolerated in a reformed and christian commonwealth, that had not warrant in so many syllables from thence. Sufficient it is, if in like case as there come into question, we retain the substance and equity as it were the marrow of them. And in the rest which it leaveth unspoken of, we suffer nothing repugnant to the law of nature or light of reason.[4]

[1] Bodl., Rawlinson MS. C. 43: 'Nomotexnia' or 'Of the common law', fols. 4–15; 'A Conference or Reformation', fols. 16–33.
[2] Ibid., fols. 2–3; cf. my 'The Dialectical Origins of Finch's Law', *Cambridge Law Journ.* xxxvi (1977), 331–2.
[3] P. D. L. Avis, 'Moses and the Magistrate: A Study in the rise of Protestant Legalism', *Journ. of Eccl. Hist.* xxvi (1975), 149–72.
[4] Bodl., Rawlinson MS. C. 43, fol. 18.

All authority is denied to what can be safely discounted as merely ceremonial parts of the law, such as the death penalty for sexual intercourse with a menstruating woman, or for fornication with a priest's daughter ('respect of persons being extinguished with us, who are a royal kingdom and a holy priesthood'). This same principle of individual equality before the law asserts that the freedom of Hebrew masters to kill their alien bond slaves 'bindeth us not as straightly to such respect of persons, but that we may (as concerning life and death) account all sorts alike'. Scriptural precedent must also be weighed against long-continued custom and professional consensus, which upheld the common-law doctrines of deodands and manslaughter, despite their admitted minor variance from Old Testament authority.[1]

Professor and Mrs. George have described the Old Testament legalism of the Elizabethan Protestant clergy as the result of a 'bookish isolation from the real issues of social fact'.[2] But Finch's arguments for specific changes in the common law show considerable social awareness. Adultery and the dishonouring of parents deserve capital punishment because they stand condemned by the light of nature as well as the explicit word of God. Both undermine the integrity of the family and the authority of the father; adultery also breaks 'holy bonds so solemnly entered before God and his congregation' (although marriage is to Finch no sacrament but 'a mere civil contract') and perverts inheritances from rightful heirs to bastards. Even more explicit social considerations dictated that mayhem should be punished by the *lex talionis*—'who sees not, what a bridle it would be to the untamed stomachs of our swashbucklers and Smithfield quarrellers'.[3] Yet while the family must be preserved and upper-class hooliganism firmly curbed, Finch is not an uncompromising advocate of greater penal severity. Thus benefit of clergy and sanctuary are condemned as popish innovations unknown to the Jews, but also because 'under the vizards of mercy' they are 'cloaks of partiality', discriminating against 'the poorer sort and most pressed with

---

[1] Ibid., fols. 21ᵛ, 27ᵛ, 28ᵛ, 32.

[2] C. H. and K. George, *The Protestant Mind of the English Reformation* (Princeton, 1961), 231.

[3] Bodl., Rawlinson MS. C. 43, fols. 26–7, 29ᵛ–30ᵛ, 31.

need which . . . can least skill of reading and hardliest keep sanctuary . . .' Moreover Finch uses his command of Hebrew to urge mitigation of the capital sentence for theft, urging that the words of King David reported in II Samuel 12: 5–6 were 'not any judicial sentence' but 'a hyperbolical or excessive speech', and thus 'our law making the stealth of 12^d value a capital and deadly crime, is without all question a cruel and deadly law, written rather with the bloody pen of Draco or Lycurgus than by the merciful finger of the Lord Jehovah.'[1]

Most defects in English law are unhesitatingly attributed to 'the general corruption of the religion of God, under the popish and anti-christian tyranny'. Fornication was originally punished by the common law courts ('as by ancient records may yet appear: The book of Domesday in the Exchequer'), until the popish hierarchy deprived them of their rightful jurisdiction over sexual offences, marriage, and matters testamentary. Times of 'popish darkness' also saw the infection of the common law with such canonist impurities as the maxim 'bastard eigne et mulier puisne', permitting an illegitimate son to inherit before the legitimate heir, 'which proceeded first from a gross ignorance of the word of God'. Some of these abuses have already been reformed; others, most notably benefit of clergy, still remain to be rooted out, along with the very names of those legally disabled persons, monks, 'abbots, priors and the rest of that rabble . . . *pereat memoria eorum*'.[2]

No strategy for reform is presented, although the call to 'the magistrates (fathers of the country)' to protect parents against their insubordinate children may indicate that Finch regarded Parliament as the most likely agent of change. But he was also well aware of the political obstacles, complaining that the prelates 'cease not to charge us as sowers of sedition, enemies to the state, disorderers of the commonwealth . . .'[3]

Finch's view of English law as essentially grounded upon the law of God revealed in Scripture was neither new nor unorthodox. It had been expounded at length by Christopher St. Germain and would be further endorsed by Sir Edward Coke. According to Professor Pocock, Coke was also responsible for

[1] Bodl., Rawlinson MS. C. 43, fols. 25–25^v.
[2] Ibid., fols. 16–17^v, 22^v–23, 26–26^v, 29^v–30^v.
[3] Ibid., fols. 30^v–31.

crystallizing the potent concept of the common law as immemorial custom, henceforth the chief political weapon of the common lawyers and their parliamentary allies. Yet it is not clear how widely this concept was accepted and enunciated before the Civil War; and we may wonder whether the high claims often made for the common law did not depend as much upon its supposed descent from and consonance with the laws of Israel as on its immemorial (hence unknowable) antecedents. If the former, it becomes easier to understand both the importance attached to the law's antiquity as a token of its legitimacy (unaffected by popish corruptions), and the increasing vigour with which the actual or apprehended intrusions of other codes and jurisdictions were resisted from the mid sixteenth century onwards.[1]

The appeal to Scripture could equally be used to criticize the common law. Indeed if God's word was final arbiter, why should the Golden Rule and 'Moses' judicials' not be substituted for the lawyers' 'obsolete precedents'? That position was widely canvassed during the 1640s and '50s (although, understandably, by few lawyers).[2] Following Thomas Cartwright, Finch however sought not an abrogation of the common law in favour of Mosaic law, but a return to its proper relationship with God's law, as part of a continued process of reformation directed towards the creation of a godly church and commonwealth.[3]

It seems unlikely that Finch would have embarked upon his task had he not felt some confidence in the general prospects for reform. In fact, as we now know, the defeat of the Elizabethan Presbyterian movement slammed the door on such hopes. Finch accordingly lost interest in the closer integration of the common law with the law of God. The revised and expanded versions of 'Nomotexnia' which circulated in manuscript from

---

[1] Cf. G. L. Haskins, *Law and Authority in Early Massachusetts* (New York, 1960), 143–7; J. G. A. Pocock, *The Ancient Constitution and the Feudal Law* (Cambridge, 1957), ch. 2; M. A. Judson, *The Crisis of the Constitution* (New Brunswick, 1949), 335–9; *Christopher St. German's Doctor and Student*, ed. J. L. Barton and T. F. T. Plucknett (Selden Soc., 1974), 27–31.

[2] Cf. D. Veall, *The Popular Movement for Law Reform* (Oxford, 1970), chs. 3–4; *Winstanley. The Law of Freedom and other Writings*, ed. C. Hill (1973), 377–8; T. G. Barnes, *The Book of the Generall Laws and Liberties of Massachusetts* (San Marino, 1974), 6–7.

[3] Cf. D. Little, *Religion, Order and Law* (Oxford, 1970), 101–4.

1604 and in print from 1613 onwards are simply systematic descriptions of existing law. No trace survives of the 'Conference or Reformation' or its reforming purpose.[1] The ambitious attempt to combine a Ramist exposition with a religious critique of English law had been the work of a young Presbyterian barrister at the beginning of his professional career. Henceforth the realms of nature and grace are clearly segregated in his writings.

The Sacred Doctrine of Divinitie

The unsigned preface to Finch's first published book, *The Sacred Doctrine of Divinitie*, which was issued at Middleburgh in 1590 by the Puritan printer Richard Schilders, claims that it was written before the appearance of Dudley Fenner's *Sacra Theologia* (1585).[2] If so, it must have been composed around the same time as the manuscript 'Nomotexnia', and indeed the two works are closely related in aim and form, for *The Sacred Doctrine of Divinitie* is a brief exposition of the main tenets of reformed Protestant Christianity, organized on Ramist principles. Fenner's longer Latin text had a similar purpose, and Finch obviously made considerable use of the work of his brilliant young Cambridge contemporary, fellow-Ramist, and co-religionist, sometimes translating him virtually word for word. But as the anonymous preface to his book justly pointed out, Finch was no mere plagiarist:

the same is made English, which before was in Latin, and brought into the artificers shop, which before was in the studies and closets of the learned alone . . . he hath brought Mr. Fenner's book, for help of memory, into a great deal smaller room. . . . And notwithstanding the author's both modesty and wisdom is such as he would not have passed by the advantage of a further garnishment of his work by Mr. Fenner's labours . . . he hath for the matter, a stock of his own, and for the form and manner of delivery of it, art and cunning of his own, to have finished some commendable work in this kind, if he had had no such pattern before his eyes.[3]

---

[1] 'The Dialectical Origins of Finch's Law', 339–40.

[2] The confusion which has previously surrounded the authorship and dating of Finch's book (*STC* 10774) and its two *sequelae* (*STC* 10775, 7148) is fully resolved in the forthcoming revised edition of *STC* vol. i; I am most grateful to the editor, Miss Katherine Pantzer, for a sight of the relevant proof sheets.

[3] *The Sacred Doctrine of Divinitie* (1590), 7–9.

Not surprisingly, the tone and content of *The Sacred Doctrine* (as well as the appended 'Short explication of the Lord's Prayer', a separate work which seems to be entirely from Finch's own pen) are uncompromisingly Presbyterian. The treatise consists of three books, the first dealing with the sovereignty of God, the second with the law (mainly the Commandments and man's duty to obey them), the third with the Gospel, or Christ's mission for the salvation of the elect. Finch followed Fenner in expounding a modified Calvinist covenant theology and the classic Genevan form of church government. Thus ministers of the church, appointed by 'common consent', are said to be either elders or bishops:

An elder is he which is to govern only. A Bishop is he which is to preach . . . Preaching is the public instructing of the church concerning Christ. Whereunto are annexed public prayers and the administration of sacraments. . . .
A Bishop is a teacher or pastor. Teacher which is to teach only. Pastor which is to exhort. These are the governors. Church servants are those who are to attend the poor: as deacons and deaconesses.[1]

While obviously accessible to a far wider audience than Fenner's lengthy Latin treatise, Finch's curt and dogmatic exposition was better suited as a credo for the converted than a means of attracting potential adherents. His prose style relaxes a little only in the following commentary on the Lord's Prayer, as for example where he recounts the blessedness of the righteous, who may confidently solicit in 'testimony and assurance of Thy love . . . all the good things of this present life . . . maintenance, health, credit, friends, comfort of wife, children, servants; a blessing upon our labours; the fruit of magistracy and government and good order in the world . . .'[2]

This last assurance was not granted, either to Finch himself, or his fellow Presbyterians, during the two following decades. Finch's professional career seems to have been closely tied to the city of Canterbury, where he was appointed fee'd counsel to the Corporation as early as 1590. Over the next three years he was similarly honoured by the Cinque Ports, added to the commission of the peace for the county of Kent, and elected to represent Canterbury in the Parliament of 1593. In a Lower House dominated for the first time in Elizabeth's reign by religious moderates and conservatives (among them Henry's elder brother, Sir Moyle Finch), he attacked the anti-separatist Act 'to retain the Queen's subjects in obedience' (35 Eliz. c. 1) with what Sir John Neale describes as 'the authentic Puritan voice from the past'.[1]

As leading spokesman for the small Puritan parliamentary remnant, Finch was reinforcing a public stance which dated back at least to 1584, when he had been among the more vocal members of a delegation of Kentish gentry to Archbishop Whitgift, protesting against the suspension of Nonconformist ministers. He evidently played an equally activist role in the internal politics of Canterbury, where his election in 1593 seems to have been aided by a Puritan faction campaigning on his behalf against the rival candidacy of John Boys, the town's new-appointed Recorder, a conscientious member of the local diocesan High Commission and steward to five successive archbishops. But by now the godly cause was everywhere in retreat, as Finch found shortly after the dissolution of Parliament, when he appealed for Robert Cecil's support to displace four councillors who had supposedly been elected in breach of the city's charter, only to see the Privy Council declare the elections valid three months later. Finch sat once more for Canterbury in 1597, when Boys gained the other seat; but while the latter continued to represent the borough until his death in 1612, Finch was never again chosen and on Sir John Boys's death it was his fellow M.P. Mathew Hadde, rather than Henry Finch, who replaced him as the town's chief legal officer.[2]

Finch's private fortunes were also dogged by a series of expensive lawsuits with his elder brother. Before her death in 1587 Lady Katherine Finch had been persuaded by her

---

[1] Canterbury Cathedral Archives, City Burghmote Minutes Book 2, fol. 158; Edward Boys, *Antiquities of Sandwich* (1791), 779; J. E. Neale, *Elizabeth I and her Parliaments, 1584–1601* (1958), 272, 282, 289.

[2] Dr. Williams's Library, MS. Morice L, pt. 5, pp. 7–11; BL, Lansdowne MS. 43, fol. 7; Canterbury Cathedral Archives, Burghmote Book 2, fols. 222ᵛ, 236ᵛ–8; *HMC, Salisbury*, iv. 350–1; BL, MS. M 484/5 (Hatfield MSS., vol. 23, pt. 90); C. Mason, 'Men of Kent; 1. Boys of Bonnington', *Archaeologia Cantiana*, lxxxix (1964), 70–2; E. Hasted, *The History of Canterbury* (1801), ii. 611.

second husband to bequeath a five-year lease of Eastwell Manor near Canterbury to Henry's wife, probably with the aim of blocking Sir Moyle Finch's claim to the property. If so, the plan misfired, for shortly after Henry took possession he was forcibly evicted by Sir Moyle. Henry was said to have borrowed heavily to meet the cost of the ensuing litigation, which dragged on until at least 1598 and may have laid the seeds of his eventual bankruptcy.[1] In any event the combination of financial pressures, domestic responsibilities, the demands of his legal and theological studies, and a generally unsympathetic politico-religious climate probably explains Henry Finch's retirement into almost complete obscurity during the first decade of James I's reign.

In 1613 Finch broke his silence, publishing a law-French version, much revised and expanded, of his first manuscript analysis of the common law, prefaced by a fulsome dedicatory epistle to James I and including a studiously non-partisan account of the powers and jurisdiction of the spiritual courts. This is the only one of Finch's books published during his lifetime under his own name, although one variant of the new edition of *The Sacred Doctrine of Divinitie* which he also brought out that same year contains a signed dedication to Lord Chancellor Ellesmere, couched in equally obsequious terms.[2] The self-censored text of this second edition omits every passage from the original 1590 version which criticized the existing system of church government directly or by implication. The commentary on the Lord's Prayer is replaced by a new treatise of 112 pages entitled 'The Olde Testament, or the Promise', an elaboration of covenant theology based on the premiss that the Old Testament comprehends 'one half, or rather one whole, and the entire body of Christian doctrine; for substance the same that shall be in the Church for ever . . .' In accordance with Cartwright's teaching, Finch maintained that it differed from the covenant of the New Testament only in the 'many figures,

---

[1] PRO, SP 12/146/35; STAC 5/F11/33; C2/Jas.1/F10/21. I am indebted to Mr. P. Clark for his most helpful comments and references on the matters discussed in this and the previous paragraph.

[2] See above, p. 102; *The Sacred Doctrine of Divinitie, Gathered out of the Word of God, and comprehended into two volumes. Whereof this First Volume containeth a description of all that Holy Doctrine according to the Rules of Art* (1613); the dedicatory epistle is at sigs. q–q2v of the BL copy (1478.d.31).

rites, ceremonies and shadows', of which his book provides a detailed analysis.[1]

While constituting significant evidence of Finch's deepening interest in the divine plan for the Jewish nation, the doctrinal content of the 1613 edition of *The Sacred Doctrine of Divinitie* remains entirely within the bounds of Anglican-Calvinist orthodoxy. We may indeed suspect that Finch's double-barrelled literary salvo was aimed at securing the preferment which had so far eluded him, despite his early professional and political prominence. Coincidentally or not, within the next twelve months Finch was created serjeant-at-law, nominated to a Crown-controlled seat for the Addled Parliament, and chosen against the competition of Mathew Hadde and another barrister to be 'assistant to Mr. Maior' of Sandwich 'in points of law', succeeding Sir John Boys, deceased.[2]

It is not clear whether the second companion volume fore-shadowed in the full title of the 1613 *Sacred Doctrine of Divinitie* was already written, and the precise date of its subsequent publication is unknown, since *The Summe of Sacred Divinitie First Briefly & Methodically Expounded: And then more Largely & cleerely handled and explaned published by John Downham* is undated, although a marginal reference in Finch's last book, *The Worldes Great Restauration*, shows that it must have been in print by 1621. The Puritan minister of Blackfriars Church and fellow-Ramist, William Gouge, Finch's other clerical 'publisher', also served with him as executor of Thomas Whetenhall, a pious London merchant who bequeathed a substantial legacy for the estab-lishment of church lectureships in the City. No such personal ties have been traced between Finch and Downham, although both doubtless formed part of the informal network which linked the Inns of Court with the City's Puritan preachers; but it is worth noting that Downham, like his elder brother George, the author of a standard commentary on Ramist logic, was yet another graduate of Christ's College, Cambridge.[3]

As with Finch's published law books, and despite its title,

---

[1] 'The Olde Testament', 1; *Cartwrightiana*, ed. A. Peel and L. Carlson (1951), 110–11.

[2] William Dugdale, *Origines Juridiciales* (1666), 103; T. L. Moir, *The Addled Parliament of 1614* (Oxford, 1958), 50, 148; Kent AO, Sa. AC/7, fol. 24.

[3] PRO, C 3/549/28; W. K. Jordan, *The Charities of London 1480–1660* (1960), 286; *DNB s.n.* 'Downham, George and John'.

The Summe of Sacred Divinitie is a much enlarged version of an earlier outline. Ramist methodology is represented by an 'Art' or abstract of the whole work, printed both as a prefatory synopsis and a running marginal gloss to the main text, which comprises 551 octavo pages. The doctrinal content is markedly Calvinist, although once again not Presbyterian, for as in 1613 Finch explicitly eschews all 'deep and difficult questions' concerning the ministry: 'their calling, election, ordination, the keys of the church committed into their hands, their power of binding and loosing, and the whole order and government of God's house: I will leave them all, and hold me only to that of preaching and administering sacraments'. Otherwise there is nothing in Finch's overview of the Christian religion which his Puritan teachers and contemporaries from Cambridge in the 1570s could not have fully endorsed. Preaching is said to subsume the offering of public prayer and to be the 'only instrument that God useth ordinarily to beget faith'; the two sacraments, baptism and communion, are 'only signs and seals, they signify not confer grace, having no inherent force and power to sanctifie . . .'. Finch's comprehensive exposition of covenant theology includes a sharp attack on Pelagians and semi-Pelagians, with the assertion that the elect cannot fall from grace—there are absolutely no signs of any compromise with the increasingly fashionable Arminian theology.[1]

But a significant innovation occurs in the closing pages, where Finch outlines the course of events which will precede the resurrection and last judgement. After the church is delivered from the tyranny of the Roman Antichrist, the darkening of the heavens will signify 'a notable change to fall out'. Then will follow the downfall of the Turkish empire, the conversion of the Jews, and a general, glorious publishing of the gospel to all mankind.[2]

It is difficult to fit this passage into the development of Finch's eschatology. Apart from its unknown date of composition and publication, the scenario is based on a New Testament source (Matthew 24: 23–30), rather than the classic prophetic books of the Old Testament, and lacks both the considerable detail and some of the main components of the schema to be expounded

---

[1] *The Summe of Sacred Divinitie*, 308, 364, 366–7, 377–8, 396–8, 411.
[2] Ibid. 529–35.

in *The Worldes Great Restauration* (most notably the literal gathering-in of the Jews to the Holy Land). The basic chronology and sequence of apocalyptic events expounded in that work were derived from Thomas Brightman's influential biblical commentaries first published in 1609 and 1614. (We should note that Brightman entered Christ's College in 1576, a year before Finch left for Gray's Inn.) Yet Finch's own commentary on the Song of Solomon, which was published in 1615 although purportedly written 'long since', shows little evidence of Brightman's influence. Whereas the latter treated virtually the entire Song as literal historical prophecy, Finch mainly follows the traditional allegorical interpretation (as expounded in Dudley Fenner's translation of 1587).[1]

Finch does, however, identify a prophetic element in the last four books of the Song, which he takes to foreshadow the conversion of the Jews and 'their access in the last days to the church of Christ'. There is no explicit reference to a physical calling to Jerusalem, and none of the elaborate scriptural arithmetic which dominates Brightman's approach; but Finch follows Fenner in insisting that 'when the church of the Jews becomes the catholic church of all the world', there shall be 'a new government and discipline, new officers, pastors, teachers etc. to administer it . . . A house of Saints shall be erected by the preaching of the Gospel to be the palace of the Great King . . .'.[2]

A Present to Judah

Fascination with and a desire to emulate the historical and spiritual role of the Jewish people probably goes back to the earliest origins of Protestantism; the fifteenth-century Lollard John Seygno is said to have regarded the eating of pork as sinful and to have kept the Sabbath on Saturday.[3] Such popular heresies were encouraged by Luther's insistence on the divine inspiration and literal interpretation of both Old and New Testaments, while the post-Reformation revival of Hebrew

[1] Cf. *Puritans, the Millennium and the future of Israel*, ed. P. Toon (1970), 26–32; *The Workes of . . . Mr. Tho: Brightman* (1644), 985, 1065, 1075; [Henry Finch], *An Exposition of the Song of Solomon* (1615), 75.

[2] [Finch], *Exposition of the Song of Solomon*, 4–5, 70; Dudley Fenner, *The Song of Songs* (Middleburgh, 1587), sig. F.

[3] J. Fines, ' "Judaising" in the Period of the English Reformation—The Case of Richard Bruern', *Trans. Jewish Hist. Soc.* xxi (1962–7), 323.

studies stimulated scholarly interest which could also lead to heterodoxy. Richard Bruern, Regius Professor of Hebrew at Oxford, was deprived of his chair in 1559, but whether for adultery, homosexuality, popery, or judaism—he was accused of all four—appears uncertain; a clearer case is that of Francis Kett, Fellow of Corpus Christi College, Cambridge, burned as a heretic in 1589 for his claim that Jesus, not the son of God but a good man, was currently in Jerusalem gathering the faithful and that all God's people should go to join him there.

Meanwhile, respectable Protestant sources like the reformer Beza and the Geneva Bible were teaching that the literal conversion of the Jews to Christianity in the last days of the world would bring great glory to the church, Foxe's *Acts and Monuments* encouraged Protestant Englishmen to regard themselves as members of a New Israel, and a wide range of literary material reinforced the identification. But the strongest impulse to judaizing amongst zealous Protestants probably remained the simple desire to return to the purest possible forms and sources of God's worship.[1]

Finch's Hebrew studies began at Cambridge and continued at Gray's Inn. Thomas Brightman's writings possibly helped turn his interests to the specific subject of the conversion of the Jews, as may have Thomas Draxe's *The Worldes Resurection, or the generall calling of the Jewes* (1608), the work of yet another Puritan from Christ's, Cambridge, who looked forward to the general conversion of the Jews in the last days of the world, although not to their recovery of the Holy Land. We may also conjecture that the Ramist habits of mind which Finch had acquired at Cambridge, together with his virulent anti-Catholicism, encouraged him to take a dialectical view of the relationship between the nation of Israel (God's people) and the church of Rome (the realm of Antichrist); despite the apparent recent resurgence of Catholicism in Europe, the hand of God was about to strike down the pride of the Papacy and elevate in its place the hitherto despised and dispersed Israelites.

---

[1] Ibid. 323–6; Toon, *Puritans, the Millennium*, 20–6; Hill, *Society and Puritanism*, 202–5; E. Kobler, 'Sir Henry Finch (1558–1625) and the first English advocates of the Restoration of the Jews to Palestine', *Trans. Jewish Hist. Soc.* xvi (1951), 101–20.

Finch's worsening financial difficulties may also have im-
pelled him towards apocalyptic speculation. He had continued
to accumulate marks of honour after his elevation to the coif,
gaining a knighthood and letters patent as King's Serjeant-at-
Law in 1616 and the High Stewardship of Faversham in 1617
(when his eldest son John was made Recorder of Canterbury).
His services were sought by the Privy Council as arbitrator in
a variety of mercantile and fishing disputes, and as prosecutor
of the disgraced Lord Treasurer Suffolk. Sir Francis Bacon,
a former colleague on the bench of Gray's Inn, now Lord
Chancellor, recommended him to Buckingham and appointed
him to an unofficial law-reform working party; his services on
this seem to have secured his inclusion in the 1621 Commons'
committee for codifying the penal statutes, although he was
not an elected member of the House.[1]

Yet like many office-holders, Finch found that place was not
synonymous with profit, at least on a scale sufficient to pay off
his increasingly importunate creditors. As early as 1614 he was
being sued for money borrowed to purchase an office in King's
Bench for his sons John and Nathaniel (who had both been
called to the bar at Gray's Inn in 1611). In 1616 he was an
unsuccessful candidate for a Welsh judgeship; in 1619 he was
rumoured to be seeking the Chief Barony of the Exchequer.
It may have been his failure to secure the latter post which
finally provoked his creditors to the drastic action of arresting
Henry and his two sons (who had acted as their father's guaran-
tors). However, the Finchs still had a friend in Francis Bacon,
who in 1620 granted them Chancery injunctions for stay of
process, together with a 'bill of conformity' which obliged their
creditors to accept unfavourable terms of composition. This
dubious proceeding was attacked next year in the Commons'
debates preceding Bacon's impeachment, but it served its
immediate purpose. Although John Finch was again obliged to
seek protection from arrest for his father's debts in 1623, Sir
Henry himself seems to have practised freely, both at West-

---

[1] *CSPD, 1611–18*, 373; Kent AO, Fa/AC 3, fol. 115; Hasted, *Canterbury*, ii. 611;
HMC, Salisbury, xxii. 96; *The Works of Francis Bacon. The Letters and Life*, ed. J.
Spedding, R. L. Ellis, and D. D. Heath, vi. 71, 294–5; *The Letters of John Chamberlain*, ed. N. E. McLure (Philadelphia, 1939), ii. 203; *APC, 1615–16*, 590, 633; ibid.
1616–17, 23, 35, 76, 89; ibid. *1618–19*, 114; *CSPD, 1615–16*, 590; *Debates 1621*, ii.
73; vi. 349.

minster Hall and in Kent, until his death from the plague in 1625.[1]

Nevertheless the composition of Finch's last and most controversial book cannot be ascribed simply to the trauma of his bankruptcy, since at least one part of *The Worldes Great Restauration* was evidently already written by 1615. Indeed a draft of the whole work may have been completed by August 1616, when the Stationers' Company registered a book described as 'The prophesie of Hosea with an explanation thereof and a treatise of the calling of the Jews' to the printer John Beale. In the event it was another printer, William Bladen, who finally issued *The Worldes Great Restauration* in March 1621, after having entered it on the Stationers' Register some fifteen months before.[2]

The complex bibliographical history of Finch's other works suggests that he normally discarded numerous drafts before settling on a final version, which may help to account for the apparent long delay between the composition and printing of *The Worldes Great Restauration*. Equally significant is the fact that Finch did not permit his name to appear on the title-page of any of his five published religious treatises, and that the three published after his call to the coif were all issued by others on his behalf (and in the case of *An Exposition of the Song of Solomon*, apparently without his foreknowledge or consent). William Gouge, who brought out that work (as also *The Worldes Great Restauration*), explained in his foreword that the author was 'a man of great place and note in the commonwealth; his humility will not suffer him to have his name made known'.[3] Yet Finch's own preface to *Nomotexnia* (1613) shows no such modesty, and his wariness about attracting attention to the fruits of his religious studies probably sprang from a prudent recognition of the conservative prejudice against the lawyer who dabbled in the preserves of other professions. Moreover,

---

[1] *Debates 1621*, v. 296; *Calendar of the Wynn (of Gwydir) Papers* (Aberystwyth, 1926), 123; PRO, C2/Jas.I/F5/2, F1/2, C33/137, fols. 770ᵛ–771; J. Ritchie, *Cases decided by Lord Bacon 1617–1621* (1932), 166–7; *APC, 1621–3*, 417; *CSPD, 1619–23*, 515; Kent AO, Sa AC/7, fols. 118ᵛ–119; below, p. 115.

[2] *A Transcript of the Registers of the Company of Stationers of London*, ed. E. Arber (1875–94), iii. 274b, 307b. Gouge refers to Finch's unpublished commentary on Hosea in his preface to Finch's *An Exposition of the Song of Solomon* (1615), sig. [A5].

[3] *An Exposition of the Song of Solomon*, sig. [A3].

the subject-matter of his last book was far more likely to arouse hostile official reaction than anything he had published since the first version of the *Sacred Doctrine of Divinitie* (1590), particularly after the furore which attended the Star Chamber prosecution of the judaizing separatist John Traske in 1618.[1] In the absence of further evidence it is tempting to speculate that it was the disasters suffered by the Protestant cause in Europe during the opening stages of the Thirty Years War, and the desire to influence the Parliament called in January 1621, which finally emboldened Gouge and Finch to authorize the printing of *The Worldes Great Restauration*.

The content and theme of Finch's book are obviously indebted to Thomas Brightman's exegesis of the Apocalypse. But while following Brightman's chronology of the last days, *The Worldes Great Restauration* is far from a mere summary of Brightman's theories. Brightman sought to elucidate the historical process whereby the Jews would return to the Holy Land and destroy the Turkish empire, as a prelude to the return of Christ at the end of the second millennium (A.D. 2300). Finch is not primarily concerned with Christ's actual return, but emphasizes the establishment of the Jewish church-state as an end in itself. Unlike Brightman he claims that the returning Jews will include the ten lost tribes. He also appears to depart from Brightman's plan in proposing that the downfall of Rome will precede rather than follow the calling of the Jews, and he discusses a far wider range of biblical sources than Brightman handles.[2]

Christopher Hill has already identified some of the considerable subversive possibilities of an appeal to the primitive tribal democracy of the Old Testament.[3] We noted above (p. 108) that the Presbyterian church order which Finch suppressed from his second and third versions of *The Sacred Doctrine of Divinitie* reappears in the 1615 *Exposition of the Song of Solomon* as the constitution of the future Judaeo-Christian theocracy; the point is made even more plainly in *The Worldes Great Restauration*, where it is emphasized that the Jews will set

[1] Cf. H. E. I. Phillips, 'An Early Stuart Judaising Sect', *Trans. Jewish Hist. Soc.* xv (1939–45), 63.
[2] Cf. Toon, *Puritans, the Millennium*, 28–32; *The Worldes Great Restauration*, 1–3, 9, 75, 77, 91.
[3] Hill, *Society and Puritanism*, 204.

up not 'the legal ceremonies, but . . . the true spiritual worship of God. The form of the church policy and government you have pointed at under the name of elders, comprehending pastors, teachers and other governors of the church'. Moreover, the 'most flourishing commonwealth' of the regathered Jews will be ruled not by 'Christ the Lord', but by 'a governor which the Jews shall have set up from among themselves'—a view that scandalized Joseph Mede, the most famous of all the Christ's College millenarians.[1]

While Brightman's readers might take comfort from the foreknowledge of a coming cosmic drama which would secure the triumph of the Saints and the destruction of their oppressors, Finch's lengthy commentaries on the prophecies of Isaiah and Hosea spoke even more directly to the concerns and hopes of his fellow-Puritans. His discussion of Isaiah begins with a vigorous affirmation of God's omnipotence and man's sinfulness, 'the proper and immediate cause of all our afflictions'. Yet God has entered into a covenant 'with his servants . . . under certain conditions, as it were to contract with them for life eternal'. Those who accept this free offer of grace by faith in Christ shall be relieved of the full consequence of their sins and join the church, 'which whosoever entreth . . . remains a citizen and free burgess both here and in heaven for ever'. God's chosen must expect tribulations in this world, both on account of their own sinfulness and through the malice of the wicked, to whom 'it is meat and drink . . . to see God's people buffeted and tormented'. A state of 'truceless and perpetual war' exists between the seed of the woman and the seed of the serpent; 'our losses they take to be their own gain, and think themselves can never prosper . . . so long as the godly hold up their head'. But 'the patient expectations of the Saints shall not be deceived for ever', and the end of their enemies shall be 'lamentable, howsoever for a while they look aloft and hold up their heads':

Our way therefore is to let him alone and rest in that which he shall do. Not that we are to sit still, and neglect the means he appointeth for our good: that were not to depend upon him, but to tempt him. *But when we have done all we can . . . trust in him and he will do it.* [Emphasis added.]

[1] *The Worldes Great Restauration*, 48, 52, 91, 102, 120, 160, 163; Joseph Mede, *Works* (1664), ii. 831; T. Birch, *The Court and Times of James I* (1848), ii. 250–1.

It is perhaps not entirely fanciful to detect in these passages some echo of Finch's own earlier political and current financial difficulties. Yet their potential application was clearly not limited to the author alone, whose exhortation to the Saints to stand firm, with the sure knowledge that God stood behind them, is given added weight by his treatment of the prophecies of Hosea. These are summarized as 'a fearful denouncing of God's judgements against the people for their sins, and a sweet publishing of mercies to a small remnant . . .'. While it is hard to know how closely Finch's readers would have identified Israel and England in this context, it seems unlikely that they would have failed to detect contemporary implications in the denunciation of the intemperate princes, 'who by their gravity and wisdom should be the stays and props of the common-wealth', and the King himself, who 'quaffs as they, and joineth hands with beastly drunkards . . . who ought to make clean the commonwealth . . . but sitteth still and letteth all alone'. Finch's characterization of the religious backsliding of the Israelites was also suggestive of an obvious contemporary parallel:

> Their sins first, consociating with strangers and making a mixture of their religion with the superstitions of the Gentiles. They neither hold them to the sincerity of God's service, nor to the mere toys and fooleries of the heathen: but frame to themselves a mingle-mangle out of both.[1]

The Differentiation of Belief and Calling

James I's main objection to Finch's book was evidently its assertion that a restored Jewry would exercise 'chief sway and sovereignty' over the rest of the world. Yet given the number of other equally disquieting propositions James and his bishops might have found, official reaction to its publication in March 1621 seems to have been surprisingly restrained. After examination before the High Commission and condemnation of his work as 'too servilely addicted to the letter' by the Convocation conveniently sitting at Westminster, Finch was imprisoned without trial in the Fleet.[2] An undated petition in the State

---

[1] *The Worldes Great Restauration*, 83–146, 147, 179, 206–7.

[2] Joseph Hall, *The Revelation Unrevealed* (1650), in *Works*, ed. J. Pratt (1808), x. 102; BL, Harley MS. 389, fols. 45, 53 (printed Birch, *Court and Times*, 244, 250–1); Chamberlain, Letters, ii. 363.

Papers shows that he made a formal if rather vague disavowal of 'the opinion which the words of his book in your majesty's deep judgement and high prudence are found to import'. After two months' confinement Finch was allowed to resume practice and even retained his patent as King's Serjeant. Indeed it would appear that he went straight from the Fleet to the service of the new Lord Keeper, Bishop John Williams, who had succeeded Finch's now disgraced patron, Francis Bacon. According to his chaplain and biographer, Williams's ignorance of the common law 'was improved as far as he could' by 'the assistance of Sir Henry Finch, a most profound lawyer, whom he kept in his lodgings from May to October following, for all sorts of advice; the best heifer he could have ploughed with, to find out mysteries . . .'.[1]

Williams's appointment of Finch as resident law coach was perhaps in part a gesture of defiance to his enemies Bishops Laud and Neile (who had apparently initiated proceedings against the book and its author).[2] But the fact that in Williams's eyes Finch's professional expertise evidently outweighed his dubious religious orthodoxy illustrates the extent to which the exercise of technical legal skills was now established as an autonomous, value-free activity over which neither church nor religion exercised special rights. Of course individual lawyers were affected by the religious conflicts of the post-Reformation era; Finch's own career exemplifies the extent to which a man's involvement in those disputes could influence the course of his professional life. Nevertheless lawyers were increasingly able to insist on their professional autonomy, distinguishing both the code they professed and the manner in which they practised it from all other areas of human concern. No doubt this process of differentiation was part of that general transformation of the church's role so brilliantly delineated in Tawney's *Religion and the Rise of Capitalism*. For the lawyers it was accelerated by a vast expansion of litigation, the concomitant growth of the

---

[1] PRO, SP 14/120/96; John Hacket, *Scrinia Reserata* (1693), 60.

[2] Cf. William Gouge, *A Learned and very useful Commentary on the whole Epistle to the Hebrews* (1655), sig. [a3ᵛ]. For Laud's pulpit attack on the book, see *The Works of . . . William Laud* (Oxford, 1847–60), i. 16–19; cf. John Prideaux, *The Doctrine of the Sabbath, Delivered in the Act at Oxon. Anno 1622* (1634). The interesting article by G. W. Thomas, 'James I, Equity and Lord Keeper Williams', *EHR* xli (1976), 506–28, makes no mention of Finch's appointment.

profession in size, wealth, and influence from around the middle of the sixteenth century, the infiltration of trained lawyers into positions of administrative responsibility, the heightening of professional specialization, and the proliferation of a printed legal literature. As a result barristers developed a sense of corporate solidarity and a code of behaviour which helped to minimize the intrusion of ideological differences within the professional sphere, in relation both to colleagues and to clients.

The segregation of 'public' calling from 'private' belief, by no means unchallenged during the early seventeenth century, was temporarily checked in the later seventeenth century and is hardly absolute even today. But the tendency was clear. It helps to explain why, despite his vigorous condemnation of monopolies in *The Summe of Sacred Divinitie*, Finch could nevertheless defend the Crown's general power to grant patents in the Parliament of 1614, and later even sanction perhaps the most notorious single abuse of that power, Mompesson's patent for licensing alehouses. It also helps to clarify the readiness of many lawyers to accept Crown office during the 1630s, despite the distaste they must have felt for the government's ecclesiastical policies. Among them was Finch's eldest son, whose activities as Chief Justice of Common Pleas and Lord Keeper did much to maintain Charles I's non-parliamentary government; yet when riding north to join the King in the spring of 1640, Sir John Finch went out of his way to visit his aged former tutor Laurence Chaderton in Cambridge, an action which lends some credence to his protestations of Calvinist orthodoxy before the Long Parliament later that year.[1]

By then Henry Finch had been dead for fifteen years. His reputation as 'an eminent serjeant . . . that professed no less acquaintance with the laws of God than of man' survived a little longer, but it is mainly as a precursor of Blackstone that he is still remembered.[2] Yet the corresponding neglect of the greater part of his literary output, and some of the most interesting aspects of his intellectual biography, is perhaps neither surprising

---

[1] *Summe of the Sacred Doctrine*, 210; *Debates 1621*, v. 478–9; vii. 631; E. S. Shuckburgh, *Laurence Chaderton* (Cambridge, 1884), 19–20; Nalson, i. 693.

[2] Hall, *Works*, x. 102. Cf. Thomas Fuller, *A Pisgah—Sight of Palestine* (1650), 194.

nor unfitting; for, as we have seen, Finch himself made only one early attempt to integrate the legal and religious doctrines he professed, thereafter merely applying a common Ramist mode of analysis and exposition to the distinct realms of the Art of Law and the Law of God.

The Anatomy of a Radical Gentleman
Henry Marten

C. M. WILLIAMS

KING CHARLES I called Henry Marten an ugly rascal and whoremaster and forbade him Hyde Park. In the summer of 1643 John Pym, advocating Marten's expulsion from the House of Commons, accused him of lewdness. On the day Oliver Cromwell overthrew the Rump he denounced some of its members as whoremasters, 'looking then towards Henry Marten'. Less eminent contemporaries compared Marten with John of Leyden, Wat Tyler, Jack Cade, and Catiline. Sir Simonds D'Ewes thought him an 'Atheisticall liver' and in the next generation Cox Macro called him 'impious and vitious'.[1] Marten himself once acknowledged that, having at various times attacked the King, the Scots, the Lord Mayor, Aldermen and Common Council of London, the Assembly of Divines, the whole House of Lords, and the greater part of the House of Commons, he 'could not but expect to bee reproched and inveighed against by almost every pen and tongue, that would take notice of so mean a subject'.[2]

Archbishop Laud's detractors thought they had scored a hit when they called him a butcher's son; Oliver Cromwell's enjoyed suggesting that he was a brewer. But it seems not to have occurred to Henry Marten's many enemies that his gentility was barely skin-deep; the work of one, brilliantly successful generation.

It was Marten's father, Sir Henry Marten, whose eminence

---

[1] Bodl., Aubrey MS. 6, fol. 103; *Mercurius Aulicus*, 19 Aug. 1643; Whitelocke, i. 208; iv. 5; D'Ewes, BL, Harley MS. 165, fol. 152; Anthony Wood, *Athenae Oxonienses*, ed. P. Bliss (1813–20), iii. 1237–44.

[2] Library of Lady Fairfax, Gay's House, Holyport (Lady Fairfax's MSS.), 'Rash Censures Uncharitable' (1647), bound in 'Original official manuscripts of the Civil Wars and Commonwealth, 1641–1653' ('Original official MSS.'). I am indebted to Lady Fairfax for her kind permission to transcribe and quote Marten MSS.

and wealth established and guaranteed the family's gentle status. Himself the son of an obscure yeoman worth no more than £60 a year, Sir Henry rose by the practice of ecclesiastical and admiralty law to be Dean of the Arches, Judge of the Prerogative Court of Canterbury, Judge of the Admiralty, and the most famous (if not the most highly respected) civil lawyer of his day. Before his death in 1641 he owned or leased much of the Vale of the White Horse, had married his sons and daughters to competent fortunes derived from land, the law, or London, and was able to leave his heir a reputed £3,000 a year.[1] That heir, the younger Henry Marten, had enjoyed a gentleman's education—grammar school, University College Oxford, the Inner Temple, and continental travel—and, having married a widowed sister of Lord Lovelace, settled down to live a gentleman's life at Becket in Berkshire. It was enough: men sometimes jested that the father's fortune, built in the 'bawdy courts' upon the sins of others, was dissipated by the son back to the 'Sins and Venerie' whence it had come; but they never questioned the gentility of father or son.[2]

Until 1640, Henry Marten seemed destined to be nothing more than a rich gentleman. But in that year, at the age of 38, despite his being 'the son of a new man among them, whose father was then living',[3] Marten was chosen by the freeholders of Berkshire as one of their Knights of the Shire in the Short Parliament. It was an undistinguished beginning which has left not a recorded word for posterity; but in October of the same year he was elected again.

The next twenty years Henry Marten spent in and out of the Long Parliament. Before the outbreak of the Civil War he was already conspicuous in contradictory ways. On the one hand his energy and talents had made him one of the dozen or so members most often appointed by the House of Commons to serve on its innumerable committees. On the other hand, he had

[1] Brotherton Lib., Marten-Loder MSS., *passim*; Mrs. J. C. Cole, 'Some Notes on Henry Marten, the Regicide, and His Family', *Berks. Archaeol. Journ.* xlix (1946); C. M. Williams, 'The Political Career of Henry Marten' (D.Phil. thesis, Univ. of Oxford, 1954), appx. A.

[2] Wood, *Athenae Oxonienses*, iii. 1237–44; [W. H. Cooke], *Students admitted to the Inner Temple* ([1877]), 227; *Coll: Henry Marten's Familiar Letters to His Lady of Delight*, ed. Edmund Gayton (Oxford, 1663), sig. A3ᵛ.

[3] Lady Fairfax's MSS., 'Rash Censures Uncharitable', fol. 1, in 'Original official MSS.'.

earned the reputation of a 'fiery spirit', the most outspoken member of the emerging 'war party', an uncompromising opponent of King, Court, and Privy Council. As early as the summer of 1641 he revealed to the future Earl of Clarendon that he was a republican: 'I do not think one man wise enough to govern us all.' Nor did he admire or trust the leaders of the parliamentary opposition: he thought them knaves.

Often single-handed, Marten conducted a guerrilla campaign in the Parliament against everyone and everything that might lead to compromise with Charles I. It was a campaign that brought him into sharp conflict not only with the King's adherents but with the House of Lords, with the 'peace party', and, increasingly, with John Pym. Nevertheless, his election as one of the fifteen original members of the powerful Committee of Safety in July 1642 seemed to secure his position and influence in the House. But in August 1643 the least guarded of a series of remarks in contempt of the royal family at last gave John Pym and his friends a pretext for expelling him from the Parliament and lodging him, briefly, in the Tower.[1]

This abrupt and ignominious stop to his political career could not have come at a worse time for Marten. The war had cut off his revenues from his lands. His house at Becket was plundered and half destroyed. The regiment he was rebuilding after its failure to hold Reading against the King in October 1642 was now dispersed among the troops of the Earl of Essex and Sir William Waller. The warship *Marten*, which he and his brother George had insinuated into the parliamentary navy, seems to have been lost in November 1643. The end of his parliamentary immunities exposed Marten to his creditors.[2] With his release from the Tower in September 1643, he disappears from view, almost entirely, for twenty-eight months. He seems to have been serving in the army for at least part of that time, though not as the Governor of Aylesbury, as used to be thought.[3]

[1] Marten's revelation to Hyde, his tactics, and his expulsion are discussed and illustrated in C. M. Williams, 'Extremist Tactics in the Long Parliament, 1642–1643', *Historical Studies*, 57 (1971).
[2] Ibid.; Williams, 'Marten', 202–11, 326; *CJ* iii. 323–4; *The Journal of Sir Samuel Luke*, ed. I. G. Philip, i (Banbury, 1950), 36.
[3] D'Ewes, BL, Harley MS. 165, fol. 152; Brotherton Lib., Marten-Loder MSS., box 16, fol. 165. The Governor of Aylesbury was Colonel Francis Marten.

The Anatomy of a Radical Gentleman: Henry Marten 121

In December 1645, however, Henry Marten presented himself at Westminster as the 'recruiter' M.P. for the borough of Abingdon, a seat vacated by the delinquency of his royalist kinsman, Sir George Stonehouse. Baffled by this manœuvre, a rebel House whose earlier devotion to monarchy had grown a little tired decided, in the end, to rescind his expulsion and readmit Marten to his old seat as a Knight of the Shire for Berkshire.[1] In no time he had resumed his old campaigns. Peace by conquest, not by negotiation, was his prime objective. Anyone who stood for negotiation with Charles I was his antagonist, but especially the House of Lords, the Scots, and the Presbyterians in and out of Parliament.

By now, Henry Marten had begun to confirm and enlarge a reputation for radicalism by his friendship with John Lilburne, Richard Overton, William Walwyn, and John Wildman. His hand in some of the earliest Leveller manifestoes is suspected. His hand in the second 'Agreement of the People' is acknowledged by Lilburne himself: Marten was the only civilian member of parliament who contributed to the hammering out of the Leveller version of that remarkable constitution.[2] In May or June 1648, when it seemed likely that a 'Presbyterian' majority would commit the Parliament to a restoration of Charles, Marten left the House and, for a time, roamed the countryside at the head of an armed band proclaiming Leveller sentiments and pledged to fight against anyone, royalist, Scot, or parliamentarian, who might seek to put the King back on his throne. It was not until the day after Pride's Purge that he slipped into the House again, secured against the proper consequences of his adventure by the expulsion of many of his parliamentary enemies.[3] In due course he was a regicide.

It might be thought that the first avowed republican would have found a place of honour in the first republic: but now, as

[1] *CJ* iv. 384, 388, 397; BL, Add. MS. 31116, fol. 252ᵛ; Harley MS. 165, fol. 152; House of Lords RO, MS. Journal of the House of Commons, expunged entries of 16 Aug. 1643.
[2] John Lilburne, *Legal Fundamental Liberties*, in *Leveller Manifestoes of the Puritan Revolution*, ed. D. M. Wolfe (N.Y., 1944), 411–24. Attempts by various scholars to identify Marten's hand in other Leveller documents are discussed in Williams, 'Marten', 218–44.
[3] *Mercurius Pragmaticus*, 22–9 Aug. 1648; *HMC, Portland*, i. 495; *Cal. of Committee for Advance of Monies*, iii. 1292; Bodl., Tanner MS. 57, fol. 197; *CJ* v. 673; *Terrible and bloudy Newes from the disloyall Army in the North* (1648); Whitelocke, ii. 382, 406.

before, Marten seemed unable to attach himself to a majority. He was elected to three of the five republican Councils of State, but his growing opposition to the army's political influence helped to keep him from real eminence. At the same time, it assured him of a special allocation of Cromwellian indignation when the Captain General, afraid that the Rump might attempt a political settlement not to his liking or advantage, destroyed the regime he had sworn to serve.

The fall of the republic he had striven so hard to create spelt the end of Marten's effective political life. There is a surprising piece of evidence that he may have been summoned to Bare-bones' Parliament;[1] but he certainly did not sit. He made some effort to win election to the other Protectoral parliaments, but from early in 1655 he was hampered by confinement within the Rules of the King's Bench, the prisoner of his creditors. As one of his political agents wrote, finding a seat for 'a man in durance' was impossibly hard.[2] With the fall of Richard Cromwell and the restorations of the Rump, Marten enjoyed brief returns to parliamentary influence, but it was exercised to little purpose. At the Restoration he surrendered on the terms of the King's promise of oblivion and indemnity and stood his trial as a regicide, declining all opportunities to express any contrition for his part in the killing of Charles I. A spirited defence barely delayed his conviction. He was lodged in the Tower again, this time to await the verdict of the two Houses of Parliament. The Commons voted that he should be hanged, drawn, and quartered but, ironically, the Lords, whose House he had often treated with contempt, decided that he might live out his days in prison.[3] They were long days. It was not until 1680 that Henry Marten was at last quiet in his prison at Chepstow Castle.

Nothing distinguished Henry Marten more conspicuously from the great majority of his parliamentary colleagues than the quick, dry, irreverent wit for which he was remembered long after his death. According to John Aubrey, his speeches

[1] Brotherton Lib., Marten-Loder MSS., 'Henry Marten Papers, Political and Miscellaneous', ii (1651–1658), fols. 39–40, 1–4. This is part of a letter to Oliver Cromwell which, on internal evidence, I have little hesitation in ascribing to Marten.

[2] Brotherton Lib., Marten-Loder MSS., *passim*; Williams, 'Marten', 416–19.

[3] Williams, 'Marten', 441–5.

were 'not long, but wondrous poynant, pertinent, and witty'. To eyes and ears tuned by the BBC, much of his wit may not seem very funny; but against the prevailing solemnity, pomposity, and piety of his day it fairly sparkles. The godly member who moved that all profane and unsanctified men be expelled from Parliament provoked a typical Marten amendment: let all the fools be put out, too, and 'then there would be a thin House'. Another, who thought he had caught Marten asleep during a debate, moved to expel all members who slept and minded not the business of the House. Marten, who had only been enjoying a 'dog-sleepe', suggested that if the nodders were put out, the noddees should go with them.[1]

That sort of thing was thought 'an incomparable witt for repartees', but it could generate intense resentment in its victims. It was for constantly opposing and 'wittilie ierking at old John Pym', thought Sir Simonds D'Ewes, that Marten was expelled from the Commons in 1643. D'Ewes himself was so disconcerted by a blast of 'scurrilous and windie witt' from Marten and others that for an agonizing four months he denied himself the pleasure of speaking in the House. No wonder he complained that Marten 'used too many levities to stirr upp laughter'.[2] The Earl of Essex would have agreed. In the winter of 1642 his main army, ill-paid, ill-supplied, and ill-manned, lay immobile near Windsor while active royalists scored victories elsewhere. Marten commented that it was 'summer in Devonshire, summer in Yorkshire, and onlie winter at Windsor'. The London M.P., Samuel Vassall, can hardly have been pleased when Marten offered a meeting of his constituents the choice between fighting like men and submitting 'as Vassalls'. Later, when the Rump voted to abolish the House of Lords as 'useless and dangerous', Marten's comment was as wounding as it was dry: 'useless, but not dangerous'.[3]

The 'apt instances' for which Marten was famous were usually intended to sting. When the Assembly of Divines claimed *jure divino*, Marten compared them with the sons of Zebedee, who

---

[1] *Aubrey's Brief Lives*, ed. O. L. Dick (1950), 194.

[2] Ibid.; D'Ewes, BL, Harley MSS. 163, fols. 291ᵛ, 292ᵛ; 164, fols. 102, 273, 295ᵛ; 165, fol. 152.

[3] BL, Harley MS. 164, fol. 243; *Three Speeches Delivered at a Common-Hall, on Saturday the 28 of July, 1643*, 18; J. Forster, *Lives of Eminent British Statesmen*, iv (1838), 318.

had wanted no more than to sit on either side of Christ. The Divines, less modestly, 'would faine take Christ out of his Throne, that themselves might sit in it, and place the House of Lords on their right hand, and the House of Commons on the left'. George Monck, protesting his fidelity to the Parliament while he led into England the army that would restore the monarchy, reminded Marten of a man who swore he could make a good suit of clothes with carpenter's tools.[1] Scottish claims that the Covenant gave them a major voice in settling English affairs provoked the remark that the Covenant was 'like an Almanak of the last year [to] shew us rather what we have already done, then what we be now to do'. It was bad enough for the English to have to bear the weight of a King, Marten suggested, without the extra burden of Scottish interference: 'to be *Charge en crouppe* is that which nature made a mule for, if nature made a mule at all'. In 1660 he wrote that he would never have consented to the King's execution if he had suspected that 'the Axe which took off the late Kings head, should have been made a stirrop for our first false General'.[2]

Not all Marten's wit was barbed. When his friend, John Lilburne, offered to right a wrong he had done Marten, he was advised gently 'not to trouble your selfe . . . about repairing of mee, till I feel my selfe dilapidated'. There was more good humour than malice in his remark that the Parliament's great seal might cure the King's Evil as effectively as the touch of Charles I 'if there were an ordinance for it'. Occasionally in the House he indulged in sheer high spirits; and his letters to his mistress, Mary Ward, though written mainly in the grimmest possible circumstances, breathe a cheerfulness that helps to explain why those of his acquaintance who did not hate the man liked him very well.[3]

Henry Marten's religious position is obscure but unquestionably radical. Political opponents who called him a Saint were indulging in heavy sarcasm. Those who called him an atheist

[1] *Mercurius Pragmaticus*, 18 (25 July–1 Aug. 1648), 5; *The Memoirs of Edmund Ludlow*, ed. C. H. Firth (Oxford, 1894), ii. 207–8.

[2] Marten, *The Independency of England Endeavored to be maintained* (1648), 11, 24; *Coll: Henry Marten's Familiar Letters*, 3.

[3] *Two Letters: The One From Lievtenant Colonell John Lilbourne to Colonel Henry Martin . . . With his Answer* (1647); S. R. Gardiner, *History of the Great Civil War*, iii (1891), 57–8; *Coll: Henry Marten's Familiar Letters*.

were exaggerating. There is no clear evidence to link Henry
Marten with any church, sect, or congregation. His surviving
papers show that he was on familiar terms with parsons as
various as John Goodwin of Coleman Street, John Saltmarsh
the apostle of free grace, Hugh Peter, William Twisse (the
prolocutor of the Assembly of Divines), and Dr. Samuel Fell,
the Dean of Christ Church, but these associations tell us
nothing reliable about his own opinions:[1] the son of a judicial
pillar of the Church could hardly avoid an extensive, clerical
acquaintance. John Aubrey hints that Marten was 'of the
natural religion'—presumably a sort of deist—but is on firmer
ground when he tells us that he was 'as far from a Puritane as
light from darknesse'.[2]

At some time between 1645 and 1649, Marten decided to
publish his opinions on a wide variety of subjects. For his first
topic he chose God and wrote simply that 'what ever hath bene
said by any yet concerning him is but . . . opinion'.[3] In those
few words Marten confounded dogma, discipline, and the
exclusive claims of all churches, sects, and clergy. So it is no
surprise to find him joining John Selden in urging toleration of
the hated Papists and Hugh Peter in advocating the readmission
of the Jews to England.[4] He attacked the Assembly of Divines
for its attempts to force its opinions on parliament and people
alike, the English Presbyterians for their desire to erect a
coercive, national church, and the Scots for their support of
both. Brownists, Antinomians, and Anabaptists he thought
honest men. Presbyterians and Independents should not persecute them, or attack each other, remembering that they
themselves were heretics in the eyes of orthodox anglicans: 'if
you will . . . manage God's matters according to God's ways',
he wrote,

you must suppresse Blasphemies, Sects, and Heresies by convincing
the Blasphemer, the Sectary and the Heretick. When Christ is

---

[1] Brotherton Lib., Marten-Loder MSS., *passim*. It was in defending Saltmarsh
that Marten made the statement for which he was expelled from the Commons
in 1643.   [2] *Aubrey*, ed. Dick, 61, 193–4.
[3] Brotherton Lib., Marten-Loder MSS., 'Opinions offered by HM', box 78,
fol. 10.
[4] BL, Add. MS. 50200, fol. 19; S. R. Gardiner, *Civil War*, iii. 212; [Clement
Walker], *Anarchia Anglicana or, the History of Independency*, 'the second part'
(1649), 60.

contented to tolerate the tares among the corn I would not have you call toleration accursed especially since you may be deceived in discerning tares from corn.[1]

In Marten's opinion, the Bible was a sufficient guide to salvation. Why, then, should laymen be persecuted for undertaking to interpret that guide 'as if nobody might labour in God's husbandry though they ask no wages but such as have a human title . . . unto the tenth sheep'? It was absurd, he suggested, that 'all other good offices a man may freely do to his neighbour except contributing to the service assisting him in the ways of salvation; for that he must have a patent'.[2]

Even the Irish, Marten believed, should be left free to practise popery if they pleased. In 1647 he urged the Parliament to offer terms of peace to the Irish rebels. Those Englishmen who wanted to suppress the rebellion for the sake of Protestantism reminded him of 'those gallant ancestors that ly buryed in Palestine whither they were carryed with a fervent desire to recover the holy land and beat the wholl world into Christianity'. To try to 'make all Christendome a protestant' was a foolish ambition.[3]

In 1655 Marten wrote a vigorous defence of the Quakers, though he claimed to know as little about them as their fierce detractors did. The motto he chose for that defence was 'Felicia tempora quam te moribus opponunt'.[4] Unlike many of his opponents, Marten rarely flourished scriptural texts in his writings and speeches, but, like them, he could quote Scripture —and misquote it—when the text suited his political purpose. He was quite willing to argue with such formidable students of holy writ as William Prynne, John Lilburne, and John Goodwin.[5] But his attitude to the religious passions of his day was

---

[1] Brotherton Lib., Marten-Loder MSS., fragment of 'Rash Censures Uncharitable', box 78, fol. 1; Lady Fairfax's MSS., 'The Mistakes of the Petition . . . of the Inhabitants of Suffolk' (1647) in 'Charles I his Reign 1625–1649, Portraits and State Documents' (C3S16B.R.).

[2] Lady Fairfax's MSS., 'The Mistakes' in 'Charles I his Reign' (C3S16B.R.); Brotherton Lib., Marten-Loder MSS., fragment of 'Rash Censures Uncharitable', box 78, fol. 4.

[3] Brotherton Lib., Marten-Loder MSS., 'An additional instruction for the Ld. Lieut't of Ireland', box 78, fol. 13.

[4] Brotherton Lib., Marten-Loder MSS., 'Justice Would-bee that made himself a Ranter last week in opposition to those he calls Quakers', box 78, fols. 6–7.

[5] [Marten], *A Word to Mr. Wil. Prynn Esq; And Two For the Parliament and Army* (1649); Lady Fairfax's MSS., fragments of 'A Plea for the People' and of 'Certain

generally one of detachment, sometimes amused, sometimes not. In so far as the perfervid enthusiasms of the times were sincere, they should be respected and protected; in so far as they led to persecution, they deserved mockery and opposition; in so far as they generated divisions within the parliamentary cause and distracted men from the urgent secular problems of England, they were deplorable. The energy spent in religious controversy should be turned against the enemies of England, the King and his sympathizers at home and abroad.[1]

The imminence of death is said to clarify a man's religious convictions. If this be true, those who thought Marten indifferent to religion were perhaps not far from the mark. Most of his published letters to his beloved mistress, Mary Ward, were written from the Tower while Marten, a convicted regicide, waited to know if the Parliament would confirm his sentence to be hanged, drawn, and quartered, or commute it to imprisonment for life. Those letters are devoid of conventional piety. They show us a man deeply imbued with stoic principles, derived, perhaps, from Marten's 'little great philosopher Epictetus'.[2] For himself and for his beloved he advised being 'snugg like a Snail within our own selves, that is, our mindes, which no body but we can touch': 'The Skill is, not in being weather-wise, but weather-proof'.[3] Even at the end of his life the acrostic epitaph he composed for himself gave not even a perfunctory nod in the direction of conventional religion. It began:

Here or elsewhere (all's one to you, to me)
Earth, Air, or water gripes my ghostless dust
None knowing when brave fire shall set it free.
Reader, if you an oft tryed rule will trust
You'll gladly do and suffer what you must.[4]

Select Passages of Esqr Prynnes Plea for the Lords Improved by Henry Marten' in 'Charles I his Reign' (C3S16 B.R.); fragments of 'Rash Censures Uncharitable' and of Ἀντικρητισμός or Satisfaction dissatisfying', 'Original official MSS.'; Brotherton Lib., Marten-Loder MSS., fragment of 'Rash Censures Uncharitable', box 78, fols. 1–2.

[1] Brotherton Lib., Marten-Loder MSS., 'An additional instruction', box 78, fols. 11–13.

[2] Brotherton Lib., Marten-Loder MSS., 'Henry Marten Papers, Political and Miscellaneous', ii. Ralph Brideoakes to Marten (n.d.), fols. 63–4.

[3] *Coll: Henry Marten's Familiar Letters*, 6.

[4] William Coxe, *An Historical Tour of Monmouthshire* (1801), ii. 389.

The same good nature that brought Marten to the defence of Quakers and Jews, Catholics, Brownists, and Anabaptists alike, was the despair of his business agents and a major cause of his own financial troubles. But there was more than mere good nature in the man. 'He was a great cultor of justice,' wrote Aubrey, 'and did always . . . take the part of the oppressed.'[1]

The beneficiaries of this amiable trait were often, it is true, men of Marten's own class. The Earl of Rutland, Edmund Waller, and Sir William D'Avenant, as well as John Lilburne and Richard Overton, were among the many who appealed for Marten's help when their lives, liberties, or fortunes were in danger.[2] But his sense of justice extended far below and beyond the ranks of society to which most would have thought it proper. How many of his contemporaries had a good word to say for the wretched Irish as he had? It was to Marten that the exiled Lilburne wrote in 1652 seeking help for wounded English sailors he had found abandoned in Zealand. He counted on a sympathetic response. So did the poor prisoners for debt whose appalling plight Marten tried repeatedly to relieve; so did the widow Ellen Benson when one child died and another was starving at her breast; and hard-pressed Anne Windsor when the state did not honour the debentures of her husband away fighting in Scotland; and many 'handycrafte men poor Widdowes and servants' who had lent money to the Parliament and discovered that they were to be left in the lurch while rich creditors were to be paid.[3] 'The oppressed' were often people of inferior social rank, their oppressors men of wealth and worship. To take up the cudgels for the poor and

[1] *Aubrey*, ed. Dick, 194.

[2] Brotherton Lib., Marten-Loder MSS., Rutland to Marten (n.d.), 'Henry Marten Papers, Political and Miscellaneous', ii. fols. 42–3; D'Avenant to Marten, 8 July 1652, ibid., fols. 11–12; Waller to Marten, 1643, box 78, fols. 56–7; John Lilburne, *Two Letters Writ by Lievt. Col. John Lilburne . . . to Col. Henry Martin . . . 13. and 15 of September, 1647* and *A Copy of a Letter written to Coll. Henry Martin . . . Iuly, 20, 1647;* Richard Overton, *An Arrow Against All Tyrants*, and *The Commoners Complaint.*

[3] Brotherton Lib., Marten-Loder MSS., 'An additional instruction', box 78, fols. 11–13; Ellen Benson to Marten (n.d.), 'Henry Marten Estates, Miscellaneous Letters, Accounts', iii, fol. 35; Anne Windsor to Marten (1652), 'Henry Marten Papers, Political and Miscellaneous', ii, fols. 17–18; petition of handicraft men and others, box 67, fol. 42; James Frese, *Every mans Right: or, Englands Perspective-Glasse* (1646); Lilburne to Marten, 8 Sept. 1652, HMC, 13th Rep. appx., pt. iv. 390.

obscure, in such circumstances, was not only to offend particular oppressors but to challenge the tradition, cherished by men of rank and estates even during the Civil War, that in the face of their inferiors, gentlemen should stick together.

A strain of indifference, even of hostility, to the privileges of birth and wealth appeared early in Marten's public life. He had the bad taste to contrast the Lords' consideration for the rights of the Earl of Strafford with the summary justice meted out in the ordinary courts to poor rogues. Repeatedly he opposed bills for the conscription of common seamen, watermen, gunners, surgeons, and the like for service in the Parliament's fleet. Conscription, he argued, was 'against the liberty of the subject': the offer of decent wages would be a better way of recruiting the navy. In 1642 and 1643 he promoted in vain a bill 'for the Confirmation of the subjects liberties in their persons'.[1]

Marten consistently brushed aside the fears of men like Edmund Waller and Sir Simonds D'Ewes that to invoke the warlike energies of the common people in the struggle against Charles I would threaten destruction to all property and all social distinctions. In the summer of 1643 he was the parliamentary leader of the General Rising movement which, under the alarming slogan 'One and All!', sought to enlist every able-bodied man, irrespective of wealth or rank, for a popular crusade against the King and his adherents.[2] No wonder Sir John Maynard later accused him of 'bringing in the democraticall eliment' and of putting himself at the head of 'the skumme of the people or the Canalia'.[3]

Marten's capacity for sympathy with common people and his indifference to the exclusive pretensions of exalted and wealthy men made it easy for him to associate with the Leveller leaders and to become their 'good (or best) friend' in a parliament increasingly hostile to them and their ideas. He had no difficulty in adopting the Leveller objection to jurymen uncovering in the presence of judges: in 1648 he was even reported to have forbidden the soldiers under his command to defer to him except on the battlefield.[4]

---

[1] D'Ewes, BL, Harley MS. 162, fols. 90^v, 237, 255^v, 256^v, 363^v; *CJ* ii. 356, 922.
[2] Williams, 'Marten', 88–101.
[3] 'Speech in answer to Mr. Martyn' (MS.); BL, E. 422 (32).
[4] *A Declaration of some Proceedings of Lt. Col. John Lilburne and his Associates* (1648),

Henry Marten was no communist. He was as eager to preserve his own property, and to defend the principle of private ownership, as any man in England. But nothing in his life suggests that he valued gentility or nobility for their own sake, or that he felt any pangs of regret when he helped the Levellers to draft the second Agreement of the People, with its insistence that the law of England should apply equally to all, without respect for blood or title. Nothing suggests that he shared the deep suspicion, prevalent amongst his parliamentary colleagues, of the many-headed multitude. That in itself was enough to damn him, in the eyes of most of his peers, as an impossible radical.

He was not so obliging as to leave us a statement of the 'first principles' which brought him into conflict with most of those amongst whom he worked; but from his public acts and from a meagre corpus of writings it is possible to piece together elements of his political philosophy and vision.

'The English Nation', he once proclaimed, 'is a free people undeniably possessed of liberty in their persons, and of property in their goods.' The will of the people was the sole source of legitimate authority in England: 'it is not in the power of any person or persons to force such laws upon them as they apprehend hurtful to them, or to hinder them from having such laws as they judge good for them'. The power of legislation, which Marten described as 'the supream badge of supream power', derived solely from the people.[1]

That supreme power could be exercised either collectively or representatively: perhaps under Leveller influence, Marten seems seriously to have entertained the possibility of legislation by the people 'in the Masse, as they are inhabitants of one countrey, gatherable into a body'. But in practice it was exercised by their elected representatives. 'The Peoples consent signified by their Trustees in the House of Commons', Marten declared, 'is the only essential binding part of all our statutes, and that which makes them law.' The traditional concurrence

14; BL, Add. MS. 50200, fol. 35; *Mercurius Pragmaticus*, 21 (15–22 Aug. 1648); I. Waters, *Henry Marten and the Long Parliament* (Chepstow, 1973), 41.

[1] Lady Fairfax's MSS., 'Fundamental Rights belonging to the English Nation' in 'Charles I his Reign' (C3S16B.R.); Brotherton Lib., Marten-Loder MSS., 'Rash Censures Uncharitable', box 78, fol. 1ᵛ.

of King and House of Lords was a mere 'ornament'.[1] He found
it hard to conceive that a truly representative House of Commons *could* be oppressive. It was here, in the end, that he parted
company with the Levellers. He was on the best of terms with
them as long as they addressed the Commons as the supreme
authority of England; but, despite the manifest faults of the
House of which he was a member, he could not accept the
later Leveller view that the struggle between King and Commons was merely to decide 'which of them should domineer
over the people'.[2] The commons should remember that, though
their authority was the highest in England, it was 'but derived',
and must be used 'to advance or to conserve at least, not to
infringe, the interest of those by whom they are deputed'. With
that one proviso their power was unlimited.[3]

Behind this simple web of ideas lay an unusual degree of
faith in the civic virtue and political wisdom of 'the people'. It
enabled Marten to invoke the political energies of 'one and all'
in 1643, without fearing, as John Pym did, 'a general com-
bustion'. In 1653, attacking Oliver Cromwell for depriving the
people of their sovereignty and liberty, he maintained that the
quiet, freedom, and happiness of England were 'not to be
expected but from a popular election'. A government chosen by
and responsible to the people would have the 'hearts, persons,
and purses of the Nation' at its devotion. Only such a government promised real integrity. 'The People have this advantage
in their choyce', he wrote, 'that they are uncapable of being
bribed.' Given the choice between a man of integrity and one
not esteemed so, they would always choose the first 'though the
second bring more Wine and Venison'.[4]

So sublime a faith had need of reinforcement; and Marten
seems to have found it in a vaguely formulated notion that only
'natural' solutions to political problems could be relied upon to

[1] Lady Fairfax's MSS., 'The Rights of the People of England' in 'Original
official MSS.'; 'Fundamental Rights' in 'Charles I his Reign' (C3S16B.R.).

[2] Henry Marten, *The Parliaments Proceedings justified, in Declining A Personall
Treaty with the King* (1648), 15.

[3] Lady Fairfax's MSS., single sheet beginning 'The House of Commons in
Parliament' in 'Original official MSS.'.

[4] Pym's speech in *Three Speeches Delivered at a Common-Hall, on Saturday the 28 of
July, 1643*; Brotherton Lib., Marten-Loder MSS., Letter to Oliver Cromwell
(1653), 'Henry Marten Papers, Political and Miscellaneous', ii, second fragment,
fol. 3.

work. Conquest was a 'more naturall' way to peace than compromise. A King was but 'an artificial thing'. If they were to withstand the subtlety and evasions of man, constitutions had to be 'introduced by time and framed by necessity rather then wisdome'. New frames of laws devised even by such wise legislators as Solon and Lycurgus had always 'suddenly altered with the humour of the people'.[1] The implication for the Trustees of the English people was plain: they must remain responsive to the will of those whom they governed, or face inevitable failure. 'Common reason', argued Marten, was 'the surest ground of all law.'[2]

Unlike many of his contemporaries Marten was little interested in the origins of the liberties and sovereign powers he claimed for the English people. He could appeal to Magna Carta and the Petition of Right as occasion required, but he was one of those who made what Christopher Hill called the 'momentous transition' from seeking to recover lost (and often mythical) rights to 'the pursuit of rights because they *ought* to exist'.[3] Being a free nation, he argued, the English 'ought to live under laws of their own making'. John Aubrey tells how Marten was reprimanded in the House for a 'notorious lie' when his draft of the bill abolishing kingship declared that 'a most happy way is made for this nation . . . to return to its just and ancient right of being governed by its own representatives . . . chosen and entrusted for that purpose by the people'. Marten's response was meekly to remind the House of the biblical story of *'the man that was blind from his mother's womb whose sight was restored at last*, i.e. was restored to the sight which he should have had'.[4]

Against this background it is easy to see the logic of Marten's almost idolatrous respect for the House of Commons, which was the positive aspect of his contempt for kingship and the House of Lords. Kings represented only themselves and their families;

---

[1] Brotherton Lib., Marten-Loder MSS., Letter to Oliver Cromwell (1653); 'Henry Marten Papers, Political and Miscellaneous', ii, second fragment, fol. 4; Marten, *The Independency of England*, 15; D'Ewes, BL, Harley MS. 163, fol. 272ᵛ.

[2] Lady Fairfax' MSS., 'The House of Commons in Parliament' in 'Original official MSS.'.

[3] Hill, *Puritanism and Revolution* (1958), 75.

[4] Lady Fairfax' MSS., 'Fundamental Rights' in 'Charles I his Reign' (C3S16 B.R.); *Aubrey*, ed. Dick, 194.

the House of Lords a small, privileged élite. Neither was in any sense representative of the people or fit to guard their interests. Neither was necessary to the happiness of the people or to the conduct of good government. To allow the will of King or Lords to frustrate the will or endanger the safety of the people was a sort of treason.

It was one thing for Henry Marten to declare the House of Commons the sovereign and only essential part of the English constitution, but quite another to persuade his parliamentary colleagues of it. From the beginning of the Long Parliament until Pride's Purge, the majority in the Commons did their best to avoid laying claim to permanent, sovereign authority. Even after the Civil War began, they resisted sending envoys abroad as from a sovereign power and suffered 'grievous mischiefs' rather than invest themselves with that symbol of sovereign authority, a Great Seal of their own. It took a comforting dose of misconstrued precedents to persuade them that the Parliament might issue ordinances with the force of law. For eight years they persisted in treating Charles I as the victim of 'evil counsel' rather than, as Marten saw him, the chief of malignants 'set in his heart, upon being either an absolute Tyrant over us, or no King'.[1] Even after Pride's Purge, they tolerated for a month the equal authority of a ridiculous remnant of the House of Lords.

Marten would have none of this hesitation. As early as August 1641, he wanted an ordinance to have the force and power of an Act of Parliament. He was so eager for the Parliament to have its own Great Seal that he had an engraver ready to make it. It was he who urged the Parliament not only to give itself the power to send envoys abroad, but to 'take the people into our protection'. Naturally he was unmoved by John Pym's objection that that would be to subvert the monarchy.[2]

Subversion of the monarchy was, indeed, essential to Marten's hopes of persuading the House of Commons to assume the powers and functions of sovereign government. He scorned the fiction that Charles was the innocent captive of his advisers.

---

[1] Marten, *Parliaments Proceedings*, 14. On the sending of envoys and the controversy over the Great Seal, Williams, 'Extremist Tactics', 140, 143.

[2] D'Ewes, BL, Harley MS. 164, fols. 70, 381ᵛ–382; *CJ* iii. 162.

When he needed horses for his regiment, he took some from the King's stables, as from any other malignant. He made fun of the royal regalia, calling them useless 'toyes and trifles', and protested against his colleagues' incongruous gestures of deference to a king whose armies were trying to crush them.[1] He lost no opportunity to express his conviction that the happiness of the kingdom did not depend on the King 'or upon any of the royal branches of that root'. The Commons' shock on hearing Marten declare that it was better for the royal family to perish than for the whole nation to suffer gave Pym his chance to have this embarrassing colleague expelled.[2]

It cannot be said that Marten made much progress in his early attempts to undermine the Parliament's reverence for the monarchy. The hard realities of civil war and the failure of all attempts to come to terms with his Sacred Majesty achieved more in that way than all Marten's sallies. It was 'time and necessity', which, by degrees, overcame his fellow-members' reluctance to assume the functions of a sovereign authority. During the wars they had no choice; in the aftermath of war they discovered that the choice was between an insecure compromise with the King and an unprecedented seizure of power into their own hands. So great was their reluctance and so powerful the monarchist set of most parliamentary minds, that it took an angry and determined army to make the choice for them. There were not many confident and convinced trustees of the people in the Parliament of the Rump Republic that followed.

The creation of that republic did not alter Henry Marten's profound suspicion of power concentrated in few hands. As early as June 1641 he had moved for the abolition of the Privy Council, with the quip that anyway 'the Counsell table had been turned altar-waies'. There was no need for a 'third howse'.[3] Within the Parliament itself, he guarded jealously the authority of his House as a whole. He vehemently opposed the move to erect a plenipotentiary committee to act for the Parliament during its first recess. The more the Committee of Safety arrogated to itself the important business of the Parliament, the

[1] Williams, 'Extremist Tactics', 137–8, 141–2.
[2] Clarendon, ii. 149; *CJ* iii. 206; Whitelocke, i. 208.
[3] D'Ewes, BL, Harley MSS. 163, fol. 363; 162, fol. 375^v.

more Marten, though himself a member of the committee, sought to have it abolished. 'A pint pot', he said, 'could not hold a pottle of liquor.'[1]

Marten regarded the House of Lords as a body bent on domineering over the people and their representatives. No fewer than four of his unfinished and unpublished pamphlets are attacks on writers or petitioners who defended the authority of the Lords over commoners.[2] In the Rump he attacked Sir John Danvers for implying that the Council of State was superior to the House, and opposed the creation of the title of Lord President of the Council. The Rump's worst folly, he thought, was its allowing Oliver Cromwell to domineer. By 'putting all the power in the 3 Nations into one hand' the Rump had 'manifested to the World that they understood nothing of a Commonwealth but the name'. It was the same error that the Long Parliament had made in forbearing to inform Charles I that he was subject to the law and 'accountable to man for whatsoever he should do'.[3]

In spite of the Rump's many acknowledged faults, however, Marten regarded the constitution of the Commonwealth as 'the best frame of lawes yett extant in the world'.[4] And why not? In form, it corresponded closely with the model that can be derived from Marten's political principles. The whole power of legislation, jurisdiction, and government was vested in a single, omni-competent House to which an executive, newly elected by secret ballot each year, was responsible and subordinate. All the Rump lacked was the truly representative character that only popular elections could ensure; and Marten implied that these would have been held soon, if Cromwell had not put an end to the Rump in April 1653.[5]

[1] D'Ewes, BL, Harley MS. 164, fol. 107; Williams, 'Extremist Tactics', 147–8.

[2] For his attacks on John Selden, William Prynne (twice) and the Suffolk petitioners of 16 Feb. 1646, see Lady Fairfax's MSS., 'The Rights of the People of England' in 'Original official MSS.'; and 'A Plea for the People', 'Certain Select Passages', and 'The Mistakes of the Petition' in 'Charles I his Reign' (C3S16B.R.).

[3] *CJ* vi. 143; S. R. Gardiner, *History of the Commonwealth and Protectorate* (new edn. 1903), i. 244; Brotherton Lib., Marten-Loder MSS., Letter to Oliver Cromwell, 'Henry Marten Papers, Political and Miscellaneous', ii, second fragment, fol. 1; *Coll: Henry Marten's Familiar Letters*, 3.

[4] Brotherton Lib., Marten-Loder MSS., Letter to Oliver Cromwell, 'Henry Marten Papers, Political and Miscellaneous', ii, second fragment, fol. 4.

[5] Ibid., first fragment, fol. 40; second fragment, fol. 2.

Furthermore, that constitution had the virtues of being both natural and native. It was simply the old, English constitution stripped of all that Marten had thought corrupt and inessential. He himself was to fall briefly under the spell of Harrington's ideas,[1] but long before they were given to the world he had fixed his hopes on just such a constitution as the Rump republic adopted. His own political writings and speeches show few signs of European influences or of those Greek and Roman principles which, according to Bishop Burnet, were his inspiration. The political figures he admired were the 'faithfull Patriots' who had compelled Charles I to accept the Petition of Right; above all his father's old friend, Sir John Eliot. The political virtues he praised were those of good English parliament-men; honest, hard-working, regular in attendance to their duty, disinterested, fearless. By contrast, he had only contempt for most of the former members of the Rump whom the army nominated to sit in Barebones' Parliament. They, said Marten, were 'only fitt to hold theire peace and consent': if they had ever opened their lips in House or Committee it was to little or no purpose.[2] Marten's was a strenuous ideal. It is only fair to add that he tried to live up to it.

Strenuous ideals are no guarantee of a good reputation. Everything about Henry Marten, from his irreverent humour to his immorality, his religious heterodoxy, his indiscriminate concern for justice, and his association with Levellers and Quakers, might have been calculated to alienate a sizeable part of his noble and gentle contemporaries. But it is on his republicanism that Marten's reputation as a radical has always rested most firmly.

On the face of it, this is strange. A republic in which all power lay in the hands of a House of Commons might seem admirably adaptable to the desires of a gentry weary of having its destiny directed by one man and his 'evil counsel'. Marten's republicanism was, after all, little more than a logical extension

---

[1] Marten may have been the 'H. M.' who was one of the authors of *The Armies Dutie* (1659). Lady Fairfax's MSS., 'Original official MSS.', contains the beginning only of a defence of *Oceana* ('The Considerations on Mr. Harrington's Commonwealth of Oceana reconsidered by H. Marten').

[2] *Burnet's History of my Own Time*, ed. O. Airy (Oxford, 1897), i. 283; Brotherton Lib., Marten-Loder MSS., Letter to Oliver Cromwell, 'Henry Marten Papers, Political and Miscellaneous', ii, first fragment, fol. 40; second fragment, fol. 4.

of the very principles by which the great majority of Long Parliament men had sought to justify their initial opposition to Charles I.

Yet there can be no doubting the genuineness of the horror inspired in gentlemanly breasts by republican ideas. When Edward Hyde first heard Marten's opinions he was sure they would have been abhorred by the whole nation, 'that Gentleman being at that Time possessed of a very great Fortune, and having great Credit in his country'.[1] Six years later Hyde could not believe that

those who have good fortunes and excellent understandings, have a design to dissolve monarchy and change the government which would carry away with it so much of the common law, as would shake their own property and every part of their condition, which made life pleasant for them, or that they were not themselves now more afraid of the people than ever they pretended to be of tyranny.[2]

Republicanism was an ugly threat to property and privilege. No gentleman of fortune and understanding should ever embrace it.

Henry Marten's public life was lived among men who, as Hobbes remarked with distaste, had the bad habit of thinking the King merely the highest member of a social edifice in which they themselves enjoyed much privilege and might hope to enjoy more.[3] They were men whose favourite metaphors for the society in which they lived included the arch and the human body. Everyone knew what happened to an arch if the keystone were removed, and to a body when the head was taken off. In seeking to remove the head, even if it were on the pretext of curing the body's ills, Marten betrayed the interests of his class. He was a worrying anomaly. Gentlemen had well-tried ways of dealing with the radicalism that was to be expected of the meaner sort. But one who threatened them from within their own citadel made them apprehensive and angry. The fact that they could recognize in his ideas a family likeness to their own declarations of principle made matters worse. That in

---

[1] *The Life of Edward Earl of Clarendon* (Oxford, 1759), i. 31–2.

[2] Hyde to Jermyn, 8 Jan. 1647, quoted in B. H. G. Wormald, *Clarendon, Politics, History & Religion, 1640–1660* (Cambridge, 1951), 187.

[3] Hobbes, *Behemoth*, in *The English Works of Thomas Hobbes*, ed. W. Molesworth (1840), vi. 169.

Marten the treachery of republicanism was combined with a catalogue of other, dangerous heresies, confirmed their low opinion of him—and of republicanism.

It did not worry Henry Marten. Early in 1647 he told the House of Commons that the King had on his side 'the greater part of the Nobility, Gentry and Clergy of the kingdom', working together for their 'corrupt interests, directly opposite to the interests of the people'.[1] If that analysis was correct, who but the people themselves could save their cause? Who but the majority of their betters would be the enemy? However vaguely he may have conceived 'the people', Marten did not shrink from those questions.

Ideas are judged as much by the men who propound them as by their intrinsic merits. In the person of Henry Marten, gentlemen of property and privilege in his own generation saw proof, if any were needed, that the idea of a parliamentary republic would subvert *them*. Their heirs, it seems, have long memories.

[1] Brotherton Lib., Marten-Loder MSS., 'An additional instruction for the Ld. Lieut't of Ireland', box 78, fol. 12.

Puritanism and Democracy
1640–1642

BRIAN MANNING

ISAAC PENINGTON, the Puritan merchant and alderman who represented London in the Long Parliament, justified the right of 'mean men' to have and express views on religious questions and ecclesiastical government, and to demand radical changes.[1] Nathaniel Fiennes, Puritan gentleman and son of Lord Saye and Sele, defended in the Long Parliament, where he represented Banbury, the right of 'the multitude' to petition Parliament for sweeping changes in the church, and to assemble and demonstrate in support of their demands.[2] The influential Puritan minister Charles Herle, who preached often to the Long Parliament and wrote pamphlets in support of the parliamentarian cause in the Civil War, advised the rulers of England that

the common people are such a part in every state, as would be choicely handled by those that steer it, as not cried up, so much less trod down, no nor altogether laid aside: the moral of the serpent tells us, that though the tail must not lead, yet must it not be utterly left behind neither, lest the head be so disabled to support or raise itself by; and experience tells us, that such councillors as wholly despise the multitude, are neither safe to themselves, or serviceable to their master, but still in the end prove rather the people's sacrifices, than the prince's servants.[3]

In 1640–2 some of 'the people', even 'mean men' of 'the multitude', publicly declared their views on bishops and called for an end to their rule in the church. The agitation against bishops became the main focus for a great variety of popular grievances and passions, and it precipitated a furious controversy

[1] *D'Ewes*, ed. Notestein, 339; V. Pearl, *London and the Outbreak of the Puritan Revolution* (Oxford, 1961), 214–15.

[2] *A Speech of the Honorable Nathanael Fiennes* (1641); Rushworth, iv. 174–83.

[3] Charles Herle, *Ahab's Fall by his Prophets Flatteries* (1644), 19–20.

amongst the clergy, gentry, and members of parliament. It
became a central issue in the crisis that led to the Civil War.
But, just as the freemen of the towns were more concerned to
assert their right to vote in municipal elections than in parliamentary elections, and were more interested in the distribution
of power between the mayor, the corporation, and the townsmen at large than between the King, Lords, and Commons,[1]
the issue which more directly, and perhaps more deeply, concerned the common people, and also the gentry, than the
question of episcopacy, was the distribution of power in
their local church between the minister, the squire, and the
congregation.

   Gentlemen and plebeians alike looked to the minister for
guidance and instruction on spiritual matters, on the conduct
of their lives, and on their roles in society; they sought from him
comfort in this life and hope of avoiding hell and gaining heaven
hereafter. Thus the laity, both gentlemen and plebeians, had an
interest that their ministers should be competent to perform the
duties on which their happiness and security in this life and the
next depended. But the gentry also had interests in the church
distinct from those of the people. They were more concerned
than the people that the parson should teach obedience to social
superiors and established authority. They were anxious to keep
in their own hands the power to appoint the local minister, and
they were determined to retain the system of tithes to support
the ministry, since a substantial part of the income from tithes
had passed into the possession of the gentry. In most churches
the right to nominate the minister belonged to a gentleman,
who resented a bishop who refused to accept his nominee; and
in many churches the tithes were owned by a gentleman who,
paying out of them only a small part for a stipend to the
minister and pocketing the rest, feared bishops who might try to
recover the whole of the tithes for support of the church. These
interests also led to conflicts between the gentry and the
congregations: if a gentleman owned the tithes, some members
of the congregation might blame him for paying too low a
stipend to attract a good minister, and if a gentleman owned
the right to nominate the minister, some members of the

   [1] D. Hirst, *The Representative of the People? Voters and Voting in England under the
Early Stuarts* (Cambridge, 1975), 44–57.

congregation might object if he imposed on them a parson whose ability they deemed insufficient for the functions they expected of him, or whose opinions or conduct they disliked. Thus all the laity had an interest in how the church was run: how the parson was chosen, how he was paid, how he performed his duties. But when the gentry spoke of the role of the laity in the church, they tended to be thinking of themselves; and when they talked of giving the laity a share in the government of the church, they tended to be thinking of protecting their rights to own tithes, and of extending their own control over the appointment of ministers and over what was taught in the church.[1]

Nathaniel Fiennes complained in the Long Parliament that the government of the church by bishops meant that 'all is in the hands of one man, in the several dioceses, or his chancellors, or commissaries . . . with a total exclusion of those that notwithstanding have as much share in the church, and consequently as much interest in the government of it, as they have in that of the commonwealth'. This exclusion of the laymen from a share in the government of the church, he held, was the cause of antagonism between the laity and the clergy, between parliament and the bishops, between the common law and canon law, between State and Church.[2] Sir Edward Dering, who sought at first to voice the views of many of the 'common people' amongst his Kentish constituents as well as of the gentry, argued that as the whole nation, laity as well as clergy, was bound by the acts and canons of the church, it was neither reasonable nor just that the laity should have no share in choosing the men who made laws for the church or in the decision-making processes of the church.[3] Lord Brooke, the Puritan peer, observed that the bishops claimed to represent the church, but that could not be so because they were chosen not even by all the clergy let alone by the laity, who were as much a part of the church as were the clergy. Nor, he went on,

---

[1] On all the matters discussed in this paragraph the fundamental and irreplaceable studies are Hill, *Economic Problems of the Church. From Archbishop Whitgift to the Long Parliament* (Oxford, 1956) and *Society and Puritanism in Pre-Revolutionary England* (1964).

[2] Rushworth, iv. 174–83.

[3] Sir Edward Dering, *A Consideration and a Resolution* (1641). On Dering's position see W. M. Lamont, *Godly Rule: Politics and Religion, 1603–1660* (1969), 83–93; also A. Everitt, *The Community of Kent and the Great Rebellion, 1640–1660* (Leicester, 1966), 53–4, 62–3, 84–95.

could Convocation claim to represent the church, because the mass of the clergy did not have free choice of their representatives and, more important, 'the people choose not these convocation men, but the clergy, and so they cannot represent the whole church'. He believed that his argument was supported by the practice of the early Church and by the authority of the Bible where, he claimed, the word 'church' was not used to mean only bishops or only the clergy but embraced all the members of the church, lay as well as clerical.[1] 'The blessed apostles and their fellow labourers', added Sir Edward Dering, 'did not engross, and (as our churchmen affect to do) usurp and monopolize the word "church", as proper only to churchmen.'[2] Thomas Goodwin and Philip Nye, two important Puritan ministers, declared that the exclusion of the people from a share in ruling the church and the restriction of ecclesiastical government to clergymen only, was a usurpation, and they asserted that the people now demanded to be restored to their original and rightful share in the government of the church.[3] Some of the lower clergy hoped to increase their voice in the running of the church, and some of the gentry looked to play a greater part in its government; but the assertion by Puritan gentry and ministers of the rights of 'the people' in the church reflected a growing popular demand, especially of the more zealous in religion, and the need of the Puritan leaders to win popular support for their programme of reforms by satisfying this demand.[4]

It was a common practice of the Puritans to make analogies between the government of the church and the government of the state. Nathaniel Fiennes said that in the civil government of England power was dispersed into the hands of many men,

[1] Lord Brooke, 'A Discourse Opening the Nature of that Episcopacie, which is Exercised in England' (1642) in *Tracts on Liberty in the Puritan Revolution 1638–1647*, ed. W. Haller (N.Y., 1933–4), 54–9, 123–7.

[2] Dering, *A Consideration*.

[3] John Cotton, *The Keyes of the Kingdom of Heaven* (with an epistle by Thomas Goodwin and Philip Nye) (1644).

[4] John Stow, *A Survey of the Cities of London and Westminster*, ed. John Strype (1720), ii, bk. 4, 9–10; 'Some Memoirs Concerning the Family of the Priestleys' (Surtees Soc., 1883), 17; *The Autobiography and Diaries of Oliver Heywood*, ed. J. H. Turner (Brighouse, 1882), i. 83–4; *Memoirs of the Reign of Charles I: The Fairfax Correspondence*, ed. G. W. Johnson (1848), ii. 381–2; M. Campbell, *The English Yeoman under Elizabeth and the Early Stuarts* (New Haven, 1942), 296–7.

not concentrated entirely into the hands of one man, 'as appeareth in this High Court of Parliament, in the inferior courts of Westminster Hall', where 'there are many judges in the point of law' and juries in matters of fact, and in the assizes and the quarter-sessions in the counties, 'which are held by many commissioners, and not only by one'. 'And in short, in the civil government, every man from the greatest to the least, hath some share in the government according to the proportion of his interest in the commonwealth, but in the government of the church, all is in the hands of one man, in the several dioceses . . .', 'and that of one man proceeding in a manner arbitrarily . . .'.[1] Goodwin and Nye declared:

> In commonwealths, it is a dispersion of several portions of power and rights into several hands, jointly to concur and agree in acts and process of weight and moment . . . which makes them lasting and preserves their peace, when none of all sorts find they are excluded, but as they have a share of concernment, so that a fit measure of power or privilege is left and betrusted to them. . . . So in that polity or government by which Christ would have his churches ordered, the right disposal of the power therein . . . may lie in a due and proportioned allotment and dispersion (though not in the same measure and degree) into divers hands, according unto the several concernments and interests that each rank in his church may have; rather than in an entire and sole trust committed to any one man (though never so able) or any one sort or kind of men or officers, although diversified into never to many subordinations under one another. . . .[2]

Fiennes was not arguing that all men had the same share in the government of the country, but greater and lesser shares 'according to the proportion' of their 'interest in the commonwealth' (that is, their office, rank, and wealth); and Goodwin and Nye were not arguing that all men had the same share in the government of the church, but greater and lesser shares according to the rank they held in the church.

Thomas Cartwright, the Elizabethan Puritan leader, praised the constitution of the English state, with its representative assemblies, and observed that 'it draweth much the obedience of the subjects of this realm, that the statutes, whereby the

---

[1] Rushworth, iv. 174–83.
[2] Cotton, *The Keyes*: the epistle of Goodwin and Nye.

realm is governed, pass by the consent of the most part of it, whilst they be made by them whom the rest put in trust, and choose for that purpose, being as it were all their acts'. 'So is it also', he continued, 'when the question is to choose the magistrate, mayor, or bailiff, or constable of every town.' He argued that since it was thought expedient and reasonable that the people should have a voice in choosing their lawmakers and some of their governors in the secular sphere, there was an even stronger case for them to have a voice in choosing their lawmakers and governors in the religious sphere; and since parliaments and municipal governing bodies contained representatives elected by the people, so much more should the assemblies of the church be similarly composed. 'Which things, if they have grounds in civil affairs, they have much better in ecclesiastical', because civil affairs deal only with men's bodies and their properties, but ecclesiastical affairs deal with more important matters of greater concernment to all men—the salvation of their souls and their fate in eternity.[1] By 1640 sections of the populace had come to expect Parliament to hear their opinions and to be responsive to their wishes,[2] so much more might they expect the church to hear their views and to be responsive to their demands.

'Originally, virtually, and conclusively', claimed Lord Brooke in 1642, the government of the church was 'in the people',[3] and this principle was also asserted by the author of *The Presbyteriall Government Examined* (1641). The obligation upon the people to obey the laws of the state and submit to the jurisdiction of its courts, Cartwright thought, ought to be derived from the consent of the people. He wrote:

It is said among lawyers, and indeed reason, which is the law of nations, confirmeth it, 'Quod omnium interest ab omnibus approbari debet': 'That which standeth all men upon should be approved of all men'. Which law hath this sense, that, if it may be, it were good that those things which shall bind all men, and which require the obedience of all, should be concluded, as far as may be, by the consent of all, or at least by the consent of as many as may be gotten.[4]

---

[1] A. F. Scott Pearson, *Church and State: Political Aspects of Sixteenth Century Puritanism* (Cambridge, 1928), 44–5.

[2] Hirst, *Representative of the People?*, 157–93.

[3] Brooke, 'A Discourse', 98, 113–27.   [4] Pearson, *Church and State*, 44–5.

But the people did not give consent to the laws of the church and so were not obliged to obey them. Dering declared in 1641: 'No canons can bind the laity where we have no voice of our own, nor choice of the clergy persons who do found them, nor assent in the susception of them after they are framed.'[1] Jeremiah Burroughes, a leading Puritan minister, said that a Christian was not bound to obey a government 'that he no way either by himself or others hath ever yielded consent unto . . .'.[2] Some Puritans carried this further and argued that no man was bound to obey a church unless he had personally of his own free will consented to be bound by its laws and jurisdiction. This was the foundation principle of the separatists, who denied the validity of a national church and of compulsory membership of such a church. They considered that the only true church consisted of a group of people who believed themselves and each other to be true Christians, and voluntarily came together and made a covenant or agreement between themselves to form a church and to obey its rules and officers. But the principle that the only legitimate authority which man could create, as distinct from authority which God or Nature established, was one which the people under its jurisdiction had consented to obey, applied not only to a voluntary society of godly people but to all people in civil society, saints and sinners, for it was a principle derived from civil society and applied to the church. 'The superiority of jurisdiction either in things spiritual or temporal (if it be not natural as the paternal) must be voluntarily subjected unto, or it is usurped and tyrannical', wrote a separatist. He was not suggesting that it was a privilege only of congregations of true Christians not to be subjected to an authority to which they had not given their consent, but that it was a right of all men in civil society which he applied to the church. There it meant that in order to establish a legitimate authority there 'must be a voluntary submission of themselves one to another testified by some act, whether you call it a Covenant, or Consent, or Agreement between fit members for such ends'.[3] This became a basic principle of the democracy advocated after the Civil

---

[1] Dering, *A Consideration.*

[2] Jeremiah Burroughes, *The glorious Name of God* (1643), 94.

[3] *The Saints Apologie* (1644) ('This discourse was written some years since when the times were perilous'); A. L. Morton, *The World of the Ranters: Religious Radicalism in the English Revolution* (1970), 14–15.

War by the leaders of the Levellers, who were themselves separatists, and they called the constitution which embodied this principle 'An Agreement of the People'. They did not, however, transfer this principle from church government to civil government, but from civil government to church government, and they applied it to both spheres. In the words of John Lilburne:

Unnatural, irrational, sinful, wicked, unjust, devilish, and tyrannical it is, for any man whatsoever, spiritual or temporal, clergyman or layman, to appropriate and assume unto himself, a power, authority and jurisdiction, to rule, govern, or reign over any sort of men in the world, without their free consent, and whosoever doth it, whether clergyman, or any other whatsoever, do thereby as much as in them lies, endeavour to appropriate and assume unto themselves the office and sovereignty of God, (who alone doth and is to rule by his will and pleasure). . . .[1]

At first the need had seemed to be to establish this principle in the church, but increasingly the Levellers concentrated upon making it a reality in civil government.

There were two main areas in which a voice was claimed for the people in the affairs of the church, one in the choice of their pastors and the other in the exercise of ecclesiastical discipline. Growing numbers of the laity had come to object to the operation of the existing system by which parsons were appointed by lay patrons and bishops. 'He which have money, or the letter of some great man, or favour by other means' could always get himself a benefice, 'and so the guides of our souls are appointed unto us without our advice and counsel'.[2] Cartwright pointed out that the consequences of giving the people no say in the choice of their pastors were worse than giving them no say in the choice of members of Parliament or town councillors: 'For it is much more unreasonable that there should be thrust upon me a governor of whom the everlasting salvation or damnation both of my body and soul doth depend, than him of whom my wealth and commodity of this life doth hang. . . .'[3]

---

[1] John Lilburne, *The Free-mans Freedome Vindicated* (1646), 11; [(?)John Lilburne and (?)Richard Overton], *Regall Tyrannie discovered* (1647), 46; *Puritanism and Liberty*, ed. A. S. P. Woodhouse (1938), 66.

[2] Hill, *Economic Problems of the Church*, 53–69.

[3] Pearson, *Church and State*, 44–5.

The people had no power to prevent the patron and the bishop from appointing as their minister a man who could not preach, or who taught false doctrine, or behaved badly. Sir Edward Dering declared that it was contrary to the law of nature and reason and to the practice of the early Christian Church for the congregation to be denied the right to refuse to accept 'a man of inability, and of ill life' as their pastor, and he urged that the people should be restored to the right to have a voice in choosing the minister who was to guide and direct their souls.[1] Lord Brooke held that power in the church originally derived from the people, and so the ministers and other officers of the church should be elected by the people. This, he maintained, was the rule laid down in the Bible and the usage of the early Church. 'The election of all church officers was in the people . . . for divers ages after the Apostles . . .' and should now be restored to them, he wrote in 1642.[2] This would make the people more likely to respect and obey their ministers, because 'they have them set over them, whom above others themselves have liked, and made choice of'; and it would make the ministers more diligent because they would know 'that they are set over those by whom they before others were made choice of, and elected . . .'.[3] The main alternatives proposed to the existing system of church government in 1640–2 all made a central point of giving the people a voice—smallest amongst the Presbyterians, greatest amongst the separatists—in the choice of their minister. The Presbyterians proposed that the congregation should have the right to accept or reject the man nominated.[4] The Independents declared that the congregation should have 'the power, privileges and liberty to choose their officers . . .'.[5] In their final and definitive version of the Agreement of the People, the leaders of the Levellers laid down that there should be no 'power to impose ministers upon any the respective parishes' but that 'the parishioners of every particular parish' shall have 'free liberty . . . to choose such as themselves shall approve . . .' to be their ministers.[6] The election of ministers by the people was

[1] Dering, *A Consideration*.
[2] Brooke, 'A Discourse', 98, 113–27.
[3] *The Presbyteriall Government Examined* (1641), 10, 16–17, 20–1.
[4] *The Government and Order of the Church of Scotland* (Edinburgh, 1641), 5–11.
[5] Cotton, *The Keyes*, 12.
[6] *Leveller Manifestoes of the Puritan Revolution*, ed. D. M. Wolfe (1944), 408.

contrary to the interests of most of the gentry and many of the clergy, but some were prepared to concede it.

The second main issue which raised the question of democracy in the church concerned the exercise of jurisdiction over offences against morality, religion, and the church, especially the administration of the supreme ecclesiastical penalty, excommunication. Henry Burton complained in 1641 that at the present time

> the discipline is brought under one man . . . The Archbishop in his province. The bishop in his diocese. This is condemned flatly and expressly in the Scripture, that the power of discipline it is not left to one man, but indeed to the whole congregation . . . for the congregation had a vote in this business, of executing of censure upon such an offender. . . .[1]

Lord Brooke argued that according to God's rule and the practice of the early Church the congregation should have a voice in the punishment of offenders.[2] A Puritan pamphleteer wrote

> Who is so unequal a judge as not to think it a most equal thing, that the multitude should clearly, and undoubtedly take knowledge both of the heinousness of the crime, and incorrigible contumacy of the person, after the use of all means, and remedies for reclaiming him. This if it be not done, then doth not the church herin live by her own, but by her officers' faith; neither are her governors to be reputed as servants, but lords unto her; neither do they exercise their office popularly in the church as they ought, but tyrannically, as they ought not. . . .[3]

Under the Presbyterians' proposals the congregation would have had to consent to the excommunication of a member and would have had a right to object to the sentence.[4] Under the Independents' proposals the congregation would have had the 'power and privilege to join with the Elders, in inquiring, hearing, judging of public scandals; so as to bind notorious offenders and impenitents under censure, and to forgive the repentant . . .'. Here the role of the congregation was likened to that of a jury and the case for its participation founded upon the use of juries in the secular courts. Like a jury of neighbours the

---

[1] Henry Burton, *Englands Bondage and Hope of Deliverance* (1641), 23–4.
[2] Brooke, 'A Discourse', 98–107, 123–7.
[3] *The Presbyteriall Government Examined*, 21.
[4] *The Government and Order of the Church of Scotland*, 39–45.

congregation was expected to know the facts of the case and the character of the person involved far better than anybody from outside the locality. In the constitution of the kingdom, wrote Goodwin and Nye, the sentencing to death of any subject

> is not put into the hands of an assembly of lawyers only, no not of all the judges themselves, men selected for wisdom, faithfulness, and gravity, who yet are by office designed to have an interest herein . . . Yet they have no power to pronounce this sentence of death upon any man without the concurrence of a jury of his peers, which are of his own rank; and in corporations, of such as are inhabitants of the same place: and with a jury of these . . . two judges, yea one . . . hath power to adjudge and pronounce . . . And we of this nation . . . do esteem this privilege of the subject in this particular (peculiar to our nation) as one of the glories of our laws, and do make boast of it as such a liberty and security to each person's life, as (we think) no nation about us can show the like.[1]

The leaders of the Levellers had the same high regard for the jury system.[2] The practical reason for involving the people in the disciplinary procedure was that the effectiveness of the penalty of excommunication depended on the co-operation of the congregation in ostracizing the offender.[3] Many of the gentry were horrified at the thought of allowing to the people, or any part of them, a voice in the censures of the church, fearing that they would lose respect and authority in society if their lives and opinions were subjected to the scrutiny and judgement of their social inferiors.[4] But some of the gentry were prepared to permit the congregation to participate in the disciplinary procedure provided that there were sufficient safe-guards to assure them the gentry would have the dominant voice in the system.

Under the Presbyterian system the parish would be governed by a minister and a group of lay elders, varying according to the size of the parish from six to twelve in number. Some ten to

---

[1] Cotton, *The Keyes*, 12–15, and the Epistle of Goodwin and Nye.

[2] *Leveller Manifestoes*, ed. Wolfe, 301–2, 303, 406–8; Morton, *Ranters*, 191–2; D. Veall, *The Popular Movement for Law Reform 1640–1660* (Oxford, 1970), 100, 156–9.

[3] *The Presbyteriall Government Examined*, 21.

[4] Sir Thomas Aston, *A Remonstrance against Presbytery* (1641); *The Oxinden and Peyton Letters 1642–1670*, ed. D. Gardiner (1937), 36–7; John Bramhall, 'The Serpent-Salve' (1643) in *The Works of John Bramhall* (1844), iii. 478; Griffith Williams, *The Discovery of Mysteries* (1643), 52.

twenty neighbouring parishes would be grouped together to form a 'presbytery' or 'classis' composed of the minister and one elder chosen by his colleagues from each parish. The 'classes' would be grouped—perhaps about twenty-four of them—into a province, which would have a synod composed of two ministers and two elders elected from each 'classis'. And finally, the national synod would consist of three ministers and three elders chosen by each provincial synod. In Scotland the provincial synods were composed of representatives of the parishes and the national synods of representatives of the 'classes', but in England, because of the greater numbers involved, it was proposed that representation should be less direct, and that the 'classes' should elect the provincial synods and the latter elect the national synods. The ratio between clerical and lay representatives could be varied, and in the scheme adopted by the Long Parliament in 1645 the lay representatives were increased at every level so as to outnumber the clergy, indicating a stronger desire for lay control of the church.[1] The ministers and elders of the parish church would meet weekly to arrange public worship, catechizing, visits by the elders to every family in the parish to examine their knowledge of religion and the conduct of their lives, and the administration of the Lord's Supper, to which only those with sufficient knowledge and of good conduct would be admitted. The main part of the duty of the elders was discipline: the admonishing of all men of their duties and the reporting of scandalous behaviour and disobedience to the weekly meeting of the eldership. The 'classis' would be responsible for the training of ministers, and its approval would be necessary for the appointment of a minister to a congregation; it would have cognizance of serious offences committed by laymen or clergymen, its approval would be necessary before a congregation could proceed to excommunicate a lay member, and it alone would have the power to suspend and deprive ministers. It was on these points that the Independents fell out with the Presbyterians, the Independents objecting to the control over the congregation by the 'classis' and proposing

[1] *The Government and Order of the Church of Scotland*, 17, 20–1, 30, 36–9, 45–60; P. Collinson, *The Elizabethan Puritan Movement* (1967), 298–301; W. A. Shaw, *A History of the English Church during the Civil Wars and under the Commonwealth 1640–1660* (1900), i. 190, 195–9, 204–5.

to give greater power to the minister and elders of the congregation.[1]

The significance of the Presbyterian system was that it placed the government of the church in a series of assemblies in which every single congregation was represented directly or indirectly, and in which the laity had their own representatives alongside, and perhaps outnumbering, the clergy. 'There is no assembly wherein every particular church hath not interest and power; nor is there anything done, but they are, if not actually, yet virtually called to consent unto it.'[2] Here was a national system of church government involving the representation in theory of the whole nation. The parish church was to be governed by the minister and elders but they were to be chosen with the consent of the congregation and everything they did was to be subject to the 'express or tacit consent of the congregation'.[3] In Elizabeth's reign Archbishop Whitgift had criticized Cartwright for advocating such a system because it gave too much power to 'the people' and its democratic principles might be transferred to the state:

The reasons that you use for the popular or aristocratical government of the church, when they come among the people, will be easily transferred to the state of the commonweal, and peradventure breed that misliking of civil government that you would now have of ecclesiastical, to a further inconvenience and mischief than you and all yours will be able to remedy.

Although Cartwright insisted that his principles applied only to the church and that he was not advocating the popular election of all civil magistrates, the transference of his notions of popular consent from the church to the state was made easier by the fact that he was advocating a form of government for the church by elected officers and representative assemblies parallel with the structure of civil government at each of the levels from the local community up to the central government.[4] It was a natural extension of these principles, as Whitgift prophesied, to advocate as the Levellers did that the officers of local government as

---

[1] *The Government and Order of the Church of Scotland*, 17, 20–1, 30, 36–9, 45–60; Cotton, *The Keyes*, 20–2.
[2] *The Government and Order of the Church of Scotland*, 36–9, 64–5.
[3] Ibid.
[4] Pearson, *Church and State*, 43–7, 91–2, 127–9.

well as parsons be elected by the people, and that the supreme
authority in the nation be a legislature consisting only of
representatives of the people, without a king or a House of
Lords. The Levellers did not make a distinction between electing a minister of the parish church and a member of Parliament,
the qualification for the franchise was to be the same in both
cases.[1]

The Presbyterians in 1640–42, like Cartwright before them,
denied the democratic implications. Cartwright had justified
the popular element as a check upon the elders to prevent them
becoming a self-interested and tyrannical oligarchy, and he had
portrayed the whole system as standing for order and obedience:
it put 'the people in subjection under their governors, the
governors in degree and order one under another, as the elder
underneath the pastor, and the deacon underneath the elder';
it provided 'that a particular church shall give place unto a
provincial synod ... and the provincial to a national...'.[2] 'Here
is subjection without slavery...', said the Presbyterians in 1641.
'Here there is a superiority without tyranny ... Here there is
parity without confusion and disorder, for the pastors are in
order before the elders, and the elders before the deacons; the
church is subordinate to the presbytery, the presbytery to the
synod, and the synod to the national assembly. ...'.[3]

Goodwin and Nye pointed out that the fundamental question
in the state was the respective power of rulers and ruled, and
that this was also the fundamental question in the church,
where it resolved itself into the question of the respective power
of, on the one hand, the minister and elders and, on the other
hand, the congregation. As John Cotton, the New England
Puritan minister, wrote, the stability of the commonwealth
depended on 'the right and due establishment and balancing of
the liberties or privileges of the people ... and the authority of
the magistrate: so it is the safety of church estate, the right and
due settling and ordering of the holy power of the privileges and
liberties of the brethren, and the ministerial authority of the
elders'. Goodwin and Nye, in recommending Cotton's book to

[1] John Lilburne, *Londons Liberty in Chains discovered* (1646), 7; *Leveller Manifestoes*,
ed. Wolfe, 189–91, 269–70, 303, 408–9.
[2] Pearson, *Church and State*, 68–9.
[3] *The Government and Order of the Church of Scotland*, 36–9, 64–5.

an English public in 1644, observed that 'the greatest commotions in kingdoms have for the most part been raised and maintained for and about power, and liberties, of the rulers and the ruled, together with the due bounds and limits of either; and the like hath fallen out in churches, and is continued to this day in the sharpest contentions . . .'.[1] Perhaps this was the main ecclesiastical issue in the English civil war. At first the issue had seemed to be episcopacy, which many of the gentry were ready to get rid of and replace by a government of the church by the county gentry; but they became frightened of this as they realized that the consequence of the abolition of bishops, and the aim of many of the people who agitated against bishops, might be a greater say for the people in the running of the local church. Those who denied that the people should have a voice in the government of the church, in the choice of the ministers, and in the exercise of ecclesiastical discipline, increasingly ceased to have any alternative but to support the King and the existing episcopalian church, and this became a main reason for supporting the royalists. Those who were prepared to agree that the people should have some voice in the government of the church, were bound to accept that this involved radical changes in the government of the church, possibly the establishment of some form of presbyterianism or congregationalism, and this meant supporting Parliament in the Civil War. They differed, however, as to how much power they were prepared to concede to the people and the lines of the divisions into which the parliamentarian party fell were drawn according to whether the people should have greater or lesser share in the government of the church.

Both Presbyterians and Independents felt it necessary to defend their systems of church government against accusations of being too democratic. They may, therefore, have overstressed the checks on the democratic element in their respective church polities. At the same time it seems clear that they did indeed fear to concede too much power to the people, as may be seen in their condemnations of the sects for being too democratic, and that they regarded their own systems of church government as the best means of both satisfying and curbing popular demands for participation, of giving the people a voice while at the same

---

[1] Cotton, *The Keyes*, 12, and the epistle of Goodwin and Nye.

time maintaining order and obedience among them. In the Scottish model of Presbyterianism, at the introduction of the new form of government, the pastor chose the elders, subject to the people approving his nominations; thereafter the pastor and elders filled vacancies in the eldership as they occurred, publishing the names to the congregation to give opportunity for any objections, and if objections were made which the pastor and elders deemed valid, they put forward other names.[1] An Independent pamphleteer argued that elders ought to be elected for life and to have a legal right to keep the office for that time.[2] It was expected that the elderships would be filled by substantial gentlemen and members of the richer classes.[3] Under both the Presbyterian and the Independent system, when the pastorship of a congregation fell vacant, the elders nominated a candidate for the place, their nominee would preach to the congregation, which would be given an opportunity to make any objections. The role of the people is confined to a power to veto the proposal of the elders: they cannot put forward names themselves or nominate a candidate against the choice of the elders, and if they can persuade the elders to withdraw their nomination, they cannot propose an alternative but must wait for the elders to bring forward another name.[4] In the procedure for excommunication, under both the Presbyterian and the Independent system, the elders privately investigate the affair and decide whether the accused has committed an offence and whether it is an offence deserving of excommunication. It is they who initiate the proceedings leading to excommunication. If they decide upon this penalty they must report the case to the congregation and obtain its approval of the sentence, but in making their report they use only arguments to persuade the congregation to support their decision. The elders 'declare to the church the counsel and will of God therein, that they may rightly discern and approve what censure the Lord requireth to be administered in such a case'. The congregation has the power to veto the decision of the elders, but they are under pressure to obey the 'will of God' as voiced

---

[1] *The Government and Order of the Church of Scotland*, 14.

[2] *The Presbyteriall Government Examined*, 2, 16–17.

[3] Hill, *Society and Puritanism*, 228, 230–1, 236, 237–8,

[4] *The Government and Order of the Church of Scotland*, 5–11; Cotton, *The Keyes*, 12–17, 20–2, 41–3; *The Presbyteriall Government Examined*, 23.

by the elders.[1] The elders, under both the Presbyterian and the Independent system, have the power to meet apart from the congregation, to prepare matters for presentation to the church, to make all the decisions and put them forcefully to meetings of the congregation, at which they give permission to members to speak and silence anyone who speaks amiss, '. . . lest themselves and the church be openly cumbered with unnecessary and tedious agitations, but that all things transacted before the church be carried along with most expedition and best edification'.[1] Essentially, therefore, the initiative lay with the minister and elders: the congregation had the right to object to their decisions, and ultimately a power of veto, if they had sufficient interest and independence of mind to use it; but they could not put forward their own proposals or alternatives to the recommendations of the elders, or raise matters which the elders did not wish to have discussed; their role was the passive one of saying 'yea' or 'nay' to the resolutions and rulings of the minister and elders. The Presbyterians and the Independents both stressed that it was the task of the elders to govern and the duty of the people to obey. It was an Independent who wrote:

> It appertains to the people freely to vote in elections and judgements of the church . . . it behooves the elders to govern the people even in their voting in just liberty, given by Christ whatsoever. Let the elders publicly propound, and order all things, in the church, and so give their sentence on them; let them reprove them that sin, convince the gainsayers, comfort the repentant, and so administer all things according to the prescript of God's Word. Let the people of faith give their assent to their elders holy and lawful administration, that so the ecclesiastical elections and censures may be ratified, and put into solemn execution by the elders, either in the ordination of officers after election, or excommunication of offenders after obstinacy in sin.[1]

Some of the gentry and richer classes were persuaded towards Presbyterianism or Independency, partly by religious arguments and partly by the opinion that these systems would do better than the king and the bishops had done in containing popular demands and disciplining the people.

Richard Byfield defended and recommended Presbyterianism in 1641 as the form of church government closest to

[1] Ibid.

'aristocracy': 'It is very suitable to our sessions of justices of peace, or the sessions of the House of Commons in Parliament; and therefore may be very suitable to our civil state . . .'[1] Nathaniel Fiennes objected to episcopal government of the church as 'monarchical' and urged the bringing of the ecclesiastical government more into line with the civil government, which was 'aristocratical . . . as appeareth in this High Court of Parliament, in the inferior courts of Westminster Hall, and in the assizes and sessions in the country . . .'.[2] The author of *The Presbyteriall Government Examined* (1641) was anxious to deny that the Independents believed in a popular or democratic form of church government:

But now lest any should take occasion, either by the things here spoken by us, or elsewhere of us, to conceive, that we either exercise amongst ourselves, or would thrust upon others, any popular, or democratical church government . . . We believe that the external church government under Christ the only mediator and monarch thereof, is plainly aristocratical, and to be administered by some certain choice men. . . .[3]

In the tradition of Cartwright and Travers the Presbyterian polity was more often described as a mixed form of government—a mixture of monarchy, aristocracy, and democracy. Cartwright wrote:

The church is governed with that kind of government which the philosophers that write of the best commonwealths affirm to be the best. For, in respect of Christ the head, it is a monarchy; and in respect of the ancients and pastors that govern in common and with like authority amongst themselves, it is an aristocracy, or the rule of the best men; and in respect that the people are not secluded but have their interest in church matters, it is a democracy, or a popular state. An image whereof appeareth also in the policy of this realm; for as in respect of the queen her majesty, it is a monarchy, so in respect of the most honourable council, it is an aristocracy, and having regard to the parliament, which is assembled of all estates, it is a democracy.[4]

John Cotton, the philosopher of Independency, observed that 'it is an usual tenet in many of our best divines, that the govern-

---

[1] Richard Byfield, *The Power of the Christ of God* (1641).
[2] Rushworth, iv. 174–83.   [3] *The Presbyteriall Government Examined*, 22–3.
[4] Pearson, *Church and State*, 43, 136–8, 142–5.

ment of the church is mixed of a monarchy, an aristocracy, and a democracy. In regard of Christ the head, the government of the church is sovereign and monarchical. In regard of the rule by the presbytery, it is stewardly and aristocratical. In regard of the people's power in elections and censures, it is democratical . . .' He used this to support his view that 'the people have some stock of power and authority in the government of the church', although, he added, what the people had should be characterized as 'privilege or liberty' rather than as 'rule or authority', but in the Independent system 'the large and firm establishment of the liberties of the brethren' kept the elders from becoming a tyrannical oligarchy. By the device of making Christ the monarchical element in church government, the constitution was in practice, as the Independents Goodwin and Nye described it, 'a government tempered of an aristocracy and democracy', in which 'the people have a share, and their actual consent is necessary to all laws and sentences . . .' They drew an analogy between the elders and the congregation in the church and the aldermen and the common council in a municipal corporation.[1]

Goodwin and Nye acknowledged that the Brownists were the first to restore the people to their rights in church government, but they fell into the opposite extreme 'by laying the plea and claim on their behalf unto the whole power; and that the elder set over them did but exercise that power for them, which was properly theirs, and which Christ had (as they contended) radically and originally estated in the people only'. Thus Brownism 'doth in effect put the chief (if not the whole) of the rule and government into the hands of the people, and drowns the elders' votes (who are but a few) in the major part of theirs . . .'. Cotton argued that though the ministers and elders were chosen by the people, their offices were ordained by God and they exercised a power delegated to them by God, not by the people. The people could act only with the concurrence of the elders, and the consent of the elders was necessary to make any act binding. Goodwin and Nye argued that God had given to the elders the power of rule and authority and to the people the liberty to assent or dissent, so that

affairs should not be transacted, but with the joint agreement of

[1] Cotton, *The Keyes*, 12, 36, and the epistle of Goodwin and Nye.

both, though out of a different right: so that as a church of brethren only, could not proceed to any public censures, without they have elders over them, so nor in the church have the elders power to censure without the concurrence of the people; and likewise so, as each alone hath not power of excommunicating the whole of either, though together they have power over any particular person or persons in each.

'. . . So as without the consent' of both the elders and the congregation 'nothing is esteemed as a church act'. On the other hand the Independents objected that Presbyterianism did not give sufficient power to the people to prevent the elders from becoming an oppressive oligarchy. They regarded their position as the middle way between Presbyterianism which gave too little power to the people and the Brownism of the separatists which gave too much power to the people.

. . . And thus by means of this due and golden balancing and poising of power and interest, authority and privilege, in elders and the brethren, this government might never degenerate into lordliness and oppression in rulers over the flock, as not having all power in their hands alone; nor yet into anarchy and confusion in the flock among themselves . . .[1]

Since both the Presbyterians and the Independents gave the central role in church government and so much power to the elders, the test of how democratic they were rested upon the extent of the franchise in the election of elders. Cartwright excluded women and children from voting in the Presbyterian system: '. . . all men understand that where the election is most freest and most general, yet only they have to do which are heads of families'.[2] An Independent writer in 1641 also excluded women and children from the franchise in the church, which he restricted to 'men, and them grown, and of discretion . . .'.[3] Neither the Presbyterians nor the Independents questioned the patriarchal assumptions of their times, and nor did the Levellers after the Civil War when they also excluded women and children from the franchise in their proposed new constitution for the state. But the Presbyterians and Independents

---

[1] Cotton, *The Keyes*, 33–5, 36, 37, and the epistle of Goodwin and Nye; 'An Apologeticall Narration' (1644) in *Tracts on Liberty*, ed. Haller, ii.

[2] Pearson, *Church and States*, 48–9, 136–7.

[3] *The Presbyteriall Government Examined*, 24.

also excluded from voting in the church those who were not full church members, that is those whose knowledge of religion was so deficient or whose conduct was so immoral that they were not admitted to participate in the sacrament of the Lord's Supper.[1] The ungodly were not admitted to a separatist congregation at all and so there all the members were full members and could vote. The Puritans tended to believe that amongst the common people only the godly possessed the qualities and the capacities required for participation in government.[2] Those who made godliness a qualification for the franchise in the church, either denied the need for the state to have the same constitution as the church, or insisted that they should have the same constitution and godliness should be the qualification for the right to vote in the state as well as the church.[3] The Levellers differed in that they advocated the same franchise for both Church and State and did not make godliness a qualification.[4] They granted the franchise to heads of families, believing that a man who governed a family had the capacity to participate in the government of the community.[5] But this was itself a notion very close to the Puritan way of thinking.[6]

By the end of the Civil War, however, many Puritan leaders were unsure of their ability to control the people and they sought to limit rather than extend the participation of the people in the government of both church and state. At the same time the radicals amongst the common people felt betrayed in their expectations that victory for parliament would lead to greater participation by the people in the government of church and state. Their feelings were focused and articulated by the Levellers. The Levellers had been Puritan radicals because they had seen a greater need for changes in the church than in the state, now they became political radicals as well because they saw the need for as great changes in the state as in the

---

[1] Pearson, *Church and State*, 48–9, 136–7; Hill, *Society and Puritanism*, 241–2, 470–1, 474–5, 477–8.

[2] M. Walzer, *The Revolution of the Saints* (1966), 219–24.

[3] B. S. Capp, *The Fifth Monarchy Men* (1972), 138–9.

[4] *Leveller Manifestoes*, ed. Wolfe, 408.

[5] K. Thomas, 'The Levellers and the Franchise' in *The Interregnum: The Quest for Settlement 1646–1660*, ed. G. E. Aylmer (1972).

[6] Hill, *Society and Puritanism*, ch. xiii; E. S. Morgan, *The Puritan Family* (N.Y., 1966), ch. vi.

church. Principles of popular participation were taken by Presbyterians and Independents in part from the civil polity and
applied to the church, but in order to establish oligarchic control
in both spheres. Separatists developed less oligarchic notions
of church government. But those Separatists, like the Fifth
Monarchists, who took those notions from the church and
applied them to the state, favoured the restriction of the franchise in civil affairs to the godly. The Levellers, on the other
hand, saw that they had to reject the existing civil polity as the
model of democracy, for it was too oligarchic and centralised,
and that the principles of popular participation and democratic
control which they had derived from both secular and religious
models had to be implemented in the state as well as the church.

The Making of the War
1640–1642

DONALD PENNINGTON

WE cannot escape from the Origins of the Great Civil War. 'Evil times were at hand', wrote Gardiner of 1603; even Elizabeth 'must be judged by the Pyms and Cromwells . . . little as she would have approved of their actions'. Accounts of the 1620s are full of 'future Royalists' and 'future Parliamentarians'; and any word or deed prophesying war is sure of historical prominence. Modern analyses of classes, places, interests, and beliefs are still pulled towards the alignments of 1642 as the crucial question. It was in 1940 that Christopher Hill's title *The English Revolution, 1640*[1] carried the implication that the outbreak of fighting was not the one decisive moment. The division between two sides in August 1642 was one of a series of shifting alignments. Many who in 1641 were passionate enemies of Stuart government fought for the King a year later; many who organized Parliament's armies in the summer were demanding peace by the winter. We need to ask not only what the conflicts were about, but why at one stage within them an armed conflict began.

Organized disobedience, riots, even campaigns to overthrow a regime arose easily. Open war required two sides, each controlling forces comparable in size and resources. A prolonged civil war involving almost the whole country meant that there must be two systems of government instead of one. Before it could occur, some revolutionaries had to become administrators, and some administrators revolutionaries. Men devoted to order and stability came to accept that war was possible; and they found, clumsily, how it could be run. As usual, preparation helped it to happen. From 1640 to 1642 there were two

* I am grateful to Mr. Keith Thomas and Professor Ivan Roots for reading drafts of this article and for their much-needed advice and corrections.
[1] See below, p. 382.

G

parallel stories. The spectacular one tells of the lawful over-throw of the personal rule and the progress from remedying abuses to rejecting the whole monarchical and episcopal system. The other concerns not hopes and ideals but worries and muddles. It shows servants of Crown and of Parliament working together, when they were not the same people. They hid, at first, their rivalries and suspicions; they competed only surreptitiously for control of men and resources. Bit by bit confusion developed into confrontation. It is with episodes in this second story that we shall be concerned here.

To most of those involved, the outstanding evil in 1640 was neither royal tyranny nor Puritan disloyalty: it was the humiliating defeat of the English army by the Scots and the occupation of the north. English soldiers moving northward had already terrified the areas they passed through. If they were kept idle much longer, or disbanded without pay, there would be mutiny and plundering. Uncontrolled armies might asso-ciate with popular risings. 'The central reality for [the ruling groups] was the collapse of order.'[1] Crown and Parliament, ostensibly united in organizing pay and disbanding, gently put the burdens and blame on each other. Despite their mutual distrust, neither showed much idea of how the idle regiments might be used for a political *coup*. Military command belonged, as seemed part of the order of the universe, to great noblemen. Northumberland, Holland, Warwick, and Essex had no thoughts of revolution. They behaved with a normal mixture of legal propriety and personal spite.[2] But Parliament increasingly took over from the King and Council three matters essential to the management of a war—finance, the control of local officials, and military administration. It was not the result of any far-sighted plan for seizing power: it happened, almost unchallenged, in the day-to-day process of meeting demands, giving authority, and blaming others. The immense expansion of the work of committees of one House or both has been well examined.[3] Not even the strongest committees were eager to

[1] J. S. Morrill, *The Revolt of the Provinces* (1975), 34.
[2] On the role of the great peers, see Brian Manning, 'The Aristocracy and the Downfall of Charles I' in *Politics, Religion, and the English Civil War*, ed. B. Manning (1973), 37–82.
[3] Notably in the articles by Lotte Glow (later Mulligan), including 'Committee-Men in the Long Parliament', *HJ* 8 (1965); 'The Committee of Safety', *EHR* 80

encroach openly on recognized and specific powers of the Crown. Their relations with royal officials were cautious and, on both sides, respectful. At every level technical illegalities had to be avoided and accepted procedures maintained as long as possible.

'Chasing out rebels' (as Charles rashly called his Scottish subjects) and remedying the calamities of the north should in theory have been a smooth joint operation.[1] Parliament would raise money; the King's civil and military officers would receive it—directly or by loans from the City—and pay it to the armies and the aggrieved inhabitants; the King's commissioners would complete the treaty with the Scots; and the Houses would be kept informed of everything.[2] It was not as simple as that. Parliament's survival seemed to depend on acquiring a share in tasks that had been performed without it. It was easier to take decisions than to put them into effect. Hardly any officers were under the direct control of the Houses. The serjeants-at-arms and ushers were ready to search and apprehend—but more to deal with Parliament's recalcitrant members than as part of the government. The clerk-assistant John Rushworth—'our nimble mercury Mr. Rushforth'—became an occasional high-grade messenger for the Commons.[3] Gradually Lenthall as Speaker developed the role of distributor of orders and centre for communications. But among old parliamentarians the feeling persisted that the 'honourable persons about the chair' were the natural link with a royal source of initiative and action.[4] Most Privy Councillors were members of one House or the other, and normally accepted its formal instructions. The elder Vane, Treasurer of the Household, Secretary of State, and a member of many of the main Commons committees, was always ready to convey messages to and from the King. Edward Herbert, Solicitor-General, gave expert guidance to the Commons on its judicial powers before becoming a victim of

(1965). See also M. F. Keeler, 'Some Opposition Committees' in *Conflict in Stuart England*, ed. W. A. Aiken and B. D. Henning (1960).

[1] *The Parliamentary or Constitutional History of England* (*Old Parliamentary History*) by several Hands, ix (1762), 57.

[2] Speeches by the King and the Lord Keeper in Rushworth, iv. 11–16.

[3] Bodl., Tanner MSS. 63, fol. 43; 66, fol. 139; BL, Harley MS. 163, fol. 143^v; *CJ* ii. 265, 269, 556.

[4] e.g. *D'Ewes*, ed. Notestein, 59 n., 146 n.; *CJ* ii. 23, 28, 30, 34.

them.[1] Finch and Bristol acted as intermediaries between the Houses even when they too were candidates for the list of evil counsellors. The successive dismissals and appointments of high office-holders had on the whole no dramatic effect on the working relationship between King, Lords, and Commons.[2]

It was not through the great men that Parliament extended its participation in government. The most effective contacts between the Commons and the departments of central administration came through royal office-holders of the second rank who saw the arrival of a parliament, and their membership of it, more as a change in the circumstances of their job than a reversal of its purposes. Sir William Uvedale, already Treasurer for the Army in 1639 and Treasurer at War in 1640, was appointed by the Commons to receive both the money for the King's army and that for the relief of the northern counties.[3] Sir Robert Pye, Auditor of the Receipt in the Exchequer, was the obvious person to make effective the King's promise to provide all the financial information the Commons desired. Before long he had established himself as a financial administrator attached to Parliament and to the Crown, and gathered a small team of his own. William Wheeler and Lawrence Whitaker were other Crown servants who moved easily into the committee work of the Commons.[4] These were not men who faced agonizing decisions on whether to obey King or Parliament. They kept their contacts with both, and dealt with contradictions as they arose. Pye (aged 55), Uvedale (aged 53), and Whitaker (aged 61) had, like the elder Vane (aged 51), ample experience of the rise and fall of patrons. Pym and his friends had overthrown one dominant group of ministers and could well take control of the government through the normal

---

[1] *CJ* ii. 28, 40, 50, 108; *D'Ewes*, ed. Notestein, 87, 142, 362, 533; Rushworth, iv. 61, 97, 99. 'Vane' throughout refers to the elder.

[2] *D'Ewes*, ed. Notestein, 85, 105, 324–7; V. Snow, *Essex the Rebel* (Lincoln, Nebr., 1970), 268; S. R. Gardiner, *History of England from the Accession of James I to the outbreak of the Civil War*, ix (1891), 249, 263–4, 408–9.

[3] *CJ* ii. 38. On Uvedale see G. E. Aylmer, *The King's Servants* (1961), 38, 391–2, and *CSPD, 1640–1, passim*.

[4] G. E. Aylmer, 'Officers of the Exchequer' in *Essays in the Economic and Social History of Tudor and Stuart England*, ed. F. J. Fisher (1961), 168–9, 176; Aylmer, *King's Servants*, 311–13, 384–5; *HMC, Cowper*, ii. 230; *HMC, De L'Isle and Dudley*, vi (1966), 344; L. Glow, 'Committee-Men', 4–7.

process of acquiring office.[1] But for the moment the officials were simply adapting their work to the division of authority. 'I am so confounded with the orders of Parliament,' Uvedale told his deputy, Matthew Bradley, in December 1640, 'I fear I shall not make myself understood.' He did not always want to. 'I keep the parliament in the opinion that the army is utterly unpaid since the 10th of November' (when the Commons were supposed to take over responsibility for it). As he still had some of 'the king's money', and could arrange a few short-term loans of his own, the accounts designed for the King, the Commons, and his own office differed.[2]

Bradley was an assiduous administrator in the north while Uvedale in London maintained both his parliamentary and his Court connections. Pye too had a close collaborator outside the Commons, the former Clerk of the Pells Sir Edward Wardour. Members were uneasy but accommodating when Pye assumed he could bring this stranger into the House with him to expound his figures.[3] The King's Remembrancer, Sir Thomas Fanshaw, a member with long experience, responded promptly to the order, on 13 November 1640, that he, the auditors of Receipt, and others of 'his Majesty's officers whom it may concern' should explain how counties had been assessed in the last subsidy. Before long Fanshaw was supporting Strafford and facing charges of abusing his own office. But he was still at work on revenue in the Commons in July 1641.[4]

Another group of the King's subjects had long been accepted as administrators without office. London merchants were used to collecting royal taxes through the customs farms. They were also used to lending to the Crown, with political demands as part of their price. The immediate reason for summoning the Long Parliament was to give security to the City for additional loans it had refused the King. But there was no subtle planning or alliance of political and merchant interests. Pym and his

---

[1] Two short accounts of the moves in that direction are in *The Origins of the English Civil War*, ed. Conrad Russell (1973), 111–16 and *Politics, Religion and the English Civil War*, ed. Manning, ch. 2.

[2] *CSPD, 1640–1*, 273–4, 292–3, 553; *CSPD, 1641–3*, 22; *CJ* ii. 270–1, 336; F. C. Dietz, *English Public Finance, 1485–1641* (1932), 287–8.

[3] *D'Ewes*, ed. Notestein, 191 and n.; *CJ* ii. 56.

[4] *LJ* iv. 28–9, 214; Aylmer, *King's Servants*, 124, 129, and, for the whole question of the allegiance of officials, 379–421.

colleagues seemed surprisingly ill-prepared for the repeated negotiations.[1] The Commons' links with the City were not unlike those with the royal government: there was an assortment of personal connections and alignments, deepening political differences, but collaboration in a succession of urgent tasks. Though monopolistic merchants were denounced as ruthlessly as Straffordian ministers, both could mitigate their sins by immediate good works. Sir Arthur Ingram, courtier, controller of the customs, manager of the alum monopoly, became the principal agent for raising money in the north.[2] Another customer and monopolist, John Harrison, with his son and fellow-M.P. William, offered, 'because the City was so tedious', to raise £50,000 themselves. The Commons withdrew their threat of expulsion; the King knighted him.[3] In the twisted negotiations with and around the Harrisons that followed, one consistent objection was to the demand that they should manage the whole business themselves. Control by the City and its institutions would not be so bad. The Commons conceded that when the four subsidies were voted 'those aldermen and others that shall give security to the particular lenders of money' could receive and retain the money raised. But after long argument it was resolved that Pye, Barrington, and Sir Arthur Capel should be treasurers in addition to Soame, Vassall, Pennington, and the City Chamberlain, Robert Bateman. The Harrisons could still collect their own debt. Collectors of the subsidies were to bring the money to 'the place within Guildhall commonly called the Chamberlain's office'.[4] The Chamber of London had under James I became a regular centre for collecting and paying out loans from the merchant community. It was now an easy but vital step for it to become

---

[1] For a full examination of the successive loans see Valerie Pearl, *London and the Outbreak of the Puritan Revolution* (Oxford, 1961), chs. v and vi. Clarendon has some pungent comments in *History of the Rebellion*, i. 283–4.

[2] *CSPD, 1640–1*, 553–4; A. F. Upton, *Sir Arthur Ingram* (Oxford, 1961).

[3] M. F. Keeler, *The Long Parliament 1640–1641: a Biographical study of its Members* (Philadelphia, 1954), 205–6; *D'Ewes*, ed. Notestein, 67, 81, 86; *CJ* ii. 164; C. Russell, 'Parliament and the King's Finances' in *The Origins of the English Civil War*, ed. C. Russell, 111–12.

[4] *CJ* ii. 30, 48–9; *D'Ewes*, ed. Notestein, 185, 189; *S. of R.* v. 59, 78; Clarendon, i. 274–6, 284–5. Among the many exchequer papers on the subsidies, the report from the Sussex commissioners in PRO E179/191/388 gives a good impression of the difficulties arising from 'shortness of time'.

a national treasury, using the City's administrators and Parliament's authority.[1]

The Exchequer was not at this stage eliminated or openly challenged. Subsidy Commissioners were chosen by a Commons committee; the Clerk of the Petty Bag was to prepare the King's Commissions 'with all the diligence and speed he can'. The Barons of the Exchequer received reports of the assessment and arrears—though a sharp order from the Commons in December 1641 forbade them to pay money collected 'upon process' into the Exchequer instead of the Chamber of London.[2] Accounts of some collectors were passed in the Exchequer.[3] Pye continued such duties as handling debentures for Crown fees and annuities.[4] Vane and Jermyn drew and accounted for household revenues, undisturbed as yet by parliamentary investigation. But feeling grew in the Council that the royal financial system was running down. In August 1641 Vane and Nicholas were alarmed to find the Commissioners of the Treasury so eager to go out of town that there were too few left to sit.[5]

Politically it was essential to show that the desperately needed revenue could be raised only by Parliament. New methods of taxation must be devised, but it would be disastrous if they produced more resentment and less return than had ship-money. The first novel levy—the poll-tax—was watched by the House with obsessive anxiety. In July 1641 the London M.P.s were ordered to give an account daily at 9.0 a.m. of the latest totals, and 'where the obstruction is'. Venn announced the day's takings sporadically.[6] At the centre the machinery was supposedly better than that for the subsidies. Pye, Wheeler, and Bateman took charge of the new receipts in the Chamber of London, where, when takings were good, they were alleged to

[1] On the earlier use of the Chamber see Pearl, *London*, appx. III, and R. Ashton, *The Crown and the Money Market 1603–1640* (Oxford, 1960), 28–9, 125–6, 137–9. An instance of the Crown using the services of Bateman and the Chamber of London, in August 1641, is in PRO, PC2/53 fol. 176 (*Privy Council Registers*, facsimile reproduction, xii).

[2] *CJ* ii. 68, 333; *CSPD 1641–3*, 173–6.

[3] Examples in PRO, E179 are 187/448 (Surrey), 183/549 (Suffolk), 80/299–300 (Staffordshire). See also *CSPD 1625–49*, 633.

[4] PRO, E101/527/20.

[5] *The Nicholas Papers*, i (Camden Soc., 1886), 27, 32–4; *CSPD 1640–1*, 135.

[6] *CJ* ii. 226, 228–30, 232, 237.

be short of tellers to receive it.[1] At York Sir Arthur Ingram
and other aldermen set up a treasury which, under Uvedale's
supervision, collected the poll-money from northern counties
and provided facilities for both soldiers and citizens to claim
their dues.[2]

The greatest difficulties were not in London or York but in
the counties, the hundreds, and the parishes, where the already
uneasy holders of familiar offices were presented with the first
in a long succession of new burdens. Poll-money required an
unprecedented new assessment, and it was generally the subsidy commissioners who had to organize it. They were still the
King's commissioners, appointed under the Great Seal, though
defaulters were now accountable to Parliament, not the
Exchequer.[3] For Henry Townshend, a commissioner in Worcestershire, the task involved ordering the high constables to
assemble the petty constables, who were to call on some of the
'most sufficient and honest inhabitants of every parish'.[4]
Collecting the money and paying it into the Chambers at
London or York was the responsibility of the sheriffs, under-
sheriffs, and ultimately of the constables and their honest
allies. Long before the militia ordinance was even hinted at, the
Commons saw the need to have in the hierarchy of rural and
urban administration officers who could be trusted. But trusted
to do what? The friends of Parliament were those who had
resisted royal exactions. To the taxpayer and the collector the
distinction between the intolerable burdens of last year and the
cheerful remedying of His Majesty's necessities this year was
not self-evident. The Commons complained as bitterly as ever
the Council had of the neglect and partiality of local officials;
and some commissioners were quick to blame the Commons for
their own failures: they had been too much on the side of
the taxpayer to be good collectors now. 'The monstrous easy
receipt of petitions at the standing committees makes authority

[1] *CSPD 1641–3*, 76.
[2] Rushworth, iv. 378–9; *CJ* ii. 270.
[3] *S. of R.* v. 105–10; *CJ* ii. 214, 228, 231, 232, 237. Some poll-money accounts
were passed in the Exchequer, though the arrangement was hazy. See the accounts
for Milverton in PRO, SP28/183.
[4] *The Diary of Henry Townshend*, ed. J. W. Willis-Bund (1916), pt. ii. 32–3. For the
assessing and collecting of poll-money in various Warwickshire parishes see the
unnumbered documents in PRO, SP28/182–3.

decline', Sir John Danvers complained as he tried to assess the subsidy in Kent.[1]

There was one method by which the Commons might improve the effectiveness and political reliability of local government: M.P.s could themselves participate, and convey the sense of the House to their local colleagues. On 17 December 1640 it was resolved that the commissioners for the subsidies should be recommended not, as was the 'usual course', by the Lord Keeper, but by the knights and burgesses of each county.[2] Members, or those who were themselves trustworthy, gradually became the political supervisors of local government, choosing desirable office-holders and denouncing the ill-affected. With Parliament sitting almost continuously they were not encouraged to spend too much time in the country. But they could write letters. They wrote about the reporting and penalizing of recusants, about tumults, about the Protestation, the cost of entertaining justices in assize, and innumerable matters concerning particular counties. They wrote to sheriffs, J.P.s, lieutenants, even commissioners for sewers. But above all they wrote to collectors of money. On 16 July 1641, for instance, the Commons ordered knights and burgesses to 'signify' to the commissioners for poll-money that they should 'proceed effectually, impartially, and with all possible speed'. Commissioners were from time to time to acquaint M.P.s with their proceedings and difficulties. There were similar resolutions in August, December, and the following March, when letters from county members to the sheriffs were coupled with an approach by Wheeler to the Barons of the Exchequer to start legal proceedings. Sometimes they could intervene personally, as when the two Middlesex knights joined Lawrence Whitaker in sorting out the differences among the county's subsidy commissioners.[3]

From its first weeks the Parliament explored, amid political intricacies and constitutional scruples, the areas of military administration in which it could act. The committee 'to consider the state of the army', set up on 21 November 1640, was

[1] BL. Stowe MS. 184, fol. 31.

[2] *CJ* ii. 53, 68, 141; *D'Ewes*, ed. Notestein, 166; *CSPD, 1625–49*, 630.

[3] Examples are in *CJ* ii. 58, 135, 208, 210, 238, 277, 328, 332, 389, 497; printed orders include those in BL, 669 f 3/13, 3/15, 3/31. Typical correspondence is in Townshend, *Diary*, ii. 46; Gloucester Public Library, Smith of Nibley MS. iv. 24; Gloucester RO, d/2810/15; Northants RO, FH 3735.

the first of a dozen or so bodies of its kind that became the core of Parliament's later wartime government, and its chairman Sir John Hotham was the first powerful committee-man. He was not one of the experienced administrators linked to the Crown as well as Parliament, but 'the undisputed leader of the disaffected gentry in the East Riding' and organizer of petitions from Yorkshire to the King and the two Houses.[1] Much of the committee's early work took the form of protest and exhortation —on popish commanders, deficient musters, 'unnecessary charges', and so on.[2] It was soon doing more. 'The Parliament', wrote Northumberland on 24 December 1640, 'means to undertake the ordering of the army for the little time they intend it shall continue.'[3] On 20 January 1641 Hotham reported a scheme for the direct intervention of Yorkshire M.P.s and their gentry community in the troubles of the 'King's Army'. The Commissary-General was to choose sixteen deputies, and the Yorkshire M.P.s sixteen 'gentlemen of the county' to join in calculating and paying arrears from 10 December. The officers and some 'gentlemen of the Country' were also to receive a commission of *oyer and terminer* which would improve discipline. Parliament could hardly introduce martial law: it would raise embarrassing memories of the Petition of Right. *Oyer and terminer* was an institution of common law, and constitutional experts were worried about this unprofessional use of it. 'Some eminent Sergeants-at-Law', D'Ewes considered, or at least some respectable local lawyers, should be involved. The Yorkshire members thought they could manage quite well themselves. So having resolved that the commission was appropriate, the House had to entreat Mr. Treasurer Vane to move his Majesty to issue it.[4] Two months later Charles did so. He was ostentatiously grieved to inform the Lords of the 'difficulties, dangers, and disorders' that had arisen despite the hopes of the Commons and the Yorkshire gentlemen. Parliament would now, he hoped, settle some course for the government of the army that would not be repugnant to the law.[5]

[1] J. T. Cliffe, *The Yorkshire Gentry* (1969), 325.
[2] *CJ* ii. 68–70; *D'Ewes*, ed. Notestein, 58, 67, 87, 88.
[3] HMC, *De L'Isle and Dudley*, 353–4.
[4] *D'Ewes*, ed. Notestein, 267; Bodl., Tanner MS. 66, fol. 128; *CSPD 1641–3*, 13, 41; *CJ* ii. 70.
[5] *LJ* iv. 182; *CJ* ii. 103–4; *CSPD 1640–1*, 491–2, 499.

The Army Plot of May 1641, and the rumours of a French invasion, produced the first outright questioning of the behaviour of local magnates. Members of Parliament began to take personal responsibility for the loyalty of their areas. The Commons committee 'to consider some ways for the security of the land' was to receive reports from the knights, citizens, and burgesses of every county on the reliability of their Lord-Lieutenants and Deputy Lieutenants, on the local supply of ammunition, on the garrisons, castles, and forts. Sir Walter Erle, 'upon his own motion', was sent into Dorset to put the militia in readiness. Sir John Clotworthy and Sir Philip Stapleton were ordered to see to the defence of Portsmouth; Hugh Cholmley the younger went with all speed to Yorkshire, after his father and the already busy Sir John Hotham had been 'spared'. The Parliament which, said Denzil Holles, 'hath all this while but beaten the air' was moving closer to royal areas of government.[1]

One area where the King's claims to sole control were strong was the apparently endless negotiations with the Scots. Until a treaty was completed there was little prospect of disbanding the northern armies. Charles's 'most confounding error', in Clarendon's later view, was to move the negotiations from the north to London.[2] It produced an extraordinary diplomatic game in which the Scottish commissioners could exploit the rivalry in treaty-making of Crown and Parliament, or 'breed distractions' among the two Houses.[3] A joint select committee, managed by the Earl of Bristol and the lawyer John Crew, examined the articles drafted by the commissioners and submitted to the two Houses to be accepted, referred back for explanation, or thrown into a new morass of committees. 'It could be done in two days if they pursued it', Clarendon remarked.[4] When the Scots demanded to know 'to whom they should address themselves' to get the promised money the

---

[1] *LJ* iv. 238; *CJ* ii. 135, 138, 146; BL, Harley MS. 163, fol. 191; Rushworth, iv. 243.

[2] Clarendon, i. 215.

[3] D. Stevenson, *The Scottish Revolution, 1637–44* (Newton Abbot, 1973), ch. 7; C. L. Hamilton, 'The Anglo-Scottish Negotiations of 1641', *Scottish Hist. Rev.* 41 (1962), 84–6; BL, Harley MS. 457, *passim*; BL, Stowe MS. 187; Rushworth, iv. 367–77.

[4] Clarendon, i. 362.

answer was that an impressive list of peers and commoners would take charge of their payment in the Chamber of London. Aldermen Ingram, Soame, Pennington were among them; so, inevitably, was Pye. (Culpepper suggested that the Scots should be made to collect it 'at some place beyond the seas'.)[1] At the end of June the treaty was reported to be ready for ratification. Charles agreed that the armies of both his Scottish and his English subjects should now be disbanded.

With great caution and greater confusion the Houses began to co-operate with the King's civil and military officers in organizing the disbanding. Left to himself, they felt, Charles might take charge of what forces he could for his own purposes. On 12 June a Commons committee, again under Hotham, produced a hasty scheme. 'Regiment after regiment' would be mustered, paid, and conducted back to its county. Uvedale was still to be the channel for the uncertain quantities of money available. Detailed rules were laid down for mustering and paying the soldiers, collecting their arms, and conducting them across the country in numbers small enough to avoid major disorder.[2] The instructions were clearly the work of a committee of busy politicians, but they were taken seriously by everyone involved. Charles had made another of the blunders pointed out by Clarendon in giving command of the northern army, on Northumberland's resignation, not to Essex but to Holland. The new General's 'open hand and easy nature', and the behaviour of Mr. Lucas, his 'raw and incompetent' secretary, alarmed Uvedale, who warned that the real task of disbanding would fall to the professional Bradley.[3] For more than two months the handling of the army, the Scots, and the northern counties was divided between royal and parliamentary authorities with little conflict about constitutional principles. On 7 August the Commons were still asking the Lords to petition His Majesty to approve their plan for the speedy disbanding of the horse. Charles was again happy to oblige. He had always 'taken the advice of his parliament concerning the army', and now commended the care of disbanding

[1] Rushworth, iv. 367; BL, Harley MS. 163, fol. 339; Rymer, *Foedera*, xx. 493; BL, 669 f 3/8.
[2] *LJ* iv. 285–7; *CJ* ii. 173–4, 184; *CSPD 1641–3*, 13–16, 21–2.
[3] *CSPD 1641–3*, 21, 29; Clarendon, i. 59.

to the two Houses. He would issue another proclamation to strengthen authority against disorders. At the same time he pointed out that if Parliament expected the disbanded soldiers to return their arms to the magazines rather than keep them it had better refund the money paid for them.[1]

The greatest fear behind the delays in disbanding was that Charles would use an army in the north to support some sudden action against the parliamentary opposition. When, 'after a long tugg' he announced his final determination to set out for Edinburgh on 11 August, the Commons' scruples about intervening in military affairs dwindled still further.[2] A succession of messages was sent to the Lord General, at first setting out the directions approved by the King and moving on to Parliament's 'express order' to disband forthwith the horse regiments. Goodwin, Hotham, Anderson, and Scawen were all ordered to York; but it was Rushworth who carried the main dispatches. He could reach York in little more than a day, unless he encountered such hazards as the failure of the postmaster at Ware to have fresh horses ready, which forced him to 'go some distance on foot, carrying his saddle'. On 9 August he encountered Holland at Doncaster, where the General had assembled two regiments of horse to greet the King. On the 21st, Rushworth with the latest order from each House and a collection of letters reached York at 4.0 p.m. to find that Holland had gone to a horse-race.[3] But M.P.s, as Holland repeatedly pointed out, were in no position to complain of dilatory administration. In June, for instance, another order had been issued to the knights of the shire from Yorkshire, Lincolnshire, and Northumberland to find gentlemen of their counties who would join with army officers in assessing the billeting-money. Holland had great difficulty in discovering the names of those appointed: officers had waited to meet them, and no-one came. If civilians were as diligent as officers, he complained, the money might be paid.[4]

Parliament was not merely inefficient: its leaders were

[1] *LJ* iv. 347–8; *CJ* ii. 243; Nalson, ii. 429–30; BL, Harley MS. 163, fols. 419ᵛ, 422ᵛ, 423.
[2] Nalson, ii. 436; *CSPD 1641–3*, 81.
[3] Bodl., Tanner MS. 66, fols. 128, 132, 139, 145; *CJ* ii. 243, 250, 264–5; *CSPD 1641–3*, 71–2, 92–3; HMC 4th Report, 96–7, 100.
[4] Bodl., Tanner MS. 66, fols. 123, 128, 135, 137–8, 140–1.

prepared to delay disbanding indefinitely if the King or the Scots seemed to be exploiting the difficulties. One of the packets of papers for York was conveyed by an eminent group of messengers who were on their way to Edinburgh on a mission of great political importance. Bedford and Howard of Escrick from the Lords, Fiennes, Armyn, Stapleton, and Hampden from the Commons had been appointed emissaries of the two Houses, to see that the Scots carried out the agreement and to 'attend his majesty, that is to be a spy upon him'.[1] 'Commissioners or rather committees', Nicholas called them;[2] and the difference was important. Most members still felt more secure in the exercise of functions that verged on the sphere of the Crown if they had the status that could be derived, directly or indirectly, from a commission under a royal seal. But Charles had left London without issuing any such document for the mission to Scotland. The Lords and Commons tried to get Anthony Nicholl to overtake him with a commission drafted in Parliament. When the six reached Darlington they found that it had been rejected: they were therefore acting only on the authority, unearthed or invented in the well-known pronouncement by D'Ewes, of an Ordinance of Parliament.[3] Littleton was refusing to use the Great Seal without specific royal command. On the other hand Holland claimed that he would not take Charles's instructions about the armies without the approval of Parliament. (Ironically Holland had no legal authority at all: the Attorney-General, Sir Edward Herbert, had forgotten to arrange for his commission to pass the Great Seal.) The parliamentary leaders had not only bungled the question of the delegation to Edinburgh: they abandoned the larger schemes for a commission authorized to act in the King's name or a *custos regni* with viceregal powers.[4] It did not mean that England, in Gardiner's dramatic phrase, was left 'without a recognised government'[5]—just that there was much more confusion than usual of legal, political, and practical considerations.

[1] Clarendon, i. 370; *CJ* ii. 265–6.   [2] *Nicholas Papers*, i. 4, 17.
[3] *CJ* ii. 262–6; *LJ* iv. 366; Nalson, ii. 437, 451, 455; Bodl., Tanner MS. 66, fol. 156; BL, Harley MS. 164, fols. 15, 16ᵛ, 32ᵛ–33.
[4] Nicholas papers in *The Life and Writings of John Evelyn*, ed. W. Bray (1819), ii, appx. 2, 2–13; Nalson, ii. 412; Bodl., Tanner MS. 66, fol. 164.
[5] Gardiner, *History*, x. 3.

Fears that the King might somehow use armed force against his parliament were on a different level of thought from immediate matters of royal and parliamentary authority: they belonged to the political revolution, not yet to the practical job of government. Men whose power and status might be threatened if armed forces began to obey orders of doubtful legality hesitated to challenge the principle that command of the army must derive from the King.[1] But on the fringe of army affairs there were vital matters within the parliamentary sphere. The guard for the Palace of Westminster could be shown as an increasingly urgent defence against coercion by mob violence.[2] Tumults also enabled Parliament to extend its influence over the City trained bands. A topic constantly disputed was the manufacture and storing of gunpowder. It was raised in January 1641, not with any overt military purpose but because it was a monopoly. Vane's friend Samuel Cordwell, powder-maker to the King, had taken it over from the Evelyn family, raising the price and curtailing the supply. Besides, said D'Ewes, he stored it in the Tower and might blow up the crown jewels and the public records.[3] Eventually the Commons decided 'after long dispute' that manufacture and purchase should be free to every man. Cordwell continued throughout the summer of 1641 to sell powder, as a royal instruction had directed, to anyone who wanted it: Robert Bateman took a hundred barrels for the use of the City. The Master and Lieutenant of the Ordnance seem to have delivered it from royal stores with no political discrimination. In August, despite Cordwell's protests that independent manufacture would mean no powder at all, the bill to end his monopoly received the royal assent. He and his rivals were soon negotiating with the House's powder committee.[4]

It was not only on disbanding the northern armies that

[1] On the theories justifying parliamentary control see L. G. Schwoerer, 'The Fittest Subject for a King's Quarrel: an essay on the Militia Controversy' in *Journ. of British Studies* xi, (1971), 46, 63–71.
[2] See below, pp. 178, 182.
[3] *D'Ewes*, ed. Notestein, 299–300; *CJ* ii. 75; Aylmer, *King's Servants*, 367.
[4] PRO, WO/55/456; *CSPD 1640–1*, 119, 313, 421, 431, 503, 521; *CSPD 1641–3*, 81, 152; *Royalist Ordnance Papers*, ed. I. Roy (Oxford Rec. Soc., 1964), introd. 11; *CJ* ii. 212, 219, 250, 364, 457, 469; *LJ* iv. 316, 332, 356; BL, Harley MS. 163, fol. 154.

Charles presented Parliament with opportunities to develop its share in the management of the forces. On 28 July, after several requests from the Lords, he announced that before his departure he would make Essex 'Captain General of the forces this side Trent'. He even sought the approval of the Houses for this. Essex as Lord Chamberlain was a major royal servant. But he had been closely involved with Parliament ever since he felt snubbed by Charles after the first Scots war. With his co-operation parliamentary leaders could take military measures that appeared both loyal and lawful.[1] On 15 August the Commons set up a committee to 'prepare heads for a conference concerning the putting of the kingdom into a posture of defence'. The term was vague, but familiar. It had been applied in January to the state the King's army should be in. In June, when Charles first proposed to go to Scotland, the Commons resolved to be 'humble suitors to his Majesty to establish a general estate of defence'. The most specific recommendation in August was that authority should be given to 'some person' to establish the posture of defence. Essex was ready. 'Seeing the king hath been pleased to make him . . . Captain-General of the South', he humbly requested that Parliament would give him the means to execute the commission for levying men, raising moneys, and resisting invasion. What sort of invasion was better left unstated.[2] On Essex's initiative directions to Holland moved beyond the familiar exhortations about disbanding; he was to convey arms from the garrisons of Berwick and Carlisle by sea to London, and prevent any interference with those at Hull. There was no sense of crisis, and no attempt by the King to interfere. 'I wish', Nicholas wrote to Vane on 18 August, 'that all business may receive dispatch by the king and his parliament rather than by the privy council, which hath sat but once since his Majesty's departure.' Vane assured him that 'the affairs of state are now in his Majesty's absence in the parliament, except it be in some particular directions'.[3] Unfortunately peers and M.P.s were no less concerned than

[1] *LJ* iv. 331; Rymer, *Foedera*, xx. 479–81; Snow, *Essex the Rebel*, 269; V. Snow, 'Essex and the Aristocratic Opposition', *Journ. of Mod. Hist.* xxxii (1960), 224–33; Whitelocke, i. 94.

[2] *CJ* ii. 183–5, 257; Rushworth, iv. 99, 143; L. Boynton, *The Elizabethan Militia, 1558–1638* (1967), 295–6; BL, Harley MS. 164, fol. 33ᵛ.

[3] *Nicholas Papers*, i. 17, 25.

privy councillors to escape the plague and the smallpox. A recess was long overdue.

The six-week interval in September and October rescued Parliament from a bad period, when the Houses were at odds and there seemed to be no policy for the future. ('Even the very fiddlers made songs upon us', said Alderman Pennington.)[1] It might have been a moment for Pym's inner group to take over more of the work of the Crown. Nothing like that happened. The recess committees appointed by each House spent most of their time, as their instructions prescribed, on matters that were now familiar—disbanding, poll-money, papists and delinquents. The remark by Sir Peter Wroth that the committee's orders only lacked the letter 'R' after the name of Pym was more bitter than realistic.[2] There were no panics to give the recess committees occasion for drastic action. Disbanded troopers, long expected to terrorize London, provided some material for tales of horror and plunder, but not very much. They presented numerous petitions complaining of broken agreements, of royal interference, and of Parliament's order against recruiting by the French and Spaniards. (The Commons later responded to some of their pleas.) Pym had to report that though 'we cannot say there were any great tumults', there might have been.[3] Nevertheless both royal and parliamentary authorities showed great concern for the welfare and loyalty of London. The City government and the justices had to cope with a startling variety of directives. On 5 October the Commons recess committee produced an order, drafted originally by Pym and Rushworth, calling on the Lord Mayor, Aldermen, and J.P.s to deal with disorders and with the unquestionably real menace of the plague which was already the subject of a detailed ordinance of Parliament. A week later the Privy Council took up the question of disorders. A royal proclamation reiterated the parliamentary demands. On 20 October the Lord Mayor reported to the Council the action taken 'upon the order made by the committees of Parliament'. The Council on the same day sent its own directions to the justices of Middlesex and Westminster,

[1] BL, Harley MS. 163, fol. 419ᵛ.

[2] *D'Ewes*, ed. Coates, 1–10; *Old Parliamentary History*, x. 1–6; *CJ* ii. 288–90; PRO, SP16/484/63; *CSPD, 1641–3*, 132, 136.

[3] Rushworth, iv. 389; *D'Ewes*, ed. Coates, 11–14. (D'Ewes had to alter 'tumults which were occasioned' to 'tumults which might occasionally happen'.)

and also to Surrey, Hertfordshire, and Kent, requiring reports by the end of the month on their execution and effect.[1]

To the power of King, Lords, Commons, and the City government there was added the military authority of the Earl of Essex. As Captain General south of Trent he could claim responsibility for a task that had already acquired great political significance—the guarding of the Palace of Westminster. The 'Incident' in Scotland, when Charles was alleged to have been involved in the conspiracy that led to the ludicrous flight of Hamilton and Argyle, was the basis of a new 'popish-plot' scare. It was a good enough reason for an emergency guard. Two days before the Houses reassembled, 500 soldiers from the Westminster trained bands were assembled in the Palace Yard. The committee directed Pym to write to the Lord Mayor requiring him to place guards in the City and to obey all instructions issued by Essex ('in his Majesty's absence'). Essex, 'by virtue of his Majesty's commission under the Great Seal', wrote to his loving friend the Lord Lieutenant of Surrey requiring him to have a 'fit number' of trained horse in readiness to suppress 'disbanded soldiers and other disorderly persons' in London and Westminster. But there were few signs of major upheaval. If London, as Nicholas reported, was growing weary of the 'insolent carriage of the schismatics', it was not ready to take forceful action against them. 'It is difficult', he confessed to Charles, 'to discern who are your best servants' in Parliament.[2] Military activity and political confrontation might yet have declined.

Then the Irish Catholics rebelled. The worst fears of popish conspiracy were confirmed; and a new armed campaign became inescapable. The crisis could not be used directly against the King. Parliament, both on practical grounds and to appease the timid and the legalistic, had to organize help for the Irish Protestants in collaboration with the Crown. It was the Lords of the Privy Council who informed the Commons of the rebellion; the King sought the advice of the two Houses,

[1] *D'Ewes*, ed. Coates, 12–13 n. 4; *LJ* iv. 397; *CJ* ii. 295; *Bibliotheca Lindesiana*, v (Oxford, 1910), 230; *CSPD 1641–3*, 141–2; PRO, PC2/53, fols. 183–4, 189–91; K. J. Lindley, 'The Impact of the 1641 Rebellion upon England and Wales' in *Irish Hist. Studies*, xviii (1972).

[2] Surrey RO, Carew MS. Acc. 1263/41; Snow, *Essex* 277–9; *Evelyn*, ed. Bray, ii, appx. 31, 38; Nalson, ii. 487; Pearl, *London*, 123–4.

and gave bland assurances that he would do anything for the salvation of Ireland. Nicholas reported Parliament's 'great affection' to his service—'in this particular'. But the impassioned declarations from both Crown and Parliament contrasted with actions that seemed irresolute and trivial. Charles, despite Nicholas's warnings that he ought to return to London, stayed in Scotland, making it conveniently difficult for Parliament to obtain his 'immediate warrant' for military measures.[1]

Any notion of an expedition under commanders deriving power and directions from Parliament alone was resisted, in the Lords more strongly than in the Commons. But on the detailed management of the campaign the large joint committee for Irish affairs was soon submitting a succession of precise orders. The storing and transport of supplies, the wording of commissions, the numbers in regiments and companies, and the rates of pay were dealt with at length. Resolutions were worded carefully. Money, and the purchase of stores, were as before deemed to be under parliamentary authority. On matters closer to the command of the army the Commons 'held it fit' or, for instance, 'moved the Lords' to 'recommend to the Lord Lieutenant' the men they wished to see as officers.[2] Distinctions between the various sources of authority could be bewilderingly vague. On 7 February Walter Frost, whom Parliament had 'engaged as our servant' to be commissary for victuals at Chester, received from the Commons minutely detailed instructions ('. . . four thousand quarters of oats . . . the number, weight, and measure of every cask . . .'); he was also to take orders from the Lord Lieutenant, the Lords Justices and Council in Ireland, or such other commissioners or council as should be 'established by the Parliament here'.[3]

A further political complication was the help which the Scots had been embarrassingly quick to offer. It was in the debate on instructions for the commissioners in Scotland that Pym, on 5 November, produced the startling proposal to make Parliament's defence of Ireland dependent on Charles taking councillors they approved. The amended version—'to resolve

[1] *CJ* ii. 300–4; Rushworth, iv. [408]–[11]; *Evelyn*, ed. Bray, ii, appx. 59, 75; HMC 4th Report, 104.
[2] *CJ* ii. 304–6, 313, 318, 360–1; *LJ* iv. 424–5, 429, 445; HMC 4th Report, 105; *D'Ewes*, ed. Coates, 76, 90–1, 109.
[3] *CJ* ii. 417; G. E. Aylmer, *The State's Servants* (1973), 254–6.

on some such way of defending Ireland . . . as may concur to the securing of ourselves' struck a realistic as well as a menacing note. It would be very difficult to 'resolve on some such way' as would be generally accepted in both Houses, and in the City. Once again everything would depend on money from London, and Parliament had not yet won firm support there. Nicholas, in the suggestions he drafted for Charles's speech at Guildhall when at last he returned to London, recognized the importance of persuading the City to lend for Ireland—but to lend to the King rather than Parliament. 'King Pym will undertake the Irish war' on his own terms; but he could do little if Charles took from him the backing of the City.[1]

Mrs. Pearl has shown how Pym's supporters came to power in the City in January 1642. But that did not, as she explains, mean that loans were easily available.[2] The eventual solution included handing over the Irish war, or part of it, to private enterprise. The Irish Adventurers were investors whose capital would be repaid out of the sale of two and a half million acres of Irish land. The scheme depended on a statute, and therefore on both royal and parliamentary approval. The Adventurers' treasury aimed at collecting voluntarily a million pounds. The treasurers (aldermen soon to be deeply involved in Parliament's war finances) were to gather equipment into their own stores and raise at once a force of 6,500 men and eighteen ships. It seemed as widely acceptable as all other schemes for robbing the Irish, until the war in Ireland came to be seen primarily as a part of the preparation for war in England. In the summer of 1642 money was 'borrowed' from the Adventurers, their stores 'purchased', and their troops taken into the service of the 'state'. The investors, 130 M.P.s among them, found themselves associated inextricably with the creation of the parliamentary armies.[3]

The Scots, the Irish, the King's supposedly evil and popish

---

[1] *D'Ewes*, ed. Coates, 94, 104; *CJ* ii. 306; *LJ* iv. 431; Rushworth, iv. 424, 494; *Evelyn*, ed. Bray, ii, appx. 59; *CSPD 1641–3*, 177–8; K. S. Bottigheimer, *English Money and Irish Land: the 'Adventurers' in the Cromwellian Settlement of Ireland* (Oxford, 1971), 30–8.   [2] Pearl, *London*, chs. iv, vi.

[3] Studies of the Adventurers include K. S. Bottigheimer, 'English Money and Irish Land', *Journ. of British Studies*, vii (1967) and his book, with the same title, cited above; H. Hazlett, 'The Financing of British Armies in Ireland, 1641–49', *Irish Hist. Studies*, i (1938); J. R. MacCormack, 'The Irish Adventurers and the English Civil War', ibid., x (1956).

counsellors, the aristocratic commanders, and the tumultuous meaner sort of people had all contributed to the astonishing possibility of Parliament taking sole control of its own armed forces. Its floundering involvement with the armies in the north and in Ireland gave it contact with every aspect of warfare. But forces able to dominate large parts of England and Wales could only come by drawing more heavily on the manpower of the local communities. The trained and even the untrained soldiers of the counties and cities had to be detached from the limited obligations which generally they felt were to their county or town rather than to any central authority. Here too King Charles had done a good deal to make Parliament's first war efforts feasible. The 'exact militia' had never come up to the expectations of the Stuart government. The Council complained constantly of local neglect and inefficiency. To the communities its cost, and its association with billeting and martial law, made it a grievance as prominent as ship-money.[1] But the accounts of rusty weapons and disorderly musters underrate the increased acceptance of the militia as a part of life. In some places the shortcomings seem to have been due more to the deputy-lieutenants than to the comparatively active high constables and petty constables.[2] The procedure for assembling and equipping county forces may have been inefficient; but everyone knew what a muster involved and how troops and companies were moved across country. Foot-soldiers and even cavalry, though not by continental standards formidable, could be called out reasonably quickly by whoever won the obedience of local officials. The men who had led resistance to the militia needed now to make it the basis of a national force with an allegiance not too closely defined. In the country even more than at the centre they had to show that their military power was derived, by something plausibly close to the familiar processes, from the Crown. A change from preparing to defend the King to preparing to oppose him had to be gradual, even evasive. Armies must still be commanded by gentlemen, with peers of the realm somewhere at their head.

---

[1] Boynton, *Militia*, chs. 7 and 8; T. G. Barnes, *Somerset 1625–1640* (Oxford, 1961), ch. 9; A. Fletcher, *A County Community in Peace and War* (1975), ch. 9.
[2] D. P. Carter, 'The Lancashire Lieutenancy' (M.A. thesis, Manchester Univ., 1973), 120.

It would not be easy to keep the services of noble commanders. The difficulties were apparent on 26 November, when Essex had to inform the Lords that the King had relieved him of the command held during his Majesty's absence. He could therefore no longer obey the instructions of Parliament.[1] In face of strong opposition in the Lords to any crucial challenge to royal military authority, Pym even raised the possibility of a guard appointed by the Commons alone, but commanded by Essex. It was not yet politically feasible. But a mere 'watch' raised by the High Constable of Westminster would be better than a royal guard.[2] Charles's attempts to extend his control to the Tower was far more alarming. If parliamentary politics and popular riots had been enough to start a war it might have been fought in Westminster and London. The King's attempt to reassert his power in his capital proved, however, to be less important than the introduction, on 7 December, of the first Militia Bill—'for settling the militia or trained bands of the kingdom under a lord general'.[3]

Haselrig's bill had no prospect of immediate success. But it marked a decisive stage in the progress of the Commons towards action in defiance of legal convention and royal command. When the affair of the Five Members and Charles's departure made collaboration with royal administration still less practicable, the creation of a parliamentary army began in earnest without legislative authority. Collectively and separately, members found their tepid intervention in local military affairs turned into urgent activity. On 15 January the committee on the posture of defence demanded that M.P.s should 'by two o'clock this afternoon' deliver the names of 'noble persons' fit to be lieutenants of their counties. On 20 January it was agreed that members should send out letters calling for a campaign to complete the taking of the Protestation. An eight-month-old document was not ideal; but it was the activity that mattered. Large supplies of the Protestation and of a declaration on the Five Members affair were to be distributed by M.P.s. The

[1] *LJ* iv. 367, 452; Snow, *Essex*, 284–5.
[2] *LJ* iv. 453; *CJ* ii. 325–8; Snow, *Essex*, 285–6; Schwoerer, 'Militia Controversy', 49–52.
[3] *LJ* iv. 455–6; *CJ* ii. 328–30, 334; *D'Ewes*, ed. Coates, 244, 246; Schwoerer, 'Militia Controversy', 52–5. For the popular movements in London see Brian Manning, *The English People and the English Revolution* (1976), chs. 3 and 4.

Sheriff of Gloucester seemed surprised to receive 'two several letters under the hand of Mr. Speaker and the knights of the parliament for this county'. He duly summoned the justices to meet at Cirencester, a town already garrisoned by a body of dragoons.[1] In February members were to produce for the militia committee lists of ports and forts in their counties, and the names of persons fit to command them.[2] A single day, 13 January, shows some typical tasks. Members were to search the lodgings of a suspected papist, deal with gunners and a storekeeper, interview the officers of the Tower, peruse letters from France, go to the Lord Admiral about intercepting a cargo of ammunition, go to York to secure the arms and powder there, approach the Commissioners of the Treasury about arrears of pay at Portsmouth, and thank the Dutch ambassador for his good affections. An urgent order had to be communicated to the sheriffs and justices of five counties: Digby and Lunsford had appeared in a 'warlike manner' at Kingston-on-Thames, and the trained bands were to be called out to suppress all such unlawful assemblies. The Houses required a speedy account of the response.[3] All this was in addition to the orders, reports, and nominations of committees and the routine instructions to such functionaries as Wheeler, who had to settle an account from Thames watermen amounting to one pound.

Such an extension of Parliament's activities would have provoked deeper suspicion if it had been seen clearly as preparation for a possible civil war. It was a blessing to Puritan leaders that almost any military measures could be made part of the unchallengeable need to raise armies and supplies for Ireland and to defend England against the popish menace. The 'Committee of 52' on Irish affairs, and its sub-committee meeting at Grocers' Hall, became a tacitly recognized parliamentary executive. It was for Ireland that stores of munitions were built up. Officers of the ordnance 'humbly craved leave' to present to Parliament details of the magazines for 'muniting this kingdom' and for Ireland—without distinction.[4] On 26 February a letter from both Houses to every sheriff gave detailed instructions for taking subscriptions for Ireland. Justices of the Peace, 'ministers

---

[1] Glos. RO., MS. D/2510, fols. 12, 15; *CJ* ii. 381, 389.
[2] *CJ* ii. 427, 440.   [3] *CJ* ii. 375–8; *LJ* iv. 510, 516; BL, 669 f 3/31.
[4] *CSPD 1641–3*, 280–1.

of God's word', and persons of quality were to give active assistance. The 'posture of defence' was revived and a new committee at Merchant Taylors' Hall put in charge of it.[1] Ireland was also an excellent subject for mutual recriminations. 'I pray you', Charles pleaded, with his injured but forgiving rectitude, 'to take Ireland really into your care.' The Lords and Commons were grieved too: their efforts were being frustrated by His Majesty's absence 'so far remote from his Parliament'. They demanded the partial remedy of a Commission to act in his place, and sent him detailed instructions on how it should 'dispose all things concerning the government of Ireland'. On 14 March Charles authorized the necessary sealing. He could now 'wash his hands of the least imputation of slackness in that pious work'. Holles, Pym, Vane, Cromwell, and Kimbolton were among the commissioners; and it was Holles who raised in the Commons the practical needs of the Commission—a secretary, an auditor, a meeting-place (Star Chamber was a conveniently available room), fire, candlesticks, and paper.[2] The Commission apparently reduced the activity in Irish affairs of the old Committee of 52 and of the Houses themselves. 'They were now', Clarendon remarked, 'like to have much to do.'[3]

The Militia Ordinance itself was a cautious measure. Most of the lieutenants recommended by local M.P.s were lieutenants already, and not all proved politically reliable.[4] Any revolutionary flavour was in the method rather than the effect. It was still possible to regard the seizure of military power as a political triumph, not an irrevocable step towards war.[5] But the passing of the ordinance on 5 March was a moment when Parliament virtually abandoned the struggle to extend its control of government without defying the essentials of monarchy. Its defence of rule by Crown and Parliament was now a matter of propaganda, not reality. As right-wing parliamentarians drifted away to become 'moderate royalists', new

---

[1] BL, Harley MS. 163ᵛ, fol. 13; *CJ* ii. 457; *LJ* iv. 615, 623.

[2] *LJ* iv. 643–4, 647; *CJ* ii. 453; BL, Harley MS. 163, fol. 66ᵛ.

[3] Clarendon, i. 598.

[4] The names of previous holders are in *BIHR* Special Supplement 8 (1970); but joint tenures and grouping of counties can make comparative figures misleading.

[5] Schwoerer, 'Militia Controversy', 58.

committee-men came into prominence as the makers of the wartime administration. But the King's servants were not excluded. Giles Green, former Town Clerk of Weymouth, and the younger Vane, until December 1641 the King's Treasurer of the Navy, became both colleagues and rivals in the management of Parliament's naval forces. John Trenchard, from the Dorset gentry, emerged as a leading financial organizer alongside Pye, Wheeler, and the London merchant M.P.s. Robert Scawen, secretary to the Earl of Northumberland, presided over the main army committee. They could hardly have had a wider diversity of background.

In counties and towns the problem of conflicting orders became steadily harder to evade. One day in June the Sheriff of Essex came to the Bar of the Commons with the 'diverse' proclamations he had received from King and Parliament.[1] The House's instructions on which he should obey were not hard to predict. But no one commented on the significance of the fact that a sheriff was still there to carry them out. The lieutenancy, the justices, the grand juries, and the constables were a demonstration in every county that 'persons of quality' and the 'honest men' who worked under them remained the administrative support of the social order. Mayors, aldermen, guilds, and common councils seemed no less secure in their functions. If holders of office were ejected, and quarrels raged about their replacement, that was nothing new. But somehow, with only vague foreboding, men of authority had between them made conceivable and practicable the fighting of a civil war. Briefly Parliament became, as it has never been again, a truly governing body. It was lucky to survive its victory.

[1] *CJ* ii. 626; *A Perfect Diurnall*, 13 June 1642. For the county's activity in the summer of 1642 see C. Holmes, *The Eastern Association in the English Civil War* (Cambridge, 1974), 34–6.

'Honest' Radicals in the Counties
1642–1649

DAVID UNDERDOWN

AMONG the most striking paradoxes of the English Revolution is the fact that a parliament which could win a civil war against the King was unable to establish a stable régime without him. The traditional, 'whig', explanation of this failure is that a moderate reform movement was wrecked by a Puritan minority which could govern only by the sword. More recent theories have stressed the alienation of communities of country gentry by a centralizing government, or the inability of the bourgeoisie, through lack of a sufficiently coherent social base, to force its allies among the élite into a genuine revolution.[1] These and other theories have in common the belief that the men who led England into revolution had no effectively organized body of lay support: no 'party' of their own. It seems worth examining this assumption, and tracing the evolution of the local groups among whom the supporters of revolutionary action were to be found.

Revolutionary action: at once we run into difficulties. For, as always in the English Revolution, we need to know which revolution we are talking about: the moderate constitutional one of 1640–2; the more violent one of 1648–9 in which Parliament was purged and the King executed; or the abortive democratic one yearned for by Levellers and sectaries, but which never materialized. Historians have not always found it necessary to keep these distinctions in mind. The result is that when we look for the essential revolutionary party in the England of the 1640s we find ourselves with too many candidates for the role. The Puritan 'Saints' variously described, the godly bourgeoisie, and the Levellers of several hues have all been cast singly or together as its central component.

[1] A. Everitt, *The Community of Kent and the Great Rebellion, 1640–1660* (Leicester, 1966); B. Manning, *The English People and the English Revolution, 1640–1649* (1976).

If, however, we adhere strictly to the threefold division previously outlined, clarification is possible. The first revolution— of 1640–2—was a disturbance within the élite, and its organized local base derived mainly from the territorial influence of the country gentry or of noblemen like the Earl of Warwick.[1] The third revolution—the 'revolution which failed'—also affords little difficulty, having been illuminated by a large literature on the Levellers and a brilliant study of the even more radical groups which succeeded them.[2] It is the second revolution—the crisis of 1648–9—which remains obscure. A respectable argument can be made that it involved no organized revolutionary movement at all outside the Army and a handful of politicians: that its leaders stumbled into revolution in a fit of absence of mind, assisted by pressure from the soldiers. In this view, the provincial revolutionaries were mere cliques of power-seeking careerists, like Sir Anthony Weldon's friends in Kent.[3] If we accept this, we are left with no grass-roots party to sustain the events of 1648 and 1649: with a revolutionary head without a body.

On the face of it this seems unlikely, and it is a view contradicted by much contemporary opinion. Throughout the later 1640s there are many references to people, both at Westminster and in the localities, who wanted something more than the reforms of 1641, and something less than those demanded by Levellers and sectaries. Their enemies had a variety of opprobrious terms for them: 'the Faction', the 'Levelling Faction', the 'Holy Beggars' (Marchamont Nedham in his royalist days): 'the Sectaries, Republican, Anabaptistical, Jesuitical, Levelling party' (William Prynne); as well as the familiar 'Independent party' favoured by Clement Walker and many later writers.[4] Many of these epithets involve the old propaganda trick of identifying enemies with their most extreme associates, or derive from the myopia which led conservatives

[1] C. Holmes, *The Eastern Association in the English Civil War* (Cambridge, 1974), 21–2, 26, 28, 34–8. Manning, *English People*, describes widespread popular enthusiasm for Parliament in 1640–2; but outside London it was not *organized*, except as above.

[2] C. Hill, *The World Turned Upside Down* (1972).

[3] Everitt, *Community of Kent*.

[4] [Nedham], *Mercurius Pragmaticus* (1648), *passim*. For Prynne and Walker, see D. Underdown, 'The Independents Reconsidered', *Journ. of British Studies*, iii, no. 2 (May 1964), 65.

like Sir Simonds D'Ewes to confuse Pym's middle group with the real 'fiery spirits'.[1] There is some excuse for this confusion. Until 1647 the men who were to mark themselves off as Levellers were still perforce allied with the 'establishment' Independents. Even after that time they shared the same enemies, and there was always a large undifferentiated middle ground (which contained such people as Henry Marten) between them.

The 'fiery spirits' themselves came reluctantly to accept that there was a radical party, though they were careful to disavow its extreme, Leveller, wing when the time came. The terms they used to describe themselves are revealing. At first 'honest', 'godly', and 'well-affected' are used interchangeably, without the addition of 'party'. But the war forged a greater sense of identity. Struggling against obstruction from the neutral or faint-hearted, 'honest' men came naturally to stress their common unity. After the war, 'honest' acquired a specific political meaning, and was frequently used to describe the radical rank and file in the country. In 1645 Sir William Brereton deplored designs against 'the Committee of Stafford and honest party'. In January 1648 Cromwell warned the Commons against endangering 'the honest party of the Kingdom'. When John Downes tried to get the King's trial adjourned he was accused of betraying 'all the honest party in the nation'. The alternative adjective 'godly' was in general use over a longer period, but 'honest' rivalled it in popularity in 1648 and 1649 and is therefore an appropriate term for our purposes. The connection between honesty and godliness was universally assumed. Baxter speaks of Thomas Hunt as 'a plain hearted, honest, godly man, entirely beloved and trusted by the soldiers for his honesty'. Lilburne's arrest in January 1648, it is no surprise to learn, was much resented by 'divers of the honest godly party'.[2]

Whether godly, honest or well-affected, these were people easily recognizable both by friends and by enemies. From their own language we can deduce something about their values: honesty meant sincerity, candour, simplicity, the virtues

[1] J. H. Hexter, *The Reign of King Pym* (Cambridge, Mass., 1941), 52–4.
[2] Brereton to Ashhurst, 24 Oct. 1645: BL, Add. MS. 11332, fol. 10ᵛ; 'Parliamentary Diary of John Boys, 1647–8', *BIHR* xxxix (1966), 156; *HMC* vii (House of Lords MSS.), 158; *Reliquiae Baxterianae*, ed. M. Sylvester (1696), i. 45; W. Clarke to Lt.-Col. Rede, 25 Jan. 1647/8: BL, Stowe MS. 189, fol. 39.

associated with 'the Country' and country living since the previous century. They were also staunchly well-affected to Parliament, uncompromising towards royalists, and liable to perceive themselves as more godly than those around them. To their critics they were hypocritical, sanctimonious trouble-makers. They provided the popular support essential to the second revolution.

We must begin with the customary caution against importing anachronistic conceptions of party into a period when they were unknown. Even in the Long Parliament party is a concept of limited value: few M.P.s were consistent adherents of any of the various factions.[1] If this was so among the politicized élite, it was all the more true of the provincial population, even its gentry governors. Civil War commanders constantly complained of operating in a bog of apathy: of soldiers who deserted at the first opportunity, civilians whose previously plentiful supplies vanished at the report of an enemy victory twenty miles away. So we should not expect more than a small minority to be committed to anything resembling a political stance. And party was still a dirty word. Subscribers of the Solemn League and Covenant promised to denounce anyone 'making any faction or parties amongst the people'. This was the conventional belief: one's enemies, pursuing their corrupt ends, had formed a party, but one's own side represented the public interest of the community. Parliament's propaganda labelled the royalists 'the malignant party' or 'the Popish and Jesuitical faction'. But Parliament's supporters were simply 'well-affected people', and Parliament defended the whole kingdom—'the Country'—against this malignant clique. Only the Cavaliers were a party.[2]

Gradually the depth of the kingdom's divisions began to sink in: Parliamentarians saw that they too were a party. It is hard to sense all the term's seventeenth-century nuances, but it is clear that during the 1640s it began to take on a new meaning.

---

[1] But cf. J. R. MacCormack, *Revolutionary Politics in the Long Parliament* (Cambridge, Mass., 1973).

[2] Statements about terminology in this and the following paragraph are based on pamphlets in the Thomason Collection. For the Solemn League and Covenant, see *Constitutional Documents of the Puritan Revolution 1625–1660*, ed. S. R. Gardiner (3rd edn., Oxford, 1906), 267–71.

From 'party' in the sense of a division of a whole (we should use the word 'part') it came to signify a political grouping. Although 'the well-affected' was still the more common expression, by the summer of 1643 'the well-affected party' becomes slightly more noticeable in the newsbooks. Many people still used 'party' in the older sense, with no political connotation. Even those who spoke of 'the Parliament's party' ignored the divisions emerging within their own ranks, which were to lead to the recognition of a 'godly party', an 'honest party', more narrowly based. But beneath the façade of unity the ugly growth of faction was under way.

The distinction between 'honest' men and the rest came clearly into the open in the crisis of the summer of 1643, following the series of betrayals and defeats which culminated in the loss of Bristol. No longer could it be pretended that the war was between the virtuous majority and a perverse handful of courtiers. The official account of Edmund Waller's plot accepted a threefold division of the nation: 'the King's party . . . the well affected . . . Neutrals'. One outcome was the scheme for the 'general rising'. A citizens' army of 10,000 men was to be raised under officers who were 'godly, or men of honest life and conversation'. Recipients of the proposal were asked to com-municate it to other 'honest men'. Another result of the crisis was the adoption of Pym's old panacea, oaths of association to distinguish honest men from neutrals: first the Vow and Covenant, then the Solemn League and Covenant. National unity against 'incendiaries, malignants or evil instruments' was again asserted. Yet the warning against 'detestable indifferency or neutrality' was an admission that these things existed.[1]

Parliament's emphasis on the distinction between honest men and neutrals was echoed in the counties. The distinction had existed ever since the outbreak of war, for in every county there were committed minorities who gradually separated themselves from the large number of nominal allies who were localist neutrals at heart. But in 1643 and 1644 the gulf became clearer. The Vow and Covenant provoked a rebellion in Kent, during which the hesitations of a majority of the County

---

[1] Rushworth, v. 322; *Instructions and Propositions Drawne up and agreed on by divers well affected persons in the City of London* (1643). See also Hexter, *King Pym*, 28–32, 121–51.

Committee contrasted sharply with the vigour of the 'honest' few under Weldon and Thomas Blount. The rebellion's failure did not end the neutralist threat in Kent; signs of continuing disaffection during the following winter renewed the vigilance of the zealous minority.[1]

The now familiar conflict between nationally-minded militants and locally-minded moderates can be found in all the parliamentarian counties. In Sussex, Herbert Morley noted that he had 'ever observed neuters to turn malignants' if encouraged by the approach of a royalist army. In January 1644 the Sussex Committee warned neutrals that if they did not assist 'the common cause' they would be proceeded against as enemies to the state. Sir Thomas Pelham and several other M.P.s were among those soon accused of backsliding. Against them were ranged the leaders of an embryo 'honest party': Morley, his kinsmen the Hays, and the upstart William Cawley.[2] Nearby in the Isle of Wight in 1644 there was friction between the 'well-affected inhabitants' and the localist gentry who still ran the committee. The latter disbanded five of the six companies they had raised, to the 'great grief of the well affected', it was said. It took intervention by the Governor, the Earl of Pembroke, to compose the differences.[3]

Even more than the localist gentry, it was the presence of noblemen of dubious loyalty in important commands that gave the activists the issue needed to unite them. The campaign against the Earls of Essex and Manchester had repercussions in the counties. In Wiltshire Edmund Ludlow refused to surrender his commission from Sir William Waller, so 'the faction of the Earl of Essex' obstructed him in recruiting his regiment, and later prevented him from taking a post in the New Model.[4] And there were moves against regional commanders: Denbigh in the west Midlands, Willoughby in Lincolnshire. Denbigh, inevitably suspect because of his royalist relations, was later accused of trying to lead a 'third party' to enforce a compromise peace, and of complicity in Edmund Waller's plot. In

[1] Everitt, *Community of Kent*, 189–200, 203–4.

[2] *HMC, Portland*, i. 130, 183; *Mercurius Aulicus*, 14 (6 Apr. 1644); *CJ* iii. 607, 646; BL, Add. MS. 31116 (Whitaker's diary), fol. 167.

[3] *Kingdomes Weekly Intelligencer*, 51 (16–25 Apr. 1644); *Perfect Occurrences*, 1 (9–16 Aug. 1644); ibid. 5 (6–13 Sept. 1644); *True Informer*, 44 (17–24 Aug. 1644).

[4] *Memoirs of Edmund Ludlow*, ed. C. H. Firth (Oxford, 1894), i. 97, 116.

December 1644, aided by some 'honest' officers, Sir William Brereton arrested the leaders of the Denbigh faction at Stafford, to frustrate any attempt by 'the ill-disposed to make a party'.[1]

The breach in parliamentarian unity reflected differences in men's priorities: between winning the war and preserving social distinctions. Even the Presbyterian Sir Samuel Luke, normally obsessed by the need for men of 'worth and honour' in authority, complained of the selfish localism of many of the gentry. If they remained in power there would be 'no living for an honest man' in his county.[2] That the division between 'honest' and compromising supporters of Parliament had social implications became steadily more apparent. In the December *coup* at Stafford, Brereton replaced Denbigh's governor, the well-connected Lewis Chadwick, with Captain Henry Stone, a Walsall merchant; most of Brereton's other 'honest' allies came either from mercantile backgrounds or from the middling and lower ranks of the gentry. Although in Cheshire Brereton could rely on middle-rank gentry like Thomas Croxton and Robert Duckenfield, there too his régime depended on the enthusiasm of lesser men.[3] Cromwell's preference for 'a plain russet-coated captain that knows what he fights for' over 'that which you call a gentleman and is nothing else' is well known: 'better plain men than none'. The conservative repudiation of this attitude is also familiar. The choice, Luke thought, was between 'beggars or unskilful men' and those who 'can with their credits sustain their companies three months from mutinies'. But in 1644 Willoughby already 'thought it a crime to be a nobleman'.[4]

By the end of the war men chosen for honesty rather than rank had come to the fore in the administration of many English counties. The process by which local oligarchies were displaced has often been described and need not detain us. In some

[1] *CSPD, 1644–5,* 173–4; *CSPD, 1649–50,* 444–7; *LJ* vi. 652–4. See also *The Committee at Stafford, 1643–1645,* ed. D. H. Pennington and I. A. Roots (Manchester, 1957), lxxiv–lxxxi; C. Holmes, 'Colonel King and Lincolnshire Politics, 1642–1646', *HJ* xvi (1973), 452, 456.
[2] *The Letter Books, 1644–45, of Sir Samuel Luke,* ed. H. G. Tibbutt (1963), 96.
[3] J. S. Morrill, *Cheshire 1630–1660: County Government and Society during the English Revolution* (Oxford, 1974), 79–89.
[4] Cromwell and Willoughby as quoted in Manning, *English People,* 259, 261; *Luke,* ed. Tibbutt, 274.

counties there were conservative reactions, as in Cheshire when Brereton relinquished his grip and allowed the community-minded Booths to recover their authority. But in most places the committees were becoming increasingly Westminster-oriented, less representative of the older governing families. Even the regional committee of the Eastern Association contained such men as Edward Clench, a newcomer to his county; Humphrey Walcott, of struggling lesser gentry family; Isaac Pullar, one of the new urban gentry; and Robert Vintner, a yeoman's son.[1]

But it would be a mistake to over-emphasize the weakness of the county committee radicals before the autumn of 1646. At that time, certainly, the oppressiveness derived from their being minority régimes convinced of their own rectitude became very obvious, and provoked many demands for their abolition. However, until the last royalist resistance was stamped out, the need to guard against a revival of the King's party was widely accepted. The authority of Westminster, an uncompromising attitude towards the King, and harsh measures against local royalists could still be justified. The war had swept many into adopting advanced religious views: 'godly reformation' might be the only alternative to surrender to the clique of papists surrounding the King. But once the war was over, older community attitudes resurfaced. Honest reformers became increasingly unpopular with the gentry.

It is dangerous to read too much into by-election returns, yet the change in their outcome after the summer of 1646 is surely significant. Pendennis, the last royalist stronghold in southern England, surrendered on 17 August; only a few Welsh castles still held out. Precisely at this time the tide in the recruiter elections, hitherto quite favourable to the radicals, turned dramatically. Out of twenty-eight members elected for English counties between September 1645 and the end of August 1646, sixteen were later to take recognizably radical stances.[2] But the

---

[1] Morrill, *Cheshire*, 183–6; Holmes, *Eastern Association*, 125. I have summarized the evidence for the general point in *Pride's Purge: Politics in the Puritan Revolution* (Oxford, 1971), 29–36.

[2] For this analysis I have used the date of the original election, disregarding delays caused by disputes. Welsh seats raise special problems and are omitted. Evidence of radicalism is that used to compile the table in *Pride's Purge*, appx. A. It includes flight to the Army in August 1647, and other signs of 'Independent' sympathies.

return of peace reawakened 'country' suspicions of men who stood for high taxes and centralization. Sir Richard Skeffington, elected in Staffordshire in August 1646, was the last county recruiter for whom honest radicals can have felt much enthusiasm.[1] Eight county members were elected between then and William Morice's return for Devon in August 1648; typical among them were such 'country' Presbyterians as Hugh Boscawen and Brereton's adversary George Booth. Not one was a radical.

Borough elections, based on highly varied franchises, are less reliable indicators of opinion. Yet they suggest the same pattern: fair success for the radicals down to August 1646, much less thereafter. Of 122 M.P.s returned for English boroughs in the first period, seventy-four (roughly 60 per cent) subsequently displayed radical tendencies. Only thirty-one (less than 40 per cent) of the seventy-nine returned between September 1646 and December 1648 fall into this category. Some of the radicals' success can be attributed to traditional electioneering methods: to patrons like Lord Wharton at Appleby, or the Fairfax interest in several Yorkshire boroughs. Some can be explained by intimidation—use of the militia or threats of sequestration— some by innovative election management, co-ordinated by Edmund Prideaux at least for West Country elections. But, in the light of the behaviour of the more populous county electorates, it seems that after the summer of 1646 honest radicals had less appeal for the gentry and freeholders.[2]

This changing electoral climate was accompanied by other signs of the radicals' declining strength. The withdrawal of the old families from county offices continued. Attacks on committee misgovernment, reflecting the alienation of influential localists, rose in volume during 1646. Yet in the great crisis of the following year, the struggle between Army and Parliament, honest radicals still made a respectable showing in many counties. The crisis produced, however, clear signs of the honest

[1] Morrill, *Cheshire*, 178; D. Brunton and D. H. Pennington, *Members of the Long Parliament* (1954), 192-4.

[2] D. Underdown, 'Party Management in the Recruiter Elections, 1645-1648', *EHR* lxxxiii (1968), 235-64. The Army later accused the Presbyterians of using the Committee of Privileges to exclude 'honest men' in disputed returns; *The Humble Answer of the General Council of Officers* (1649), 5. On popular participation in elections see D. Hirst, *The Representative of the People?* (Cambridge, 1975).

party's internal division: a divergence between the 'Independent' gentry and a by now Leveller-inclined element of the rank and file.

On both sides of the Army–Parliament conflict, the mobilizing of local support followed the Presbyterian London petition of December 1646. This was the signal for a general campaign for disbanding the Army and excluding from office all who had not taken the Covenant. Whitelocke soon noted 'endeavours . . . in countries to get hands to petitions' to support the City's initiative.[1] Where radicals had the power to do so they reacted swiftly: the Kent Committee, for example, prohibited the circulation of a petition of this kind. Radicals also promoted counterpetitions. In March a printed one was being distributed in Wiltshire, which Holles's friends there believed was 'on foot in many other parts of the kingdom' and ought to be suppressed.[2]

A printed petition: we confront the suspicion that the radical petitions of 1647 were 'parrot-petitions' foisted on the counties in defiance of local opinion. The practice was often employed in the 1640s, not only by radicals. In March 1647 the Presbyterian Essex petition was said to have been printed in London and sent down wholesale for the ministers to gather signatures. Conservatives denounced the stream of 'forged petitions' generated by the radicals in the summer: 'framed in the Army and sent abroad by the Agitators . . . to a few inconsiderable sectaries'.[3] There certainly was co-ordination, but this does not necessarily prove that a particular petition had no local support. Co-ordination is discussed in a letter of early February 1647, in which a group of Hertford men (including the radical preacher Christopher Feake) explained why they could not support the petition that their neighbour Col. Alban Cox was promoting. They had recently been to London to consult 'some principal agents in such affairs' in Parliament and the City. These people (who pursued 'one and the same interest with ours') felt

[1] Whitelocke, ii. 102. The London petition is in *The Parliamentary or Constitutional History of England* (2nd edn., 1761–3), xv. 221–35. Supporting petitions included those from Suffolk and Essex; *LJ* ix. 19, 72.

[2] *Moderate Intelligencer*, 97 (7–14 Jan. 1646/7); Thistlethwaite *et al.* to Holles, 27 Mar. 1647: Bodl., Tanner MS. 58, fol. 14.

[3] *Mercurius Rusticus* (12 Nov. 1647), 6; *A New Found Stratagem* (1647); Rushworth, vi. 448, 451; *LJ* ix. 277. On 'parrot-petitions' see Everitt, *Community of Kent*, 86–7, 107; Morrill, *Cheshire*, 46, 53.

that the current Presbyterian campaign would be counter-productive and that 'their friends in the country ought to sit still and await God's providence'.[1] So co-ordination of tactics could follow mutual discussion. A rudimentary kind of party unity was emerging.

Feake's friends soon changed their line, and a major campaign to support the Army was organized in the eastern counties. The petitions were of two kinds, illustrating the honest party's growing dualism: proto-Leveller petitions from the rank and file; more moderate (but still pro-Army) ones from 'establishment' radicals. The first Leveller one came from Buckinghamshire and Hertfordshire early in March; the commissioners who presented it to Parliament were instructed to seek the release of the imprisoned Lilburne and Overton. Petitions to Fairfax in June from the same counties and from Essex, Norfolk, and Suffolk, were of a similar character. Essex complained of being 'vassalaged and enslaved in the Norman laws', while Hertfordshire asked for action on earlier petitions against tithes and for relief of copyholders from arbitrary fines. Petitions of the other type, such as those reaching the Commons in July from Essex, Norfolk, and Suffolk, avoided revolutionary rhetoric and were presented with decent respect for parliamentary procedure.[2]

Signs of friction between the two groups can be found in the diary of Ralph Josselin, minister at Earl's Colne, Essex. In June Josselin helped draft a petition that had 'special respect to our safety and the content of the army', but was also designed to undermine 'divers heady petitions that went up and down the country tending to disturbance'. On 1 July a gentry delegation took the petition to London, after conferring at the house of the eminent Independent divine, John Owen, at Coggeshall.[3] Responsible clerics, respectable gentry, and M.P.s: this element of the honest party was well rooted in Essex society. Yet it is impossible to assess the relative support for the two kinds of petition. The 'Leveller' petitions sound realistic in claiming between 1,000 and 1,400 signatures, but these figures are little

---

[1] Feake et al. to Cox, 2 Feb. 1646/7: Herts. RO, Halsey MSS. 70556.

[2] The Humble Petition of the Inhabitants of Buckinghamshire, and Hartfordshire (1647); Rushworth, vi. 520, 559, 573, 576, 600–2; LJ ix. 260, 263, 277–8; CJ v. 231.

[3] Diary of the Rev. Ralph Josselin, 1616–1683, ed. E. Hockliffe (Camden, 3rd ser., 1908), 43.

more helpful than the conventional claims to 'many thousands' in some of the others. There is, however, independent evidence that the 'Leveller' petitioners were not the propertyless outsiders some of their critics supposed. The Earl of Nottingham reported that the Norfolk and Suffolk document was brought to Fairfax by about a hundred 'ministers and others', who arrived on horseback.[1]

Honest radicals relied heavily on Army support. Most of their petitions came from areas where the Army was quartered, an easy opening for their critics. The soldiers were active propagandists, using the press, distributing pamphlets, and drafting circular letters to civilian allies. People in Suffolk, an observer thought, were so 'apt to listen to the discontented speeches of the soldiers' that they seemed ready to rise against Parliament. The June petitions were encouraged, perhaps initiated, by soldiers. At the end of May the Agitators were urged to 'stir up the counties to petition', and a few days later it was reported from the Army: 'All the honest people in the City and Country send to us, . . . you will shortly hear of several counties petitioning the Parliament that the Army may not be disbanded.'[2]

Like Feake's London friends, though, the soldiers were responding to, as well as stimulating, currents of local opinion. Most of the June petitions dealt solely with national issues. The one from Hertfordshire, however, refers to a local matter— three of Alban Cox's soldiers victimized by a 'malignant' J.P.— in a way that suggests local authorship. The Army had plenty of sympathizers outside the south-east, as Sir Henry Cholmley noted in Yorkshire, and they sometimes petitioned even without the New Model nearby to inspire them. A radical petition from Devon (provoked by an earlier Presbyterian one at the assizes) denounced the magistrates for oppressing godly men, and complained of the recent 'undue election of burgesses' in Cornwall. The Devon men quaintly professed to regard the issues between Parliament and Army as 'these out-side controversies in the land'. In the remoter counties even radicals were still confined by community attitudes.[3]

[1] *LJ* ix. 260.

[2] *HMC, Portland*, iii. 156; *The Clarke Papers*, ed. C. H. Firth, i (Camden, new ser., 1891), 101, 112, 130–2, 138; *LJ* ix. 152, 156.

[3] *Memorials of the Great Civil War, 1642–52*, ed. H. Cary (1842), i. 293; *LJ* ix. 171–2, 278; Rushworth, vii. [742]–3.

But the Army was the vital link, when there was one, between local groups at the popular level. There was talk of institutionalizing the connection. During the summer of 1647 a draft letter to 'several counties' stressed the need for better 'communion of council'. Places which had petitioned Fairfax should elect 'agitators in the behalf of the well-affected' to discuss policy with the Army Council and ensure that decisions were 'communicated to the counties'. This proposal may perhaps explain the presence of Wildman and other civilians at Putney in October: Wildman might have represented the honest party of Berkshire.[1] His constituency, in any case, was the typical Leveller one of small peasants and craftsmen. The geographical distribution of the petitions confirms that, except in the southeast, people of this kind had not yet developed any organization, outside the burgeoning Baptist congregations. Bristol is in fact the only place remote from London from which genuinely Leveller petitions have survived from 1647.[2]

As for the 'establishment' segment of the party, the petitions suggest that its local strength was variable. We have seen that in Essex it represented a respectable minority of the gentry and clergy. Buckinghamshire was run by Thomas Scot's radical friends, yet the pro-Army petition from there was not an official one subscribed by committee-men and J.P.s. When one of the many petitions from the county against tithes reached the Commons in September, it was presented by Major Thomas Shelburne; a militia officer, to be sure, but not a man of real prominence. The radicalism of the Buckingham authorities should not be exaggerated. In only two counties—Kent and Hertfordshire—were honest radicals sufficiently in control to call out their militia forces to support the Army in August.[3] The nature of the Kent oligarchy is well known, and Hertfordshire

---

[1] HMC, Portland, i. 432. Note Wildman's statement at Putney about a meeting attended by 'country-gentlemen'; Clarke Papers, ed. Firth, i. 240. Possibly 'Bedfordshire man' was another such representative. Wildman's Berkshire connections are shown by M. Ashley, John Wildman (1947), 9, 17–18, 22. The association with Marten obviously predated his marriage to Marten's niece; HMC xiii, pt. iv (Loder-Symonds MSS.), 387, 391.

[2] Rushworth, vii. 798–9; CJ v. 289; Two Petitions of divers Free-men of Bristol (1647).

[3] Perfect Weekly Account, 36 (8–15 Sept. 1647); Whitelocke, ii. 190, 194; CJ v. 271; LJ ix. 383–4. There is no record in VCH, Bucks. of Shelburne's having owned land. For Luke's view of him see Luke, ed. Tibbutt, 291.

also seems to have had a strong radical element on its committee. It may be significant that there was no 'establishment' petition from there in July: the June petition to Fairfax may have satisfied both groups.

During the winter of 1647–8 the incipient split within the honest party became clearer. Frustrated in the Army after Putney, the Levellers set about organizing nationally. A campaign to promote the *Agreement of the People* was soon under way, directed from the Saracen's Head in Friday Street, London. There were reports of the *Agreement* being circulated in Nottinghamshire, complaints of itinerant Baptists evangelizing in Rutland. One of them was Samuel Oates, father of the notorious Titus, who was alleged to be 'drawing a concourse of people after him' and trying to stir up a 'general mutiny' on behalf of the *Agreement*.[1] Meanwhile a new petition was promoted by ward committees in London. Lilburne wanted to have men elected in every town to carry on the petition, after which there would be a mass demonstration outside the House of Commons. Most of this was paper planning. However, there were Leveller cells in several Kent towns. Lilburne visited the group at Dartford, and was also reported on the other side of London, at Watford, stirring up people to subscribe the *Agreement*.[2]

The Levellers made little headway. Outside the London region their civilian supporters were too few and scattered. Their ambitious proposals had less appeal than conservative pleas for lower taxes and an end to free quarter. Rural petitions during these months, like the one from 'divers freeholders, farmers, and labourers' of the Windsor area, presented to Fairfax on 22 November, concentrate on such grievances and contain none of the radical language of the previous summer.[3] The Levellers' popular weakness was compounded by their lack of allies in the local power structures. In Berkshire they may have been encouraged by Henry Marten, and Lilburne

[1] *LJ* ix. 529, 571–3.

[2] *A Declaration of Some Proceedings of Lt. Col. John Lilburne* (1648) in *The Leveller Tracts*, ed. W. Haller and G. Davies (N.Y., 1944), 98–104; *LJ* ix. 663. See also H. N. Brailsford, *The Levellers and the English Revolution* (1961), 313–14, 325–6.

[3] *LJ* ix. 564–5.

had some hopes from Weldon and Blount in Kent, but as usual he was over-optimistic.

This does not mean that radical sentiment among the rural 'middle sort' did not exist. In February and March 1648 the 'Independent' agitation to endorse the Vote of No Addresses aroused the same support from a minority of the rural population as the Army had obtained in the previous summer. This time the radicals tried to secure 'official' grand jury petitions, which in theory expressed the sense of 'the Country'. There were the usual complaints of petitions being artificially promoted from London, of circuit judges extracting presentments from packed grand juries. In Somerset at least the charge of packing was well founded. However, while a jury of selected honest radicals may not have been representative of the county, there was still a significant number of such men to choose from. But careful precautions must have been taken to ensure that earlier resistance to the petition in the county was not repeated at the assizes. Not all county bosses were as careful. When Sir Henry Holford presented an Essex petition to an allegedly packed jury at Romford—'a whole conclave of new-model'd justices, and dirty committee-men', Nedham depicts them—it was enthusiastically approved. But a vehement speech by Carew Mildmay (one of the promoters of the Presbyterian petition of 1647) swung the freeholders against it. Buckinghamshire was another county with no grand jury petition; the best Thomas Scot could do was one that was presented to the Commons by a committee-man.[1]

The No Addresses campaign backfired. Within a few weeks the southern counties began to smoulder with the localist flame which burst forth as the second civil war. Honest radicals were soon desperately resisting conservative petitions: Ralph Josselin encountered a 'very dangerous' one at Earl's Colne in April. In the summer's violence the Weldon machine in Kent, Holcroft's group in Essex, Morley's in Sussex, even the moderate Onslow régime in Surrey, were all seriously threatened. The second civil war was the Army's victory over the local communities. But the Army was not alone in its fight. In many places

[1] For the whole campaign see Underdown, *Pride's Purge*, 93-4. For Essex, *Mercurius Pragmaticus*, 25 (29 Feb.-7 Mar. 1647/8). For Carew Mildmay in 1647, *LJ* ix. 71.

honest radicals flocked to join new militia forces. These were usually under the control of county committees, but some New Model commanders also promoted local associations to support the Army. At Earl's Colne the villagers stoutly resisted a royalist attack: 'no part of Essex gave them so much opposition', Josselin boasts.[1] Once again men were being radicalized by events. Henry Marten shed his last inhibitions and raised volunteers in Berkshire under the banner 'For the People's Freedom against all Tyrants whatsoever'. His regiment later attracted volunteers from Wiltshire, Kent, and possibly other counties. Its progress through the Midlands during the late summer was a visible reminder that scattered radicals were formidable when united.[2]

The passions of 1648 were sustained through the autumn. To frustrate the threatened restoration of monarchy a new petitioning campaign was launched. In it the honest party's earlier division was less apparent: the urgency of the crisis demanded common action. While the Leveller leaders argued with the officers at headquarters, there were few distinctly Leveller petitions except from London and the Army. The point is that 'establishment' petitions effectively dealt with the only crucial issues: the Treaty of Newport and the future of Charles I. The November petitions supporting the Army Remonstrance came mostly from the regiments, though one from Sir Hardress Waller's brigade also claimed local backing in Devon and Cornwall. There were a few civilian petitions, for example from Bristol, Berkshire, and (with some military influence) from the town of Rye.[3]

Petitions for the trial of Charles I elicited less popular support and were well subscribed only in counties already under radical control. The Baptist Thomas Collier was alleged to have composed the Somerset one; it had John Pyne's backing but not, apparently, that of other establishment radicals in Somerset.[4]

---

[1] *Josselin*, ed. Hockcliffe, 48, 50; Clement Walker, *The History of Independency* (1661), i. 106.

[2] Army Council order, 16 Feb. 1649; Worcester Coll., Oxford, Clarke MS. 72. See also Brailsford, *Levellers*, 342–3.

[3] *The Moderate*, 21 (28 Nov.–5 Dec. 1648); ibid. 23 (12–19 Dec. 1648); *A True Copie of the Berkshire Petition* (1648); C. Thomas-Stanford, *Sussex in the Great Civil War* (1910), 214–16. See also Underdown, *Pride's Purge*, 110, 131–2.

[4] D. Underdown, *Somerset in the Civil War and Interregnum* (Newton Abbot, 1973), 153–4.

The Kent petition is the only one whose signatures have survived; there are doubts about the authenticity of many of them. Still, the petition provides some clues to the nature of the honest party in Kent. One striking feature is the almost total absence of the radical leadership: William Kenwricke appears to be the only major figure who signed. Weldon's successor Sir Michael Livesey was a regicide, to be sure, as were two other Kent M.P.s, Garland and Dixwell. Thomas Blount was named to the Court but did not attend the trial, and did not sign the petition either. Such petitioners as are easily identifiable came mainly from the towns or the clothing villages. Many people signed at Canterbury and Hythe, and among those who did so at Sandwich were a minister, a collector of customs, the town serjeant, and four jurats. Several representatives of the gathered churches who in May 1653 recommended names for the Barebones Parliament can be identified with reasonable certainty among the petitioners, mostly men from Cranbrook and other Wealden villages.[1]

Whatever we may think of the Kent petition, there can be no doubting the enthusiasm of members of sectarian congregations, of scattered republicans, of honest radicals in general, during the revolution of 1648-9. The widespread millenarian expectancy, the excited gatherings of the well-affected, the relief that the Army had acted, and the belief that it alone could force Parliament to redress popular grievances: all are evident in the newsbooks and correspondence of the time. Leveller leaders might be disillusioned, but in the countryside honest radicals took practical steps to forestall possible counter-revolution. In the western counties such men formed a new association, came together in arms, and vowed to live and die with Army and Parliament. As always, close contact was maintained with the Army. Potential opponents were disarmed, the Presbyterian Militia Ordinance reversed, and local forces restored to radical control. In the process several county régimes hitherto hostile to the radicals were overthrown, most spectacularly in Herefordshire, where the powerful Harley ascendancy was destroyed. There were frequent demands for the revolution to be carried

<hr/>

[1] Two copies of the Kent petition exist, in Bodl., Rawlinson MS. A 298, and Tanner MS. 57, fols. 476-87. For the 1653 letter, see *Original Letters and Papers of State, Addressed to Oliver Cromwell*, ed. John Nickolls (1743), 96-7.

further by having J.P.s and other local officials elected by the well-affected.[1]

The impression of united action by honest radicals in these events is of course misleading. Scarcely was the first stage of revolution over than men of property recoiled in horror from the hornets' nest they had opened. But although in the spring of 1649 Diggers and 'true Levellers' were vocal in the Army, the Home Counties, and the south Midlands, outside these areas the leadership had little to fear. The revolutionary handful in Parliament was isolated as moderate M.P.s drifted back into the Rump. Even before the Army Levellers were smashed at Burford, establishment radicals were making their intentions clear. The Leicestershire Committee, for example, protested to the Army against the toleration proposed by the third *Agreement of the People*. 'Natural liberty', they argued, could never justify repealing the blasphemy laws or divesting magistrates of powers over religion. A few voices justified the Commonwealth on grounds of popular sovereignty, as Robert Bennet did at Truro Sessions in April, but most Rump propagandists relied on the pragmatic argument of obedience to *de facto* power: any government was better than none.[2]

Ralph Josselin saw the Levellers' defeat as 'a glorious rich providence of God'. The absence of upheaval in the counties during the crisis shows how few of the honest party were committed Levellers. In Somerset, where thousands had demonstrated for the revolution in January, only a few score were willing to defy Pyne's authority in May.[3] Yet even if few were Levellers, there were many whose outlook was tinged with Leveller ideas, and for whom the Commonwealth's pragmatism was a grievous disappointment. So militant activists retreated into cynicism, or transferred their revolutionary enthusiasm from the national cause of the honest party to the fragmented causes of the sects. In this sense, the exciting proliferation of radical ideas after 1649 was the final symptom of defeat.

There were still honest radicals after 1649, but the ties which

---

[1] I have described this in more detail in *Pride's Purge*, 179–81. The Army's role in communication with local radicals is evident in the fact that it was Rushworth who provided Pyne with the inside story of the Purge.

[2] *The Humble Representation of . . . the County of Leicester* [Feb. 1649?]; Worcester Coll., Clarke MS. 181; Robert Bennet, *King Charles Trial Justified* (1649).

[3] *Josselin*, ed. Hockcliffe, 65; Underdown, *Somerset*, 157.

had bound them to their leaders were gone. Those leaders might posture as honest Commonwealthmen, but republican rhetoric could not disguise the fact that only the leaders' objectives had been attained. For the rest, the Commonwealth was the best government they had, so few were tempted into open opposition; most continued to run their communities, often in highly constructive ways. Some grasped opportunities of advancement through local office, or of enrichment by purchase of confiscated lands. A typical case in which political zeal had a strong tincture of careerism is that of Miles Hill, one of the second-echelon radicals in Herefordshire. A Leominster mercer, ruined by the depressed economy of 1642, he found employment under the Harleys and rose to be county treasurer. In 1646 he made the mistake of backing Col. John Birch's challenge to the Harleys and was dismissed, but returned to office three years later in the wake of the revolution. There are some signs that Hill may have had radical Puritan sympathies, but his career is also marked by some devious twists which bear the stamp of self-interest.[1]

We should not make too much of the careerists. More typical of the honest radicals were zealous Puritans like William Barret, the Cheshire sequestrator who was a lay preacher and elder of Samuel Eaton's congregation; or his namesake David, the Wells shoemaker who became marshal to the County Committee and founder of a Baptist congregation. We know all too little about such men, but enough to suspect that it was from the rank and file of the honest party that the radical sects of the 1650s drew many of their converts. Men like the Cumberland sequestrator John Head and the Berkshire commissioner Thomas Curtis (who had been appointed on Henry Marten's recommendation) are two examples among many possible ones of minor parliamentarian officials who were in trouble for their beliefs later in the decade.[2]

The honest party became a head without a body. But until 1649 it had adherents at all levels of English society, from the

[1] J. Tombes to Sir R. Harley, 20 June 1642: BL, Welbeck MS. 29/121; G. E. Aylmer, 'Who was ruling in Herefordshire from 1645 to 1661?', *Woolhope Naturalists' Field Club Trans.* xl (1972), 373–87.

[2] Morrill, *Cheshire*, 207, 266; Underdown, *Somerset*, 126, 172–3, 186; Joseph Besse, *Abstract of the Sufferings of the People call'd Quakers* (1733), 8, 48; *Cal. Comp.* 232, 524.

Weldons and Pynes at the top to the (to us) faceless many who signed petitions and volunteered in local associations. In the south-east many such men tended to Leveller behaviour, but only in the south-east. Rather than sweeping social reconstruction, most wanted 'godly reformation' completed and a more representative political system established. They were guided and directed not only by the county bosses, but also by the large number of lesser men—the Hills and the Barrets—who occupied the middle and lower rungs of local government. Though they often had Leveller support, they were not Levellers. They were the revolutionary party of 1648–9.

Puritans and Poor Relief
The London Workhouse, 1649–1660

VALERIE PEARL

UNTIL recent years, our views of poor relief in the sixteenth and seventeenth centuries and of attitudes to the poor were formed by the writings of five eminent modern social historians. Their interpretations were influenced in different ways and degrees by the times in which they wrote. Indeed, upon their work a wider criticism of society was sometimes mounted. Miss E. M. Leonard in *The Early History of English Poor Relief* in 1900 described the institutional history of the poor down to 1660, drawing mainly on the records of the Privy Council, of Parliament and occasionally of Quarter Sessions but thinly on parochial sources. The old Privy Council ceased to be effective after 1642 and Parliament rarely concerned itself with the poor. The dearth of formal evidence during the heyday of the Puritan Revolution led her to believe that these latter years saw the virtual collapse of the Elizabethan poor law. Her work, impressively documented for earlier periods, had a profound influence on the four historians who followed her.

In *Religion and the Rise of Capitalism*, R. H. Tawney in 1926 produced a justly famous account, sensitive and percipient, of those attitudes to the poor which had inspired the institutions. He described the ambiguities in Puritan thought in which the intellectual debris of medieval society, collective and near-communitarian ideas, and notions of individualism mingled to inspire measures of social reform whose purpose was to exercise discipline, tempered by humanitarianism, over the labouring poor. This section of his work was less commented upon by his successors than the apocalyptic account with which he followed it of the years from 1640. Influenced by Miss Leonard and by his own focus on nascent capitalism, Tawney saw the Puritan Revolution as a time of repression and collapse and of the triumph of bleak *laissez-faire* views. 'Charity and relief', he wrote, 'fell on evil days'; the redoubled emphasis on punishing vagrants was 'the new medicine for poverty'. A year later in 1927, Sidney and Beatrice Webb, active social reformers and advocates of state and municipal direction themselves, provided a fuller narrative in their *English Poor Law, History: Part 1. The Old Poor Law*. They described the fourteenth and fifteenth centuries as a time of repression followed by a more humane and reforming attitude on the part of government as revealed in the legislation enacted from the 1530s. They, too, saw a change in 1640 although they characterized it as a change from centralized direction to decentralization. Cautiously admitting that too little work had been done for a full assessment of the mid and late seventeenth century, and convinced of the *a priori* virtues of strong central government, the Webbs branded the period from 1640 as a 'relapse into anarchy' or, more temperately, as inactive.[1] This cautious note was rejected by Margaret James in 1930. Her *Social Problems and Policy during the Puritan Revolution, 1640–1660* presents the period as a time of repression, relieved occasionally by faint attempts at reform but giving way ultimately to an even greater reliance on the vagrancy laws and to a shift from humane work schemes to heartless inefficiency. 'The general impression which the Poor Law policy of the Interregnum leaves', she concluded, 'is that of harshness coupled with failure.'[2]

More recently, some of these views have been sharply criticized. It has been suggested that the institutional framework of the Poor Law did not collapse in 1640: indeed that J.P.s were just as vigilant and that parishes were raising as much money and as regularly after that date as before.[3] My research on London parishes shows that compulsory monthly collections for the London hospitals had taken place from the 1560s, and for the parish poor, irregularly at first, from the 1570s.[4] The sums raised by these and other activities challenge

---

[1] S. and B. Webb, *English Local Government: English Poor Law History: Part 1. The Old Poor Law* (1927), 95–101.

[2] M. James, *Social Problems and Policy during the Puritan Revolution, 1640–1660* (1930), 301.

[3] E. M. Hampson, *The Treatment of Poverty in Cambridgeshire, 1597–1834* (Cambridge, 1934), 44. See also below, p. 208 n. 4.

[4] Here and in the early part of this article, I draw on material from the City of

one of W. K. Jordan's main conclusions, drawn from a study of ten English counties, that between 1540 and 1660 something like 93 per cent of poor relief derived from charity and 7 per cent from doles.[1] Recent research has shown that in one London parish more than half of the sums raised came from the rates.[2] This finding is confirmed by my study of two other middling-to-rich parishes where the endowments were unusually large,[3] and future work will, I believe, show that this was the pre-dominant pattern in mid-seventeenth-century London. But Jordan's work, so valuable in certain respects, has also reminded us that the charitable impulse, far from declining as Tawney believed, was encouraged and remained effective even in the troubled years after 1640.[4] It is wrong to conclude that opposi-tion to indiscriminate almsgiving implied a negative attitude to charity. The view taken by many authorities as expressed in legislation, in sermons, and in exhortations by parochial officials was that alms must be centralized and controlled so as to direct aid where it was most needed: to the impotent,

London's archives in the Guildhall Library and the Corporation RO, including Vestry Minute Books, Churchwardens' Accounts, Journals of Common Council, Repertories of the Aldermanic Bench, and the Records of Christ's Hospital. Only brief citations are given for reasons of space, but I am writing a fuller account for later publication.

[1] W. K. Jordan, *Philanthropy in England, 1480–1660. A Study of the Changing Pattern of English Social Aspirations* (1959), 140. Jordan estimated that his figure would probably be true for the whole of England.

[2] St. Antholin's Budge Row; R. W. Herlan, 'Poor Relief during the Great Civil War and Interregnum, 1642–1660' (Ph.D. thesis, State Univ. New York, Buffalo, 1973), ch. iv, *passim*.

[3] E. Freshfield's edns. of *The Vestry Minute Book of the Parish of St. Margaret Lothbury in the City of London, 1571–1677* (1887); *The Account Books of the Parish of St. Bartholomew Exchange in the City of London, 1596–1698* (1895); and *The Vestry Minute Books of the Parish of St. Bartholomew Exchange in the City of London, 1567–1676* (1890), *passim*.

[4] *Philanthrophy in England, passim*. See also his *The Charities of London, 1480–1660* (1960); 'The Forming of the Charitable Institutions of the West of England: A Study of the Changing Pattern of Social Aspirations in Bristol and Somerset, 1480–1660', *Trans. Amer. Phil. Soc.* new ser., l (1960); 'Social Institutions in Kent, 1480–1660: A Study of the Changing Patterns of Social Aspirations', *Archaeologia Cantiana*, lxxv (1961); *The Social Institutions of Lancashire: A Study of the Changing Patterns of Aspirations in Lancashire, 1480–1660* (Chetham Soc., 1962); M. Coate, *Cornwall in the Great Civil War and Interregnum, 1642–1660* (Oxford, 1933), 328; J. S. Morrill, *Cheshire 1630–1660: County Government and Society during the English Revolution* (Oxford, 1974), 247–52; A. L. Beier, 'Poor Relief in Warwickshire 1630–60', *P. and P.* 35 (1966).

to children, and to the aged, and away from able-bodied vagrants, who by law were classified as criminal.

The imposition of work discipline has been a central theme of systems of poor relief, at least until the Beveridge Report indicated that the two were not indissolubly linked. Christopher Hill in a brilliant essay has suggested that aid to the poor came to be associated with, and subordinated to, the inculcation of the new attitudes to work and that this notion pervaded the formal system of pauper apprenticeship and schemes for providing employment.[1] The desire to impose discipline is also seen in other ways. Superficially, parish doles ('pensions') in London provided a system of social security not basically dissimilar from that which is in operation today. However, the dole, often supplemented by parish housing, grants of bread, cheese, clothes, and fuel, and by education for pauper children provided a modest, means-tested subsistence provision which was given not of right like today's payments but out of the statutory obligation of the parish to provide for the indigent. It is sometimes assumed that in London only freemen were eligible to receive alms. My continuing studies on parish records suggest that 'housekeepers' (equivalent to today's householders) and also tenants born in a parish or living there for three years were regarded as eligible; 'inmates' (unauthorized tenants and lodgers) were not so regarded. Partly because there was no declared level of entitlement (aid was discretionary), and partly because of the nature of the evidence, it is difficult to discover how many of the indigent poor were supported in this way or how much was received, in total, by each almsman. Moreover, the amount of alms provided depended to some extent on the wealth and endowments of the parish. In London the system was modified by a rate-in-aid (or equalization) scheme operated in the seventeenth century with a degree of regularity and efficiency unusual for the time. Even parish doles, however, could help to make the poor more tractable: alms were often given on terms which explicitly enjoined behaviour in strict conformity to the *mores* of the ratepayers. Conventional sentiment laid down a strict code which could be brutally indifferent to the wayward or to their offspring. City hospitals and the parochial overseers were disinclined, for instance, to help

[1] C. Hill, *Puritanism and Revolution* (1958), 215–38.

children born out of wedlock or to aid pensioners who committed adultery, a bar extended at times to those who married
without permission. But such were the long-accepted conditions
of relief. There is no evidence that they were challenged by
any body of opinion at this time.

If provision for the poor in London and the philosophy
which moved such ends during the Puritan Revolution were
not much different from what they had been before, there was
one group of activities which marked an important advance:
the conceiving and execution of schemes for employing the poor
and educating and training orphans and poor children. There
had been earlier plans enjoining the provision of stocks and
work, from the Orders for the Poor drawn up by Common
Council in 1579 to the Proclamation of 1629. But not since the
creation of the London hospitals in the 1550s had they led to
such an ambitious scheme as that projected in the 1640s. The
vagrancy laws (not to be identified with the poor laws as they
sometimes are) continued to prescribe punishment for tramps
and beggars and by one legal clarification in 1657 they were
probably strengthened.[1] No doubt also, as J. P. Cooper has
remarked, there must at any time have been greater enthusiasm
on the part of the authorities for harassing vagrants than for
more constructive efforts.[2] The emphasis on work schemes,
however, was undoubtedly greater than it had been, a concern
reflected also in Professor Jordan's evidence that such proposals
attracted more charitable requests from the 1630s than in any
earlier period.[3] The present article focuses primarily on the
most important of these work schemes: the establishment and
operation of the Corporation of the Poor in 1649. Important
as a forerunner of the workhouse movement in the late seventeenth century and subsequently, of great intrinsic interest itself
and in its socio-economic implications, the subject has been
neglected and misunderstood.

Professor Tawney described the Corporation of the Poor as
a 'Company with power to apprehend vagrants, to offer them
the choice between work and whipping, and to set to compul-

[1] Firth & Rait, ii. 1098.
[2] J. P. Cooper, 'Social and Economic Policies under the Commonwealth', in
The Interregnum, ed. G. E. Aylmer (1972), 128.
[3] Jordan, *Charities of London*, 177 et seq.

sory labour all other poor persons, including children without means of maintenance'.[1] The Webbs recognized the importance of the foundation while regretting that so little was known about its history. Margaret James in her pioneering study discovered the rare pamphlet whose author, Rice Bush, had helped to promote the undertaking. Unfortunately, she did not find the further evidence which would have filled out her picture. She did not examine the project in the context of the London hospitals system and the parochial relief of the time. Above all, she missed evidence on the way the scheme worked as described in a hitherto unrecorded broadside published by the Corporation which is discussed below and she was apparently unaware of the link between the Corporation and the plans of Samuel Hartlib and his friends for the educational and vocational training of the poor.

There exists no study of the hospital system, or indeed of poor relief, in sixteenth- and seventeenth-century London. Yet without a brief account of the first, the purpose and function of the Corporation of the Poor cannot be understood. Since the refounding of the monastic hospitals under Edward VI, the City had enjoyed a roughly co-ordinated system of poor relief. The population of the hospitals is a very complex matter. Enumeration depends on the definitions of long-term, casual, and in- and out-patients. A rough measure of population between 1640 and 1660 shows that the city provided annually for over 2,000 sick and aged persons at St. Thomas's and St. Bartholomew's, for between 450 and 900 orphans at Christ's, and for about 1,000 vagrants and other offenders, as well as around 200 apprentices, at Bridewell. Bethlehem (or Bedlam), its twin foundation, housed about thirty lunatics.[2] In addition to the help provided by these municipally established and run charitable foundations (which received large private endowments), even greater numbers were aided by outdoor parish relief and by livery company housing and doles.

[1] R. H. Tawney, *Religion and the Rise of Capitalism* (Harmondsworth, 1938), 263.

[2] A. L. Beier, 'Vagrants and the Social Order in Elizabethan England', *P. and P.* 71 (1976), 130–4; E. G. O'Donoghue, *Bridewell Hospital, Palace, Prison, Schools* (1923–9), *passim*; E. H. Pearce, *Annals of Christ's Hospital* (1901), *passim*; James, *Social Problems*, 246–7. These are very rough figures derived from the Court Books and from histories of the hospitals, and are given to suggest a general impression. See also below, p. 212 n. 3.

The refounding of the hospitals took place at a time when idealistic and humanitarian ideas were fermenting in men's minds. Harking back to an older tradition, they owed much to the new humanism and to a similar Protestant concern. Two documents attest to the strength of this spirit: the ordinance establishing the hospitals and the memorial which John Howes wrote about their early history.[1] But good intentions are not enough to run charitable institutions. The pressures which the growth of the city, the increase in the numbers of poor, and the intractable nature of the problem combined to exert on the new foundations is shown in the early history of Bridewell. Established for the punishment of vagrants, idlers, and the disorderly, and for training them and a few more innocent poor in 'honest labour and work', it became the model for all later houses of correction. Yet its earliest name, House of Occupations,[2] as well as the provisions in the indenture of the covenant between Edward VI and the City show that the founders also had it in mind to instruct and habituate certain 'institutionalized' men and women in regular patterns of work. Bridewell Hospital retained until the late eighteenth century workshops for young apprentices drawn both from its own inmates and from the city hospitals in which training was given in different trades. At times the effort was considerable. During the Interregnum years, for instance, the number being trained in this way might reach two hundred in a year and it was rarely less than one hundred.[3] But its chief function remained penal: a common gaol with its barbaric accompaniments of public whipping, boring through the ears, branding, carting through the streets, working the treadmill, and forced labour generally.

Christ's Hospital, according to its first set of ordinances, was founded for orphans over four years of age, of sound limb, born in London of lawfully wedded parents. Its exclusivity was

[1] John Howes, 'A ffamiliar & frendely discourse' (1582) and 'A [second] . . . discourse' (1587). Both were first printed in *Contemporaneous Account . . . of the Foundation* (Christ's Hospital, 1889).

[2] O'Donoghue, *Bridewell*, i, ch. xviii.

[3] A series of reports gave a yearly account of the hospitals. See *A true Report . . . 1644*, BL, 669 f 10 (2); *1645*, BL, 669 f 10 (26); *1647*, BL, 669 f 11 (5); *1649*, BL, 669 f 14 (11); *1650*, BL, 669 f 15 (27); *1653*, BL, 669 f 16 (94); *1655*, BL, 669 f 19 (71); Thomas Bowen, *Extracts from the Records and Court Books of Bridewell Hospital* (1798), 29–33.

qualified by the provision that no child was to be turned away if its life would thereby be endangered.[1] A generous admissions policy was adopted, lasting until at least the end of the sixteenth century, when it was gradually eroded.[2] Foundlings, including babies of a few days old and, exceptionally, infants from outside the city, were nurtured, but pressure on resources imposed a stricter adherence to a policy of selectivity.[3] Despite the relatively small numbers involved, the system of co-ordination between the four foundations was impressive. The intention to set up an integrated service is seen by the election of the Governors and Assistants of all four on the same day in Christ's Hospital. It is evident also in their long-continued meeting together to decide which hospital was best suited for those who came before them, occasionally transferring an inmate from one institution to another.[4]

In these early days, finance was the most critical matter faced by the London hospitals. Originally, they had been provided for mainly by the grant of the lands of the dissolved Savoy Hospital together with the income from charitable endowments, monthly collections in the parishes, and occasional levies on the livery companies. These funds were insufficient to meet rising costs caused by inflation and population growth. Difficulties were exacerbated by the Poor Law Act of 1598 which placed the chief responsibility for rating for the parish poor on the Overseers.[5] Such parochial officers, their authority strengthened by legislation, were more and more unwilling to expend funds beyond their own boundaries. Christ's Hospital felt the change most acutely as it witnessed the decline in the moneys raised by parish collections. Protests from the Governors to the Lord Mayor and Aldermen brought no permanent alleviation, forcing the hospital to reduce its intake and, no doubt, inclining

[1] R. M. Beachcroft, *Cases of the Appellants, the Governors of Christ's Hospital*, i (1889), 91. The constitution is given at pp. 87–93.

[2] Christ's Hospital, *Christ's Hospital Admissions, 1554–1559*, i (1937), *passim*.

[3] Beachcroft, *Cases*, 149–50, 161, 162; Guildhall Lib., Records of Christ's Hospital, Court Minutes, 1592–1632 (MS. 12806/3), 105; 1632–49 (MS. 12806/4), 303.

[4] Beachcroft, *Cases*, 87–90.

[5] Webb, *Old Poor Law*, 64. The Webbs state that the J.P.s' part in the levy was reduced to a formal acceptance of the rate set by the Overseers. This practice seems to have been followed thereafter in the London parishes, although the J.P.s (i.e. the senior Aldermen) directed the parish equalization system.

it towards the policy of turning itself into a grammar school
rather than a workhouse.[1] Margaret James mistook the general
crisis in the London hospitals for a particular situation caused
by the Civil War. In fact it went back to the beginning of
the seventeenth century at the latest, and earlier in the case of
Christ's because of its failure to retain a share of the Savoy
lands, for which the revenue from fines from Blackwell Hall
and from the operation of carts and carmen granted by the City
did not compensate.[2]

The relationship between the municipality and the parishes
changed at the close of the sixteenth century. Decentralization
brought about an advance in parish self-government in
respect of fund-raising at a time when metropolitan needs were
increasingly demanding central control and administration.
By the 1640s attention was focused on two necessities: first, the
need to strengthen the City's control over the parishes (not
over the hospitals, as Miss James suggested[3]—they were already
run by leading Aldermen and Common Councilmen); second,
the City's need to provide a centralized and practical scheme
for training the unemployed and providing work for them.
Only thus would it be possible to complete a unified system of
poor relief begun when the hospitals had been municipalized
in the first flush of Protestant power under Henry VIII and
Edward VI. Miss Leonard sometimes mistook official exhortation for action in this field. Such provision as existed hitherto
was fitful and piecemeal. As we have seen, Bridewell had made
some arrangements for apprenticeships. In 1579, Common
Council issued ambitious orders for the poor which would
have extended such training into organized industrial schools
for the unemployed,[4] but these and later attempts in the
early seventeenth century came to nought. Parochial provision,
enjoined since 1576, was rare, to judge from the records. In
1623, unsuccessful attempts were made by the Lord Mayor and
Aldermen to promote a scheme, particularly associated with

---

[1] Corporation RO, Repertories of the Aldermanic Bench, Rep. 37, fol. 141;
Rep. 38, fol. 178ᵛ; Rep. 45, fols. 105ᵛ, 547 et seq.; Rep. 55, fol. 73; Rep. 57, fol.
98; Christ's Hosp. Court Minutes, MSS. 12806/3, 66; 12806/4, 182, 223, 303.

[2] James, *Social Problems*, 247–8; Corporation RO, Journal of the Court of
Common Council, 22, fol. 38.   [3] James, *Social Problems*, 296.

[4] Journ. Common Council, 20, fols. 498, 499ᵛ. These orders were printed under
the date 1587.

the puritan Sir Thomas Middleton, President of Bridewell, to persuade parishes to group together to build hemp and flax houses to provide local employment.[1] In 1632, there was a more ambitious attempt to raise money for extending the apprentices' workshops at Bridewell.[2] Concern among some leading citizens was expressed by the amounts which were bequeathed for the purpose in the 1630s and 1640s: a total of £8,000, more than half of the entire sum provided by the City funds in the century before 1660, but including one munificent and much talked-about gift of £2,000 left in Sir James Cambell's disputed will.[3]

Unfortunately we do not have the details of the bill for the relief of the poor and the punishment of vagrants proposed by the Lord Mayor, Aldermen, and Common Councilmen in 1641.[4] This measure was subsumed in a debate which led to the draft of the first ordinance for the Corporation of the Poor in December 1647. It would have been instructive to isolate the original intention of the municipality and compare it with the outcome. We can interpret much of the story, however, from Rice Bush's pamphlet.[5] It appears that the City's proposals merged with those of a committee of citizens who convened a meeting in 1644 to discuss the provision of work for the poor and henceforth acted as a pressure group. It was decided that everyone should send their ideas to William Steele, a lawyer and a Baptist, later to be Recorder of the radical municipal government from 1649. An undated set of proposals written and signed by him exists in the House of Lords Record Office and can be ascribed from internal evidence to a date after 1645.[6] The proposals are drawn into a single coherent plan so that if they were meant to represent the views of a meeting they must have been thoroughly worked over and reorganized by Steele. It is more probable, however, that they represent his own views since they differ in various ways from the ordinance setting up the Corporation.

---

[1] Journ. Common Council, 32, fols. 146ᵛ–147.
[2] Ibid. 35, fol. 465.   [3] Jordan, *Charities of London*, 177–80.
[4] Journ. Common Council, 40, fols. 6, 31ᵛ.
[5] Rice Bush, *The Poor Mans Friend, or A Narrative of what progresse many worthy Citizens of London have made in that Godly Work of providing for the Poor* (1649) (Guildhall Lib., Pamph. 4706), 2, 3; Journ. Common Council, 40, fol. 145ᵛ.
[6] House of Lords MSS., Main Papers 1641.

Steele, who entitled his draft 'the maintenance of the impotent and aged poor, and for imploying and punishing of Beggars and Vagabonds', transferred the main responsibility for the poor from the Overseer to the J.P. and to the county, a view which reflected the City's desire to strengthen municipal control over the parishes. He wanted to set up workhouses and houses of correction, which he explicitly stated were to be kept separate in every county and were to be financed by taxing all the inhabitants and occupiers of houses and lands. As we shall see, the separation he advocated was made effective in the Corporation of the Poor, which did not include a house of correction. Owners of land of 100 acres or more were to be enjoined to sow two acres with hemp or flax for the poor. The able poor were to be compelled to labour, as were all beggars, vagrants, and all who did not contribute to the poor rate. Any almsmen who refused to allow their children aged ten or over to learn a trade would also be sent to the workhouse—with their children. The notion of compelling *all* the able poor to labour, contained embryonically in sixteenth-century legislation, was to become a commonplace by the end of the next century. Meanwhile, Steele's compulsory power was embodied in the second ordinance establishing the Corporation of the Poor, although, as I shall show, it was not stressed in any of the early broadsides issued by the Corporation. His tough attitude found further expression in a proposal that vagrants should not be sent to their place of birth or their last residence but should be dispatched instead to the nearest workhouse, where they would be made to work—a seemingly hard-nosed premature Benthamism, but one that was probably more realistic and no less humane than the prevailing one of transporting vagrants round the country, each parish disputing as far as it was able the paternity of its native sons and daughters. Indeed, concerning the training of children, Steele expressed an enlightened view: poor children, he wrote, 'from the time they are capable, till that age [ten years] be at the charge of the parish taught to read, and after continued at it in the workhouse'.

There is evidence of a planned campaign. At least six pamphlets orchestrated the programme for employing the poor. Two were humane and compassionate pleas, but were not meant to delineate practical blueprints. Leonard Lee, who dedicated his pamphlet to the Lord Mayor and Aldermen, called for such a committee as was established, but suggested that it should also include Westminster, Southwark, and Middlesex 'in regard in those parts most of the poor do lie',[1] an enlargement of jurisdiction which would have almost doubled the population involved, as had the differently inspired, short, and ineffective incorporation of the suburbs of 1636. *Stanley's Remedy* was a reprint of an earlier tract advocating workhouses, and stressing the saving of rates which would ensue, an argument which was to be much favoured in the early eighteenth century. It professed to have come out again in print as a means 'for stirring up the Committee of Aldermen and Common Councilmen of the Citie of London', who were trying to find employment for the poor.[2]

The third pamphlet written to publicize the scheme was that of Rice Bush, about whom very little is known. The pamphlet is important because it reveals the background of the movement. Its dedication gives the names of the small pressure group, composed of people within and outside the municipality, which had been active for some years. It included Thomas Andrews, the most radical Puritan amongst the Aldermen, Lieutenant-Colonel Walter Lee, a leading Presbyterian and one of several Common Councilmen active in the movement, Alderman George Witham, probably a fellow-Presbyterian, Samuel Hartlib, Dr. Edward Odling, a physician in the new Model Army, and Thomas Jenner, a well-known bookseller and map dealer, who was also a pamphleteering advocate of the expansion of the fishing trade. It is interesting to note that neither this group nor the group of Governors of the Corporation of the Poor can be identified as a whole with either religious Presbyterians or Independents (each contained a fair sprinkling of both parties) and that the first ordinance went through a predominantly Presbyterian court of Aldermen and Common Council, admittedly under a radical Lord Mayor, John Warner. Indeed, the existence of a common ground between political

---

[1] Leonard Lee, *A Remonstrance humbly presented to . . . Parliament touching the insupportable miseries of the poore* (1645).

[2] *Stanleyes Remedy: Or, the way how to reform wandering Beggars, Theeves, high-way Robbers and Pick-pockets* (1646), 5–6.

extremes on such programmes of relief is indicated by the appearance of an advertisement for Bush's pamphlet in *The Moderate*, an organ of the Levellers. The issue for 21 March 1649 stated that the pamphlet was sold by Thomas Underhill at the sign of The Bible in Great Wood Street. He was the leading publisher of religious presbyterian literature in London, an active member of the classis and, in political matters, naturally stood well to the right of the Levellers.[1] As Margaret James recognized, Bush's pamphlet went further than the ordinance in suggesting what was needed, but the ideas offered were only the familiar stock-in-trade of contemporary debate and one or two of them had been tried out previously in the city. Thus, his suggestion that all the poor should be listed and sent out to appropriate institutions according 'to their severall abilities and imployments' had been pursued irregularly and in part. The appointment in each ward of a place for collecting food and raw materials for the poor was also known. Bush was ahead of his time in wanting to see four workhouses established, one in each quarter of the city, so that provision could be made over a wider area than the parish. He also anticipated and advocated existing social reforms and some of the future: free medicines, the relief of large families before small, grants of alehouse licences to 'aged' and 'decaied' applicants, and consultation with the 'severall trades' of London about their grievances and how to remedy them. These suggestions and others were prefaced by a compassionate plea for the poor based on the text 'Blessed are the merciful, for they obtain mercy', in which pity for their plight outweighed the condemnation of idleness.[2]

Much more carefully constructed plans appeared in three pamphlets written by Samuel Hartlib between 1646 and 1650 which prefigured the actual working of the Corporation of the Poor. They have an additional significance in coming from the most active member of a group of Baconian social planners and scientists with European connections. Hartlib, his fertile imagination nourished by the group to which he belonged, was

---

[1] *The Moderate*, 37 (21 Mar. 1649); 'The Records of the Provincial Assembly of London, 1647–1660', ed. C. E. Surman (1957; typescript in Dr. Williams's Lib.), *passim*.

[2] Bush, *Poor Mans Friend*.

already the author of schemes for national improvement and more would follow. Some would anticipate educational and welfare reforms not achieved until the twentieth century. His plans for the London poor express a mood closer to his time and are essentially empirical, marked by hard-headed notions of social discipline far removed from the utopianism with which he is sometimes charged.[1] They are truly of their time too, in harping on the inculcation of those moral values associated with Puritan godliness and self-advance, features which appear in many contemporary pamphlets devoted to the subject.

The chief purpose of the Corporation of the Poor, to whom along with the Governors of Bridewell his second pamphlet was dedicated, was, Hartlib thought, to educate and train the children of the poor, 'to civillise and train them up, in their books, and so by degrees to trades, that so they may be fit servants for the Commonwealth'.[2] The idea of sending orphans and poor children to school was not so innovatory as it might seem. Many parishes had long done so, meeting the expenses themselves. The workhouse, into which he would put them, had some of the characteristics of a 'mixed' institution of the early eighteenth century, since it would house both children and the adult poor, although it was designed primarily for the young. His aim was to effect a moral improvement, particularly among the children, who now 'lye all day in the streets playing, cursing, swearing', while in the Corporation they 'would be kept under a godly government which is an excellent step in reformation'. Similarly, in his first pamphlet he had urged the enforcement of six rules, against swearing, filthy talk, cursing, despising their food, stealing, and slovenliness in dress.[3] Anyone refusing to live in such an orderly and decent fashion was to have a spell in Bridewell before being returned to the workhouse. 'This project', he thought, 'will either reform them that are stubborn or make them run [out of] the country.'

---

[1] See, for example, Q. Skinner's review of C. Webster, *The Great Instauration* (1975) in *TLS*, 2 July 1976, 810–12.

[2] S. Hartlib, *Londons Charitie Stilling the Poor Orphans Cry, Providing places and provision, by the care and indeavour of the Corporation appointed by the Parliament* (1649).

[3] S.H[artlib], *The Parliaments Reformation Or a Worke for Presbyters, Elders, and Deacons, to engage themselves, for the education of all poore Children, and imployment of all sorts of poor, that no poore body of young nor old may be enforced to beg within their classes in City nor Country* (1646).

In this first pamphlet written in 1646, ideology and reform go hand in hand. Hartlib wanted to see a workhouse set up in every classis[1] (the Presbyterian church government was just being established) and there can be no doubt that he thought the workhouse would flourish under the vigilant eye of the church elder, as in the French and Dutch churches in London, whose treatment of the poor was much commended by reformers. His rigid 'moral' injunctions were combined with humanity. The dedication of the second pamphlet declared his aim to be 'to clothe the naked, feed the hungry, instruct the ignorant and employ the idle'.[2]

His third pamphlet, published when the Corporation was already being organized, presented a plan for the education of 100 children between the ages of five and fifteen. A Head or Steward was to be paid £50 a year, a schoolmaster £20, and nine others (nurses, cooks, and officers) smaller minimum wages ranging from £3 to £12 a year eked out by the addition of bonuses dependent on the amount of saleable commodities produced by the children under their supervision,[3] a provision for payment by results which was to reappear at the end of the seventeenth century in John Locke's scheme for the poor. Hartlib's plan goes into some minute detail. The schoolmaster was to be provided with a serge suit out of the children's spinning work. Pupils would be taught reading and writing for two hours a day and when boys (girls are not mentioned) were aged between ten and fourteen they were to be bound as apprentices. The schoolmaster was to be a religious and moral instructor: besides teaching he was to pray with the pupils once a day and read them the workhouse rules because 'the law read is a terrour to mild children'. Rewards as well as punishments were available. Quick-witted children, which we may interpret perhaps as dutiful, obedient, or studious pupils, were to be promoted. Hartlib says they are to be called 'scholars', by which he must have had in mind the practice at Christ's Hospital, where such promotion was common, although unlike

---

[1] S. H[artlib], *The Parliaments Reformation* . . . 1.   [2] *Londons Charitie Stilling.*
[3] *Londons Charitie inlarged, Stilling the Orphans Cry. By the liberality of the Parliament, in granting two Houses by Act, and giving a thousand pounds towards the work for the imployment of the Poor, and education of poor children* (1650), 13. Thomason has inscribed '15 April 1649', but he is surely wrong because the tract mentions Parliament's gift to the Corporation of the Poor, which was after April 1649.

the Corporation all the children were, in theory, the sons and daughters of freemen. Pupils were to be given recreation regularly (again boys are considered rather than girls): some 'warlike exercise', partly a training for the militia, and in winter 'other recreations . . . as the Children of Christ's Church doe, for the sharpening of their wits, reviving their spirits and preventing them [from] . . . scurvyes and dropsies and such like'. This usage of children, he continues, 'serves to confute the thoughts of some that thought the Corporation would not be so kind and tender-hearted to poor children', an interesting observation which suggests that opponents of the reformers may have included some who feared greater harshness to the poor. Their diet, too, was to match that of Christ's Hospital, where, according to Hartlib, the allowance consisted of bread, cheese, and pottage daily, and a weekly ration of a quarter of a pound of beef and two servings of fish. Other evidence suggests that children at Christ's had meat four times a week.[1]

There is no suggestion that the poor were to be compelled to enter the workhouse, although stubborn behaviour once there would lead to a spell in Bridewell before being sent back. Nor, as far as one can see, was it envisaged that all children (and certainly not the adults) should live in. Probably Hartlib thought that some would come on a daily basis, returning at night to their parishes, as happened in the Corporation. His plan would have created a far less 'institutional' organization than the nineteenth-century workhouse or even the types envisaged in the late seventeenth century, when the schemes canvassed were more humane than anything that would emerge over the next two hundred years. In the proposals of Sir Humphrey Mackworth presented to Parliament in 1704 and in the Knatchbull Act of 1723, all paupers were obliged to enter the workhouse on pain of forgoing parish relief.[2] The penalty was renewed in the workhouses of the late 1830s, the hated 'Bastilles' of working-class radicals.

It would be a mistake to suppose that Hartlib ignored the financing of the scheme. In his early pamphlet of 1646 he recognized that even after voluntary collections and the allocation of fines paid by the disorderly (drunkards, swearers, and adulterers would thus, he thought, effect a 'double

---

[1] Pearce, *Christ's Hospital*, 176.   [2] Webb, *Old Poor Law*, 114 and n. 1.

reformation'), money would have to be voted by Parliament, a grant which he urged upon the nation. Nor was he so impracticable as to think that it could immediately pay its way. He considered that eventually quick-witted children aged six might earn about 1s. a week and 1s. 4d. or 1s. 6d. at the age of seven.[1] This would entail a financial loss, but in terms of orderliness and the reformation of manners the Commonwealth would gain. Indeed, the economy would clearly profit in the end, he argued, since with the expansion of the labour force and the improvement of industry 'we shall not only assist our own Plantations with Commodities, but be helpful to other nations also, if they need us'. In his last pamphlet of 1650, he was even more optimistic in presenting his precursive utilitarian calculus, anticipating many of the later arguments of such men as Sir Matthew Hale and predicting that the educational provision might pay for itself.[2] But neither Hartlib nor his successors made sufficient allowance for the inefficiency of a mode of production which employed the weakest and poorest members of the population and found difficulty in finding honest and skilful organizers and supervisors of labour. Hartlib was not deterred by questions of low productivity: 'when children come to earn 2s and 2s 6d per week for three four or five years . . .', he wrote, 'this will raise in a few years, a considerable stocke to the Parish; where many are set out to work, thus the charge of 6s 6d [*per annum*] paid by the Parish for teaching will be paid many times over . . . to the Parish by the child's labour.' His keen sense of economy and realism is seen in his proposal to boost the fishing trade by setting out busses to employ the poor and using part of the catch to feed the inmates of the workhouse, presumably cheaper than buying fish in the open market.[3]

How far did the Corporation of the Poor develop as Hartlib and other reformers wanted? How far were Tawney and James right to dismiss it as being concerned essentially with punishing vagrants and for having left no mark? Their views were based primarily on the two ordinances setting up the Corporation and they did not see other crucial evidence about its way of working. The ordinance of 1647 established a Corporation

---

[1] *Londons Charitie Stilling*, 7; *Londons Charitie inlarged*, [18].
[2] *Londons Charitie inlarged*, [19].   [3] Ibid. 12 et seq.

with powers to set up one or more workhouse and one or more house of correction. It proposed the appointment of three principal officers, a President, a Deputy, and Treasurer, and forty Assistants (of whom eight were to be Aldermen and thirty-two freemen) elected annually in Common Council. It granted powers to hold lands and houses up to an annual value of £2,000, to tax the citizens, and to divide the city into four quarters to balance rich and poor parishes.[1] The second ordinance of 1649[2] strengthened the legal and judicial authority of the Corporation by permitting it to distrain for taxes and by enlarging the number of Aldermen who could exercise the power of J.P.s. The second ordinance also increased the already large number of Assistants to fifty-two (ten Aldermen and forty-two freemen), an indication of the optimistic expectations of the founders in managing a very large undertaking. We may also see in the extraordinary size of the governing body (nearly the same number as in the other four hospitals combined) the desire of a newly founded and controversial organization to present the broadest possible front to a fairly critical public chary of making a suitable financial contribution. The objects of the foundation were reiterated: employing the poor and punishing vagrants, but the ordinance of 1649 was somewhat harsher than the earlier measure in its definition of the Corporation's work. It was now stated that the Corporation should set all the parish poor on work with the power to punish as vagrants any who refused. We do not know whether these compulsory provisions were effected, although both Tawney and James assumed that they implied a generally more repressive attitude.

The ordinances were short and formal, the official records no longer exist, and we have to look elsewhere to see what kind of institution developed. We know that what was established were workhouses and *not* houses of correction. There is no evidence for the existence of the last. In fact, the Corporation warders, disciplinary officers similar to those employed by the hospitals, sent offenders to Bridewell; apart from that the Court Books of Bridewell reveal surprisingly little co-operation between the two institutions.[3] In an official broadside, acquired a few

[1] Firth & Rait, i. 1042 et seq.
[2] Ibid. ii. 104–10.
[3] [Corporation of the Poor], *At a court held by the . . . Lord Mayor President, and the rest of the Governers of the Corporation for the Poor of London, the 6th of February 1655* ['Signed

years ago by the Guildhall Library,[1] the purpose of the Corporation was stated by its clerk, John Marsh: 'it is not simply the present suppression and setting to work of idle Vagrants and Beggars of all sorts' that could bring about a reformation, but some method of prevention for the future. That was to be achieved, he proclaimed, by education, training, and discipline. The parishes are described as caring only for the material provision of the poor so that they are brought up 'like Atheists, after a sordid, loose and undisciplined manner . . . by meanes whereof, so much dissoluteness, idleness, thefts, whoredomes, prophane cursing, swearing, and almost all kinds of wickedness do generally abound in that sort of people'. The broadside distributed to all the parishes of London called for all children over six years of age who were in the care of Overseers to be brought to the Corporation, carrying their luncheons with them, to be taught to read and write and to be instructed in such trades 'as they are capable of'. It was expected that after the first three months they would be paid for their work at the rate of 1*s.* a week, which would supplement whatever was already received from the parish (in the richer parishes, doles for the maintenance of orphans ranged from 1*s.* to 4*s.* a week in the 1640s and '50s, depending on whether they were at nurse or at school). The broadside recognizes that there would be no profit in the venture, an unexpectedly realist and humane note which is a far cry from the spirit of 'cash nexus' ascribed to the founders by later historians. Even that enlightened early protagonist of co-operation, the Quaker John Bellers, thought that his College of Industry would produce a surplus. Another aspect which reduced its 'institutional' character was that work was provided without requiring

by William Haslope Clerk to the Corporation'], Guildhall Lib., broadsides 8.99. A joint committee of Bridewell and the Corporation of the Poor was established to discuss how 'the younger children and the sturdy idle vagabonds might be sett on worke and imployed', but nothing came of it, to judge from the records; Bridewell Royal Hospital Court Books, Oct. 1642–July 1658, roll 6. I am grateful to Dr. A. L. Beier for allowing me to read his microfilm of the Court Books. The original archives, deposited at King Edward School, Witley, Surrey, by the Governors of Bridewell Royal Hospital, are not available for study.

[1] *Severall Propositions tendered by the Corporation for the Imploying the Poor of the City of London, and Liberties,* ['Signed Jo. Marsh, Cler. 1650']. I discovered this broadside, which is not in Wing, in 1969 and at my suggestion it was acquired by the Guildhall Library (no. 2424).

residence. Thus, it was arranged that children were to be accompanied to the workhouse by the parish pensioners (ten children to an adult) who would also be responsible for taking them home at the end of the day. Nothing was said about arranging formal apprenticeships when the appropriate age was reached. It was usual for the parish of origin to make such arrangements. The Bridewell Court Books show that very occasionally children were sent there from the Corporation for formal apprenticeships. Adults, too, would not be forced to leave their homes. They could be given out-work under the guarantee of their Overseers and be paid by the piece with a system of tickets or they could do piece-work on the premises each day. As was usual in the London parishes and hospitals at this time, all the children and adults employed were to wear the badge of the Corporation upon their sleeves. An interesting clause stated that the 'stragling poor' (presumably the non-vagrant, sc. lawful wanderers who were not parish pensioners) should be given an allowance by their parish and then allowed to work for the Corporation on the conditions set out for children; this meant that they were opening their doors very much wider than, for example, Christ's Hospital.

Two premises (both confiscated royal properties) were presented by Parliament to the Corporation of the Poor—Heydon House in the Minories, recently in the possession of Sir John Heydon, Master of the Ordnance, and the Wardrobe building in Vintry. They also gave £1,000 out of the estate of the Duke of Buckingham towards the purchase of stock.[1] According to another official broadside,[2] the first act of the Corporation was to list the poor, as had been suggested by Rice Bush, compiling a census of all such persons over seven years of age, much as was being done by the French Church in London in the quarterly *Grand Tour* conducted by the deacons. A newspaper report in 1655 stated that 80 children, clothed in a uniform of orange coats and green caps, were maintained at the Wardrobe, where they were taught by their tutor, Mr. Harmar.[3]

[1] *CJ* vi. 226; *CSPD, 1653–1654*, 144. James mistakenly gives this sum as £100,000; *Social Problems*, 298.
[2] *A Perfect Diurnall of some Passages in Parliament* (27 Aug.–3 Sept. 1649), 2737.
[3] *Perfect Proceedings of State-Affaires* (7–13 June 1655); *At a Court held by the . . . Lord Mayor.* Harmar may be the Samuel Harmar who wrote *Vox Populi; or, Gloucestershires Desire. With the way to make a kingdome happy by setting up of*

Yet another official broadside reported in the following year, 'for some years together [they] did employ about one thousand Poor at work, besides the Poor Children that are educated . . . in Learning and the Arts'.[1]

An educational feature of the Corporation which went beyond the three Rs was that the children were taught to sing. Music was one of the main intellectual activities in seventeenth-century London. Christ's Hospital children, who sang professionally at city burials, were famous for their fine voices. They also sang on days devoted by the Church to charity, such as the Spital Sermon on Easter Monday. Such material is particularly evanescent and we are fortunate in having the words of two songs produced by the Corporation of the Poor. A verse of one is openly political. The pressure group which we have seen as the promoters of the Corporation were also the backers of national legislation for the poor then being debated by the Rump and again in Barebone's Parliament. What better voice to strengthen Parliament's resolve than the sweet sound of these reformed, scrubbed, and uniformed orphans of London? The group evidently thought so, for the verse ran:

> Grave Senators, that sit on high
> Let not poor English children die,
>> and droop on Dunghill with lamenting notes:
> An Act for Poor's relief, they say,
> Is coming forth; why's this delay?
>> O let not Dutch, Danes, Devils stop these VOTES!

An earlier verse has the more characteristic note of gratitude to their guardians although it too can be seen as a propagandist work, much as Dr. Barnardo's Home in its earliest days showed touched-up 'before and after' photographs of its rescued waifs.

> In filthy rags we clothed were
> In good warm Raiment now appear
>> from Dunghill to King's Palace transferred
> Where Education, wholesome Food,
> Meat, drink and Lodging, all that[s] good
>> for Soul and Body, are so well prepared.[2]

Schoole-masters in every parish (1642). A Samuel Harmar acted as [Bible] Reader in St. Bartholomew Exchange in 1661.

[1] *The Public Intelligencer* (11–18 Feb. 1656), 326.
[2] *Poor out-cast Childrens Song and Cry* (1653). See also the petition of Dr. Edward

It can be inferred that the Corporation had ambitions to extend its operation vastly, setting the whole of the London poor on work. It asked Common Council for the very large sum of £12,000 in 1650, much more than was needed to run an institution containing about 1,000 adults and 100 children, as it had settled down to five years later. Moreover, its huge governing body may be seen not only as a means of making the widest appeal but also as a necessity for the management of so large an undertaking. The most intractable problem faced by the Corporation, and one which it never solved, was finance. In April 1650, Common Council agreed that the £12,000 would be provided in three equal instalments. It attempted to raise two such instalments between 1652 and 1657 but both fell short.[1] To free itself (and the wards) from the unpopular and burdensome task of providing additional local taxation, Common Council was compelled to seek new sources of revenue. The most promising seemed to be a national postal service operated from the city.[2] Such a monopoly looked as though it would be immensely profitable but unfortunately there were other contenders for the licence in the field, among them the Attorney-General Edmund Prideaux, who had powerful backing in Parliament, although his claim was a matter of dispute. The City's attempt to enter this minefield of interest and political intrigue came to nought despite the advocacy of an M.P. and Common Councilman, Colonel Thomas Pride, one of the Corporation's pressure group, better known for his purge of the Commons. The £15,000 a year which Prideaux was reported to be making would have to be sought elsewhere. Relief of a kind came from Parliament when it offered for use as fishing busses to employ the poor, three of the Dutch ships captured by Blake.[3] One was appropriately named *The Poor's Vessel* but no one could pretend that even a fleet of them would

Odling, the Corporation's Solicitor, entreating Parliament 'to call upon the Grand Act for imploying, and releiving [*sic*] the Poor of the whole Nation' and also to pass 'an additional Act for the Corporation of the Poor of the City of *London*, without which the newly laid foundation of their work (in which by the blessing of God they have made some good progresse) will be in danger to be demolished' [Thomason's inscription: 'December 1654', but probably 1653 was meant]; BL, 669 f 19 (48). The other song is entitled *The Cities Corporations Poor* (1652).

[1] Journ. Common Council, 41, fols. 23, 25, 158, 158ᵛ.
[2] Ibid. 41, fols. 5ᵛ, 6, 9, 10, 19ᵛ, 22, 64ᵛ, 65.
[3] *CSPD, 1651–1652*, 390, 397; *1652–1653*, 15; *1653–1654*, 144, 435; *1654*, 245.

have solved the City's money troubles over the Corporation. In 1655, Common Council made another attempt to run an industrial undertaking on behalf of the poor, accepting a plan placed before it by the Corporation for the daily cleansing of the streets, markets, and public places in the city and the liberties. The project was adopted and it was contracted out for twenty-one years to John Lanyon, entitled 'Surveyor-General of the streets'. The rates normally levied in the parishes and paid to the scavengers were to go to Lanyon, who would remit a proportion of his profits to the Corporation. The scheme operated for a few years before ending in financial disputes between the contractor and the Common Council.[1] One more attempt was made to establish a municipal enterprise but that too ended in failure. In 1658, Common Council proposed to pass over to the Corporation the oversight of carts and carmen previously in the hands of Christ's Hospital. It was a dubious gift: the Woodmongers' Company had never ceased to dispute the hospital's entitlement, a subject of litigation since the late sixteenth century.[2]

In the conditions of the time it is easy to see that such primitive forms of 'municipal socialism' hardly had a chance when any large undertaking was involved. Powerful, well-established trading and manufacturing interests had to be placated, farming-out was the accepted method for speculative ventures, public works hardly existed, and taxation was strongly resisted. London was no stranger to collective municipal endeavour, as the supply of water, the stockpiling of grain, the assize, and the regulation of standards had attested for centuries. But the public organization of manufactures and commerce was a different matter. In the 1520s a remarkable attempt to set up municipal bakeries in London had been routed,[3] and the Corporation of the Poor never undertook or suggested any-

[1] Journ. Common Council, 41, fols. 111ᵛ–112ᵛ, 116ᵛ, 119, 120ᵛ, 121, 123–5, 126, 127, 168ᵛ, 199ᵛ–200; *An Act of Common Council made the Eleventh day of September . . . 1655. For the better avoiding and prevention of Annoyances within the City of London and Liberties* (1655).

[2] Journ. Common Council, 41, fol. 194; Rep. 20, fol. 320ᵛ; Journ. Common Council, 22, fol. 38; *Analytical Index to the . . . Remembrancia . . . 1579–1664*, ed. W. H. and H. C. Overall (1878), 56; Rep. 37, fol. 141; Rep. 38, fol. 178ᵛ; Rep. 45, fol. 105ᵛ.

[3] S. Thrupp, *A Short History of the Worshipful Company of Bakers of London* [1933], 79–80.

thing so radical as the municipal brewery run by the Puritan municipality of Salisbury in the 1630s;[1] it is doubtful if an undertaking so competitive with, and subversive of, established interests would have been acceptable.

The Corporation of the Poor came to an end when the King, on his restoration in 1660, took back his properties, the Wardrobe and Heydon House. In May he granted the Wardrobe to the Earl of Sandwich and in June Pepys recorded that he visited 'the Governors of some poor children in tawny clothes who have been maintained there eleven years, which put my lord to a stand how to dispose of them—that he may have the house for his use. The children did sing finely and my lord did bid me give them five pieces in gold at his going away.'[2] Because the Restoration Parliament failed to re-enact the ordinances of the Corporation, it ceased to exist in a legal sense. No doubt the failure to establish a sufficient and regular income was the real cause. Common Council ordered on 28 June 1660 that the children belonging to the late Corporation should be taken into the hospitals, and that the money and stock be paid to the Treasurer.[3] On 31 December 1660 the Treasurer of Christ's told his Court that he had taken in 119 children and asked it to appoint some person to assist 'in disposing of the said children to the severall schools of the hospital'.[4] It is an illustration of the 'educational' nature of the Corporation that the children should have gone to Christ's and not to Bridewell. The stock, too, reflected an orphanage rather than a house of correction. It consisted of many kinds of cloth, fustian, flax, and hemp to the value of £475. 12s. 1d. and household goods, mainly beds, bedding, and furniture, worth £234. 17s., but no penal instruments of any kind such as the treadmill and stocks which were to be found in houses of correction. Christ's Hospital also took over legacies worth £1,356. 14s. 5d., a substantial sum for a new and controversial institution founded in troubled times; naturally, such bequests could not compare with the endowments of Christ's, the most prestigious of the city hospitals, which always drew the largest

[1] *Crisis and Order in English Towns, 1500–1700*, ed. P. Clark and P. Slack (1972), 182–91.
[2] Samuel Pepys, *The Diary*, ed. R. Latham and W. Matthews, i (1970), 180.
[3] Christ's Hosp. Court Minutes, 1649–1661 (MS. 12806/5), 826, 827.
[4] Ibid. 834.

benefactions, gaining £10,000 in the 1640s and £12,000 in the next decade.[1]

Thus ended the institution in which so many hopes had been placed: a pioneering educational and workhouse foundation rather than the prison for vagrants into which it was turned by historians of our own day. Its abrupt end seems also to have hidden from later students of the period the influence which it exerted on similar developments at the end of the century. There was a direct if tenuous line of descent between it and the Corporation of the Poor founded by the municipality in 1698 in Bishopsgate: both constitutional and organizational links connect the two. The terms of the ordinance of 1649 were incorporated in part in the 1662 Act of Settlement, which permitted the erection of workhouses in London, Westminster, Middlesex, and Surrey.[2] The workhouses of Middlesex and Westminster were established in 1664 and 1666, respectively, although as far as is known they did not operate with the earlier emphasis on education and both were markedly unsuccessful.[3] The Corporation of the Poor, re-established in the city in 1698 under the same Act, resembled the original Corporation in operating as an orphanage which emphasized limited education and training. Then in 1700 it opened another wing to deal with vagrants, which was run like a house of correction but was separated from the children.[4] The example of the earlier Corporation may also have helped to inspire Thomas Firmin, who in the 1670s ran a workhouse in Bishopsgate in which the training of the unemployed poor was more important than profit or punishment. Like the Corporation, he expected the parish to continue to pay doles to those whom he helped, although he was prepared to bear himself the inevitable financial losses which would ensue.[5] Some of the ideals which inspired the first Corporation were expressed in the writings of two of the ablest reformers of the later seventeenth century,

---

[1] Christ's Hosp. Court Minutes, 1649–1661 (MS. 12806/5), 828, 829, 830; Jordan, *Charities of London*, 193.　　　　　　　　　　[2] *S. of R.* v. 401–3.

[3] Calendar of Middx. Sessions Books (typescript in BL 10360 t 1), no. 194, 194; no. 217, 8, 23, 67; no. 362, 2–3.

[4] *A Short State and Representation of the Proceedings of the President and Governors for the Poor of the City of London* (1701); *An Account of several Work-Houses for Employing and Maintaining the Poor* (2nd edn. 1732), 1–3.

[5] Thomas Firmin, *Some Proposals for Employing of the Poor* (1678), 5.

Sir Matthew Hale and Sir Josiah Child. Both stressed the social advantage of educating and training the poor. The only solution to the problem of poverty, wrote Hale in 1659 in a work which he published nearly twenty years later, was the 'industrious education of our poor'.[1] Both also thought that employing the poor would increase national wealth in the long term and that the problem of making it pay in the short term was of less significance. Child and Hale saw the need for a larger unit than the parish, and Child urged the establishment of a Greater London workhouse including the area of the Bills of Mortality, an idea with vision beyond that of the sponsors of the Corporation although his proposals for organization were closer to theirs. Powers to provide work should be taken from the Overseers and transferred to Guardians of the Poor, popularly elected and modelled on the city hospitals. Only men of independence and status, he thought, would attract charity on the scale needed.[2]

It should not be thought that the existence of the Corporation of the Poor and the advocacy of the workhouse meant the triumph of that idea in the middle of the seventeenth century. Those who advocated it were fighting against strong opposition from many quarters. Prime amongst these was the fear by small masters and manufacturers of intensified competition in a limited market. The view, so ably put forward by Daniel Defoe in his pamphlet *Giving Alms no Charity and employing the poor a Grievance to the Nation* (1704), that employing the poor would cause economic ruin to small masters was strongly urged in 1649 on the setting-up of the Corporation. The attack appeared in a moderate 'middle group' newspaper[3] edited by the Fleet Street tailor, John Dillingham, the friend of Oliver St. John and other highly placed politicians. In an editorial written in March 1649 at the height of the debate on the second ordinance, he warned Parliament against ambitious and unrealistic schemes:

Handicraftsmen can tell the learned Grandees, that handicraft is a work of time, and cannot make the actors thrive in new places

---

[1] Sir Matthew Hale, *A Discourse Touching Provision for the Poor* (1683), 19–26.

[2] Sir Josiah Child, *Proposals, For the Relief and Employment of the Poor* [1670?], 4–6.

[3] *The Moderate Intelligencer* (1–8 Mar. 1649), 207, (15–22 Mar. 1649), 209, (22–9 Mar. 1649), 210.

without more damage to some-body . . . Hath not experience told England long, that such commodities may be bought cheaper than the matter which set the poor on worke cost before working, besides, how many thousands that are in the way of trade, that have not two dayes worke in the weeke, so that . . . the employing one takes the bread of life from the other, besides, the poor artificer will aske you, where's the buyer? Who will take off my labour?

Such contrivances, he thought, must surely be made by 'some arithmetician' rather than by one who got his bread by the sweat of his brow. 'Let these childish conceits lately on foot in London be pursued no farther', he cried. These arguments and others like them had often been employed against the City's work schemes, even the apprenticeships arranged by Bridewell which Rice Bush cautioned against if they led to the 'destruction of a trade'. Both he and Hartlib felt the need to rebut the arguments about price-cutting.[1] We have seen how hard it was to establish municipal enterprise in London. The Privy Council reports in the 1630s tell of stocks of work being provided in numerous country parishes, but there is no mention of similar provision in London. Perhaps the same fear of the consequences of providing employment is to be seen in the preference shown by Christ's Hospital for education rather than for work schemes, a preference displayed also by donors from the mid 1640s. The low response by the already heavily burdened tax-paying citizens of London to the financial demands of the Corporation may also be a reflection of a widespread uneasiness about the threat that training schemes offered to established trades and services. The fear of competition may also be seen in quite another sphere: the vociferous opposition to the naturalization of foreigners long expressed in the city. Xenophobic and economic prejudices would diminish or be controlled as would the opposition to work schemes. Not until the 1720s, with the greater industrial development and urbanization of the early eighteenth century, did the workhouse become a commonly recognized remedy for poverty and an accepted feature of society.

[1] *Londons Charitie Stilling*, 8; Bush, *Poor Mans Friend*, 18, 19.

Wales during the Commonwealth
and Protectorate

A. M. JOHNSON

WALES was arguably the darkest of the 'dark corners of the land' when the Commonwealth came into being in 1649.[1] For an amalgam of economic, social, geographical, and cultural reasons, Wales had proved particularly unreceptive to change and innovation since the Reformation. The governments of the Interregnum were thus provided with a wide variety of problems in their attempts to puritanize the Principality and to administer a backward region.

Because the Welsh were predominantly royalist in their sympathies Parliament had been unable fully to assert its authority in Wales before the end of the Second Civil War. Before 1649 the parliamentary position was mainly dependent upon a small number of minor gentry aided by English military commanders and a few dedicated Puritan preachers, most of whom continued to sustain and advance the parliamentary cause in the region during the Interregnum, though the effective exercise of government authority in Wales even in this period owed much to the acquiescent posture adopted by the majority of the Welsh gentry.[2]

The governments of the Commonwealth and Protectorate never developed a coherent policy towards Wales nor made provision for it within the framework of a wider Celtic policy. Wales was simply regarded as one of the outlying regions urgently in need of firm government and spiritual regeneration.

[1] Christopher Hill is, of course, responsible for the currency of this phrase in recent years as a result of his essays 'Puritans and "the Dark Corners of the Land"', *TRHS*, 5th ser. xiii (1963), and 'Propagating the Gospel' in *Historical Essays, 1600–1750*, ed. H. E. Bell and R. L. Ollard (1963). Both are reprinted with additional material in Hill, *Change and Continuity in Seventeenth-Century England* (1974), 3–47.

[2] For commissioners and J.P.s during the Interregnum, Firth & Rait, ii; J. R. S. Phillips, *The Justices of the Peace in Wales and Monmouthshire, 1541–1689* (Cardiff, 1975).

Central government was obliged by the circumstances of the political situation to recognize the difficulties of organization within the Principality so that most ordinances which depended for their implementation upon local action were administered on a regional rather than on a county basis. On two occasions only were enactments introduced to meet particular problems in Wales though in all other respects the Principality was accorded no special recognition. There was nothing novel in this, however, for Parliament from 1642 had often tailored its ordinances relating to the provinces to meet local contingencies. The two ordinances were the Acts for General Composition of £20,500 and £24,000 imposed on the six counties of south Wales and Monmouthshire and the six northern counties respectively, to compensate for parliamentary inability to sequester delinquents' estates before 1649,[1] and the Act for the Propagation of the Gospel in Wales of February 1650.

In order to meet the doubtful loyalty of provincial officials, especially in Wales, and concerned at the independence assumed by county committees in parliamentary strongholds during the civil wars the government endeavoured to exercise tighter control over the localities by appointing separate militia and assessment committees, though in practice this division of function was often little more than a technicality because the leading personnel tended to serve in a dual capacity.[2] Further, in January 1650 sequestration procedure was reorganized and control of sequestration taken out of the hands of county committees. In England, which included Monmouthshire on this occasion, power to sequester delinquents' estates was given over to three special commissioners in each county who were directly responsible to the central committee in London, though in Wales the commissioners were appointed on a regional basis.

For at least two years the attempt to implement at the same time the Acts for the General Fines and the Act for the Propagation of the Gospel in Wales, and to operate the new centralized

---

[1] Firth & Rait, ii. 14–16, 207–12 (Feb. and Aug. 1649).

[2] See the valuable thesis, T. M. Bassett, 'A Study of Local Government in Wales under the Commonwealth with Especial Reference to its Relations with the Central Authority' (M.A. thesis, Univ. of Wales, 1941), appx. 5.

sequestration procedures, introduced a wide variety of problems, arising from the conflicts in authority between the three sets of officials. Appeals from the various commissioners in Wales to the central committees in London for guidance reflected the difficulties which the recent ordinances had introduced, though eventually there evolved the general rule that the benefits of the General Fines should be confined to persons who could prove they were domiciled in Wales, and the propagators were allowed the revenues from impropriate tithes.[1]

John Penry in the late sixteenth century had led the attempt to secure special consideration for the spiritual needs of Wales, but during the Civil Wars the inspiration derived from a new generation of dedicated preachers led by Walter Cradock and Vavasor Powell. There was little enthusiasm in the Rump for propagation schemes and only one Welsh M.P., the regicide John Jones of Merionethshire, could unreservedly be described as radical. The pressure for implementation of a bill for the propagation of the gospel in Wales came essentially from outside the Rump. Petitions from north and south Wales were aided by a few sympathizers in Parliament. Eventually, an Act for the Propagation of the Gospel in Wales was passed in February 1650 and it is arguable that for the Rump the attractions of both of the Propagation Acts—for Wales and the northern counties—derived more from an awareness of their political advantages than from a care for the spiritual well-being of those regions.[2]

In recent years the Propagation Committee has been described by Professor Dodd as 'the real government of Wales' during 1650–3, and its authority has been compared by Christopher Hill with that of the defunct Council in Wales and the Marches.[3] Both these views, however, overstate the coherence, the organization, and the powers entrusted to the Propagation Commissioners.

John Walker claimed that the Propagation Commission was

---

[1] Ibid. 149–50, 156–7, 246.

[2] B. Worden, *The Rump Parliament* (Cambridge, 1974), 234–5. Prof. H. R. Trevor-Roper sees the Propagation Commission as an example of the attempts by Cromwell and the Independents to decentralize government and religion; *Religion, the Reformation and Social Change* (1967), 413.

[3] A. H. Dodd, *Studies in Stuart Wales* (Cardiff, 1952), 148; Hill, *Change and Continuity*, 33.

created 'according to the plan laid down by Hugh Peters'. The Act provided for the appointment of seventy-one commissioners to serve as propagators in the Principality, twenty-eight of whom represented the northern counties and forty-three the southern counties including Monmouthshire.[1] A high proportion of those nominated had already served Parliament in a number of capacities in the Principality. They represented a wide variety of backgrounds and were not appointed on any sort of county basis. Several of them were English militiamen who had found themselves in Wales in the service of the parliamentary armies.[2] The commissioners were empowered to examine and eject, where necessary, the incumbents of livings for delinquency, malignancy, and non-residence while those convicted of pluralism were obliged to choose one living.

The provision of a well-equipped ministry was entrusted to twenty-five approvers, who included Walter Cradock and Vavasor Powell, to recommend to the vacancies of the ejected ministers. Each approver was entitled to a salary not exceeding £100 per annum, which was to derive from sequestered livings and from the estates of convicted royalists. As with the commissioners, no attempt was made to appoint approvers on a county basis and at least six of them had no connection with Wales before the Propagation Act.

Although Major-General Harrison is usually seen as the leading figure in the Propagation Commission, he played no part in its implementation. In practice the work of Propagation in Wales was conducted by two small groups of about fifteen commissioners in each of the regions led by a trusted nucleus of about six. Those in the south were led by the four Glamorgan men who dominated south Wales politics during the Interregnum: Colonel Philip Jones, Bussy Mansell, Rowland Dawkins, and John Price. A similar situation existed in the six northern counties with the essential difference that most of the dominant figures, including John Carter, George Twistleton, and Thomas Madrin, were English military men.[3] Propagation business was

---

[1] Firth & Rait, ii. 342–8.

[2] This led Dr. T. Richards to assert that 'Wales during the Propagation regime was governed by a military middle class'; *A History of the Puritan Movement in Wales* (1928), 94.

[3] This and what follows is based on Lambeth Palace Library MS. Comm. VIII/I ('Orders of the Committee for Propagating the Gospel, 1653'); Bodl.,

conducted on a well-delineated regional basis. Regular meetings of the propagation commissioners were held in various towns throughout the north and south of the Principality to co-ordinate their work, and although each county was allowed its own treasurer, over-all supervision of the revenues of each of the regions was entrusted to a regional treasurer. Each region employed its own solicitor, and one Price Vaughan acted as solicitor in London on behalf of both sets of com-missioners.

The commissioners entered upon their work immediately, and Bulstrode Whitelocke recorded that as early as June 1650 many ministers had been ejected in north Wales, so that the Rump at one stage was moved to consider the appointment of 'more moderate men' as approvers in the region. Such was the zeal of the propagators that a high proportion of the ejections which took place in the Principality during the three years of the Act's life had been effected before the end of 1650. During 1650-3 the propagators ejected a total of 278 ministers, 82 of whom were from north Wales and 196 from south Wales and Monmouthshire. In the southern counties 127 were declared satisfactory and left in their places, though in the north far fewer were left undisturbed.

The implementation of the Propagation Act was fraught with numerous problems. There was little uniformity of view concerning doctrine, church organization, or the matter of a state-supported ministry. Further, there was no prescribed religious test to determine the suitability of incumbents either to continue under the Propagation or to be recruited to it. Indeed, the grounds for nearly all ejections were moral lapses and political disaffection rather than religious unsuitability.

There is little evidence of appointments to settled livings in the Principality during the Propagation. Only twelve ministers are known to have settled in south Wales, while a few medium-term appointments of several months are recorded in the north. Though strenuous efforts were made to recruit suitable

Rawlinson MS. C 261 ('The Proceedings of the Commissioners for North Wales', printed in *An Act for the Propagation of the Gospel in Wales, 1649* (Cymdeithas Llen Cymru, reprint, Cardiff, 1908)); Richards, *Puritan Movement*, 113, 115–33, 220, 235–6, 134–5, 144–5; A. M. Johnson, 'Politics and Religion in Glamorgan during the Interregnum, 1649–1660' in *Glamorgan County History*, iv, ed. G. Williams (Cardiff, 1974), 283–92.

replacements for the ejected clergy, especially in London and at the universities, they met with little success. The problem of finding adequate replacements was exacerbated, as Vavasor Powell recognized, 'partly because that at the time, there was the like Act for several Northern counties; but especially because they wanted the Welsh tongue'.[1] Many otherwise suitable preachers had gone north rather than to Wales because they were unable to speak Welsh which was an essential qualification if the Propagation Commission was to achieve its aim of puritanizing Wales. Although Welsh was proscribed as an official language by the Act of Union of 1536, it remained the only language of the majority of the population in Wales of perhaps 400,000 throughout the seventeenth century.[2] It was therefore vital to recruit educated Welsh-speaking preachers and to produce Welsh religious literature, especially cheap Welsh versions of the Bible.

The Propagation Commission met the shortfall in educated Welsh-speaking preachers by the use of itinerant ministers. Hugh Peter envisaged itinerant preachers working alongside a settled ministry in which no more than six itinerants would operate in any one county. In fact, there were probably about ninety itinerant preachers in Wales during the Propagation. Included in this number were some of the twenty-five approvers named in the Act and at least sixty-three who were recruited at some time during the life of the Propagation. The leading proponent of this style of ministry was Vavasor Powell, described by his great adversary Alexander Griffiths as the 'metropolitan of the itinerants'. They were supposed to serve some sort of probation to determine their fitness to preach, but so wide-ranging were their opinions that any such test served little purpose. The majority of the itinerants were unlearned and had not received the benefit of any sort of formal certification for their task. The itinerants were probably more effective in north Wales because of the influence of Vavasor Powell, though in the south they were clearly much less successful and the evidence leads the best judge of the matter to pronounce

[1] Vavasor Powell, *Bird in the Cage Chirping* (2nd edn. 1662).

[2] O. Williams, 'The Survival of the Welsh Language after the Act of Union of England and Wales: the first phase, 1536–1642', *Welsh History Rev.*, ii (1964–5), 67–93; D. Williams, 'A note on the population of Wales, 1536–1801', *Bulletin of the Board of Celtic Studies*, viii (1935–7), 359–63.

that the itinerant system proved quite ineffective in meeting the spiritual needs of the countryside.[1]

While the majority of preachers were quite ready to accept state support a substantial minority were troubled at the prospect, and rejected it. Indeed, it was claimed in 1652 that there were as many as eighty unpaid preachers at work in south Wales. Thus there was in existence an 'official' Propagation embracing all those who accepted state support as either approved ministers, or itinerants, working alongside an 'unofficial' Propagation of preachers who received support from other sources.[2]

In tandem with their attempt to establish a Puritan ministry in Wales the commissioners were ordered to found new schools. Relatively fewer schools had been established in the Principality than in England since the Reformation and they were closely associated with the Anglican Church. Through the founding of new schools it was hoped to puritanize the young and to sustain the missionary work of the preachers. The approvers were empowered to select men of 'approved piety' to act as schoolmasters, who were to be funded out of sequestered revenues of the Church, and within three years over sixty new schools were established in the Principality; thirty-seven in south Wales and twenty-six in the north. In all, the Propagation represented a considerable advance in contemporary views of school education, introducing state-supported salaries for schoolmasters, free schooling for all social groups, and, in some schools, even co-education.[3]

An unregarded, but extremely important, duty imposed on the Propagation commissioners was to act as commissioners of indemnity. The principal of indemnification against liabilities incurred in Parliament's service was recognized in 1647. Under the Propagation the power to act as commissioners of indemnity was devolved upon the propagators probably to save those involved in such cases the burden of long journeys and the expense of attending in London. The propagators acting as commissioners of indemnity conformed to the well-established pattern of other aspects of their work in that they conducted

---

[1] T. Richards, *Religious Developments in Wales, 1654–1662* (1925), 10.
[2] Ibid. 182, 203; Richards, *Puritan Movement*, 162–5.
[3] Richards, *Puritan Movement*, 233.

their business on a regional basis. As if to emphasize the distinction between indemnity and other Propagation business, the commissioners met at different times and, on occasions, even in different locations.

Whether or not the opportunity to prosecute cases locally rather than petition in London stimulated Welsh resort to indemnity procedure is a matter of conjecture, though there is no doubt that the indemnity side of the propagators' duties was very onerous. The commissioners dealt with a wide variety of cases. There were disputes about the tenancy or ownership of sequestered lands, petitions for restitution of damages incurred in the Civil Wars, and a number of allegations brought against persons who were reputed to be disqualified from office in Wales because they had been royalists or royalist collaborators.

Appeals from the commissioners in Wales were heard in London, and a familiar stratagem employed on the one hand to slow down proceedings by those against whom petitions had been brought, and on the other by petitioners who were dubious of the authority of the propagators, was to appeal to London for the case to be heard there by claiming that the commissioners for indemnity in Wales rarely sat. The central commissioners usually referred such cases back to Wales and often upheld decisions taken by the local commissioners.[1]

Indemnity was the one major aspect of the work of the Propagation Commission which escaped contemporary criticism, though one pamphleteer pointed out that none of the commissioners had received any sort of legal training for this task.[2]

The most often repeated allegations against the commissioners suggested that they were incompetent to eject ministers, and unable to find suitable replacements, and that there was widespread corruption in the administration of Propagation finances. Many of these objections were incorporated in a pamphlet from south Wales and Monmouthshire which was presented to the House of Commons in March 1652, and was said to have received the support of 15,000 persons.[3] In July 1652 efforts

---

[1] This account is derived from the Order Books of the Committee of Indemnity in London, PRO, SP 24/1–14 (June 1647–June 1653); and the bundles of cases in SP 24/30–87.   [2] Richards, *Puritan Movement*, 99.
[3] *The Petition of the Six Counties of South Wales and the County of Monmouthshire* (16 Mar. 1652); The history of the *Petition* is in Alexander Griffiths, *A True and*

were made by Sir Thomas Myddleton to promote a petition against the propagators in north Wales but it appears never to have got off the ground.[1]

The inspiration behind the south Wales petition came from two former Breconshire sequestrators, together with Colonel Edward Freeman, Attorney-General for south Wales and M.P. for Hereford, all three of whom had been critical of the conduct of sequestration business in south Wales.[2] A distinguished promoter of the petition, and possibly its author, was Alexander Griffiths, the vehement anti-propagationist. Although Dr. Richards's careful analysis of the petition has shown that as evidence of the workings of the Propagation Commission in south Wales the pamphlet is unsatisfactory,[3] this, and other anti-Propagation literature achieved a good deal of success in putting the supporters of the Propagation on the defensive throughout the Interregnum.

While the Rump was fast losing what little enthusiasm it ever entertained for propagation schemes, Major-General Harrison was urging the leading Welsh propagators to come to London to press the Rump to advance the propagation of the gospel in England. Thus it is probably fair to say, as Christopher Hill has inferred, that the more cautious members of the Rump came to see the methods of the Commission for the Propagation of the Gospel in Wales in the conduct of religious affairs as a recipe for chaos and even social dislocation if the scheme was extended to the rest of Britain.[4]

The report on the south Wales petition came from the Committee for Plundered Ministers for debate in the House on 25 March 1653 and though the committee effectively dismissed the allegations against the propagators,[5] the predominantly conservative members of the House on 1 April refused to continue the Act beyond its expiry date and thus it lapsed.

Perfect Relation of the Whole Transaction concerning the Petition of the Six Counties (1654).

[1] *Calendar of the Wynn (of Gwydir) Papers, 1515–1690* (Aberystwyth, 1926), no. 1988, p. 32.

[2] Johnson in *Glamorgan County History*, iv. 282.

[3] Richards, *Puritan Movement*, chs. xvii, xviii.

[4] Ibid. 198; Hill, *Change and Continuity*, 35.

[5] The evidence of the south Wales commissioners before the Committee is in *A True and Perfect Relation* (1654).

Harrison, who had drifted into the ranks of the Fifth Monarchists, regarded the failure of the Rump to continue the life of the Propagation Commission as further proof of the lack of determination of the M.P.s to advance the cause of Godly Reformation, and stiffened his resolve to press for an immediate dissolution of the Rump.

The period of the short-lived Barebone's Parliament which succeeded the Rump in July 1653 had few implications for Wales. Though there was a shift to the left in the personnel of local governors in many areas, there were relatively few changes in the Principality. The local governors in the southern counties continued much as before, though a few new faces appeared among the commissioners and J.P.s in the north. The most significant aspect of these months was the nature of Wales's representation in Parliament, which consisted of six M.P.s. In practice the army leaders merely selected those whom they regarded as most suitable: Major-General Harrison personally chose the three Welsh M.P.s who were based in north Wales. Although only four of the Welsh M.P.s could be described as Fifth Monarchists they constituted one-third of the number of their party in Parliament and were active in its affairs. Two of their number, John Williams and Hugh Courtney, were added to the Council of State and helped to strengthen Fifth Monarchy representation there.[1]

Although Cromwell personally encouraged the former propagators to continue in their work until new arrangements were made, the tenuous apparatus established during the Propagation years collapsed and no official provision was made to tackle the spiritual condition of Wales until a new system of appointment of ministers throughout England and Wales was introduced in 1654. Until that time the situation in Wales was very confused and many ministers resorted to various central bodies to try to secure confirmation of their appointments and the salaries awarded under the Propagation, though, as far as the evidence allows, the petitioners generally failed in their attempts or at best were granted somewhat below their entitlement.[2]

By an Act of March 1654 the task of providing and approving ministers throughout England and Wales was entrusted to the

[1] B. Capp, *The Fifth Monarchy Men* (1973), 69.
[2] Bassett, 'Local Government', 261–2.

Commission for the Approbation of Public Preachers, which was based in London. Thus no longer were special arrangements made to meet the spiritual condition of Wales. The commission consisted of twenty-nine ministers and nine laymen, of whom only two members were Welsh, Walter Cradock and Jenkin Griffiths. The commissioners were generally men of moderate religious views and represented a wider spectrum of Puritan opinion than the former Propagation ministers. All new ministers had to be approved as fit for the ministry by the commissioners, often known as Triers. They were empowered to review all previous appointments and to approve all persons they thought worthy to preach. Under the new system no provision was made for a state-paid itinerant clergy which was so distinctive a feature of the Propagation years: the emphasis was on a return to a settled ministry to which many of the former itinerants were recruited.

To provide local evidence for the Triers there were nominated throughout England and Wales commissioners for ejecting scandalous ministers. They were appointed on a county basis, except in Wales, where the task was entrusted to two regional committees, and on this occasion Monmouthshire was treated as an English county and was given its own committee. The two committees—forty-three members in the south and twenty-three in the north—consisted of the well-trusted nucleus of government support in the Principality; about half of all the committee-men had sat on other parliamentary committees in recent years. Attached to the commissioners were a number of ministers or 'assistants'—sixteen in the north and twenty-four in the south—and among those nominated for the southern counties and Monmouthshire was Walter Cradock, who was also a member of the Commission for the Approbation of Public Preachers.[1]

In practice the Commissioners for the Approbation of Public Preachers and the Committee for the Ejection of Scandalous Ministers interfered little with appointments in Wales because the propagators had carried out their work with great thoroughness, though their approval was necessary if a minister's salary was to be continued. The payment of ministers accepted by the Commission for Approbation was in the hands of the

[1] Firth & Rait, ii. 855–8, 973, 976–7, 981, 983–4.

Trustees for Maintenance of Ministers, a body of thirteen members established in 1649, but until the expiration of the Propagation Act it did not exercise any authority in Wales. The trustees appointed four 'Receivers of Wales' whose duty it was to collect rents and profits from sequestered church lands and to pay out of the proceeds the salaries and augmentations sanctioned by the trustees.[1]

It was soon apparent that the arrangements embodied in the Protectorate Religious Settlement, even more than those prescribed in the Propagation Act, failed to meet the aspirations of a substantial minority of preachers. Sixty-nine preachers have been identified as preaching without the benefit of state support during the Protectorate. Most of them were Baptists of various shades of opinion who were concentrated in south Wales.[2] The only group whose disillusionment was politicized in any significant way during these years was the Fifth Monarchists. Though essentially an urban movement, Fifth Monarchy gained a firm foothold in the rural area of north-east Wales, largely through the dynamism of Vavasor Powell.

Alexander Griffiths alleged that at the beginning of 1654 there were about '700 parishes in the thirteen counties unsupplied with any Ministers',[3] and in the event the Protectorate system proved just as inadequate as the Propagation in making good these deficiencies, so that the Triers were obliged unofficially to condone the activities of a number of preachers who worked as itinerants. The system of Triers and Ejectors remained in existence throughout the Protectorate and the verdict on their efficiency must be that they were 'absurdly far' from meeting the spiritual needs of Wales.[4]

Though no provision was made for schoolmasters under the aegis of the Commissioners for the Approbation of Public Preachers, the commissioners did endeavour to maintain the system established under the Propagation Act with the financial supervision of the Trustees for Maintenance of Ministers in London. In spite of this, the great effort during the Propagation years to establish schools in Wales was not sustained during

---

[1] Lambeth Palace Lib., Comm. VIa/6, p. 171; Richards, *Religious Developments*, 83; Bassett, 'Local Government', 261.

[2] Richards, *Religious Developments*, 199–203.

[3] Alexander Griffiths, *Strena Vavasoriensis* (1654) (Cymdeithas Llen Cymru, reprint, Cardiff, 1915), 5.   [4] Richards, *Religious Developments*, 135.

the Protectorate so that by 1660 there remained in existence only one-third of the sixty schools established between 1650 and 1653.[1]

Although the Propagation scheme ended early in 1653, it continued to excite considerable controversy throughout the life of the Protectorate much of which focused on two of its principal activists, Vavasor Powell and Philip Jones. These accusations owed much to the zeal of Alexander Griffiths, himself ejected under the Propagation from his parish of Glasbury, Breconshire, for alleged drunkenness and lasciviousness.[2] Griffiths produced two particularly effective tracts in which he repeated and developed the charges made against the propagators in the south Wales petition of 1652.[3]

The accusations against the propagators were wide-ranging and often exaggerated, but it was the constant insinuation that the leading officials had misappropriated the considerable revenues for which they were responsible during the three years of the Propagation Commission which struck most effectively. Although Powell's friends produced a tract of their own to defend him against the allegations of his misappropriation of finances and other misdeeds, they failed to stem the wave of criticism and suspicion which had been built up against Powell and the Commission by Griffiths.[4]

The south Wales petition of 1652 alleged that the total revenue from their seven counties was £20,000 annually, while Griffiths put the figure for the thirteen counties at £40,000 a year and claimed that for the period of the Propagation a sum of about £160,000 was unaccounted for. Evidence from an investigation of the church revenues of the counties of south Wales and Monmouthshire at the Restoration confirmed the sums alleged by Griffiths and it is reasonable to assume that his figures for the thirteen counties were similarly accurate.[5] Much of the criticism was based on the presumption that because only

---

[1] Ibid. 54–62.
[2] Richards, *Puritan Movement*, 133.
[3] *True and Perfect Relation* (1654); *Strena Vavasoriensis*. Closely associated with these is (author unknown) *Gemitus Ecclesia Cambro-Britannicus* (1654).
[4] *Vavasoris Examen, and Purgamen: or, Mr. Vavasor Powell's Impartiall Triall* (1654).
[5] Bodl., Clarendon MS. 75, fol. 412; Johnson in *Glamorgan County History*, iv. 297–8.

a little of the revenue was used to propagate the gospel, since so few people were recruited to fill the vacancies of those ejected, and because only small allowances were paid in fifths to the ejected ministers, the surplus moneys must have been misappropriated by officials.

The constant pressure of the allegations by Griffiths and his colleagues persuaded Cromwell in August 1654 to support the establishment of a commission of thirty-three to investigate Propagation finances. The impartiality of the commission was seriously questioned, however, because Jones helped to draft the Act and placed some of his supporters among those who 'passed' the accounts of Glamorgan at Neath in 1655.[1] The surviving evidence of income from church property is limited to south Wales, but these figures suggest that perhaps only one-half of the anticipated revenues were received during the Propagation years. The Propagation commissioners for south Wales conceded before the Committee for Plundered Ministers in London in 1652 the allegation that the income of £19,936. 10s. 8d. for the two years 1650 and 1651 was about one-half of the potential total, but excused themselves by pointing to the inexperience of minor officials 'who for reasons best known to themselves did not use their wonted rigidness in Collecting and Receiving the same'.[2] The Neath accounts furnished no evidence of actual corruption, but they and the figures admitted by the propagators for south Wales demonstrate that the values of vicarages were seriously under-realized and that church properties were not managed efficiently.

Further attempts to reduce provincial independence were a feature of the Protectorate period. In general the government was less inclined, and had less need, to make special provision for Wales than for any of the English provinces, as is evidenced by the absence of special measures to deal with the spiritual condition of Wales during the Protectorate.

Although in England there were growing signs of a return to positions of responsibility in local government of persons previously disaffected towards the parliamentary regime, there was less evidence of this in Wales, where regional government

---

[1] Bodl., MS. J: Walker C. 13, fols. 16–32; Johnson in *Glamorgan County History*, iv. 297.

[2] *True and Perfect Relation* (1654), 42.

remained under the control of small groups of experienced men well tried and trusted on Parliament's behalf.

The reapportionment of constituencies under the Instrument of Government left Wales with only two borough seats, one for Cardiff and one for Haverfordwest. All counties were given two seats, except Merionethshire, which was granted one. Thus the total number of Welsh M.P.s was raised from the 1640 figure of twenty-four to twenty-five. With the notable exceptions of Edmund Jones, Recorder of Brecon and, since 1652, Attorney-General of south Wales, and John Vaughan, both of whom were former royalist delinquents who employed corrupt methods to secure their return for the counties of Breconshire and Merionethshire respectively, those elected for Welsh seats were soundly representative of the governing class of both regions of the Principality.[1]

Cromwell's dismissal of the first Protectorate Parliament in January 1655 gave the royalists renewed hopes for a series of successful risings planned for March 1655 to overthrow the Protectorate regime. Wales was an area expected to lend support to the risings but in the event provided no assistance at all. The government was perhaps more concerned with the activities of Vavasor Powell and Morgan Llwyd and their Fifth Monarchy supporters—the one radical religious group in Wales whose disillusionment at the government's rejection of the demands of the Saints was translated into political action. Powell was known to be organizing a force in the Principality against the Protectorate, though in face of the royalist threat he even assisted the government by rounding up suspected royalist plotters in north Wales.[2]

Even before the abortive risings in March 1655, Cromwell had been persuaded of the failure of his policy of reconciliation. Central to his determination to strengthen his control of the localities was the reorganization of the militia in the counties in order to place the burden for defence more squarely on them rather than persevere with an unpopular and expensive standing army.

¹ *The Complaint of the County of Brecon* (1654); PRO, SP 18/73/73; *CSPD, 1654*, 271–2, 299; PRO, SP 18/74/49; W. R. Williams, *Parliamentary History of the Principality of Wales* (Brecknock, 1895).
² R. T. Jones, 'Vavasor Powell and the Protectorate', *Trans. of the Congregational Hist. Soc.*, xcii (1952–5).

There were no obvious principles underlying the appointment of militia commissioners in Wales in March 1655.[1] A commission of twenty-three was appointed for the six counties of south Wales and a separate commission of sixteen for Monmouthshire. No commissions were issued for the counties of north Wales, where the commissions of 1651 presumably remained in force. The appointment of the major-generals in the autumn, which coincided with measures designed to restrict the power of town corporations, marked the high point of government control over the localities. The command of Wales and the border was entrusted to Major-General James Berry, whose own solution to the administrative problems of the Principality was to retain the north Wales region as one unit and split the six southern counties into two areas.

Though Berry could write at the end of 1655 that he had not come across one refractory person in Wales, there remained very little positive support for the government in the Principality. The great majority of the population was acquiescent and too unreliable to be entrusted with positions of responsibility. Berry was obliged to rely on the small nucleus of trusted allies of the government who had been active since the beginning of the Commonwealth.[2]

In December Vavasor Powell's known hostility to the Protectorate could be contained no longer; he produced his *Word for God*, which was a wholesale denunciation of the Protectorate government for reviving all the ills which the Godly party had fought against in the civil wars. Powell's petition attracted the signatures of 322 persons, but close analysis has shown that most of them came from north Wales and at least half of them were closely associated with Powell and Morgan Llwyd.[3]

That the Protector and the religious arrangements over which he presided were more popular than Powell's inflammatory words would suggest is evident in at least three pamphlets, the most significant of which was Walter Cradock's *Humble Representation and Advice* of February 1656 in which he strongly condemned *A Word for God*. This attracted 762 signatories

[1] PRO, SP 25/76a/32–3 (14 Mar. 1654/5).

[2] J. Berry and S. G. Lee, *A Cromwellian Major-General* (Oxford, 1938), 117; Bassett, 'Local Government', 295–6.

[3] Thurloe, iv. 380–4; A. H. Dodd, 'A Remonstrance from Wales, 1655', *Bulletin of the Board of Celtic Studies*, xvii (1956–8).

representing a much wider range of political and religious views in Wales, and it seems that the government took advantage of this and encouraged the distribution of Cradock's pamphlet.[1] Major-General Berry adopted a very tolerant attitude towards Vavasor Powell, perhaps conscious of the fact that Powell had secured the support of only a handful either of the approvers then at work or of the former propagators. Berry took the view that only persecution would enable *A Word for God* to flourish.[2] His reactions further emphasize the fact that the religious radicals in the mid-1650s represented no more than a small minority who proved little or no threat to the government's position in the Principality. His reports to Thurloe also demonstrate that the provision of an adequate preaching ministry in Wales had been a disastrous failure.[3]

Powell's *A Word for God* represented the high point of millenarian activity in Wales in the seventeenth century. He was bitterly disappointed that so many Welsh Puritans should have taken exception to this publication,[4] but the reality of its appeal had been clearly revealed and from this point both he and the Fifth Monarchy movement went into decline.

The outstanding absentee among the signatories to *A Word for God* was Morgan Llwyd who, before the publication of the tract, had turned to the more moderate ways advocated by Walter Cradock, though the estrangement between Powell and Llwyd did not become final until 1657. The response to the pamphlets issued by Powell and Cradock provided additional evidence that the moderates were far more numerous than the radical millenarian followers of Powell and that Welsh Puritanism had effectively divided on the issue of the Cromwellian Protectorate.[5] Llwyd's departure from the millenarian creed was symptomatic of a general decline in interest even among the leaders of the movement. During the late 1650s the ranks of Powell's supporters were so thinned that 'of all the ministers, more or less Puritan, working in North and Mid-Wales, only fourteen subscribed the *Word for God* and before

---

[1] Thurloe, iv. 540, 545, 551.   [2] Richards, *Religious Developments*, 218.
[3] Thurloe, iv. 565, 334.
[4] R. T. Jones, 'The Life, Work and Thought of Vavasor Powell, 1617–1670' (D.Phil. thesis, Univ. of Oxford, 1947), 154 and appx. 8. Dr. Jones has published a shortened version of his thesis in Welsh: *Vavasor Powell* (Abertawe, 1971).
[5] Jones, 'Vavasor Powell', 150, 155.

1660 all these had apostatized from their affected faith in a coming millennium'.[1]

Dr. Tudur Jones has argued that the division between Powell on the one hand and Cradock and Llwyd on the other profoundly affected the course of nonconformity in Wales. It sharpened the divisions between north and south Wales, which were not easily repaired. In the south nonconformity established a firm basis for its development, but in the north the differences among its leaders rendered it ill equipped for future growth.[2]

Berry was quick to recognize the need for a Welsh-speaking and educated preaching ministry, and Richard Baxter said that he offered his 'best assistance' to the proposals of John Lewis, himself a former propagator, to create a college in Wales closely associated with the two universities. In a pamphlet on the subject Lewis expressed the hope that his proposals would merit the support of the Protector, since 'to have a dispensation for a College or two among us in Wales, would doubtless highly advance us for a supply of able ministers'.[3]

In the elections of the summer of 1656, the government had every cause for satisfaction at the results in Wales. Fourteen of the twenty-five elected in 1654 were returned and most of the remainder can be regarded as sympathetic to the government. The tense debates in the first half of 1657 concerning the offer of the crown to Cromwell reflected the precarious position of the government in the Commons. The acceptance of The Humble Petition and Advice in June 1657 foreshadowed a return to the pre-Civil War constitution, while more immediately Cromwell's selection of prominent M.P.s to sit in the new Upper House further undermined government support in the Commons. Among those selected by Cromwell from Wales were the M.P.s Philip Jones and Edmund Thomas of Glamorgan, the regicide John Jones of Merionethshire, and the former Major-General, James Berry.

By means of more traditional constitutional methods and a more conciliatory policy towards those previously alienated from the governments of the Interregnum, it was hoped that

---

[1] Richards, *Religious Developments*, 228.

[2] Jones, 'Vavasor Powell', 157.

[3] J. H. Davies, 'An Early Attempt to Found a National College in Wales' in *Wales*, ed. O. M. Edwards, iii (1896), 121–4.

a permanent settlement could be achieved. The government's policy of widening the membership of county committees and commissions of the peace in the provinces during 1657 to accommodate some of the traditional governing families did little to extend the circle of political control in Wales. Thus, though 'the county committees of 1657 were the most representative Wales had had since the war'[1] (Sir Thomas Myddleton was among those nominated for north Wales), control of local affairs in both north and south remained in the grip of loyal and experienced government supporters.

The political confusion which brought about the dissolution of the Parliament in February 1658 renewed the hopes of all those who longed for the overthrow of the Protectorate. It seems that Parliament made contingency plans to raise troops for the defence of north Wales under the command of Colonel John Carter, described as 'governor of these six counties', with Thomas Madrin as his deputy.[2]

Cromwell's death in September 1658 put further into jeopardy hopes for a political settlement. Some indication of its effects on the political life of Wales can be derived from the elections to Richard Cromwell's short-lived Parliament. Those acquiescent for a decade or more asserted themselves to return, in a majority of Welsh seats, either former royalists or members distinctly lukewarm towards the Protectorate. Royalists managed to gain seats even in the most Puritan parts of Wales, as in John Jones's county of Merionethshire, where an old royalist, Lewis Owen of Peniarth, was returned. A few government supporters were returned, mainly in the south, though Rowland Dawkins, one of the most powerful figures in south Wales during the Interregnum, was defeated in Carmarthen by David Morgan, a disillusioned former propagation commissioner.[3] In Parliament, Morgan in alliance with Edward Freeman, the chief promoter of the south Wales petition of 1652 and now M.P. for Leominster, and with the support of republican M.P.s, secured the appointment of a committee to

---

[1] Dodd, *Stuart Wales*, 161. Prof. Dodd seems to accept at face value that the new nominations of 1657 afford sufficient evidence of a sharp change in local power structures in Wales.

[2] *Calendar of Wynn Papers*, no. 2156, p. 349.

[3] Richards, *Religious Developments*, 304–6.

examine how north and south Wales might be better supplied with a conscientious preaching ministry, and attempted to get re-examined the whole matter of Propagation finances. A pamphlet probably under the aegis of Freeman set out the arguments for an attack directed primarily at Philip Jones. It was alleged that 'above £150,000' remained unaccounted for and that Jones repeatedly abused his authority in south Wales. Edmund Jones the former royalist fell a victim of the same attack. It was alleged that he held his position as Attorney-General for south Wales because of the influence of Philip Jones, and on 12 February he was disabled from his seat for Breconshire.[1]

Richard Cromwell's fall in April 1659 followed by the revival of the Rump began a further period of disruption in the personnel of both national and local politics. The most notable casualty of the new political climate in Wales was the 'supreme Cromwellian', Philip Jones.[2] Further allegations were made against him, this time by Bledry Morgan, a former Carmarthenshire treasurer of sequestrations, who, in alliance with the redoubtable Edward Freeman and other dedicated adversaries from the Propagation era, presented Parliament with a catalogue of grievances against Jones. Though, as in the past, no specific evidence could be adduced against him, the criticisms forced him to retire from Parliament, from which he was soon formally dismissed for non-attendance.[3]

The changed political climate was reflected in the commissions of July 1659 issued to raise and reorganize the militia to meet the threat of renewed royalist agitation. On this occasion appointments in south Wales were made on a county basis while north Wales had a joint committee for the whole region. The membership of the southern committees was reduced by about one-third and the associated committee for north Wales was roughly one-third of the size of the combined membership of the separate county commissions of 1657.[4]

---

[1] *The Distressed Oppressed Condition of the Inhabitants of South Wales* (1659); A. G. Veysey, 'Colonel Philip Jones, 1618–1674', *Trans. of the Hon. Soc. of Cymmrodorion* (1966), 327–8.

[2] Richards's description; *Religious Developments*, 219.

[3] Veysey in *Trans. Cymmrodorion Soc.* (1966), 328–9; Johnson in *Glamorgan County History*, iv. 305.

[4] Firth & Rait, ii. 1328, 1335–6.

In both north and south Wales those left off the militia commissions of 1659 were invariably those who had been added in 1657 when Cromwell's policy was at its most conciliatory. Suitable replacements were difficult to come by and the government was obliged to nominate a number of rank outsiders to serve as commissioners. This was especially true in north Wales, where perhaps one-third of the new commissioners were quite unknown.

With few exceptions the inner core of long-serving committeemen were kept on and accepted as zealots by the Rump. Thus in north Wales Colonels John Jones, Thomas Madrin, and George Twistleton were very much in evidence, though the Cromwellian knight, Sir John Carter, described recently as 'the Philip Jones of the north', was left off.[1] The feature of the new commissions was the complete eclipse of Philip Jones and his close colleagues Rowland Dawkins and John Price, together with a number of his dependants. The decline in the fortunes of Philip Jones marked the end of his decade of ascendancy in south Wales and the end of stable political leadership to which the region had been accustomed during the Commonwealth and Protectorate. Jones's supreme position in the region was taken over by Bussy Mansell, whose membership of Barebone's Parliament undoubtedly stood him in good stead, even though at this very time he was holding out hopes to the royalists that he might assist them on behalf of the King in south Wales.[2]

Bussy Mansell secured control of the militia throughout south Wales, which in the event was quite unaffected by threats of armed uprising. The danger to the government came from the north, where Sir Thomas Myddleton in league with Sir George Booth hoped to secure north Wales for the King. The response to Myddleton's overtures was encouraging for the royalists; and several leading county families as well as a number of minor gentry are known to have supported the short-lived insurrection.[3]

From early in September sequestration commissioners were nominated to deal with malcontents in the Principality

---

[1] Prof. Dodd's description; *Stuart Wales*, 172.

[2] Johnson in *Glamorgan County History*, iv. 305–6; A. M. Johnson, 'Bussy Mansell (1623-1699), political survivalist', *Morgannwg*, xx (1976), 20–2.

[3] G. R. Thomas, 'Sir Thomas Myddleton II, 1586–1666' (M.A. thesis, Univ. of Wales, 1967), 167–8.

Twenty-eight were nominated for north Wales, seven for south Wales, and three for Monmouthshire.[1] Most of the north Wales sequestrators were in the militia commission of July 1659, though it appears they met with little success.[2] The assessment committees nominated in January 1660, but this time on a county basis for the whole Principality, contained a few moderates along with the radical members. Philip Jones, for example, found himself nominated for the Breconshire committee but left off the commission for his own county. In the north Sir John Carter was restored to the committees of Anglesey, Denbighshire, and Flintshire, along with old colleagues George Twistleton and Thomas Madrin, while John Jones was also nominated to the Merionethshire committee.[3]

The revival of the Rump in May 1659 and the precarious political situation provided fresh hopes for radicals. In the town of Brecon, in September and October 1659, two close supporters of Vavasor Powell, Captains John Jenkins and John Morgan, combined to intimidate the electors to try to secure their own nominee as bailiff. With Jenkins and Morgan was the recently disabled M.P. for Breconshire, Edmund Jones, who had his own scores to settle with several persons in the town. The attack on the independence of the corporation was utilized to demonstrate the tyrannical methods employed by the extreme Puritans, and Powell was portrayed as the instigator of a design against the liberties of the people which he had begun under the cloak of the Propagation Commission.[4]

The return to Parliament in February 1660 of those surviving Presbyterian members excluded in 1648 effectively prepared the way for the Restoration of Charles II. Except for dedicated and unrepentant radicals like John Jones, long-standing committee-men made strenuous efforts to make themselves acceptable to the new regime, while others who by choice or proscription had not participated in county politics for a decade or more were now available again for positions of responsibility in local affairs. These pressures brought together all the conflicting and apparently irreconcilable strands in the

---

[1] PRO, SP 23/264/52 (19, 27 Sept. 1659).   [2] *Cal. Comp.* i. 773.
[3] Firth & Rait, ii. 1382–4.
[4] *An Alarum to Corporations* (1659); PRO, SP 18/205/48 (? Oct. 1659); *CSPD, 1659–60*, 288–9.

political spectrum and were reflected in the nominations of the militia commissioners made by the presbyterianized Rump in March 1660.[1] Once again the northern counties were associated while the southern counties and Monmouthshire were nominated individually. One of the distinctive features of these committees was the almost wholesale removal of those on the assessment committees of January and the return of representatives of the old-established families, now that the Restoration was all but assured. The old millenarian strongholds were severely dealt with. Only four Montgomeryshire and four Radnorshire commissioners survived from January, while only one remained from Merionethshire. In the south Philip Jones and Rowland Dawkins made a brief reappearance, though these stalwarts of the Interregnum years had now lost all their previous authority with the re-emergence of the traditional governing families.

That the Propagation Commission remained a living issue a decade after its establishment was illustrated when the Rump on the last day of its sitting in March passed an Act for taking account of Welsh tithes and church livings. In April the Council of State nominated a commission including Bussy Mansell and Colonel Edward Freeman to undertake an investigation into the Propagation in Glamorgan, though the imminence of the Restoration seems to have rendered the attempt redundant.[2]

Despite the upheavals in local politics from 1659, some made the transformation from Interregnum to Restoration with great skill, none more so than the elusive Bussy Mansell in the south and Colonel Sir John Carter in the north, both of whom were returned to the Convention Parliament in April 1660 to welcome Charles II to the throne in the following month. Carter even received confirmation of his Cromwellian knighthood at the hands of Charles II in June 1660.

The Restoration was welcomed in Wales. There was, in general, very little retribution practised against former committee-men, the majority of whom had done little more than co-operate with the governments of the Interregnum and were absorbed without difficulty into post-Restoration Welsh society and politics. Only the most uncompromising suffered more

[1] Firth & Rait, ii. 1447–8.
[2] Johnson in *Glamorgan County History*, iv. 397–8.

than a temporary removal from positions of influence in local affairs, and even a figure as prominent as Philip Jones was able to make his way back after a few years to become a pillar of the south Wales gentry.[1]

When the dust had settled it was clear that the Revolution had had little lasting effect on Wales. Welsh political and social structure had proved very resilient and been little affected by the changes introduced during the Interregnum. Neither the principal official weapons for extending the Revolution into Wales, the Propagation Commission and its successor the Protectorate religious settlement, nor the unpaid and unofficial preachers combined made much progress in puritanizing Wales and supplying the spiritual needs of the Principality. The spearhead of this effort was dependent upon the dynamism of a relatively small number of dedicated Puritan preachers the most prominent of whom were by the time of the Restoration either in decline, in prison, or dead. In the longer term, however, enough of the Puritan congregations which they had founded or nurtured during this period survived to provide inspiration for the steady progress of nonconformity in Wales from the end of the seventeenth century.

[1] Veysey in *Trans. Cymmrodorion Soc.* (1966), 335–40.

The Puritans and Adultery
The Act of 1650 Reconsidered

KEITH THOMAS

Adultery is a fire which will root out, but the gentiles,
the nations of the world, will never be proved capable
of such laws and punishments as that holy nation, bred
up and fed with miraculous dispensations, were fit for.

Roger Williams, 16 Dec. 1649.[1]

IF any single measure epitomizes the triumph of Puritanism in
England, it must surely be the Commonwealth's act of 10 May
1650 'for suppressing the detestable sins of incest, adultery and
fornication'.[2] This was an attempt, unique in English history,
to put the full machinery of the state behind the enforcement
of sexual morality. Spiritual misdemeanours were reclassified
as secular crimes and severe penalties prescribed for behaviour
which had previously been left to the informal sanctions of
neighbourly disapproval or the milder censures of the ecclesiastical courts. Incest and adultery became felonies, carrying
sentence of death without benefit of clergy. Fornication was
punished by three months in gaol, followed by a year's security
for good behaviour. Brothel-keepers were to be whipped,
pilloried, branded, and gaoled for three years; for a second
offence the penalty was death.[3] 'In those days', drily remarked

---

* I am indebted to Dr. Alan Macfarlane and Mr. J. A. Sharpe for references
to Essex records, to Mr. Conrad Russell for help with the parliamentary history
of the 1620s, to Dr. J. S. Cockburn for information about assize records, to Dr.
M. J. Ingram for permission to cite his unpublished thesis, and to Mr. D. H.
Pennington for constructive criticism.

[1] *Collectns. of the Massachusetts Hist. Soc.* 4th ser., vi (Boston, 1863), 276.

[2] Firth & Rait, ii. 387–9.

[3] The death penalty for those convicted a second time of 'any of the said last
recited offences' may have been intended to apply to fornicators as well as brothel-
keepers. This was assumed by some contemporaries (e.g. *Mercurius Pragmaticus*,
14–21 May 1650) and is implied by the index to Henry Scobell, *A Collection of Acts
and Ordinances* (1658), *s.v.* 'fornication'.

8224397   K

an eighteenth-century commentator, 'they went roundly to work.' It was, David Masson agreed, 'a tremendous act'.[1]

It was, of course, much too tremendous to be put fully into effect. In the late nineteenth century the researches of J. C. Jeaffreson and F. A. Inderwick revealed that, in Middlesex and on the Western Assize Circuit, death sentences for incest or adultery were scarcely ever imposed.[2] Trials for incest were understandably rare, but even for the commoner offence of adultery only four death sentences could be found, one at least of which is unlikely to have been carried out. The judicial records of the 1650s have not been fully searched and are in any case very incomplete. But all the evidence so far examined suggests that, although most counties had a small trickle of successful prosecutions for fornication,[3] the conviction of adulterers was exceedingly rare.[4] So far as its more drastic prescriptions were concerned, the act was very largely a dead letter. In 1660 it lapsed and was not renewed.

How then did it come to be passed in the first place? Was the act a bizarre aberration, the isolated product of an excessive outburst of Puritan zeal? Or was it the culmination of a long sequence of historical development? The ordinance of 1650 poses in microcosm the question which faces all historians of the English Revolution: were its spectacular events the outcome of an essentially transient combination of circumstances or did they reflect pressures which had been at work for many previous decades?

There was nothing new about the act's hierarchy of sexual

---

[1] James Burgh, *Political Disquisitions* (1774–5), iii. 137–8; D. Masson, *The Life of John Milton* (new edn. 1881–94), iv. 179.

[2] F. A. Inderwick, *The Interregnum* (1891), 33–9; *Middlesex County Records*, ed. J. C. Jeaffreson (1886–92), iii, pp. xxii–xxiii.

[3] They can be found in Cheshire, Derbyshire, Devon, Essex, Hampshire, Lancashire, Middlesex, Norfolk, Northamptonshire, Nottinghamshire, Somerset, Sussex, Warwick, Westmorland, Wiltshire, Yorkshire, and no doubt elsewhere.

[4] In addition to the four cases discussed by Inderwick, an elderly couple was said to have been convicted at Monmouth Assizes in 1653; *Mercurius Politicus*, 25 Aug.–1 Sept. 1653; and a woman was convicted but reprieved in Essex in 1658; PRO, Assi 35/99/2. A man was condemned in Yorkshire for incest and committed suicide in prison; Jonathan Clapham, *A Full Discovery . . . of the . . . Quakers* (1656), 51. Another was condemned for incest in Essex in 1653, but reprieved; PRO, Assi 35/94/1. In Scotland there were executions for both adultery and incest; see, e.g., *Mercurius Politicus*, 26 June–3 July 1656.

offences. For penitential purposes the medieval Church had regarded fornication as less serious than incest and adultery.[1] The Reformers reduced the range of prohibited degrees defining incest,[2] while denouncing Catholics for being too indulgent towards fornication. But their ranking of sexual sins remained unaltered. Adultery, as a Jacobean bishop put it, was 'worse than fornication, and incest worse than adultery'.[3] (Sodomy, which was even worse than incest, had been a capital offence since 1534.)[4]

But Tudor and Stuart moralists had new reasons for condemning these old offences. Their period saw a growing idealization of married love and domestic life. Although divines still regarded procreation as the primary purpose of marriage, Protestant and Catholic alike laid increasing emphasis on the blessings of mutual society and companionship.[5] It was this preoccupation which strengthened their desire to safeguard the family against the disruptive effects of sexual licence. 'If anything ought to be taken for holy in the whole life of man,' wrote Calvin, 'it is the faith which the husband plighteth to his wife and the wife to her husband.'[6] What adultery destroyed was love. The adulterer, wrote William Tyndale, robbed the husband of 'the preciousest gift that a man hath in this world . . . the true heart of his wife, to abide by him in wealth and woe'.[7] The guilty husband, said John Downame, fills his wife's heart 'with grief and jealousy and her face with shame when she seeth herself rejected and set at naught'.[8] The children also

[1] William Lyndwood, *Provinciale* (Oxford, 1679), 314.
[2] Edmund Gibson, *Codex Juris Ecclesiastici Anglicani* (1713), 494–500.
[3] Arthur Lake, *Sermons* (1629), iii. 12.   [4] 25 Hen. VIII, c. 6 (1533–4).
[5] W. and M. Haller, 'The Puritan Art of Love', *Huntington Lib. Qtly.* v (1941–2); R. M. Frye, 'The teachings of classical Puritanism on conjugal love', *Studs. in the Renaissance*, ii (1955); J. T. Johnson, *A Society ordained by God. English Puritan Marriage Doctrine in the first half of the Seventeenth Century* (Nashville, N.Y., 1970). Cf. J. T. Noonan, *Contraception* (N.Y., 1967), 310, 377. Sensible cautions against exaggerating the change or seeing it as peculiarly 'Puritan' are offered by J. Halkett, *Milton and the Idea of Matrimony* (New Haven, 1970), ch. 1; and by K. M. Davies, 'The sacred condition of equality—how original were Puritan doctrines of marriage?', *Social History*, 5 (1977).
[6] *The Sermons of M. Iohn Calvin upon . . . Deuteronomie*, trans. Arthur Golding (1583), 224. Cf. George Joye, *A Contrarye (to a certayne manis) Consultacion: That Adulterers ought to be punyshed wyth Deathe* (n.d. [1549]), Sig. Gvᵛ.
[7] [William Tyndale], *An Exposycyon upon the v. vi. vii. chapters of Mathewe* (?1530), fol. xxxixᵛ.
[8] John Downame, *Foure Treatises* (1613), 180–1.

suffered. Adultery intruded bastards into the family, depriving lawful heirs of their rightful inheritance, or producing illegitimate cast-offs to be neglected and despised. 'The children which are so begotten,' declared Thomas Cartwright, 'having oftentimes less care and cost bestowed upon them in their education, become hurtful members of the commonwealth.'[1] Fornicators, wrote Downame, 'make the poor infant bear the punishment of their sin . . . They also rob it of their own love'.[2] Similarly, the objection to incest was not that it was thought to have disastrous genetic consequences, but that it seemed a threat to the reverence and respect which ought to exist between members of the same family.[3]

The act of 1650 thus asserted 'the principle that monogamy is the most salutary institution for the joint welfare of men and women, and ought to be strictly enforced by law'.[4] As Christopher Hill has said, it was 'part of the battle . . . for love in marriage'—'an attempt to impose new social patterns on the easier-going sexual habits of traditional society'.[5]

These 'easier-going sexual habits' need little documentation. Such figures as are available for illegitimacy and premarital conception in Tudor and Stuart England show that the Church's sexual code was never universally observed; and further allowance must be made for the successful practice of contraception. Courting couples enjoyed much freedom; perhaps a fifth of all brides were pregnant when they married.[6] No wonder that moralists lamented that fornication was lightly treated as 'but a trick of youth'.[7] There were many delinquents,

[1] *The Second Replie of Thomas Cartwright: agaynst Maister Doctor Whitgiftes Second Answer* (1575), ci.

[2] Downame, *Foure Treatises*, 145–6. Cf. Aquinas, *Summa Theologica*, II. ii. 154. 2.

[3] See, e.g., Lake, *Sermons*, iii. 12.

[4] L. O. Pike, *A History of Crime in England* (2nd ser., 1876), 183.

[5] *The World Turned Upside Down* (1972), 248; 'Science and Magic in Seventeenth Century England' (typescript of lecture at J. D. Bernal Peace Lib., 19 Oct. 1976), 7.

[6] M. J. Ingram, 'Ecclesiastical Justice in Wiltshire, 1600–1640, with special reference to cases concerning sex and marriage' (D.Phil. thesis, Oxford Univ., 1976), ch. vi; P. E. H. Hair, 'Bridal Pregnancy in rural England in earlier centuries', *Populn. Studs.* xx (1966–7); id., 'Bridal Pregnancy in earlier rural England further examined', ibid. xxiv (1970); P. Laslett, *Family Life and Illicit Love in Earlier Generations* (Cambridge, 1977), chap. 3.

[7] George Estie, *A Most Sweete and Comfortable Exposition, upon the Tenne Commandements* (1602), sig. Q8; William Perkins, *The Workes* (Cambridge, 1616–18),

like the almsman expelled from Dulwich College in 1632 for trying to seduce one of the almswomen, who reasoned 'that fornication was not sin at all if both parties are agreed'.[1] Adultery was notoriously an occasion for ribald laughter; villages mocked the cuckold, but often ignored the adulterer. Even some of the clergy condoned marital infidelity: an Elizabethan vicar of Hitchin said that, when a man committed adultery, 'he doth it not of himself, but that God makes him do it'.[2] A Lincolnshire rector affirmed in 1631 'that lechery was but a love sin', while an Essex clergyman, accused in 1636 of kissing a woman who was not his wife, retorted that 'change of pasture made fat calves and a bit abroad was worth two at home'.[3]

There were also more theologically-based variations upon this eternal theme. Some of the Lollards had denied the sinfulness of adultery, while early Protestants noted the example of the patriarchs: in 1551 an offender informed the Bishop of Gloucester's court that 'The law is for me to have children by adultery: I would wish Moses's law to be again'.[4] In 1646 Thomas Edwards accused sectaries of teaching that 'when either of the parties married is asleep, the other is free of the bond of matrimony . . . so that if a woman should have to do with any other man, her husband being asleep, she committeth not adultery'.[5] Like most of Edwards's allegations, the charge had some basis; back in 1588 an inhabitant of Tollesbury, Essex, had been cited for declaring 'that it is no sin, if his own conscience doth not oppress him, to have carnal company with a man's wife if the husband be asleep'.[6]

It was against such doctrines that the adultery act took its stand. Yet it too followed Old Testament precedent in defining adultery as the adultery of the married *woman*. Intercourse by a married man with a single woman was only fornication.

i. 551; Arthur Dent, *The Plaine Mans Path-Way to Heaven* (16th impn. 1617), 56; D[aniel] R[ogers], *Matrimoniall Honour* (1642), 340.

[1] W. Young, *The History of Dulwich College* (1889), i. 104.
[2] Bodl., University Coll. MS. 152, iv.
[3] Lincs. AO, court papers 69/2/26; Essex RO, D/ABD/7, fol. 127.
[4] J. A. F. Thomson, *The Later Lollards, 1414–1520* (1965), 64, 177; F. D. Price, 'Gloucester Diocese under Bishop Hooper, 1551–3', *Trans. Bristol & Glos. Archaeol. Soc.* lx (1938), 145.
[5] Thomas Edwards, *Gangraena* (2nd edn. 1646), ii. 141.
[6] Essex RO, D/ACA 16, fol. 64ᵛ.

This was not a distinction which many Protestant moralists had upheld. On the contrary, they had defined adultery as sexual misconduct by *either* partner. Like St. Augustine, they held that adultery was, if anything, a greater sin in the man, because he had superior reason and should set an example.[1]

The act of 1650, by contrast, embodied a double standard which modern historians understandably regard as 'iniquitous'.[2] Yet (unlike the common law) it did not allow injured husbands to sue for damages and it did not necessarily imply an unequal conception of the marriage relationship. For even those moralists who regarded adultery by either sex as equally sinful had observed that the temporal consequences were very unequal. It was the wife and her lover, not the married man and his mistress, who made adultery such a 'notorious theft'[3] and thereby a threat to the whole system of property relations. 'What else will remain safe in human society', Calvin had demanded, 'if licence be given to bring in by stealth the offspring of a stranger? to steal a name which may be given to spurious offspring? and to transfer to them property taken away from lawful heirs?'[4]

No doubt a wife's adultery was also regarded as more serious because she dealt her husband's honour an irreparable blow, a cuckold being vulgarly regarded as 'a fool, a coward and all that is bad in a man'.[5] But the ordinance was exclusively concerned with adultery as a public crime, not as a private injury. The man's sin might be greater, but 'in regard of the commonwealth, the woman's fault is more dangerous'.[6]

For these reasons the adultery of married women and their lovers required severe punishment. Moralists (following

[1] e.g. Estie, *Tenne Commandements*, sig. Q8ᵛ; Andrew Willet, *An Harmonie upon the Second Booke of Samuel* (Cambridge, 1614), 70; id., *Hexapla in Leviticum* (1631), 501; and refs. cited in K. Thomas, 'The Double Standard', *Journ. Hist. Ideas*, xx (1959), 203–4.

[2] G. E. Aylmer, *The State's Servants* (1973), 307.

[3] [Lancelot Andrewes], *The Morall Law Expounded* (1642), 778.

[4] John Calvin, *A Commentary on Genesis*, trans. and ed. J. King (1847: reprinted 1965), ii. 286–7.

[5] Margaret Cavendish, Marchioness of Newcastle, *The Worlds Olio* (1655), 75. Cf. Downame, *Foure Treatises*, 181; *Complete Prose Works of John Milton* (New Haven, 1953–), ii. 336–7.

[6] Willet, *Harmonie upon Samuel*, 72. Cf. Thomas Timme, *A Plaine Discoverie of Ten English Lepers* (1592), sig. I1ᵛ; [Heinrich Bullinger], *The Goldē Boke of Christen Matrimonye*, trans. M. Coverdale (1543), fol. xxiiii.

Proverbs 6: 22–5) agreed that adultery was worse than theft; some even thought it worse than murder.[1] Yet the theft of goods worth a shilling was a capital crime, while the adulterer usually escaped altogether. The discrepancy did not escape commentators; neither did its social implications. 'Silly thieves are sharply handled everywhere,' noted Willet, whereas 'adultery is but the sport of great men'.[2]

There was also the argument of self-protection. For if the magistrate did not act, then God would bring his judgements to bear, both upon the adulterers who had broken his holy ordinance and upon the community which condoned their perjury. Remissness on the magistrate's part, warned William Gouge, 'hath been one cause of sundry severe judgments which have been from time to time inflicted upon this kingdom.'[3] Part of the case against Charles I was to be the King's 'capital breaking of God's laws in not punishing and suppressing those horribly and openly known . . . adulterers, whoremongers, and what not sins'.[4] It was in response to such warnings that the preamble to the ordinance of 1650 began by citing 'the abominable and crying sins . . . wherewith the land is much defiled and Almighty God highly displeased'.

For many centuries the punishment of sexual misconduct in England had been the business of the church courts. In the Middle Ages offenders were whipped or sentenced to do penance. After the Reformation corporal punishment was abandoned and the normal censures became public penance (which could sometimes be commuted into a fine) or excommunication for the contumacious. To many ecclesiastics these penalties seemed inadequate; and one of the explicit reasons for setting up the High Commission was the desire to impose heavier sentences on notorious sexual offenders.[5] The *Admonition* of 1572 denounced the commissaries' courts for their 'toyish

[1] e.g. [John Dod and Robert Cleaver], *A Treatise or Exposition upon the Ten Commandements* (1603), sig. Oii; Matthew Griffith, *Bethel: or, a Forme for Families* (1633), 298–9; Henry Hammond, *A Practical Catechism* (16th edn. Oxford, 1847), 143–4.

[2] Willet, *Hexapla in Leviticum*, 503.

[3] William Gouge, *A Learned and Very Useful Commentary on the Whole Epistle to the Hebrewes* (1655), iv. 36.

[4] John Blackleach, *Endevors aiming at the Glory of God* (1650), 43.

[5] John Strype, *The Life and Acts of John Whitgift* (Oxford, 1822), i. 266.

censures'; and the 'light punishment of adultery' became a standard Puritan grievance against ecclesiastical justice.¹ Punishments for sexual offences, Queen Elizabeth was told in 1585, were 'so small and slight, and executed so little upon them of the meanest degree, and nothing at all upon them of the higher, that . . . God must therefore be angry with Your Majesty'.² 'I am sorry so renowned and famous a church as this of England', lamented a Norfolk parson, 'should have no sharper censure for adultery than a white sheet.'³

Many orthodox churchmen shared these views. Preaching before the Queen in 1563, Alexander Nowell, Dean of St. Paul's, called for 'some other sharper laws for adultery', while Matthew Hutton, a future archbishop of York, told Whitgift in 1589 that he wished 'a more sharp punishment were by law appointed'.⁴ In keeping with such sentiments, the *Reformatio Legum Ecclesiasticarum* (1552) prescribed severe punishment for adultery: perpetual imprisonment or exile, the forfeiture of all property rights gained by marriage, and, in the case of the husband, the surrender of half his goods to his wife.⁵ But the code was never implemented; and nothing came of proposals in the Convocation of 1563 for 'sharper laws' against adultery, incest, and fornication, including imprisonment for life.⁶

By 1640 the soft treatment of sexual offenders had become one of the leading charges against the bishops. The Root and Branch Petition blamed 'the great increase and frequency of whoredoms and adulteries' upon corrupt and inefficient ecclesiastical justice. The bishops, it was said, concentrated their energies on enforcing hated ceremonies, while ignoring the more urgent task of moral reformation.⁷

¹ *Puritan Manifestoes*, ed. W. H. Frere and C. E. Douglas (1907), 34; *A Parte of a Register* (n.d.), 61; [Anthony Gilby], *A Pleasaunt Dialogue* (1581), sig. M1ᵛ; Philip Stubbes, *The Anatomie of Abuses*, ed. F. J. Furnivall (New Shakspere Soc., 1877–9), 98; Downame, *Foure Treatises*, 130–1.
² *The Seconde Parte of a Register*, ed. A. Peel (Cambridge, 1915), ii. 54.
³ W. Yonger, *Iudahs Penance*, in *The Nurses Bosome* (1617), 51.
⁴ Alexander Nowell, *A Catechism*, ed. G. E. Corrie (Parker Soc., Cambridge, 1853), 226; Strype, *Whitgift*, iii. 225. Cf. *The Workes of . . . Gervase Babington* (1615), i. 480, 111.
⁵ *The Reformation of the Ecclesiastical Laws*, ed. E. Cardwell (Oxford, 1850), 49–51.
⁶ John Strype, *Annals of the Reformation* (2nd edn. 1725), i. 351; W. P. Haugaard, *Elizabeth and the English Reformation* (Cambridge, 1968), 72, 173.
⁷ *The Constitutional Documents of the Puritan Revolution, 1625–1660*, ed. S. R. Gardiner (3rd edn. Oxford, 1906), 142; *Complete Prose Works of Milton*, i. 134.

Feelings were intensified by the belief that clerical jurisdiction was itself a usurpation, part of the Popish darkness which the Reformation had not fully dissipated. There was some historical justification for this view, for it was only during the century and a half after the Norman Conquest that the Church had achieved its monopoly.[1] Antiquarians observed that Anglo-Saxon kings had made laws against adultery and that their penalties were severe. The flabby practices of the church courts compared unfavourably with the sterner rule of Cnut, under whom adulteresses were liable to lose their goods and have their noses cut off. 'In those days,' wrote William Lambarde, 'the bishops had not wholly gotten into their hands the correction of adultery and fornication, which of latter times they have challenged from the laity with such pertinacity and stiffness, and have punished . . . with such lenity, that not only the Prince's commodity is thereby greatly decreased, but also incontinency in his subjects intolerably augmented.'[2]

The ordinance of 1650 was thus an attempt to resume secular jurisdiction in an area which had for five hundred years been under clerical control. But the breach with the immediate past was less abrupt than might appear. Of the four offences listed in the act, brothel-keeping was already under lay jurisdiction. At common law it was a nuisance to keep a house of ill fame; bawds and prostitutes had long been 'carted' or sent to the house of correction by justices at quarter sessions.[3] The only innovation of the 1650 act in this area was that it greatly stiffened the penalties.

The extension of secular jurisdiction to cover adultery, incest, and fornication was also a step for which legal developments had paved the way. In the reign of Henry VII the courts upheld the doctrine, rooted in the custom of London, that adultery was a breach of the peace which the officers of the law were entitled to avert.[4] Many legal handbooks taught

---

[1] Cf. Sir Edward Coke, *The Third Part of the Institutes of the Laws of England* (1817 edn.), 205.

[2] William Lambarde, *A Perambulation of Kent* (1596), 224. Cf. William Harrison, *The Description of England*, ed. G. Edelen (Ithaca, N.Y., 1968), 190; Sir Henry Finch (Bodl., Rawlinson MS. C 43, fols. 26–7; and W. R. Prest, above, 100).

[3] Coke, *Third Institute*, 205; *Reports and Cases collected by the learned Sir John Popham* (1682), 208.

[4] *Year Books*, 1 Hen. VII, 6–7; 13 Hen. VII, 10.

that constables could arrest would-be fornicators and that
J.P.s might bind them over to good behaviour.[1] At courts
leet, petty sessions, and even quarter sessions, adulterers and
fornicators were bound over or punished by carting, stocking,
whipping, or imprisonment in the house of correction.[2] The
towns, in particular, were active against sexual offenders. Their
jurisdiction usually rested on local custom, but was occasionally
recognized by royal charter, as at Boston, where Elizabeth I
gave the mayor and burgesses authority to punish whore-
mongers, panders, and 'all others whatsoever living lasciviously
and incontinently'.[3]

Armed with such powers, zealous local magistrates could
build up a powerful machine for the punishment of sexual
vice. In early Stuart Norwich the mayoralty court carted
bawds, sent the incestuous to Bridewell, and ducked and
whipped those found guilty of 'lewdness'.[4] At Bury St. Edmunds
in 1579 a group of J.P.s drew up a code for the moral reformation of the town: fornicators, adulterers, and the incestuous
would be tied to the whipping-post for twenty-four hours,
have their hair cut off (if female) and receive 'thirty stripes
well laid on till the blood come'.[5] Such claims to lay jurisdiction
were often challenged by the local clergy. In late fifteenth-
century Exeter, the mayor, John Hooker, proceeded with
great severity against whore-mongers and adulterers, thus
provoking 'some difference between him and the clergy, who
claimed the punishment and correction of such offences to be

---

[1] Michael Dalton, *The Countrey Iustice* (1618), 160; William Shepheard, *The
Whole Office of the Country Justice of Peace* (1650), 45, 129; John Godolphin, *Repertorium Canonicum* (2nd edn. 1680), 474.

[2] Examples are cited by A. Cleveland, 'Indictments of adultery and incest
before 1650', *Law Qtly. Rev.* xxix (1913), and G. May, *Social Control of Sex Expression*
(1930), ch. 8. For others see *Court Leet Records*, ed. F. J. C. and D. M. Hearnshaw
(Southampton Rec. Soc., 1905–7), 356; R. Welford, *History of Newcastle*, ii (1885),
402; R. H. Morris, *Chester in the Plantagenet and Tudor Reigns* (Chester, n.d.), 189;
HMC, Var. Collns. i. 288; iv. 265; F. G. Emmison, *Elizabethan Life: Disorder*
(Chelmsford, 1970), 29, 178, 200; *Somerset Assize Orders, 1640–1659*, ed. J. S. Cock-
burn (Somerset Rec. Soc., 1971), 29; A. Fletcher, *A County Community in Peace and
War: Sussex 1600–1660* (1975), 159–60.

[3] P. Thompson, *The History and Antiquities of Boston* (1856), 72.

[4] *Minutes of the Norwich Court of Mayoralty, 1630–1631*, ed. W. L. Sachse (Norfolk
Rec. Soc., 1942), 25–6.

[5] BL, Lansdowne MS. 27, fol. 155; E. Rose, *Cases of Conscience* (Cambridge, 1975),
160–2.

incident only unto their charge and office'.[1] In 1627 another ex-mayor of Exeter, the godly Ignatius Jourdain, renowned for his zeal against adulterers, swearers, and sabbath-breakers, was prosecuted in the Star Chamber for exceeding the letter of the law when punishing 'an unclean person'. Jourdain successfully pleaded that, by local custom, the magistrates of Exeter had the right to whip adulterers. The court ruled that his actions had been free of malice and upheld the local custom.[2] Like the legislation relating to sabbath-breaking, drunkenness, and swearing, the ordinance thus put on a national basis what was often well-established municipal practice.

The way had been further prepared by the bastardy legislation, which had had the effect of giving the justices at quarter sessions a share in the sexual business previously handled by the church courts. By an act of 1576 J.P.s could set maintenance orders upon the parents of chargeable bastard children and punish them as they thought fit. For women whipping became the usual penalty, though in 1593 the Commons rejected a proposal that the men be whipped too, for fear the penalty 'might chance upon gentlemen or men of quality, whom it were not fit to put to such a shame'. A later act of 1610 consigned the mothers of bastards to the house of correction for a year.[3] By comparison with this, the three-month sentence for fornicators prescribed in 1650 was relatively mild; and it was free from the social discrimination of the bastardy acts, which affected only those parents too impoverished to maintain their illegitimate offspring. The church courts had also tended to concentrate their attentions on those whose sexual lapses threatened to constitute a charge upon the parish.[4] 'The law of bastardy', said a preacher, was like a spider's web: 'the little flies are caught and hang by the heels, but great ones burst through'.[5]

[1] W. J. Harte, *Gleanings from the Common Place Book of John Hooker* (Exeter, n.d.), 19. See also W. T. MacCaffrey, *Exeter, 1540–1640* (Cambridge, Mass., 1958), 98 n.
[2] BL, Lansdowne MS. 620, fols. 47ᵛ–9; Ferdinand Nicolls, *The Life and Death of Mr. Ignatius Jurdain* (2nd edn. 1655), 49, 78–80.
[3] 18 Eliz., c. 3 (1575–6); BL, Cotton MS., Titus F ii, fol. 81ᵛ; 7 Jac. I, c. 4, s. 7 (1609–10).
[4] Ingram, 'Ecclesiastical Justice in Wiltshire', 214–15, 219–20, 223, 247, 261.
[5] Yonger, *Iudahs Penance*, 50. Cf. Robert Burton, *Anatomy of Melancholy* (Everyman edn. 1932), i. 63.

More spectacular than the resumption of secular jurisdiction in 1650 was the severity of the new penalties. Yet violent death or mutilation was known as the conventional fate of adulterers among many civilizations of the world. Antiquaries and ethnographers listed such punishments with relish:

Some did burn them alive, as Lucian reports . . . Some did use to quarter them, as Euclidos makes mention of . . . Others pluckt out their eyes, as Valerius reports it. Others did whip them and cut off their noses, as Siculus shows it of the Egyptians. Others, saith Caelius, did hang them. Others did tie them to two trees, which, being bowed down by violence, letting them suddenly go did with a jerk rent one limb from another. Others did stone them to death . . .[1]

Persians and Egyptians, Greeks and Romans, Arabs and Indians: all had favoured the death penalty. In contemporary Europe examples could be cited from Germany, Bohemia, Spain, Switzerland, Poland, even Rome.[2] It seemed that the very law of nature prescribed death for adultery. Even the beasts and birds of the air killed adulterers, declared Philip Stubbes.[3]

In England, there was a well-established tradition that a husband could lawfully kill an adulterous wife caught *in flagrante delicto*. Angevin kings permitted injured husbands to emasculate their rivals, while the common law of a later age accepted that the shame of being called 'cuckold' justified violent retaliation.[4] George Joye exaggerated when he affirmed that the courts would exonerate husbands who killed their rivals *in flagrante*. The deed was still manslaughter and men could be hanged for it.[5] But offenders could secure benefit of clergy and the courts might be lenient. When the King's Bench found one avenging husband guilty of manslaughter, he was allowed his clergy and ordered to be burned in the hand. But 'the court

---

[1] BL, Harley MS. 980, fol. 74ᵛ (collections by Thomas Gibbons).

[2] Joye, *A Contrarye*, sig. Bviᵛ; *Shakespeare's Europe*, ed. C. Hughes (1903), 88, 293; Fynes Moryson, *An Itinerary* (Glasgow, 1907–8), iv. 298–9; *HMC, Rutland*, i. 505; John Evelyn, *Diary*, ed. E. S. de Beer (Oxford, 1955), ii. 527 and n. 4; L. Pastor, *The History of the Popes* (Eng. transl., 1891–), xxi. 90–1.

[3] Stubbes, *Anatomie*, i. 92.

[4] Sir F. Pollock and F. W. Maitland, *The History of English Law* (2nd edn. Cambridge, 1911), ii. 484 and n.; *Year Books*, 1 Hen. VII, 6, 7.

[5] Joye, *A Contrarye*, sig. Aiiij; Sir Matthew Hale, *Historia Placitorum Coronae*, ed. Sollom Emlyn (1736), i. 486; Emmison, *Elizabethan Life*, 154.

directed the executioner to burn him gently because there could not be greater provocation than this'.[1]

One did not therefore need to be a Puritan to favour drastic measures against adultery. Polydore Vergil, Erasmus, and other humanists had deplored the prevailing leniency towards adultery, by contrast with the severe treatment of theft.[2] Thomas More in *Utopia* made slavery the punishment for adulterers, with death for a second offence. William Harrison also favoured slavery.[3] Other advocates of severity included such diverse figures as John Jones, the physician, Robert Burton, the anatomist, and Sir William Segar, the herald.[4] The romantic Margaret Cavendish felt that unfaithful wives deserved death 'and their executioner ought to be their husband'.[5]

But the most influential precedent came from the Old Testament. By the law of Moses (Leviticus 20: 10; Deuteronomy 22: 22), death was the penalty for both parties involved in the adultery of a married woman, just as it was for incest, idolatry, blasphemy, or murder. But was this law of Moses still binding upon the Christian magistrate? The issue was complex, for the Mosaic law fell into three distinct sections. There was the moral law, enshrined in the ten commandments, and recognized by all save the most desperate antinomians to be of perpetual validity. There was the ceremonial law, comprising religious and dietary regulations, which all but a handful of eccentric 'judaizers' agreed to be irrelevant to Christians. Finally, there was the judicial law, the civil and criminal code, about whose continuing validity controversy raged.

In England the official view, cogently expressed by Archbishop Whitgift, was that the judicial law had been wholly abrogated by the coming of Christ. As James I told Parliament in 1610, the law of Moses was the law of Israel, 'only fit for that country, that people and time'; other nations could vary

---

[1] Sir Thomas Raymond, *The Reports of Divers Special Cases* (1696), 212.

[2] *The Complete Works of St. Thomas More*, iv, ed. E. Surtz and J. H. Hexter (New Haven, 1965), 315, 483.

[3] Ibid. 190–1; Harrison, *Description of England*, 190.

[4] John Jones, *The Arte and Science of Preserving Bodie and Soule* (1579), 37; Burton, *Anatomy*, i. 105; W. Segar, *Honor Military, and Civill* (1602), 21.

[5] Marchioness of Newcastle, *CCXI. Sociable Letters* (1664), 49.

its rules to fit local circumstances.[1] As for adultery, Christ's
mercy to the adulteress (John 8) showed that the severity of
the Old Testament was no longer required.[2] In 1548 John
Foxe accordingly urged that the judicial law had been abrogated. Foxe did not deny the ruler's right to make adultery
capital in extreme cases. But, in his view, so grave a step could
not be taken on biblical grounds, but only for reasons of state
(*ratio reipublicae*).[3]

This was not the interpretation offered by most leading
continental reformers. For Zwingli or Bucer or Bullinger, death
was the appropriate penalty for adultery because it was the
one prescribed by God.[4] Their attitude was shared by many
English theologians. Few maintained that the judicial law
obliged in every detail, but it was common to hold that the
substance of some of the laws was binding and that death for
adultery was part of that substance. The case of Christ and the
woman taken in adultery was dismissed as irrelevant: Christ's
apparent mercy indicated no mitigation of the penalty, but
was merely a refusal to intervene in the business of the magistrate. Death for adultery was a penalty which the magistrate
was by perpetual equity obliged to enforce.[5] This was the
view urged by Martin Bucer in his scheme for godly reformation in England and by William Bullein in his description of
an ideal city.[6] It was supported by the boy-king Edward VI
and by most of the Edwardian reformers.[7] Through Thomas
Becon's contribution to the *Homilies*, innumerable congregations were pointedly acquainted with ancient laws for the

[1] *The Works of John Whitgift*, ed. J. Ayre (Parker Soc., Cambridge, 1851–3), i.
273, 278; *Proceedings in Parliament, 1610*, ed. E. R. Foster (New Haven, 1966), i. 47;
ii. 60.

[2] Willet, *Harmonie upon Samuel*, 72–4.

[3] *De non Plectendis Morte Adulteris Consultatio Ioannis Foxi* (1548), esp. sig. Bvii^v.

[4] P. D. L. Avis, 'Moses and the Magistrate', *Journ. Eccl. Hist.* xxvi (1975).

[5] Joye, *A Contrarye*; John Foxe, *Acts and Monuments*, ed. S. R. Cattley (1837–41),
viii. 323; Cartwright, *Second Replie*; *The Writings of Henry Barrow, 1587–1590*, ed.
L. H. Carlson (1962), 599, 659–60; *HMC, Rawdon Hastings*, i. 437.

[6] *Martini Buceri Opera Latina*, xv^bis, ed. F. Wendel (Paris, 1954), 186–91, 276,
279–80; William Bullein, *A Dialogue against the Fever Pestilence*, ed. M. W. and A. H.
Bullen (Early Eng. Text. Soc., 1888), 108.

[7] *Literary Remains of King Edward the Sixth*, ed. J. G. Nichols (Roxburghe Club,
1857), i. 128–30; *Sermons by Hugh Latimer*, ed. G. E. Corrie (Parker Soc., Cambridge,
1844), 244, 258; *The Sermons of Edwin Sandys*, ed. J. Ayre (Parker Soc., Cambridge,
1841), 50.

punishment of adultery.[1] In the reign of Elizabeth the death penalty was urged by Cartwright and his allies. Later it gained the support of William Ames, John Downame, Thomas Gataker, Sir Henry Finch, William Prynne, and many other leading Puritans.[2] Some urged leniency if the injured spouse was prepared to forgive the guilty party, but many thought death the appropriate punishment, particularly when, in the absence of any procedure for divorce, it was the only way by which the injured party could gain the right to remarry. Lancelot Andrewes summed up opinion: 'Howsoever politic men have not punished it with death, yet it is the joint consent of all divines that it is capital.'[3]

There were also the influential examples of Scotland and New England. In Scotland the *First Book of Discipline* (1561) had demanded the Mosaic penalty and in 1563 the Scottish Parliament under clerical pressure passed an act imposing death for 'notoure and manifest' adultery. This was less extreme than some reformers would have liked, for a clarificatory act of 1581 explained that by 'notoure and manifest adultery' was meant only those cases where a child was conceived or where the adultery was 'notoriously known' or where the parties had refused to give up their association after admonition by the Kirk.[4] But it seemed a step in the right direction and it was accompanied by other acts imposing death for incest and heavy punishments for fornication.[5]

In the North American colonies death for adultery was prescribed by the first Virginian legal code of 1610.[6] It became the law in Massachusetts in 1631, being subsequently codified in John Cotton's model of 'Moses his judicials' (1636) and enacted in the *Body of Liberties* (1641) and the *Laws of Massachusetts*

[1] Thomas Becon, *Early Works*, ed. J. Ayre (Cambridge, Parker Soc., 1843), 41; *The Two Books of Homilies*, ed. J. Griffiths (Oxford, 1859), 129–30.
[2] William Ames, *Conscience* (1639), iv. 210–11, 221; Downame, *Foure Treatises*, 187; Thomas Gataker, *Of the Nature and Use of Lots* (2nd edn. 1627), 373; Sir Henry Finch in Bodl., Rawlinson MS. C 43, fol. 26ᵛ; William Prynne, *Histrio-Mastix* (1633), 382–3.
[3] Andrewes, *The Morall Law Expounded*, 778.
[4] *The Works of John Knox*, ed. D. Laing (Wodrow Soc., Edinburgh, 1846–64), ii. 227, 248–9, 338–41; *The Acts of the Parliaments of Scotland* (1814–75), ii. 539 (1563/10); iii. 213 (1581/7); HMC, *Rutland*, i. 85.
[5] *Acts of the Parliaments of Scotland*, iii. 25–6 (1567/14, 15).
[6] [William Strachey], *For the Colony in Virginea Britannia. Lawes Divine, Morall and Martiall* (1612), 5.

(1648). Similar legislation was passed in Connecticut and New Haven.[1]

By the 1640s the case for the Mosaic law was gaining ground. The Westminster Assembly ruled that the judicial law of Moses obliged 'no further than the general equity thereof may require', but Archbishop Ussher's *Body of Divinitie* (1645) urged the implementation of those parts of the judicial law to which the death penalty was attached.[2] In January 1648 an extract was republished from Cartwright's argument that the magistrate had no power to abrogate the Old Testament penalties for incest, adultery, and blasphemy; and at the Whitehall debates in December of that year the issue was debated by Philip Nye and Thomas Collier in terms unchanged from those employed by Whitgift and Cartwright seventy years earlier.[3]

In the event, the adultery act did not mirror the Mosaic law in every respect; and consequently failed to satisfy the legalists. It had been issued as a mere act of parliament rather than as the immutable law of God, complained John Brayne; it said nothing of the Mosaic rule that the fornicator should marry the girl he had seduced; and it ignored the text in Leviticus (19: 20) which excused a 'bondmaid' (which Brayne took to mean apprentice) from the full penalty for adultery.[4] Worst of all, it was not followed by a reduction in the punishment for theft. Nevertheless, the act testified to the influence of the Mosaic tradition. 'The late act of adultery', declared John Spittlehouse in 1653, 'doth clearly manifest that the late Parliament was carried on, though in darkness, to put in execution the aforesaid laws of God.'[5]

The ordinance itself had been in gestation for over a century.

---

[1] *Records of the Governor and Company of the Massachusetts Bay*, ed. N. B. Shurtleff, i (Boston, 1853), 92, 225, 301; G. L. Haskins, *Law and Authority in early Massachusetts* (N.Y., 1960), chs. viii and ix; W. E. Ohlson, 'Adultery: a review', *Boston Univ. Law Rev.* xvii (1937).

[2] *The Confession of Faith . . . agreed upon by the Assembly of Divines* (1651), 40; James Ussher, *A Body of Divinitie* (1645), 204.

[3] *Helpes for Discovery of the Truth in point of Toleration: being the Judgment of that eminent scholler Tho. Cartwright* (1648); *Puritanism and Liberty*, ed. A. S. P. Woodhouse (1938), 165, 168.

[4] John Brayne, *The New Earth* (1653), 61.

[5] John Spittlehouse, *The First Addresses* (1653), 23–4.

Since 1543, when the House of Lords considered bills 'for true keeping of matrimony', 'for the incontinency of women', and 'for women lawfully proved of adultery to lose their dower, goods, lands and all other possessions',[1] there had been numerous parliamentary efforts to make adultery a criminal offence. The 'bill for adultery' introduced in the Commons in 1549 may have been designed only to allow the innocent party to remarry, but the intentions of the Lords' bill of 1576 'for the punishment of avowtrie and incest' were clearly penal.[2] So were those of a Commons bill of 1601 which provided that an adulterous husband should lose his tenure by courtesy of his wife's lands and that a guilty wife should lose her tenancy in dower.[3] In 1604 another measure 'for the better repressing of the detestable crime of adultery' got as far as a second reading in the Lords.[4] In 1614 the Commons had a bill prescribing that wives who left their husbands for adulterers should lose 'their jointures, etc.'[5] In 1621 a draft act against scandalous ministers proposed that adulterous clergy should be fined 40s. for the first offence and lose their livings for the second.[6] In 1626 the Commons gave two readings to two successive bills against adultery and fornication.[7] In 1628 a bill 'for the further punishment of adultery and fornication' was given two readings and sent to committee; a similar measure was given a first reading on 24 January 1629, six weeks before the Parliament's sudden dissolution.[8]

Most of these bills were milder than the final enactment of 1650. In 1628, for example, the proposed penalty for adultery was a hundred marks' fine for gentlemen and a whipping for others.[9] 'As yet, we have not that law among us', declared a preacher in 1610 of the Mosaic penalty, 'and . . . there is no great likelihood neither that ever we shall hereafter have it'.[10] Yet Puritan reformers had urged Parliament to make adultery a felony in 1584; the idea was canvassed again in 1604, and in

[1] *LJ* i. 215, 221, 224, 226.   [2] *CJ* i. 6 (cf. 9); *LJ* i. 740.
[3] Sir Simonds D'Ewes, *The Journals of all the Parliaments during the Reign of Queen Elizabeth* (1682), 641.
[4] *LJ* ii. 271, 272, 273.   [5] *Debates 1621*, vii. 629.
[6] Ibid. ii. 439.   [7] *CJ* i. 823, 830, 838, 844, 850, 859, 865.
[8] Ibid. i. 880, 886, 922.
[9] BL, Stowe MS. 366, fols. 53ᵛ–4; Harley MS. 2313, fol. 35 (*Debates 1628*, ii. 329, 331).
[10] Edm. Bunny, *Of Divorce for Adulterie, and marrying againe* (Oxford, 1610), 162.

1626 death was proposed for adulterous clergy.[1] This was all part of a wider campaign for moral reformation, expressed in parallel attempts to legislate against drunkenness, swearing, sabbath-breaking, and blasphemy; and the pressure came from the godly.[2] In 1614 it was the Puritan lawyer Nicholas Fuller who introduced the bill against adulterous wives, while in 1626 and 1628 many leading Puritan gentry sat on the committees to which the adultery bills were assigned. At the head of the list was that godly Devonshire magistrate, already the terror of Exeter's moral delinquents, Ignatius Jourdain. On 9 July 1625 he informed an unsurprised House 'that divers places, *viz.* Clerkenwell, Pickehatch, Turnmill St., Golden Lane, Duke Humfrey's at Blackfriars, are places of open bawdry'.[3] In 1626 and 1628 he championed the adultery bills, undeterred by the flippancy of his colleagues.

When he made a motion in the Parliament concerning the bill against adultery some one or more in the House cried out, 'Commit it, Mr. Jourdain, commit it!' Upon which a great laughter was occasioned. He then presently said to them (in a zealous manner like himself), 'Do you laugh, when a man speaks for God's glory?' Thereupon there was more than an ordinary silence in the House. The bill was then laid aside, but was called for in an after Parliament by the name of 'Mr. Jourdain's bill' . . . He was a great stickler to have the bill passed for the punishment of adultery with death, but those times would not bear it.[4]

Yet the failure of the bills against adultery does not necessarily indicate lack of support for their general intentions. The measure of 1601 was criticized on grounds of detail: it left the ecclesiastical courts to decide who was guilty of adultery and its penalties were unequal, for a man without land would go unpunished. The Lords committee rejected the bill of 1604 because they found it 'rather to concern some particular

---

[1] John Strype, *Annals of the Reformation*, iii (1728), appx. 77; Charls George Cock, *English-Law* (1651), 36; *Original Letters illustrative of English History*, ed. H. Ellis (1824), iii. 223; Cambridge Univ. Lib., MS. Dd. 12. 20–1, fol. 83ᵛ.

[2] See J. R. Kent, 'Attitudes of members of the House of Commons to the Regulation of "Personal Conduct" in late Elizabethan and early Stuart England', *BIHR* xlvi (1973).

[3] *CJ* i. 807.

[4] Nicolls, *Life*, 73–4. For a slightly different account of the episode; BL, Stowe MS. 366, fol. 97ᵛ (*Debates 1628*, iii. 26). See also F. B. Troup, 'An Exeter Worthy and his Biographer', *Repts. & Trans. Devonshire Assoc.* xxix (1897).

persons than the public good', but they referred the general issue to the House's further consideration. The special punishment for adulterous clergy proposed in 1621 was unacceptable because it implied different laws for the clergy and the laity.[1]

It was predictable that the Long Parliament should return to a matter which had preoccupied so many of its predecessors. On 16 November 1640 the Commons Committee for Religion received a petition from the clergy of Lincoln demanding among other things 'some severe law against fornication and adultery'.[2] Three months later Nathaniel Fiennes declared roundly that the cognizance of adultery belonged to civil jurisdiction and should be taken from the clergy.[3] Yet though Parliament in 1641 proceeded to strip the bishops and the church courts of their authority, it put nothing in their place. Royalists were quick to point out that there was now no way of dealing with 'heinous crimes, inquirable by those courts, as adultery, incest, &c.'[4] The abolition of High Commission, observed Clarendon, left 'adultery, and incest as unpunishable as any other acts of good fellowship'.[5] The lack of punishment for sexual offenders was also remarked upon in petitions from the gentry and ministers of the counties; and not only in those from parliamentary supporters. In Cornwall it was the royalists who demanded in 1642 that 'there may be penal laws enacted for punishing of adulteries and divers other offences not punishable by common law'.[6]

In December 1641 the House had seemed ready to take action against whoring, swearing, and drinking,[7] but not until 11 December 1644 did the Commons order the bringing-in of the bill for repressing incest, adultery, whoredom, drunkenness, swearing, blasphemy, and other vices.[8] It

---

[1] D'Ewes, *Journals*, 641; *LJ* ii. 273; *Original Letters*, ed. Ellis, iii. 223.

[2] *D'Ewes*, ed. Notestein, 38.

[3] *A Speech of the Honorable Nathanael Fiennes* (1641), 12.

[4] *The Remonstrance of the Commons of England to the House of Commons* (1643), 4.

[5] Clarendon, i. 373.

[6] Bodl., Rawlinson MS. C 789, fol. 57 (also in *A Collection of Sundry Petitions presented to the Kings most Excellent Majesty* (1642; 1681 edn.), 16). Cf. the similar demand from Kent (ibid. 14).

[7] *D'Ewes*, ed. Coates, 308, 343; *CJ* ii. 348, 356.

[8] *CJ* iii. 721. In 1643 a writer had claimed that Parliament intended to punish 'adulterers &c.' 'according to the Word of God and not by the Pope's canon law',

received a first reading on 16 December and a second one six weeks later, when it was sent to committee. Other business intervened and the matter lapsed for over two years. On 28 May 1647 the bill was at last recommitted and split into two separate ordinances, one against incest, adultery, and whoredom, the other against drunkenness, swearing, and blasphemy.[1] The new adultery bill got a first reading on 31 March 1648, but the Second Civil War intervened. The Rump inquired into the bill's progress on 23 March 1649 and again, more peremptorily, on 2 November. Finally, on 8 February 1650 the measure received its first and second readings and was committed. After extensive debate and amendment it was passed on 10 May and was ordered to be printed and a copy distributed to every parish.[2]

Such long delays were typical of much of the legislation projected by the Long Parliament. What was it in this particular case which finally stirred the House into action? For S. R. Gardiner the adultery ordinance was an attempt by the Rump to woo the Presbyterians in order to avert the threatened alliance with the royalists.[3] Undoubtedly, the act was part of a larger programme of legislation in 1650 designed to conciliate moderate Presbyterians by showing the Rump's desire for moral reform. It belongs with the acts for the Propagation of the Gospel in Wales (22 February) and Ireland (8 March); for the maintenance of ministers (5 April); for the better observance of the Lord's Day (19 April); for the prevention of swearing and cursing (28 June); and against atheistical and blasphemous opinions (9 August). There was also attempted legislation for the Propagation of the Gospel in England (29 January), against immodest dresses and patches (7 June), and against drunkenness (6 September).[4]

But the adultery act also reflected the pressure of opinion

but had been 'hindered by men that hate to be reformed'; *A Disclaimer and Answer of the Commons of England* (1643), 10.

[1] *CJ* iii. 724; iv. 35, 184, 189; BL, Add. MS. 31, 116, fol. 311.
[2] *CJ* v. 478, 523; vi. 171, 317, 354, 359, 385, 396–7, 404, 408, 410–11, 413.
[3] S. R. Gardiner, *History of the Commonwealth and Protectorate* (new edn. 1903), i. 255–6; ii. 2.
[4] Firth & Rait, ii. 342–8, 355–7, 369–78, 383–7, 393–6, 409–12; *CJ* vi. 352, 421, 464.

outside the House.[1] On 6 February 1649 the Leveller-influenced *Representative of divers well-affected persons in and about the City of London* demanded that all brothels, bawds, whores, panders, and pimps be 'duly punished and not tolerated as . . . hitherto'. It was followed by a petition presented to Parliament on 4 December 1649 by the Lord Mayor, Aldermen, and Common Council of the City of London, urging stringent legislation against swearing, cursing, drunkenness, sabbath-breaking, and 'all uncleanness now abounding as if there were no law'. The Rump promptly affirmed the need for effective laws against these vices and instructed a committee to meet City representatives to discuss the matter.[2]

It was no coincidence that the City's petition was delivered only two days after the Mayor and Aldermen had heard a sermon by Vavasor Powell, urging them to 'labour to suppress vice more'.[3] Such exhortation by the preachers had been continuous throughout the 1640s. On many fast days, Parliament had been warned that sexual sins left unpunished would provoke God's judgements; and it is noticeable that it was on fast days that the adultery bill tended to make most progress. With the threat of sexual licence among the antinomian sects the pressure grew. The decision on 2 November 1649 to resuscitate the bill was taken after Peter Sterry had been thanked for a sermon with a long preface attacking the Ranters.[4] The order for the presentation of the bill was made on 1 February 1650, immediately after the House had condemned Abiezer Coppe's Ranter tract, *A Fiery Flying Roll*; three days later Parliament ordered a fast to bemoan sins committed 'under pretence of liberty and greater measure of light'.[5] In the summer the blasphemy act prohibited the 'execrable opinion' that adultery, incest, and fornication were free from sin and 'in their own nature as holy and religious as the duties of prayer, preaching or giving thanks to God'.[6] The adultery

---

[1] See B. Worden, *The Rump Parliament, 1648–1653* (Cambridge, 1974), 234.

[2] *CJ* vi. 328; Corporation of London RO, Journ. of the Common Council, xli, fos. 18ᵛ–19 (I am grateful to the Deputy Keeper of the Records for furnishing me with a summary of the petition).

[3] Vavasor Powell, *God the Father Glorified* (1649), 59.

[4] *CJ* vi. 317; Peter Sterry, *The Commings Forth of Christ* (1650), esp. sig. aiᵛ.

[5] *CJ* vi. 354; Worden, *Rump*, 233.

[6] Firth & Rait, ii. 409–12. Cf. Edwards, *Gangraena*, iii. 14, 107.

act was passed at a time when men and women were pleading conscience to justify adultery,[1] divorce,[2] and bigamy;[3] when the very concept of prohibited degrees had been attacked as unscriptural;[4] and when sectarian religion had become notorious as a cover for unscrupulous sexual adventures.[5] Ranting, it was said in a parliamentary committee, was 'a sad principle, which, if not routed, all honest men will have their wives deluded'.[6] The fear of licence propelled the Rump to drastic measures; and it was appropriate that an early victim of the new ordinance was the Ranter Thomas Webbe, who had justified free love and was tried at the Wiltshire Assizes for adultery with a married woman.[7]

Yet the act was exceedingly controversial. Within the Rump it encountered a vigorous opposition led by Ludlow and Henry Marten, the latter arguing, perhaps disingenuously, that its very severity would cause the sins it proscribed to be committed more frequently, because people would take greater care to conceal their offences 'and being undiscovered would be emboldened the more in the commitment of them'.[8] In the end, the measure was substantially modified, almost entirely to the advantage of the accused, whose position was made well-nigh impregnable: he could produce witnesses for the defence; the indictment had to be filed within twelve months of the offence; the penalty for adultery did not apply to a man who did not know that the woman concerned was married; nor did it touch a married woman whose husband had been overseas for three years,[9] or[10] was by common fame reputed dead, or whose whereabouts had been unknown to

---

[1] *The Letter Books of Sir Samuel Luke*, ed. H. G. Tibbutt (Beds. Hist. Rec. Soc., 1963), 197.

[2] K. Thomas, 'Women and the Civil War Sects', *P. and P.* 13 (1968), 49–50; Colchester Borough Records, Examination Book, 18 Dec. 1647 (case of Mary Pickis).

[3] *Puritanism and Liberty*, ed. Woodhouse, 146; and the striking case of John Petts, discovered in Colchester Examination Book (29 Oct. 1647) by Mr. J. A. Sharpe.

[4] *Little Non-Such* (1646); *The Counter Buffe* (1647).

[5] Laurence Clarkson, *The Lost Sheep Found* (1660), 22, 26, 28. Cf. *CSPD, 1634–5*, 371–2, and, of course, Hill, *The World Turned Upside Down*, esp. 159, 173–4, 182, 192, 253–6.

[6] Clarkson, *Lost Sheep*, 31 (who adds that 'one of them said he feared not his wife; she was too old').

[7] Edw. Stokes, *The Wiltshire Rant* (1652).　　　　[8] Whitelocke, iii. 190.

[9] Originally five years; *CJ* vi. 397, 404.　　　[10] Originally 'and'; ibid. 404.

her for three years. Most crippling of all, the confession of one party was unacceptable as evidence against the other; nor could husbands and wives testify against each other. (There was even an attempt to extend the prohibition to include masters and servants.)[1]

It was immediately obvious that these limitations meant that convictions for adultery would be few indeed. Who was to prosecute? asked a royalist journal: injured husbands were debarred from giving evidence, and there was no reward for informers.[2] Besides, who could ever prove that the woman did not believe her absent husband to be dead? The act, wrote a contemporary,

is so penned that few or none will ever be convicted upon it. Insomuch that it hath been thought that that statute was made only or chiefly for guarding of women's credits, that lewd persons might not dare to boast of their own filthiness to the discredit of women's persons . . . which act is so cautiously penned that a man shall not be (in strictness of law) in danger of death, unless it appear there was *Res in Re* and that the adulterer knew the whore to be a married woman, which none can tell, but such as were present at the marriage, and besides one of the parties cannot be a witness against the other, as being *particeps criminis*. This law ought to be amended.[3]

Proposals for amendment were common enough. One reformer suggested that the courts should convict on a basis of reasonable presumption of adultery and cease to insist on certain proof (which was virtually unobtainable without either the offender's voluntary confession or recourse to what Milton called 'unmanly indignities').[4] In 1656 William Sheppard agreed that the act was defective, 'the way of conviction being so difficult that it is very hard to prove'.[5] But no change was made, though in August 1655 the government had issued a proclamation for the ordinance's 'speedy and due execution'.[6]

---

[1] Ibid. 411. An attempt to limit the operation of the act to three years was also defeated; ibid.

[2] *Mercurius Pragmaticus*, 14–21 May 1650. But for a case of attempted blackmail see *Hertfordshire County Records*, v, ed. W. Le Hardy (Hertford, 1928), 482.

[3] *Examen Legum Angliae: or, the Laws of England examined* (1656), 127–8.

[4] D[aniel] T[aylor], *Certain Queries* (1651), 9–10; *Complete Prose Works of John Milton*, ii. 337. Cf. Cock, *English-Law*, 70.

[5] William Sheppard, *Englands Balme* ('1657', actually 1656), 159–60.

[6] BL, 669 f. 20(11).

The rarity of convictions for adultery is usually attributed to the humanity of judges and jurors.[1] But the sheer technical difficulty of securing proof is alone a sufficient explanation. Fornication was easier to prove, particularly when pregnancy resulted. As a result the main effort of the 1650s was concentrated upon the bastardy laws, perhaps to greater effect than in previous decades.[2] It was because the penalties laid down by the bastardy acts were inconsistent with those in the act of 1650 that a parliamentary committee was appointed in 1656 to review 'the acts and laws touching bastardy, adultery, and fornication; and to reduce them into one law, with such alterations and additions as shall be necessary to supply the defects in those laws'.[3] But nothing came of this.

Meanwhile the prosecution of those sexual irregularities which did not result in chargeable bastards was desultory indeed. As in New England, where death sentences for adultery, though legally mandatory, were exceedingly infrequent,[4] the importance of the 1650 act was primarily symbolic. It was a public assertion of offences to be abominated. But it was not an effective part of the criminal code.

To modern commentators, for whom sexual morality is a private matter, the very aims of the adultery act appear alien and tyrannical: the Oxford History of England describes it as a 'draconic law'—'definitely a step in the wrong direction'.[5] Many contemporaries also thought the death penalty for adultery 'too hard and too cruel',[6] while some considered it preposterous to punish people for fornication.[7] It was never more

---

[1] Cf. Jeaffreson in *Middlesex County Records*, iii. p. xxiii; G. Davies, *The Early Stuarts* (2nd edn. Oxford, 1959), 172; Aylmer, *State's Servants*, 306.

[2] Laslett, *Family Life and Illicit Love*, 119–20; and the impression given by many quarter session records. Even so William Sheppard in 1656 thought bastardy 'very common and little punished'; *Englands Balme*, 152.

[3] *CJ* vii. 433. Mr. D. Veall is surely wrong to suggest that this step was taken 'because of widespread feeling about its [the ordinance's] absurdity'; *The Popular Movement for Law Reform, 1640–1660* (Oxford, 1970), 141.

[4] E. Powers, *Crime and Punishment in early Massachusetts* (Boston, 1966), 279–81, 291–2.		[5] Davies, *The Early Stuarts*, 172.

[6] Joye, *A Contrarye*, sig. B1; (Bullinger), *Christen Matrimonye*, fol. xxxii; Timme, *Plaine Discoverie*, sig. Ii; *Leveller Manifestoes*, ed. D. M. Wolfe (1944), 302.

[7] See the fascinating exchange between Lord Morley and the zealous Puritan J.P. who proposed to whip one of his tenants; A. Searle, 'Two Elizabethan justices', *Essex Journ.* ii (1967), 211–14.

than a determined minority who wanted the Mosaic penalty; and there was always a gap between Puritan doctrine and popular attitudes, particularly on the subject of premarital intercourse. Some theologians held temporal punishment irrelevant: it was in the next world that adulterers and fornicators would meet their deserts. Others observed that the essence of adultery lay not in the physical act but in the adultery of the heart. No one could legislate against this; instead Milton was to urge a different remedy: divorce for incompatibility. 'Natural unmeetness' between married persons was worse than 'adultery, though repeated'.[1] Long before Milton, Puritan commentators had argued for the right of the innocent party to divorce and remarriage. They had also undermined the double standard of morality implicit in the ordinance of 1650. Such attitudes were to make the punishment of marital infidelity increasingly anachronistic. 'The more marriage is regarded as a state of life into which two persons enter upon equal terms,' wrote a later commentator, 'and the less the wife is looked upon as being the husband's property, the less will people be inclined to punish as a crime this most grievous and disgraceful of all private wrongs.'[2]

Yet the act of 1650 was not an anomaly. Although owing its final passage to the special circumstances of the newly established republic, anxious to conciliate the Presbyterians and fearful of sectarian licence, it represented the culmination of more than a century's legislative pressure. It was also part of a wider, though partly unachieved, programme of reform, intended to redefine the prohibited degrees, to introduce divorce, to raise the age of consent, and to punish clandestine marriage.[3] Its ideals were not forgotten after 1660. To many it continued to seem wrong that wealth should be 'a privilege for lewdness' and nobody punished 'but those who have no money in their pocket'.[4] Some pressed for the death penalty for adulterers;[5] others favoured fine, imprisonment, or mutilation.[6]

[1] *Complete Prose Works of John Milton*, ii. 591, 674.
[2] Sir J. F. Stephen, *A History of the Criminal Law of England* (1883), iii. 318.
[3] See *CJ* v. 189, 478; vi. 385.
[4] Jeremy Collier, *Essays upon General Moral Subjects*, iii (3rd edn. 1720), 134.
[5] *A Letter to a Member of Parliament with Two Discourses enclosed . . . The one shewing the Reason why a Law should pass to punish Adultery with Death* (1675).
[6] *The Petty Papers*, ed. Marquis of Lansdowne (1927), ii. 213; Thomas Short,

In 1689 William III, in a letter to the Bishop of London, referred ominously to the absence, 'as yet', of 'sufficient provision made by any statute law for the punishing of adultery and fornication'.[1] The societies for the Reformation of Manners emphasized the common-law right of local justices to proceed against sexual offenders, while many later Evangelicals favoured severe penalties for adultery: 'as it was punished capitally by the Jewish law,' wrote John Bowdler in 1796, 'some think it ought to be so punished among us'.[2] In 1800 the Bishop of Rochester observed that 'although he loathed and held in utter abhorrence every thing that passed in the time of the Commonwealth, yet the law which prevailed in that time was not peculiar to it'; death for adultery was the law in pagan times, among the Hebrews, and in 'the best and purest days of Rome'.[3] In the same year a bill to punish adulterers by fine and imprisonment, proposed by Lord Auckland, with the support of Pitt, Eldon, and Spencer Perceval, passed the Lords and was only narrowly defeated in the Commons.[4]

Similar measures were suggested intermittently during the nineteenth century, notably during the divorce reform of the 1850s.[5] In the U.S.A. nearly all the states kept adultery as a crime until recent times. Indeed it is not the punishment of adultery in 1650 but the subsequent growth of sexual *laissez-faire* which makes England distinctive. An attempt to correct the impression that the adultery ordinance was an isolated aberration is a slight, but it is hoped appropriate, offering to the historian who has done most to strip Puritanism of obfuscating mythology and to reveal its position as a central element in the mainstream of English history.

New Observations . . . on . . . Bills of Mortality (1750), 157; James Foster, *Discourses* (1749–52), ii. 51; Josiah Tucker, *The Elements of Commerce and Theory of Taxes* (1755), 27; Burgh, *Political Disquisitions*, iii. 141.

[1] *Documentary Annals of the Reformed Church of England*, ed. E. Cardwell (Oxford, 1839), ii. 328.

[2] *Memoir of the Life of John Bowdler* (1824), 165.

[3] *The Parliamentary History of England . . . to the year 1803* (1806–20), xxxv. 235.

[4] Ibid., 236–326; S. Walpole, *The Life of the Rt. Hon. Spencer Perceval* (1874), i. 78–9.

[5] *Hansard's Parliamentary Debates*, 3rd ser., cxlvii (1857), 378. Cf. 'A country parson', *Adultery, Felony, Penal Servitude* (1882).

The Tactics of the Commonwealthsmen in Richard Cromwell's Parliament

IVAN ROOTS

'THE game of quotations may be played in many ways', says Dr. Christopher Hill.[1] His own ploy is to bring to bear, on a particular point, a mass of citations from a rich variety of contexts, ranging in time and place. This article *per contra* cites mostly a couple of much-used sources, Burton's *Diary*[2] and the *Commons Journals*[3]—concentrating on a few days' debates in the Commons during February 1658/9. The subject there was the Bill of Recognition of Richard Cromwell as Lord Protector. The objective here is to establish the tactics of the Commonwealthsmen at a critical moment in their fortunes.

Richard Cromwell's succession was peaceable—to many a surprise and a disappointment. On 4 September 1658 a proclamation, endorsed by councillors and leading army officers, announced his proper nomination under the terms of the Humble Petition and Advice. Loyal addresses flowed in from the localities, congregations, and—it was an imperial succession —from 'the Armies in England, Scotland and Ireland'. But at once, as Secretary John Thurloe had feared, there were 'secret murmurings' among the soldiery, many of whom suspected that Richard was already dominated by civilians, a view confirmed by the decision (3 December) to call a parliament.[4] Some grandees, perturbed by the army's lack of pay, were sure money must be raised, but doubted that it had to be by Parliament. Some could contemplate collecting taxes on their swords' points. It was bad enough for the regime to be

[1] Reviewing M. J. Lasky, *Utopia and Revolution* (1977) in the *Guardian*, 27 Jan. 1977.
[2] *Diary of Thomas Burton M.P.*, *1656–59*, ed. J. T. Rutt (1828). The edition used here is the reprint (1974) with Introduction by I. Roots and annotated index of speakers by P. Pinckney and P. H. Hardacre.
[3] *CJ* vii. 593–644.
[4] *Old Parliamentary History* (*1751–62*), xxi. 228–9, 233–6; Thurloe, vii. 374.

ringed with dissidents—royalists, Fifth Monarchists, Levellers, Commonwealthsmen—without giving them a platform at Westminster. Moreover, the indiscipline of under-officers and rank-and-file might be increased by contact with parliament-men sharing similar political outlooks. The civilian councillors were prepared to take the risk. To have a counter to hardened military men was appealing in itself, and they expected the enemies of the Protectorate to be too divided to provide a coherent opposition. The grandees' reluctance was not in fact immovable. Not every soldier sees force as the sole political weapon. Some officers could hope to be returned to put their point of view. So the writs went out for a parliament to assemble on 27 January 1658/9.[1]

The Commons was to be chosen not on the novel arrangements of the Instrument of Government but 'according to the ancient rights of the nation in the late king's time'. The Humble Petition and Advice had enjoined the Protector merely to ensure that 'the laws and statutes of the land be observed', a formula vague enough to allow a range of options. The changes made by the one chosen were substantial, chiefly increasing borough representation at the expense of the counties. For Scotland and Ireland to be represented as under Oliver was, of course, an anomoly, but the Commons itself was to decide on their permanent inclusion—a likely source of controversy. There was also a second chamber, with Oliver's pseudo-lords summoned. As the dissolution of his second Parliament had been an abrupt response to the Commons' unwillingness to accept any 'screen or balance' to itself, here was another likely quarrel-centre. In addition, the legitimacy of the new Protectorate itself would be open to question even by members who had not hesitated to stand on its writs.

Elections were fought vigorously on a variety of issues, as always many local, some by no means peculiar to the strained circumstances of the late 1650s.[2] Particular efforts by 'the courtiers' to get the right sort of men returned were reported and the electoral influence of some patrons was effectively

---

[1] See G. B. Nourse, 'Richard Cromwell's House of Commons', *Bulletin of John Rylands Library*, lx, and references there. I am grateful to Dr. Nourse for allowing me to read his article in typescript.

[2] See G. Davies, 'Election of Richard Cromwell's Parliament', *EHR* lxiii (1948), and Nourse, op. cit.

exploited. The House's protracted consideration of disputed
contests suggest that in some places 'unjust proceedings' were
pursued. Evidently the republicans, though of various outlooks,
attempted some kind of co-ordination. Thurloe's reference
to clandestine meetings mentions specifically Thomas Scot,
John Weaver, Henry Neville, and Edmund Ludlow. His
inclusion among them of the secluded member, Col. John
Birch, who would act as teller for 'the court' in some divisions,
and failure to mention Sir Arthur Hesilrige raises doubts about
the reliability of his information upon this as upon other aspects
of his concerns. His anticipation that the Commonwealthsmen
would work to have voting within the House by 'ballating box'
was never realized. He expected difficulties over 'the other
House' and the succession itself. 'What these men will be able
to effect in the House, I know not; but certainly no endeavours
will be wanting to put us into trouble'—a prediction anyone
could have made.[1]

In the event all of his troublemakers got in, but so did a mish-
mash of others—major-generals and swordsmen of a range
of political persuasions, many Presbyterians, certainly some
ex-royalists and more crypto-royalists, office-holders, and men,
obscure and prominent, of less established attitudes. More than
half the members were new to Westminster; many were very
young, too, and, it was thought, ready to be manœuvred by
experienced players of the parliamentary game. At least three
members would survive to sit in the early eighteenth century.
A few had appeared in Jacobean times or in the early Parliaments of Charles I. There were about thirty original members
of the Long Parliament, including the ancient Sir Walter Erle.
Rather more recruiters survived. There were twenty-five
'saints' from the Nominated Assembly and a fair number who
had sat in or been excluded from the Oliverian Parliaments.
Socially the composition was much like that of any seventeenth-
century Commons, though at any other time an elected marquis, a viscount, a few earls, and barons would not have been
encountered. 'Gentlemen of the long robe', official and otherwise, were as usual conspicuous. There was a sprinkling of other
professional men, citizens and merchants, and as ever country
gentlemen galore. The Scots and Irish members, for all the

[1] Thurloe, vii. 550.

government influence upon their selection, were also a mixed bag.[1]

Prominent in confidence, energy, and noise were Commonwealthsmen, civilian and military, able to enlist the support from time to time of other members, particularly disappointed army officers like Col. Packer. The so-called moderates—many of whom did not in fact occupy any sort of middle ground but were really crypto-royalists or conservatives drifting towards monarchy in the old line—were politically, religiously, and socially very diverse. The still-smarting secluded members were hardly likely to join with the Rumpers. Some of them preferred a Protectorate to a Commonwealth, either for itself or as the thin end of a wedge to split opposition to a return to the 'ancient constitution'. There were certainly other members besides the officials and courtiers who might develop a genuine regard for the regime established by the Humble Petition and Advice. In the men and in the issues there was material for all kinds of disagreement to be set off and kept alive by skilled and determined politicians. In this the Commonwealthsmen were from the start prime movers. They accused the courtiers of chicanery, but employed without shame, often without finesse, the very methods they condemned. Opinionated, long-memoried, well-read, they had a sense of mission which would release them from restraint. They would join no matter whom against a common enemy and as easily abandon old as new friends. To a Hesilrige, a Lambert could be as acceptable for a while, at least, as a Neville.

When Parliament assembled on 27 January 1658/9, the Commons' first business was to choose a Speaker. The appointment of Chaloner Chute, a Middle Temple barrister who had been excluded in 1656, was generally acceptable. Hesilrige, overlooking Chute's pre-Civil War 'royalist' activities, was even ready to second the nomination. Whitelocke remarks that no one expected that Chute would join 'the Protector's party, but he did heartily'. In fact, the Speaker did little to help Thurloe, and his feeble handling of the debates, in which he was often at a loss, gave more opportunities to the Commonwealthsmen than to the councillors. As soon as he was in the chair, the

---

[1] For constituencies of members and indications of biographical sources see the index of speakers in Burton (1974 edn.), iv. (1)–(43).

customary bill on a trivial matter held over from the last parliament was given a formal first reading to demonstrate that the House did not have to wait for a government legislative programme before getting on with its own business. It was a more than symbolic gesture. Almost immediately Hesilrige, to impress the new members with his easy mastery of procedure and contempt for parliaments called since the expulsion of the Rump, objected to the phrase that the Clerk, John Smyth, 'be continued' and secured the amendment that he 'be the Clerk'. Hesilrige went on to assert categorically that this or that was the order of the House. Contrary opinions were soon heard and the Speaker remarked tartly that well might he himself be ignorant of the orders of the House seeing 'both sides' so confidently contradictory. But Sir Arthur and friends were not unhappy about disagreement. Any sort of conflict would keep things in train, holding up the matters of substance for which Secretary Thurloe might want priority. Hesilrige then argued that no business ought to be taken until the House itself was full. (Some members were slow to arrive and there was a crop of disputed elections and double returns to be resolved.) What was essential now was a Committee of Privileges, an admirable venue for arguments over and above those on the floor of the chamber. The Commons adjourned overnight with no decisions taken—not a bad start for the 'opposition'.[1]

Meantime, in the other House the Lord Protector had made a brief sensible speech 'from the throne', giving the obvious, and now almost traditional, reasons for calling this parliament—army pay, foreign policy, internal security, and unity. A windy discourse by the Lord Keeper, Nathaniel Fiennes, added only an emphasis on the Humble Petition and Advice, unwelcome both among the sprinkling of M.P.s standing at the Bar and to those who had deliberately stayed away.[2]

Next day began with the Commons flaring up into what Burton calls 'a great debate' about the preachers to address the House on a day of humiliation the following week. Commonwealthsmen Hesilrige and Weaver nominated Edmund Calamy, who was soon to advocate a Restoration. His rival, John Owen, was backed by Major-Generals Kelsey and Lambert,

---

[1] Burton, iii. 3–6.
[2] Burton, iii. 7–11; *Old Parliamentary History*, xxi. 265–81.

who would not always see eye to eye. Owen was, of course, somewhat tarnished by close association with the late Protector. But he was chosen, an indication perhaps that the Commonwealthsmen were in a minority, but as Calamy had also been supported by the Presbyterian, Thomas Clarges, Monk's brother-in-law, himself moving towards royalism, the vote revealed rather that cross-voting in divisions was to be expected. Unabashed, Hesilrige bounded back with strong views over the location of the service. Not for him, St. Margaret's, 'the Commons' parish church', but the House itself. It would be crowded and stuffy, certainly, but it was *the* House and the proper place for members to be reminded privately of their faults and duties, not publicly before 'a promiscuous auditory'. This last phrase seems somewhat jaundiced, coming from so vocal an exponent of 'the rights and liberties of the people'. Hesilrige's definition of 'the people' was in fact a narrow one, taking in hardly more than the members of the Commons who happened to agree with him. Scot, too, was one who kept reminding the Commons that they sat for the people of England, but sometimes gave the impression that he himself was the people. Henry Neville, more loosely attached to Rumper commonwealthdom than either, would make a Harringtonian interpretation which was perhaps more precise. But 'the people' was a phrase that came to everybody's lips as readily as 'the fundamental laws' had in the Long Parliament, and was as elusive of definition. Hesilrige clearly enjoyed these preliminaries of Parliament, bustling about like a prefect out to impress new boys at school. When on 1 February a procedural matter arose about the relative status of the judges at Westminster Hall and that of the Commons, he underlined the latter's superiority by telling Mr. Speaker that he looked upon him 'as the greatest man in England'. (So much for my Lord Protector.) He then precipitated a discussion in which he and many others aired very diverse legal and historical knowledge, a trend to be pursued throughout this parliament. In such matters he became so opinionated that there was a protest that he was inventing orders of his own, which he was.[1]

---

[1] Burton, iii. 11–20. For Owen, see P. Toon, *God's Statesman, Life and Works of John Owen* (Exeter, 1971). For Clarges's relationship and relations with Monck, see M. Ashley, *General Monck* (1977).

Reports from the Committee of Privileges (constituted on 28 January) concerning disputed elections gave further opportunities for a crash-course in parliamentary ways. Adam Baynes, a former associate of Lambert who had sat in the 1656 Parliament but was now actively supporting the Commonwealthsmen, wanted an offending returning officer, a mayor, hauled up over the objections of moderates that time was being wasted on trivial matters. Clearly the Commonwealthsmen were out to make themselves conspicuous upholders of privilege, to bring home to the rest that by experience, grasp of what Parliament was for, and how it should work, they deserved leadership. Moreover, all this hampered the introduction of a government programme. Members of all outlooks would get swept into the filibuster, sometimes because they saw openings for their own political purposes, often—and this should not be forgotten—because there was an intrinsic appeal to all these points of detail and protocol for men with a smattering of law, a sense of the past, and an urge to do things and to see things done in a parliamentary way. It would be difficult to overstate the part played by procedure in the attitudes of the Stuart generations, who cast themselves as present trustees of the past to posterity. The very deficiencies of the auspices under which they came to Westminster were an incentive to have things there done properly. Hesilrige need not have worked quite so hard to get the House bogged down. Members would have got there quickly and happily enough of their own accord. Older men, prolix like Sir Walter Erle, sharply legal-minded like John Maynard, were ever ready to demonstrate their special knowledge, while new men were willing and apt to learn. Debates would drag out almost of their own volition, particularly as the councillors and office-holders were mostly very diffident about hurrying the House along and very reluctant to appear as 'pilots of the Commonwealth'.[1]

Certainly no member could fairly claim that this parliament was abridged of 'the ancient liberty of freedom of speech and just censure'. There had been no exclusion (or even the suggestion of one) of members of unwelcome political views. Some members certainly sat without taking the requisite oath (e.g.

---

[1] Burton, iii. 14, 22–4. For instances of Erle's and Maynard's interventions, ibid. 14, 19, 25, 50, 248, 435.

Edmund Ludlow).[1] Though Hesilrige and company only rarely admitted it, this was a far freer and more comprehensive parliament than that Rump whose virtues and achievements they would rehearse *ad nauseam*.

Perhaps the government members should have taken a more positive approach. Parliaments have always needed some sort of management—whips, scorpions, or carrots. If the executive does not give a lead, someone else will, and may, if only temporarily, take over. But Thurloe's mistake is understandable. It looks as if he remembered how well things had gone in the first session of the 1656 Parliament, which had produced a spate of legislation, public and private, votes of revenue, and, in the Humble Petition and Advice, a revised constitution, the present 'government', and forgot the tone of the second aborted session, with its changed membership which included some dynamic men now present.[2] The court had clearly decided that to prevent the Hesilriges and Scots from sitting would make them martyrs and bring contumely on the government. Once the House had assembled it would have been madness to attempt simply to expel anyone. Subtle management was beyond Thurloe; it might be beyond the Commonwealthsmen too. The courtiers in the event were neither inconspicuous, nor puerile or ineffective in their interventions in the debates. What is more they could win divisions—or at any rate not lose them to the republican opposition. This was an additional reason why the latter tried to prevent issues from coming to a rapid vote.

It was reasonable too for the government to let the House gradually reveal itself. Who in this puzzling linsey-woolsey assembly were friends, who enemies, who uncommitted? When the answers came the court might slip into the appropriate managerial posture. With the power of dissolution in the Protector's hands, time and he might be a match for any two. But unfortunately there were those other uncompliant groups, whose responsibility was only to an undefined 'people' and who were well endowed with confidence and righteous indignation about the past. So the debates were prolonged, side-tracked, interrupted, renewed, lulled to sleep by Hesilrige and his allies.

[1] *Memoirs of Edmund Ludlow*, ed. C. H. Firth (Oxford, 1894), ii. 50–3.
[2] See I. Roots, 'Lawmaking in the second Protectorate Parliament' in *British Government and Administration*, ed. H. Hearder and H. R. Loyn (Cardiff, 1974).

Sometimes these voluble orators almost took over, but never quite, and it would be a misreading of the discussions on Recognition, negative voice, the other House, and anything else to see the opposition really triumphant. Eloquence, cogency, concern, energy, political sense, and certainly good manners were not their monopoly. Some courtiers and moderates shared all or some of these qualities. Considering the situation at home and abroad it is hard to absolve the Commonwealthsmen from a charge of political frivolity. Apart from the goings-on in the House they got involved with forces outside, notably among the tough under-officers of the army, at whom they might upon reflection have looked somewhat askance. Their encouragement of discontents brought on a dissolution which should have been the last thing they wished for, unless they were utterly negative. Perhaps some of them already were. True, the Commonwealthsmen would soon be back when the Rump was restored by the grandees, but by then their prospects of being free agents had already dwindled. When Monck marched south in early 1660 the possibilities disappeared completely. The Commonwealthsmen were, of course, not solely responsible for the failure of this parliament. If they overestimated their own strength, so did the government its own, allowing the neuters to see through both sides. In the very short run with the dissolution the uncommitted conservatives and moderates might seem to have lost as much as government and Commonwealthsmen. In the long run—and it turned out to be not a very long one—they would win.

John Thurloe has been mocked for his rather minor part in this parliament.[1] His first major intervention came on 1 February after the House had indulged in one of its many minute electoral post-mortems. (Could a healthy under-sheriff be sent for to answer the misdemeanours of the ailing sheriff?)[2] 'Suddenly and abruptly', the Secretary stood up, 'You have spent some time about the forms of your House. It is now time to mind other things.'[3] He then introduced a short Bill of Recognition, whereby the Parliament would acknowledge formally the succession of Richard Cromwell as Lord Protector.[4]

---

[1] H. R. Trevor-Roper, 'Oliver Cromwell and His Parliaments' in his *Religion, the Reformation and Social Change* (1967), 387.   [2] Burton, iii. 21–2.
[3] Burton, iii. 25.   [4] The text of the bill is in Thurloe, vii. 603–4.

Just as in former kingly days Parliament had recognized in the interests of unity and security the succession of Elizabeth I and of James I, so now. The bill asserted that, to the general consent and approbation of the people of the three nations—Wales as usual subsumed in England—and of the armed forces by land and sea, Richard had lawfully assumed office and dignity 'immediately after' Oliver's demise. Although this in itself was an ample satisfaction, the two Houses requested that their 'hearty recognition and agreement of your Highness's right to succeed in government shall remain for ever among the records of the High Court of Parliament'. The rest of the bill renounced 'in the name of all the people of the commonwealth' all allegiance to Charles Stuart and his kin, who were 'absolutely and utterly' excluded from any title or authority. The emphasis of the draft bill is certainly on the pretensions of the Stuarts. Thurloe ought to have made more of this than he did. Many who in ensuing debates turned out to be critics of Recognition were certainly still committed against the Stuarts and it might have helped for them to be reminded more particularly now about the sleepless common enemy.

It comes as no surprise that Hesilrige should leap at once to his feet. The bill was 'not seasonably offered now'. The great requirement was circumspection, to take care 'within these walls' rather than stray abroad. The Commons still had committees of grievances, trade, religions to set up. So far they had achieved only one thing—the appointment of the Committee of Privileges. Hesilrige then swung into a rhapsody about the 'pulling down' done by the late Long Parliament (especially, of course, the Rump), a favourite theme from now on. What was wanted now was an accounting for everything done and spent since they were turned out in 1653. Not that he did not honour 'the person' (Richard), whom he patronized as without either 'guile or gall'. But a bill of this significance should not be taken before other business or until after the Fast, which was clearly a device for delaying as well as praying. The strategy of the opposition was already revealed.[1]

Government supporters thought it a greater honour to build up than to pull down. But Thomas St. Nicholas and Thomas Scot (almost as frequent a speaker as Hesilrige) rapped back: first,

[1] Burton, iii. 26–7.

seek God: do not fish before casting your net. Scot then flung in the argument that the position of the Scots and Irish must be settled before any bill of Recognition (implying, as this one did, the existence of an imperial parliament) could be considered, let alone passed. Recognition of Richard could not be separated from acceptance of the whole constitution—the Humble Petition and Advice itself. Col. John Birch, who had taken it as read and a matter for congratulation that these members had been 'admitted into oneness with us', would not have the bill set aside for a day or even an hour. The debate had already started to flow along a slow, meandering, and muddy course. The Solicitor-General naïvely confessed that he had not expected any discussion on the Recognition at all. 'Is this any more than we are sworn to at the doors?' (Some members had, in fact, already slipped in without the oath.) The first formal reading taken, the Attorney-General moved briskly for a second the very next day. His request for 'no coldness' was ignored by Hesilrige who, ostentatious as ever in his urge 'to serve posterity in this generation', moved to defer the next reading 'til Monday sennight' and demanded meantime copies for M.P.s to ponder over. (At this point Burton records that an unnamed young member told 'a story of Cain and Abel' and made a speech 'nobody knew to what purpose'—an ironical comment perhaps on Hesilrige's already thickening clouds of rhetoric.)[1]

Robert Steward could not blame those who urged delay. They obviously needed time to make up arguments against Recognition. Hesilrige's rejoinder that no one knew whether he himself would come out for or against the bill was unconvincing, so his ally Adam Baynes quickly got on to points of substance. He might, he said, have acquiesced in the bill 'if nothing else were in the belly of it'. But it was big with dangers—the negative voice and the other House at least. 'The consequence must be that you will either bring the government to your property or your property to the government. The balance will be too great for the people and if the army turn mercenary farewell property.' The language with its Harringtonian echoes is obscure. 'Does the good captain mean we stand in no need of an

<hr/>

[1] Burton, iii. 28–32. The Solicitor-General was Sir William Ellis, the Attorney-General Sir Edmund Prideaux.

army?' asked John Trevor. But one argument is plain: concentrate on dangers not from Charles Stuart but from the
present regime. From the other side Thomas Manby wanted
quick Recognition followed by 'a bill in my pocket' for enabling
the Scots and Irish members. Though it was his side who had
dragged them in, Hesilrige would have none of that. Go back
to the proper—his own—order of proceedings. He then got into
a niggling, procedural argument—one of many to come—with
Serjeant Maynard. Finally, 'Lord' Lambert, who 'liked the
thing but not the haste', felt that 'something touching your own
privileges and the people's rights'—a sort of Instrument of
Government perhaps?—should go along with it and he referred
to a Grand Committee. Meanwhile study moderation. Lambert
was not trying to help a regime which had long drifted away
from his requirements. He would speak and act as teller on a
number of matters in a way that made him at least a prospec-
tive ally of the Commonwealthsmen. Finally the second reading
was voted to be taken on the following Monday (7 February).[1]

Every day of the discussion to come on Recognition, or the
other House, etc.—they cropped up in many contents quite un-
related to the bill—deserves close study. (This article considers
only the first couple of weeks.) Nothing was cut and dried,
the unforeseen overtook the expected; no one, least of all the
harassed Speaker, took command. The 1st of February had set
the pattern: diffuseness and volubility. It had rehearsed both
major arguments and attractive side-issues. It had introduced a
corps of leading contributors, though from time to time quieter,
unthrustful men did get a word in.

Quickly reference in the bill to 'the chief magistrate' had
come to mean a full agreement to lodge the former royal
prerogatives in the Lord Protector, to accept two Houses of
Parliament and to equate the other House with a House of
Lords with its ancient powers and privileges, to consent to the
union of the three nations and to the unimpeded admission of
the Scots and Irish. Slingsby Bethel later claimed that all these
things were covertly wrapped up in the bill 'to have carried
undiscovered'.[2] It may be so. If it were then those 'more

---

[1] Burton, iii. 31–3. For Lambert as teller, *CJ* vi. 611, 619, 621.
[2] Slingsby Bethel, *A Brief Narrative of the Parliament called by Richard Cromwell* in
The Interests of the Princes and States of Europe (1694), 335.

careful of the liberties of the people' were gratuitously provided with an opportunity for a display of virtue. In the process they offered—and stimulated—commentaries on a range of constitutional, political, and institutional history and theory. Extravagant always, Hesilrige would go back to the Heptarchy and might have begun at the Flood, but there were others almost as anxious to trot out almost as much history. All this makes these debates of interest not only to the student of the events of 1659–60, but of the Interregnum in general. Burton's *Diary* proves an almost inexhaustible quarry.

The bill itself might be put off but the issues would not sleep. The very next day (2 February) on another matter Henry Neville was offering his thoughts that something should be done to amend—of course, 'for the liberties of the people'—'the great flaws' and uncertainties in 'the Government', specifically 'the negative voice' and the militia. There must be no veto in either Lord Protector or other House—and control of the army must rest in the Commons. George Starkey replied that on the contrary these things had already been settled in the Advice. 'We ought to keep singly to the Recognition and not perplex what is clear or ought to be meddled in more seasonably.' Hesilrige's horror that anyone could believe that 'the militia and the negative voice are not in this House' stirred him to recall and (worse) to relate his own part in the Militia Bill of 1642, his exclusion from the Oliverian parliaments, and so on, all for the edification of the younger members. He may have been aware that the royalist M.P.s at the outbreak of civil war had been rather younger than the parliamentarians and many of them had lacked direct experience of the events of the 1620s.[1] Guibon Goddard comments in his *Diary* that Neville and Hesilrige were letting 'the Court know that they were not asleep' and, suspecting that there were members ready 'to 'surfeit the Protector with too much kindness in the Bill', were resolved to 'involve the Court in this labyrinth, that either they must not make that speed with the Recognition which they intended or look that what promotion they made with the one, it was expected the like should be in the other' (i.e. the people's liberties).[2]

---

[1] Burton, iii. 34–6; D. Brunton and D. H. Pennington, *Members of the Long Parliament* (1954), 20.

[2] Goddard's diary (BL, Add. MS. 5138) cited in Burton, iii. 35–6. An edition

John Trevor was amazed (as well he might be) by Hesilrige's effrontery. Having thus won his point that nothing should be done with the bill till the standing committees were established, the Rumper was now dragging in veto and militia, claiming that the latter was 'the beginning of the quarrel between the King and the Parliament'. Trevor hoped 'it shall not be the quarrel between his Highness and the Parliament'. But that was what the Commonwealthsmen did want and they were already working on it inside and outside Parliament. For the moment attention passed to other matters—among them a breach of privilege, always a fascinating topic for the privileged. *En route* Hesilrige treated the 'gallant young gentlemen' to a further lesson in parliamentary history and procedure. (His constant and gratuitous patronage of youth was later adversely commented upon.) This minor debate is illuminating on diversities of outlook and attitude. None of the groupings were rigid or homogeneous. Serjeant Maynard, so often inimical to Hesilrige, joined him in fervent vindication of privileges, 'lest from 20 you come to 12'. (Did the Commons ever have as many as a dozen privileges?)[1]

Consideration next day (3 February) of the continued imprisonment of the radical Col. Overton and of the case of Henry Neville against the 1656 sheriff of Berkshire—a long-festering electoral dispute—revealed and encouraged further rifts. In the Overton debate army members, already incensed by remarks which had led one of them to snap that it would soon 'be a crime to be an army man', stood up for their brother officer and the court had to go warily. Hesilrige did not help by tackling the Protector's opening speech, now in print. Cutting through the present dangers alluded to in it, he was soon in full spate on the glories of the Rump and the need for accountability about everything done since. He was surprised and distressed that the army should be in want. That must not continue. 'Necessity will make them break through stone walls.' (The walls of this House?) Here surely was a ploy to win the

of the Goddard diary is in preparation by Ivan Roots. An edition of the diary of Sir John Gell for this parliament is in preparation by W. A. H. Schilling. For sources for the parliamentary history of this period see the Introduction to Burton (1974), i. (1)–(12).

[1] Burton, iii. 36–41.

army to the Commonwealthsmen. But the impact was weakened by the sour reflections on the Rump of Col. Birch, who never forgot he had been secluded. 'If that glorious time had lasted a little longer we must have sold two thirds of our estates to keep the third.' Thurloe followed up by being pleased that everyone was so keen to look into the necessities of the nation and how they might be supplied. 'To look forward will be more necessary for the peace of the people than to tell what was done either in 1648 or 1653.'[1]

The Secretary spoke with some justification. There had been little constructive so far in the plethora of Commonwealthsman reminiscences. They seemed to have forgotten nothing and learned nothing. Yesterday's men, they would stop the clock in fumbling to set it back. That was something they never understood. So, unrepentant, they went on, Scot demanding details of past expenditure, 'the better to estimate what to provide'. 'The people'—the Commons—'are the purse of the nation.' It was resolved to have the accounts of the army and navy shortly rendered—providing further opportunities for obstruction and Rumper self-righteousness.[2]

The 4th of February was Fast Day. On the 5th the question of members sitting without taking the oath was raised. It soon spilled over into the qualifications of the Scots and Irish. In a comical interlude it was discovered that 'a gentleman in grey clothes', a simpleton, had sat for three whole days unnoticed. A practical joker had told him that he had been chosen 'a parliament man'. Somehow or other this debate, differing features of which were unwelcome to court and Commonwealthsmen, petered out. For once Hesilrige successfully pressed the House to take pity on itself and to rise, to get ready for Monday and the full resumption of the Recognition debate.[3] That morning (7 February) in a very full House—the Serjeant-at-arms had fetched the lawyers back from Westminster Hall[4]—the second reading was met by a silence. Hesilrige—who else?—broke it, though with seeming reluctance, with what turned out to be 'a very long harangue', designed, as someone said, to educate further those gentlemen who had been 'at school during the late troubles'.[5] In it 'for method's sake' Hesilrige contemplated 'what

---

[1] Burton, iii. 45–60. [2] Burton, iii. 61. [3] Burton, iii. 68–84.
[4] Burton, iii. 87. [5] Burton, iii. 87–105. See especially 87.

we have been, what we are, and what we shall be'. As always the past had the most appeal. This time he began with the Conquest, when Kentishmen had resisted that 'single person', William of Normandy, 'and in some sort preserved liberty to all the rest'. Then came Magna Carta, won by the barons in opposing the suppression of the people's liberties. Soon government was 'in King and Parliament, Lords and Commons sitting together'. Then the Lords made a separate and superior House, leaving the Commons only 'the power of the purse'. But that turned out to be the very preservation of the rights of the nation, particularly as the Commons acquired a greater share in lands and possessions. (There is a watery Harringtonianism here. Perhaps Hesilrige had been listening to Neville as well as preparing his own speeches.) This situation had lasted 300 years —but in time abuses crept in. Hence the Civil Wars, of which he proceeded to give an account playing up the role of ex-General Fairfax, who, it was noted, 'always sat next to him'. (Soon Fairfax would be urging Monck to restore Charles II. If at present Hesilrige was using him, he was probably using Hesilrige.) Eventually Hesilrige re-created the golden age of the Rump:

We continued four years before we were put an end to. In which time I appeal to you if the nation which had been blasted and torn began not exceedingly to flourish. At the end of 4 years scarce a sight that we had had a war [or were having one with the Dutch?]. Trade flourished; the City of London grew rich; we were the most potent by sea that ever was known in England. Our navy and armies were never better . . .

Hesilrige never appreciated what a heterogeneous collection of men the Rump was—radical moderate, conservative; many hardly shared the philosophy of Hesilrige and Scot, let alone that of Harringtonians and more revolutionary bands of Commonwealthsmen. It would have upset Sir Arthur to learn that if there was a typical Rumper it was not himself but the even more boring Bulstrode Whitelocke.[1] Hesilrige had still not finished. The story of the Protectorate must be told yet again. From two protectoral parliaments they had dared to keep him out. 'During the second the [Instrument of] Government grew

---

[1] For analyses of membership of the Rump see D. Underdown, *Pride's Purge* (Oxford, 1971), and B. Worden, *The Rump Parliament* (Cambridge, 1974).

dangerously sick and it died. Another foundation was laid. The Petition and Advice must be the law and foundation of all.' Never! It was the work of a forced, imperfect, tame, dismembered parliament, whereas 'We are the freest and clearest and most undoubted representatives that ever were since the dissolution of the three estates, King, Lords and Commons. I know not one member kept out . . . I hope God will direct us to get out of this great darkness.'

If not God, Sir Arthur Hesilrige will. Here was an irony. If they were free it was because Richard had called them and let them be, because government management was so loose it has been dismissed with contempt by modern historians.[1] Hesilrige had yet more to say. 'The people of England were never more knowing and sensible of their privileges and liberties' nor readier for a settlement from their representatives. 'We can do here whatsoever is for the good of the people. We have power over their purses and persons; can take away whole laws, or part of them or make new ones.' He almost took off in his exuberance. Returning to earth, he went on to tell those still listening, 'what we cannot do . . . Set up any power equal to the people either in one person or in another House.'

Back, then, to the bill. For Richard the man he had the greatest affection, but he could not recognize him as Protector by simply taking for granted the validity of what had not been given in a free parliament. 'The people are not pleased' . . . so we must look into it. 'Never begin with the person first, but agree what trust he shall have. There is no danger to the nation so long as this representative sits here.'[2]

There was the rub. The court had one weapon left—dissolution. The great problem that Hesilrige, like so many advocates of Parliament as the embodiment of the nation, never really faced was that to achieve their work they must continue to sit. In the early seventeenth century parliaments had been advised to handle their business 'so as they might make the king in love' with them.[3] It might have been enough for him to be only half in love. His needs could have done the rest. The Commons did

---

[1] See Trevor-Roper, 'Oliver Cromwell and his Parliaments'.

[2] Burton, iii. 105.

[3] Cranfield in 1621, cited in C. Russell, 'Parliamentary History in Perspective 1604–1629', *History*, lxi (1976), 14.

not have to be supine or abject, rather the leadership should have a realistic, informed, and reasoned appreciation of a government's situation and make appropriate gestures. That would be to compromise, a term unpleasant to men of principle. To compromise is, in fact, not always to fall below one's principles. It might mean rising above them. Even revolutionary and extremist politics must at times become the politics of compromise, just as all parties, even the most seeming monolithic, are coalitions and to that extent at least pragmatic. (Has there ever been a more pragmatic politician than the revolutionary theoretician, Lenin?) But the awareness of these things during intense conflict is usually flickering. Hence under the young Charles I there had been three abrupt dissolutions, symbols of his failure certainly, but also of the inept tactics of leaders like Sir John Eliot, and seen by Clarendon as sources of the troubles of the 1640s. In the 1650s to drive Cromwell to expose the force that lay at the base of his power by bringing on irate dissolutions in 1653, 1654/5, and 1657/8 was no doubt a propaganda triumph. But if an effective Cromwellian settlement had been put off, so just as surely had other versions. The republicans were no nearer a permanent agreed Commonwealth early in 1659, or even after the Rump was restored in May 1659, than they were in 1653. If any interest had improved its position it was that of the royalists, who might discern in the struggles of courtiers, republicans, and army groupings Charles Stuart's coming moment. Not that *the* Restoration of 1660, or any restoration, was inevitable, but during 1659 the possibility of a commonwealth under Hesilrige, Scot, and Ludlow or the metamorphosis of England into Oceana was increasingly remote.

Richard's sensible resignation (25 May 1659) and the military auspices under which the Rump was recalled should have aroused republican misgivings. Instead of providing money to end free quarter, or introducing and passing legislation, private and public, to win over all manner of folk to a continued parliamentary sitting, the Commonwealthsmen had encouraged the Commons to wrangle over the Recognition, the other House, the Scots and Irish members. It may have been satisfying to see Richard forced to harangue some troops as 'a company of mutineers . . . men that will go about to undermine me',[1] but it was dangerous to encourage (as George Monck knew) any group in the army to become even more political than it already was. 'A knowing army' could turn out to be more demanding than a knowing people. The Good Old Cause of military men must ultimately be different from that of the civilian sort. The habit of ranging over the years is contagious. Turning back to Burton's *Diary* we find John Bulkeley, supplying from acquired knowledge, not experience, omissions in Hesilrige's partial narrative. There were, he understood, more causes of the Civil War than control of the militia: they included the King's protection to delinquents, church exorbitancy, toleration of popery. There was more to events, too. What of Pride's Purge, which had spawned a 'monster' rather than a healthy commonwealth? Nor was the Instrument of Government all bad, though certainly 'that liberty was not left you which is your due', 'not' he went on—'not that I would set the crown on the head of the people'. What Bulkeley wanted to promote was a House of Lords, but meantime he would 'hold fast to the head of government'—a single person. Concentrate on the Recognition of Richard singly, and come to the rest by and by. (Perhaps Charles Stuart might have been among 'the rest'.)[2]

Bulkeley made no impact on Thomas Scot. The House had liberty to propound any Government. Scot, too, could not resist the appeal to history. 'The first rape committed on the House' was not Pride's Purge but one in April 1648 by London apprentices demanding the King's return in safety to London, 'otherwise our guts should be about our ears'. But God had borne witness against 'that cursed family', the Stuarts. So long as he was 'above ground', Charles I had encouraged daily army revolts and local risings. It was impossible to keep him alive. It was his blood or ours, but (echoing Oliver) 'we did not assassinate or do it in a corner'. The execution ushered in the Commonwealth when 'we never bid fairer for being masters of the whole world'—not that he himself favoured extension of England's borders. But the Rump had been disgracefully dissolved on that never-to-be-forgotten day in 1653, leading to the late Protectorate and now the new. Like so many, Scot

[1] Cited in G. Davies, *The Restoration of Charles II, 1658–60* (1955), 64.
[2] Burton, iii. 105–7.

professed no objection to Richard the man: 'If you think of
a single person I would have him sooner than any man alive.'
But, there it was, Recognition needed to be committed and
so on.[1]

Major Robert Beake, deploring 'all the stories' so far told,
felt obliged to add one more. For him Rumper England had
not basked in halcyon days; rather it was a period in which
errors, opinions, and blasphemies had taken root, among them
'levelling' agreements of the people—'nothing monstrous but
that time produced. We may bless God we are out of it.' The
debate dragged on. Commit the bill. Accept the fundamentals
of the Humble Petition and discuss circumstantials by and by.
Accept the whole bill, and so obviate what was working out
doors to obviate government itself. All that could be got that
day was an adjournment till the morrow, 'nothing to intervene'
(8 February).[2]

The war of words began again with the republican St.
Nicholas assailing the Humble Petition as 'a sandy foundation',
passed on a quick narrow vote in an unparliamentary way.
(There had in fact been protracted debates.) It was 'the most
destructive [law] to the nation' ever, because it placed both
militia and negative voice in a single person. Once confirmed,
Richard would have all the dead king's powers. 'If the people
shall ask us what we have done for their liberties, we can answer
only *ruina Angliae*.' They needed a healing parliament, new
foundations. Sir John Lenthall was more modest: 'I had rather
a cottage here, than a glorious palace in the sky.'[3] This is always
a problem—is a half-loaf now better than a whole loaf to come,
which may in fact be no loaf at all?

Hesilrige and Scot could not see the difficulty. Nor could they
understand that they held no blank sheet of paper upon which
to write whatever they fancied. The Rump had never found
one, nor had the Protectorate. The Instrument of Government
had drawn on the Heads of the Proposals. Moreover, time was
running out, for them as for the government. There was
impatience out of doors and it was not enough to snort 'we
should be above it'. If it was right not to 'huddle over' the
constitution in haste when setting foundations, it was also good

---

[1] Burton, iii. 107–13.   [2] Burton, iii. 113–17; *CJ* vii. 601.
[3] Burton, iii. 118–22.

sense not to linger over the past. An obscure member did well to point out that 'we cannot bring the constitutions of the Saxons, Romans or Normans to our purpose' in 1659. The hope that 'we shall look forward' was politic. This Mr. Thomas Edgar was tactless enough to remember that 'the people'— those for whom Hesilrige claimed to be the oracle—seemed content so far with Richard's rule. Members, known and unknown, reinforced such points, while as many in speeches long and short raised fresh issues or refurbished old ones. The very style of the bill was criticized; it was 'very dark and imperfect', not at all 'in a parliamentary state', 'plain and perspicacious'. Brushing that aside, the Attorney-General saw their own doubts breeding worse doubts in a nation at present willing to forgive and forget. It might not always be. But Henry Neville could not forget that he had read *Oceana*, and offered another survey from Conquest to the Dissolution of the Monasteries and on again to the Civil War. 'It was not the civil war that altered our government but tendencies in the government that caused the civil war', neatly put but hardly helping a decision on Recognition. Let Richard, he declared, be chief magistrate but 'under such rules and limitations as you shall agree upon' in a Grand Committee. Hesilrige and Scot must have been relieved to hear that—it had looked as if with all his talk of an Oceanic senate and hard words about the oligarchical nature of the Rump Neville would sail out of their sight.[1]

A pro-government member, Griffith Bodwrda, argued that to abandon the Humble Petition, as freely made as any law since the Long Parliament first met, would endanger 'private acts, acts of oblivion and diverse public acts of consequence' such as the sale of lands. Bodwrda had been conspicuous in the first session of the 1656 Parliament and was proud of its enormous legislative achievement. Settle things now, he pressed, lest the Protector feel obliged to use his power to dissolve, snatching away yet another opportunity to unify the nation. He meant to freeze the young members' blood when he mused that the major-generals might return 'with a breach in the city and the country'. But the passion to discuss, decry, amend, commit, modify, extend, and expound was still too hot. Col. Birch saw two ways to kill a bill: one by a grand committee, 'the other like

[1] Burton, iii. 123–35.

a pin in the wall—if you cannot knock it down with an axe, hang so much on it as to break it down . . . When I was in the army some said, "let us not go this way, lest the war be ended too soon".' Hesilrige confirmed his fears by confessing that though he had spoken much yesterday 'to the trouble of the House', he would speak as much more today—and did, drifting back again over 500 years, flaying the late Protectorate and appealing that lest they be made slaves, 'this little world [the Commons] should give laws to the great world'. His shameless proposal after all that of an adjournment for dinner was ignored. Samuel Gott, who had been excluded in 1656, refused to go back to 'times past' or to look forward 'to Oceana's Platonical commonwealth, things that are not and never shall be', and claimed a Recognition lay already in the oath. After the irrepressible Hesilrige had asked for windows to be opened, Adam Baynes slipped in another Harringtonian analysis of power. 'The people were too hard for the king in property and then in arms too hard for him.' The Harringtonians did not in fact make many converts to their slick view of politico-social development. Not until 4 p.m. was adjournment agreed. But the Commonwealthsmen could rejoice that things were still being spun out, regardless of pleas for a limit on the length and number of speeches a member might make. No vote was taken and tomorrow would be another day.[1]

Some observers now felt that the House was drifting towards Recognition, an impression confirmed by the Burton record of the debate. Hesilrige was the more determined to drag in other issues and to exploit every procedural device. The Speaker was no hindrance. He dithered, and when on 9 February John Swinfen, an experienced member, complained about his lack of control, he could only reply weakly that 'it is hard to know your [the House's] sense'. They had already that day got pulled aside from the 'great business' by arguments over a petition. The historical disquisitions continued over Sjt. Maynard's objections that they were not often relevant. Recognition Vane saw as a pair of stairs to ascend a throne, and to check that and a stack of other inconveniences urged yet again committal and adjournment. Thomas Gewen, who had always thought 'a well-regulated monarchy best', warned that a new common-

[1] Burton, iii. 135–51.

wealth was impossible 'unless with an army they rake out all members that are against returning'. Lambert remarked sagely that every man told that part best which concerned himself most and gave a version of the late troubles omitting the Instrument of Government. Congratulating the House on its assiduity, Hesilrige trusted that for their own safety they would not sit too late; 'peradventure 40 or 50 more [members] would speak'. At that ghastly thought the House soon rose.[1]

The 10th of February found them increasingly at sea. 'Put the question whether you will put the question', one member begged the Speaker. Another, who had sat in three parliaments and had never dared 'speak to the order of the House', complained that some who had never sat before were boldly doing just that. Sir Walter Erle searched his soggy memory for precedents and would not have men speak four or five times, as some certainly had done, notably, of course, Hesilrige, Scot, and Vane. Disingenuously, Hesilrige recommended both sides not to be jealous of one another. 'If I surprise any I desire never to be heard again.' It must have been a wish shared by many. At three o'clock the House had had enough for the day.[2]

Discussions of disputed elections and points of procedure, increasingly absorbing, interrupted the next day's (11 February) 'great business'. The usual mixture of the trivial and the vital flowed on. More Harringtonian snippets, biblical references, English history. An anonymous member rejected Scot's version of parliamentary development: 'Those that know history, know they [kings] were kings before Parliament declared them so . . ., and by the same token Richard was Protector before we came. Someone claimed that the Humble Petition had been buried with Oliver. Anthony Ashley Cooper, a peer in the making, warned against the other House, and demanded decisions certain and clear, since Englishmen, 'better taught' these days in their liberties, expected things to be clinched by Parliament. If Richard was confirmed there must be stated limits in 'additions' to the vote. Though Hesilrige found the provisos 'exceedingly short', the Commonwealthsmen were, of course, all for them and for more. Suspecting that in a vote the additions might be lost, Hesilrige turned to his old tactic of pointing out

[1] Burton, iii. 155, 161–2, 171–80, 181, 185–91, 193.
[2] Burton, iii. 195–6, 197–8, 199, 200, 201.

how late it was. When the general opinion was that it was best to go on, he moved, 'that every man may have liberty to speak again'. 'We must consider what we were, what we are, what we will be' (an almost exact echo of his demand of 5 February).[1] We need not follow him and the rest too closely. Ludlow would claim later that the courtiers were driving 'furiously'[2] at this point, but Burton's reportage, admittedly growing rather curter, gives the impression of a still diffident approach. By two o'clock the Commons adjourned gratefully without a question put.

The 12th of February provided distractions in moves to expel some members for past delinquency—both court and Commonwealthsmen worked to reduce each other's numbers by this way. An anonymous gentleman upset a good many when he said cogently that if they were to cast out everyone who had aided the King's cause at one time or another they would have 'a thin house'. There was no time that day for further exchanges on the Recognition.[3]

Sunday's rest gave Hesilrige renewed vigour. On Monday (14 February) he was all set to stroll again through the last five centuries in justifying his assault on Protectorate maladministration. *En passant*, he made remarks shedding light on what he meant by 'people'. 'The people care not what government they live under, so they may plough and go to market . . . Lawyers, officers, commanders of the army, that have great incomes, besides their rents, may be able to pay their rates; but the poor freeholder, the ploughman, the labourer that hath nothing but the sweat of his brow, how shall we take care for these, how shall they be able to live.' A genuine concern for economic welfare no doubt but no indication of independent political rights. His points were not taken up, and the debate followed its erratic course. Richard Knightley, assailing the Rump and praising the present regime, observed that people outside were beginning to notice their lack of progress: 'When posts go up and down they say you are where you were.' Even so, the *brouhaha* was not over. Though some fully supported the present regime and others, not wedded or glued to particular forms, were for posterity's sake willing to cling to even a bad government until

---

[1] Burton, iii. 203–33, 222, 226, 227–9, 229, 230.
[2] Ludlow, *Memoirs*, ii. 55.   [3] Burton, iii. 233–56, 238.

another, presumably better, was certain, the opposition still argued every point. They precipitated 'a long sermon' by John Stapleton, praying that landmarks (i.e. limitations) might be set on his Highness that he 'may not be split', that the people's liberties be cared for and for Parliament's and unity's sake they might both be joined. At this point the Speaker had to confess that 'we are indeed in a wood, a wilderness, a labyrinth. Some affirmative, some negative, which I cannot draw into one question.' The historian who has sat with him through the debates must sympathize.[1]

Yet there was more to come. What had been meant by 'Recognition' of Richard II and Henry IV? The word was French, a strike against it. So, someone objected, were 'parliament' and 'declaration'. 'If we exclude all French and Latin words we will not have words left in our own language to express ourselves.' Samuel Gott exploded, 'We have been debating by wholesale; now in words; next time will be in syllables and we shall, I hope, at last, come to the syllables *yea* and *no*, to determine all.' It was too much for the Speaker, who withdrew for an hour for dinner. When they trooped back, the topic was still 'words', Hesilrige helpfully offering 'two other English words which our laws know', 'constitute' and 'appoint'. John Sadler, fearing that 'recognise' would stay in, claimed that in France (where, ironically, that unwelcome word came from) there was a law 'that after a man lost his suit, he may speak nine days and nine nights'. He would do the same, not going to his closet even to pray, 'but I will pray here'. Thankfully that promise was broken. Shortly afterwards by 191 to 168 —with Hesilrige and Neville tellers for the *Noes*—'recognise' was voted to stand in the question. A further procedural discussion to which Vane, Weaver, Scot, Hesilrige, Ludlow, Baynes, and St. Nicholas all contributed and during which candles, of which Hesilrige 'never knew good', were brought in, a major vote was taken—'that it be part of the Bill to recognise and declare his Highness, Richard, Lord Protector, to be Lord Protector and Chief Magistrate of England, Scotland, and Ireland, etc.', and at the initiative of Col. Trevor and 'to the end the other party might not go away displeased', it was resolved that before committal that 'such additional clauses . . . be part

[1] Burton, iii. 256–60, 262, 266–9, 269.

of the Bill as may bound the power of the Chief Magistrate and
fully secure the rights and privileges of Parliament and the
liberties and rights of the people and that neither this, nor any
other previous vote, that is or shall be passed in order to this
Bill shall be of force or binding to the people until the whole Bill
be passed.'[1] The bill was, of course, never to be completed.
Burton mentions that there was 'but one negative' to this vote,
usually ascribed to Thurloe. Slingsby Bethel blames the courtiers for the ensuing collapse of unanimity, but that is not the
only story that can be made of the rest of the session, or, indeed,
the most convincing.[2]

This seems an apt point at which to leave the early debates on
the Recognition Bill. Much remains in a further volume and a
half of Burton and in the *Commons Journals*. But the shape, pace,
tone, and direction of the discussions are apparent and the
strategy—if such tactics add up to one—of the Commonwealthsmen has been exposed. No doubt some parts of the vote
gave them a momentary discomfiture but they clearly hoped
for success not only in future divisions but in their shady
negotiations out of doors. Much would be made of the dangers
from the Other House, which was in fact doing nothing of
significance, and of the unacceptability of the 'alien' members.
They would pick away at the government's financial accounts
and object with virtuous backward glances to current foreign
policy. There were also the almost daily reports on disputed
elections. An excise bill—the only other piece of legislation
offered in this addled session—encouraged more wordy indignation. When Parliament was abruptly dissolved by Richard
under military pressure they were still talking about the past
(22 April).[3]

Soon Richard made his exit, while the Commonwealthsmen
came back in the restored Rump, without the 'young gentlemen' whom they had at once deplored and patronized. It was
a heady moment. But they were not really free and they had

---

[1] Burton, iii. 275, 276, 277, 279, 281, 287; *CJ* vii. 603.
[2] Bethel, *A Brief Narrative*, 337–9.
[3] Burton, iv. 482–3; *CJ* vii. 644. Compare the first session of the second Protectorate Parliament, where the progress of the Humble Petition and Advice and
other public legislation was held up by a spate of 'private business', which benefited
at least some individuals and groups of interests within the community. See Roots,
'Lawmaking', *passim*.

already wasted too much time. The battle for their Commonwealth—for some the Rump itself (modestly augmented), for others the fictional institutions of *Oceana*—had already been lost to grandees, who were themselves in those 'ticklish times' all set to be losers too. Within a year or so they were all either in the political wilderness, in hiding or exile, or marked out for execution. The year 1660 confirmed the lesson they might have learned in 1659: that history can be for the politician a useful tool, but, as a weapon, may turn in the hand. It is harsh but true to say that like Charles I, whose dignity and courage in death they emulated, Vane and Scot were their own executioners.

Sir Johannes Rothe: English Knight
and Dutch Fifth Monarchist

K. H. D. HALEY

FROM Portugal to Sweden, and from the Germany of the Thirty Years War to the England of the Civil War, millenarianism was widespread in seventeenth-century Europe, and the Dutch Republic—an entrepôt for ideas as well as goods—had its share. Though Article 37 of the official Confession of faith, on the 'last things', made no reference to a Fifth Monarchy, and Voetius, the champion of unbending Calvinist orthodoxy, included attacks on such teachings in his voluminous writings, widespread literacy, the absence of a censorship, the generally tolerant attitudes of a regent class which was far from being rigidly Calvinist, and the looseness of the political constitution had contributed to the spread of sects. Easy contacts with Germany and with England had helped, though a connected study of those between Puritan England and the Netherlands has still to be written. There were Mennonite Baptists, 'Brownists' and Quakers (stimulated by British preachers such as Stephen Crisp); close-knit communities like followers of Jean de Labadie, and relatively informal groupings such as the Collegiants. Millenarian ideas were to be found amongst the Quakers and in Labadie and Antoinette de Bourignon; while amongst those influenced by the Collegiants was the Amsterdam burgomaster and ambassador to Paris and London, Coenraad van Beuningen, whose conviction that the coming of Christ's kingdom on earth was at hand was so great that one night he got up and raged through the streets of Amsterdam, banging on doors as a demonstration of urgency, and found it significant of the people's lethargy that though it was in the early hours and absolute quiet reigned, no one woke up.[1]

* I am much indebted to Professor D. J. Roorda of Leyden University for bibliographical assistance.
[1] C. B. Hylkema, *Reformateurs* (Haarlem, 1900–2), ii. 203 and elsewhere;

Van Beuningen was an exception among the regents, and the appeal of millenarian ideas was greatest lower down in the social order. But the sects were essentially quietist, not revolutionary, in their outlook. Occasionally they might be capable of radical ideas—the Labadists were credited with unorthodox views on property ownership and the relations between the sexes—but for the most part their gospel was more personal than social, and in order to preach it they did not need to revolt against an oppressive political and ecclesiastical establishment. On the contrary, their best safeguard against persecution lay in the indulgent attitude of the regents, and between 1650 and 1672 the only feasible political alternative to de Witt's regime would have been a *coup* by the Orangists and their less tolerant Calvinist supporters. There was no political party with whom millenarians could identify themselves, and no crisis which provided opportunities like those open to Fifth Monarchists in England in 1653.

There were also various individuals who felt a personal call to travel up and down the Dutch provinces preaching repentance and the coming of God's kingdom like the Jewish prophets of old.[1] To one of these, Johannes Rothe, the catastrophes of the disaster-year of 1672 gave a sudden prominence.[2]

The Rohdes or Rothes originally came from Danzig, the city with which Amsterdam conducted much of its 'mother-trade' in Polish corn, until Thomas Rothe sent his son Hans to Holland to seek his fortune. Settling in Amsterdam in 1580, he took a wife who had a connection, albeit illegitimate, with the prominent family of Boelens, and before his death was an elder of the Calvinist Church. Two of his sons became ministers in it; but another, Zacharias (1595–1656), enjoyed a much more successful commercial career as corn merchant, sugar refiner, and director of the East India Company: at his death he left a fortune of 269,000 florins. Twice he married into prominent Amsterdam families. His first wife, Maria, was the daughter of Dirck Bas, thirteen times burgomaster, several times ambassador,

---

L. Kolakowski, *Chrétiens sans Église* (Paris, 1969), 719–97; C. W. Roldanus, *Coenraad van Beuningen, Staatsman en Libertijn* (The Hague, 1931), 158–93.

[1] Cf. Hylkema, *Reformateurs*, i. 33, 43, 74; ii. 193–210.

[2] There is a Dutch article by M. G. de Boer, 'Johannes Rothe, een onrustige geest', in *Tijdschrift voor Geschiedenis* (1900), 201–19.

and the owner of a fortune of about 500,000 florins; and his second wife, Catherine, was the daughter of Pieter de Vlaming van Oudtshoorn (four times burgomaster) and sister-in-law of another well-known citizen, Dr. Nicholas Tulp. The child of a successful merchant could have had no more useful connections.[1] Zacharias's eldest child was born in 1628, and, like the son of an earlier Zacharias, was named John (Johannes); in later years the parallel with John the Baptist seemed more than coincidence. Three weeks later the baby's mother died, after blessing him: 'The Lord sanctify him to his service, or take him quickly into his kingdom.' The words were carefully preserved, and, like the name, had their influence on a highly impressionable boy as he grew up.

According to his own account all his pleasure in youth was in solitude and in walking with God, though his father and friends wanted to make him worldly-wise, and the spirit of Satan and the world drew him to this. In a second version he added that he had travelled, learned languages, studied politics, law, history, and theology, frequented academies and paid attention to everything relating to earthly and divine wisdom; yet so far as possible kept away from their accompanying sins and the company of raucous youth, 'so that I did my studies by myself for the most part, after a small foundation from my teachers. The knowledge which I might have of theology came to me more as a gift from God . . . The reading of the Holy Scriptures and consulting them day and night was for me the only means of imparting the fear of God and the knowledge of that same Holy Word.' He steeped himself in those parts of the Bible which related Jacob's wrestling with the angel, the persecution of Job, and the trials of David and the prophets. Often he prayed that he might suffer the same trials and chastisements, and be spared nothing that might make him a fit instrument

---

[1] For the Rothe family cf. J. E. Elias, *De Vroedschap van Amsterdam, 1578–1795* (Haarlem, 1903–5), ii. 894–8. Johannes Rothe himself left three autobiographical accounts, in *Eenige Prophetien en Revelatien Godts* [2nd edn.], *Neffens eenige Annotatien tot nader verstant* (Amsterdam, 1672), 3–30, W. P. C. Knuttel, *Catalogus van de pamfletten-verzameling berustende in de Koninklijke Bibliotheek* (The Hague, 1889–1926), no. 9933; in the third edition of the same pamphlet (Amsterdam, 1673) with additional notes at pp. 3 n., 4 n. (not in Knuttel, but to be found in a collection of Rothe's pamphlets, bound as his *Works*, in the Koninkljk Bibliotheek at The Hague, catalogued as 514 G 29); and in *Een Geschenck aen de Werelt van een Koningh* (Amsterdam, 1674: also in *Works*), 25–7, 33–40.

for God: this from the age of twelve, when he read a Book of Martyrs[1] and composed prayers that he might be permitted to suffer the same fate. Between the ages of eighteen and twenty-five there were few nights when he was not visited by the Evil Spirit. He found no comfort until 1652, when he was living in The Hague, at his father's desire, 'to learn the things of the world' where the States-General and the States of Holland assembled. For eight months he often went out into the woods of the Haagse Bos (presumably the nearest to a wilderness that the neighbourhood could afford) to meditate on the bloodshed of the Anglo-Dutch war with prayers, sighs, and tears, until late one evening God appeared to him in a tempest, 'and I saw his face as in a fire, out of which he said to me: "I accept you as my servant to make known my judgements to the world: humble yourself, and put on sackcloth and ashes." ' Before dawn he began, like the prophets, to wander through the cities of Holland, calling them to repentance; and to write letters to the authorities, churches, and foreign rulers warning them to prepare to give place to a king who would come. After travelling in France, he obeyed a second divine call to go and preach in England in 1654, but was no more successful. At Exeter, his message that 'God would come from on high and give a King to his people' was misinterpreted as a reference to Charles II, and he was promptly put into prison, where he was consoled for 'daily threats of death' by God's presence and the reception given to his teachings of the Second Coming by the soldiers who guarded him. His influential relations came to his rescue through the Dutch ambassadors, and he was soon set free.[2]

Between 1654 and 1663 'the Spirit ceased in great measure to prophesy through and in me', and Rothe spent his time in prayer, in watching the course of political events, in travel to Denmark and the ancestral home in Prussia, and in living quietly on an estate at Oude wulven in the province of Utrecht. In 1660, however, he accompanied Charles II to England, where, either because his father had had Orangist sympathies or

---

[1] Probably a Dutch one such as that by Haemstede rather than that by Foxe, though he knew English and came to believe, like followers of Foxe, that Providence had assigned to England a special part in the divine plan.

[2] *Verbaal gehouden door de Heeren H. van Beverningk* (etc.), pub. H. Scheurleer (The Hague, 1725), 564–5.

possibly because he had given some financial assistance, he received a knighthood on August 5/15 1660.[1] This is a little incongruous in view of his later career, and other company which he was keeping at the time. For he frequented the home of Samuel Hartlib, who with his friends Dury and Comenius had supplied to his Puritan friends many ideas with a strong millenarian element. Hartlib had been born in Elbing not far from Danzig where the Rothe family originated (and where Dury too had lived from 1625 to 1630),[2] and lived in Axe Yard near Pepys; and the diarist's comment on Nan Hartlib's marriage, which took place on a grand scale at Goring House on 10 July 1660, was that Rothe was 'a great fortune for her to light on, she being worth nothing in the world'.[3] Exculpating himself from the charge that the attraction was a settlement of £6,000 at a time when the future of the Hartlibs was distinctly uncertain, Samuel Hartlib wrote that he liked his new son-in-law's 'manners and comportments' and simply wanted the Lord to make this providence a covenant mercy to the married couple and himself.[4]

Sir John and Lady Rothe returned to the Netherlands (in a royal ship arranged by Pepys), and when Dury followed he was invited to make their Utrecht house his headquarters for his work towards the union of the Protestant churches as a preliminary to the coming of a new age. In the summer of 1661, the Rothes returned to London (where a son was born), and there was a serious possibility that he might become a naturalized Englishman and seek either a post at Court, or a place 'in subordination to the King here [in the Republic] in reference to the Prince of Orange, of whom the King is the Chief Tutor'. Dury drafted a petition for him, stressing his devotion (and his father's) to the Stuart cause when it was at its lowest ebb, the knowledge acquired by his travels, and his linguistic skills.[5] Nothing came of this, however, and Charles II's

---

[1] W. A. Shaw, *The Knights of England* (1906), ii. 231.
[2] For Hartlib, cf. the article in *DNB*; G. H. Turnbull, *Hartlib, Dury and Comenius: Gleanings from Hartlib's papers* (1947), *passim*; H. R. Trevor-Roper, *Religion, the Reformation and Social Change* (2nd edn. 1972), 249–93; C. Webster, *The Great Instauration* (1975), *passim*.
[3] Diary, 1 July 1660; 10 July 1660; 7 Aug. 1660.
[4] Hartlib to J. Worthington, 3 Aug. 1660; Turnbull, *Hartlib*, 110–11; and cf. 2.
[5] Turnbull, *Hartlib*, 10–11, 112–13.

religious policy began to turn in directions of which Rothe could not approve.

His knowledge of international politics was relevant when in 1663 the Spirit of God began to move him again. For predictions of the coming of Christ's kingdom were accompanied by 'revelations' of Louis XIV's forthcoming conquests in the Spanish Netherlands as one of the divine scourges that must be expected. He resumed a life of wandering through the cities of Holland, writing admonitory letters about events that were imminent. The response was negligible and he 'often complained to God and my wife with great sadness of heart and sometimes tears, that I thought the Lord had forgotten me'.[1] Though the Lord's prophets must expect to be scorned and to suffer from the hardness of heart of men, scorn or indifference was harder to bear than direct persecution would have been, and Rothe imbibed a comprehensive bitterness about magistrates, clergy, and teachers which was reflected to the full in his later pamphlets. His prophecies of doom began to become more sweeping. In the winter of 1667–8 he wrote to the States of Holland and the consistories of Amsterdam, Haarlem, Leyden, and The Hague asking for a day of prayer, and when this met with no response he published a letter to the people, urging them in the name of God to flee from the wrath to come, for all four cities would be destroyed by fire from heaven. 'The Lord be witness between you and me.'[2]

There is no sign that this had any immediate impact. But in March 1672 the English attacked the Dutch Smyrna fleet; in May Louis XIV's armies began to move; within a few weeks they were encamped in the middle of the Netherlands, with only the water-line to protect the cities of Holland from them; and by the autumn De Witt had been overthrown and lynched, and there had been upheavals in many cities. For a short, panic-stricken period the Dutch state seemed to some people to be in dissolution. In this apocalyptic situation Rothe suddenly found readier hearers.

---

[1] *Eenige Prophetien en Revelatien Godts . . . Neffens eenige Annotatien*, 10 n.; *Een Geschenck aen de Werelt van een Koningh*, 35; and for a glimpse of him and his wife in this period by the English minister at The Hague, J. Price, *Satan in een Engel des Lichts* (Knuttel, no. 11247), 22.

[2] *Aen de Gemeynte in de Nederlantsche Provincien . . . 26 Jan. 1668* (one page; Knuttel, no. 9705). A letter of 6 April 1668 to the States-General is printed in *Eenige Briefen van hoogen gewicht (Works)*, 28.

Early in 1672, before the outbreak of war, he had published *Eenige Prophetien en Revelatien Godts, aengaende de Christen Werelt in dese Eeuw*. Over the signature *JOANNES, Den Diensknecht Godts* (John, the servant of God), he proclaimed that Daniel's fourth monarchy was shortly to be replaced by the fifth: the Kingdom of Rome would be torn in pieces by the 'Emperor of the Mahometans'. The King of France was a Nebuchadnezzar to punish Jerusalem for its sins, and unless the Netherlands repented they would be punished like Jerusalem, for they had mocked the man of God who had been sent to them. The King of England too would visit them with ships; but his own time of judgement was approaching, when the Lord would punish his house for his ingratitude; his subjects would throw off his yoke and his kingdom would be given to the Prince that should come, and his dominion should be for ever. 'Out of you, O England, comes a people forth, and the same shall capture the whole earth.' The time was come, that the saints should possess the kingdoms of the earth. 'The Lord goes before the host of his people: who shall be afraid?' The Turkish Emperor would drive Louis XIV back to his kingdom, and then be driven back and killed in his turn, and the Turks would then accept Jesus as their Lord—Gog and Magog were ready. The Netherlands would suffer desolation to the point that not a third of the people would remain; but the King of England's fleet would be sunk in a great storm from the north, and the Lord would appear in Britain in glory. The time for this monarchy was at hand, as soon as Israel had been purified.

From this medley of predictions, not unlike some of the Old Testament passages on Israel's relations with neighbouring peoples, those on France and England seemed on the point of fulfilment when the crisis came. Before the end of 1672 a second edition of the pamphlet appeared, extended from 16 pages to 40 by a description of Rothe's life and divine call; and in the following year a third edition was filled out to 72 pages. It called the clergy a limb of the Beast. The fifth monarchy would admit no false priests, but truth and righteousness would reign in a new heaven and earth, into which the wise professors and teachers in the high schools would not be admitted either, for they had called the fifth monarchy a daydream. The Lord would lead his saints out from Amsterdam, as in the time of

Moses, under the Servant of God, and there would be a similar exodus from England, which would flow over the whole world. On the penultimate page there were a few sentences only about the social consequences for the Dutch people: an end to heavy taxes, devastation, and bloodshed. Import and export duties would be reduced—not abolished, for even in the new heaven and the new earth one had to be realistic—and the people's labour would be lightened and their gain increased. In later pamphlets the increasing burden of wartime taxation was reflected, but the social content of Rothe's works occupied a very small proportion of the total space apart from vague and general attacks on the wickedness of people in high places.

These editions of Rothe's prophecies all appeared under the imprint of Pieter Arentsz., a bookseller at the sign of the three turnips in the Beursstraat, Amsterdam, who was also responsible for some of the unorthodox publications of the Collegiants. The first edition was translated into German, and thence into English by E. R. (Edward Richardson, minister of the English church at Leyden) in November 1672.[1] Other pamphlets followed in 1673, notably *Een Nieuwe Hemel en Aerde* (two editions, the latter of 88 pp.) and *Spiegel voor alle Menschen* (120 pp.).[2] It is difficult to summarize these vast, sprawling documents in a way which will make clear their appeal. Not only do they consist of a number of very loosely connected sections, possibly written at different times, with a great deal of repetition, but their essence is the skilful appropriation of the biblical language in which Rothe was steeped in a way which suggested that he must be a new prophet of the Lord. His use of the Bible was extremely selective, with more reference to the Old Testament and Revelation than to the Gospels (and no reference to any Christian writings outside the Scriptures). There are references to the mysterious King Melchizedek and the forthcoming setting-up of the Standard of the Lord, which was to be regulated by 'the servant of the Lord who makes this description' in accordance with the Lord's instructions. All forms of authority in the Church were attacked (including Bishops and Superintendents, though these were scarcely relevant to the Netherlands)—'all supreme power in a Christian church is Antichrist,

[1] See his letter of 8/18 Nov., printed at the beginning of *Satan in een Engel des Lichts*.   [2] Knuttel, nos. 11023 and 11022 respectively.

and there is only one Head in Christ'. 'Pilate [the regents] and Caiaphas have become friends and crucify the holy members of Christ'. The true church of Christ on earth was: 'where I see the life of Christ, and this I find in no public churches and assemblies: but a few believers scattered through the whole earth and fleeing before the Dragon in the wilderness, these form the true church of Christ till God comes and all is restored through Christ.' The Calvinist preachers were corrupt hirelings who owed their places to promises of money and the intrigues of factions—'a Cartesian wants a Cartesian'; they were proud and arrogant; synods, classes, consistories, and the whole apparatus of discipline were causes of dispute, envy and hatred, and 'form-work'. For a renewal new regents were needed—and indeed a Sovereign, a new David chosen by God, not man; and therefore not to be identified with William of Orange. He consoled himself for the attacks on him by an appearance of the Lord on 20 October 1673, in which the Lord (face to face) showed him a clock with the sun shining on it as a sign that the time was at hand when the Sun of Righteousness would shine over the whole earth; and by citing his enemies to take part in a trial like that of Elijah, on Mount Carmel, in which both parties would call for the voice of God from the heavens, and the defeated party would suffer the same fate as that of the prophets of Baal. (This challenge, several times repeated in the next year, was never accepted, much to his scorn.)

The concluding pages announced his intention to summon all those who wanted to be inhabitants of the new heaven and earth to assemble early in 1674, in readiness for a new Exodus. They would leave England, Scotland, and the Netherlands on a journey to the northern part of the world (for the north had a special part to play in the messianic prophecies). There were no precise instructions, nothing in the shape of a programme. In December 1673 a one-page summons followed.[1]

The publication of his first pamphlet may well have been financed from Rothe's own ample private fortune, but the reprintings, translations, and publication of longer new pamphlets are fair indications that he found numerous readers. Readers are, however, not necessarily supporters, and the extent of the

---

[1] *Den Optocht en het Uyttrecht van de Helden Godts* (in *Works*); cf. *Het Leger des Grooten Godts Wort* [also Dec. 1673, in *Works*].

support which he received (ephemeral as it was) is difficult to assess. Some pamphleteers rushed to support his claim to be sent from God: *Joh. Cornelisz. Haesevens Kenteecken aen den waer Gesant Godts* (1673)[1] defended 'John the third' as the successor to the Baptist and the Evangelist. This pamphlet's attacks on Mennonite Baptists and Quakers, and Rothe's own attacks on the Labadists, suggest that the sects were no better disposed to Rothe than the Calvinist Church.

On January 1674 Everard van Someren, a schoolmaster, nervously entered the pulpit of the main church at Rotterdam and began to preach on Daniel 2: 44–5. The words of the printed version[2] are sober enough (more sober than Rothe's) but the Calvinist clergy, notably Franciscus Ridderus (significantly, a zealous Orangist), warned beforehand of the line which the sermon was to take, interrupted his attacks on the orthodox clergy and shouted that he was a Quaker. The Burgomaster summoned van Someren from the pulpit to put an end to the excitement, and then he and the town council tried to patch matters up between van Someren (who had influential relatives and friends) and the consistory. But van Someren recanted from the letter of apology which he had signed under pressure from his brothers, and left his school and the town to join 'the people of the standard' at Amsterdam.[3]

Van Someren had previously translated a treatise on the kingdom of Christ by Alhardt de Raadt, the publication of which had, according to one account, been financed by van Beuningen.[4] De Raadt had some reputation as a young and talented scholar, as had Quirinus Kühlmann, an ardent enthusiast for the millenarian prophecies of Jakob Boehme, who published a book describing how they were reinforced by Rothe's prophecies—'Boehme speaks of the future, Rothe of the present'—gave up his studies at Leyden, went to Rome to win over the Pope, to Constantinople to convert the Sultan, and eventually to Moscow, where he was burned at the stake.[5]

---

[1] Knuttel, no. 11024.

[2] *Predicatie over de Woorden Daniels* (Rotterdam, 1674); Knuttel, no. 11250.

[3] Ridderus's own account is appended to Esaias Clement's orthodox *Predicatie over de Woorden Daniels. . . . Gedaen den 7 February, Anno 1674* (Rotterdam, 1674); Knuttel, no. 11251.

[4] Ibid. 3; Hylkema, *Reformateurs*, ii. 423; Roldanus, *van Beuningen*.

[5] Q. Kühlmann, *Neubegeisterter Böhme, begreiffend Hundertfünftzig Weissagungen*

Most of the clergy and virtually all the regent class remained aloof. Rothe had relatives amongst the Amsterdam patriciate who would seek to protect him from the consequences of his actions, but they would give him no positive support. The crisis of 1672, which had seemed to give him his chance, was very different from that which had stimulated the English Fifth Monarchy men. It sprang from foreign invasion rather than from acute dissension over domestic policy, and most people sought salvation in William of Orange with whom the orthodox Calvinists were allied. The former followers of de Witt either co-operated or lay low, and were in any case far removed temperamentally from millenarian ideas and from anything which might lead to disorder and interfere with trade. There was nothing comparable with the New Model, for the Dutch army was entirely professional, in part composed of foreign mercenaries, and devoted to William, and so there was no prospect of protection from any soldier like Harrison—still less one like Oliver Cromwell. There was no political cause on to which Rothe could effectively latch, and in any case both his religious attitude and his well-to-do regent background prevented him from developing genuinely radical political and social ideas: his message was simply that the standard of the Lord should be raised, that this should be followed by an exodus, and that thereafter the Lord would give his instructions to his servant. Had the crisis been longer drawn-out as in England, more radical ideas might have developed; but by the end of 1673 the French had evacuated all Dutch territory except Maastricht. In February 1674 Charles II withdrew from the war (without his fleet having been sunk in a storm as Rothe had predicted), and thereafter the fighting was in Flanders. The time and the mood for apocalyptic speculation were passing, as Rothe completed his preparations.

The episode which contemporaries remembered longest was that of Theodorus Hubi, whom he chose as Melchizedek to his own Abraham. To Hubi he brought about 1,000 rijksdaalders, and a later supplement of 500–600 guilders to make up the

---

mit der Fünften Monarchi oder dem JESUS REICHE des Holländischen Propheten JOHAEN ROTHENS übereinstimmend und mehr als 1 000 000 000 Theosophische Fragen allen Theologen und Gelehrten zur beantwortung vorgeleget (Leyden, 1674), esp. chs. xiii–xvi.

tithe that he owed to Melchizedek. Hubi allowed himself to take this money, and to be circumcised, as Timothy had been circumcised by Paul, as a preliminary to the conversion of the Jews which all knew was supposed to come before the establishment of the kingdom. This operation was not only painful but resulted in an infection, from which Hubi had to be nursed back to health at further expense to Rothe.[1]

The flow of writing continued unabated. *Een Geschenck aen de Werelt van een Koningh*[2] extended to 232 pages. It is a medley of repetitions (naïvely stated by the author to be deliberate, on the ground that reading the same thing several times brings conviction). Amsterdam is promised, or threatened with, purification by fire, pestilence, hunger, death, and mourning. Three pages relate to the oppression of the people: fraud was so common that there was scarcely a single upright regent to be found; the subjects are the body of a country, and there can never be a healthy body so long as the head (the Prince of Orange) and the members (the States) are not healthy, 'and if they be so, let every man inquire, and learn to know the tree from its fruits'; they had given offices to godless men who did not follow a good conscience but ruled according to passion and self-interest. But this was a prelude to nothing more specific than a call for God to give a sacred leader to the people, and change those in power. A spiritual autobiography culminated in recent visions of a maiden burning in a fire without being consumed, of the world in a flame of fire with its cities burning, of Jesus descending from heaven with many angels to greet him, and of an angel who talked about the conversion of the Jews and shared a meal with him; of God as the Ancient of Days, coming down from a high mountain with a walking-stick, of the Lord handing him a sceptre and sword from the skies, and of Jesus with Moses and Elijah in the clouds showing him to the Jews. Returning to the everyday world, Rothe stated the Christian duty of a subject to the magistrate: he must pay his taxes without murmuring, but must resist idolatrous commands; he could wage war (unlike the Mennonites) but only in a defensive war, without any form of compulsion upon him, and after satisfying himself that he was not being deceived. He

---

[1] *Hollandtse Mercurius* (1677), 95; Hylkema, *Reformateurs*, ii. 35.
[2] In the volume of *Works*, not in Knuttel.

then attacked sabbath-breaking, dancing, and swearing, the frivolity of children disrespectful to their parents (a fault which, like other contemporaries, he thought commoner in the United Provinces); avarice, idleness, the sale of pardons to criminals, and extravagant expenditure on churches. The kings of England and Scotland were much worse than the regents: a review of the Tudors and Stuarts contained little that was complimentary, and Charles II was said to be living in constant adultery, lust, and vanity, in spite of divine chastisement. In both countries a reformation was necessary, and the last sixty pages of the pamphlet rhapsodized on the glorious kingdom of Jesus Christ which was at hand.

Such words of exaltation alternated with periods of depression in which doubts were interpreted as temptations and the voice of sanity as that of the Devil, until they were stilled by reassuring visions which became steadily more frequent as the time for the Exodus approached and as he faced greater hostility. He had an illness lasting six weeks, in which he could scarcely move for weakness and pain, until his prayers were answered by God appearing and healing him with a touch of his finger. From the beginning of January 1674 he seems to have kept a record of his visions and the hours at which they took place—usually early in the morning, in that time which lies between sleeping and waking. He could not distinguish between visions and dreams (or nightmares), which were unusually vivid. He saw a crowd of clergy dressed like the Pope with his cardinals, and sticking out from the sky an outstretched arm with a sword; he saw a man standing on a mountain dressed like Moses, with a walking-stick in his hands, dividing out the cities in the valley, with the Ancient of Days speaking encouraging words from the clouds; he saw the Hebrew alphabet, with all the letters changed into armed men; he saw a burning woman, representing alike Rome and the Whore of Babylon, and a prince on a great stage, monstrous of face, whose consigning to the flames was followed by Melchizedek's arrival to give a mission to Rothe. On the evening of 25 January there was a vision of Jesus coming to judge the quick and the dead, and early next morning Michael bound the Devil in chains. He was instructed to restore the old Hebrew calendar, beginning on the first of Abib in the year 5434 from the Creation. 'Do all you who read these prophecies think that they come from a man who is silly?'[1]

There is no evidence that Rothe intended his raising of the Lord's Standard to be a prelude to armed rebellion. He protested loudly and sincerely that in proclaiming God's word he used no sword but the sword of Elijah.[2] Yet the books of the Bible in which he was steeped were far from pacific, and the language which he took over from them included not a few references to swords, armies, standards, and the driving-out of Antichrist and of wicked rulers; and it is not very surprising that he came to be regarded as a madman who ought to be locked up.

Rejecting Rothe's petition for leave to appear before them the States of Holland issued orders for him to be taken into custody.[3] He embarked upon a series of farewell letters to The Hague, to the Netherlands as a whole, to the citizens of Amsterdam, to churchmen and politicians, and to the brethren who were not taking part in the forthcoming exodus from Egypt and Sodom.[4]

Gradually Rothe became convinced, though his family background was Orangist, that his real enemy was William. On 23 July 1672, in the crisis when William had first gained a dominating influence, Rothe had written warning him not to try to obtain sovereignty by force and bloodshed, on penalty of eternal punishment to both soul and body; and accused the Prince of also trying to bring in Popery, but this was because he had been 'tempted by sweet words', and conversion was not impossible. Since then Rothe's tone had become progressively more severe. There were uncomplimentary contrasts between the army of the Lord and William's army, 'a collection of godless and evil men'. Even in February 1674 there were still references to William's youth and his being led astray by persons unnamed, and on the 2nd he wrote summoning him to the Banner like everyone else to help to bring in the glorious kingdom of Christ. But it steadily became clearer that the Prince was personally behind the orders to take him into custody, and

---

[1] *Eenighe Prophetien en Revelatien Godts, gegeven en vertoont aen sijnen Knecht* . . . (1674: in *Works*, not in Knuttel).
[2] Ibid. 7.
[3] Resolutions of the States of Holland, 6 Feb. 1674.
[4] *Eenige Fragmenta of Gebroocken Stuckjes* (in *Works*), 10–12, 18–19; *Een Zeedige en Christen Beantwoordinge* (in *Works*), 67–70.

a further letter gave William only a few months before he died with many lamentations for persecuting the servant of Almighty God.[1]

His visions began to include William. He saw William fleeing in terror with his courtiers and calling 'Where is the man of God that he come and help us?' only for Rothe to strike the earth twice with his staff: the earth opened and a terrible many-headed dragon emerged, and Death with him. Again Rothe saw William as a young and fierce lion, and Pensionary Fagel as a fox, both slain by Jesus as a great old lion with a sword in his paw.[2] On 24 March, the day before the exodus was to take place, he wrote a parting letter to the Prince: 'You allow yourself to be worshipped like a God, and you aim at power.' He enclosed a print showing William as 'the great idol of Holland', standing on one leg on a pedestal outside the Binnenhof at The Hague, near the place where the De Witts had been lynched. In one hand he held a sword and in the other a sceptre; from his mouth issued the word *Geveinstheyt* (insincerity); surrounding him the citizens of The Hague knelt in adoration, while troops approached; but lightnings emerged from dark clouds, aimed directly at him. Promising to distribute copies throughout the country, Rothe told him: 'when you see judgements falling from the heavens upon the land, think of my writings, and be afraid'.[3]

On 25 March, Easter Sunday, the exodus took place. On the previous day there had been an encouragingly apocalyptic combination of weather conditions, thunder, lightning, hail, and snow, which could not be coincidence. Neither his wife nor his children seem to have been among the small party. He had proclaimed that the period of exile would be only forty weeks: forty years, like the wanderings of the children of Israel, would have been far too discouraging, and forty days, like Jonah's stay before Nineveh, would scarcely have been worth the journey. As it was, there was murmuring among the children of Israel even before they left Amsterdam, and Rothe later said

[1] *Eenige Briefen van hoogen gewichte* (Sept. 1674: not in Knuttel; in the copy in *Works* only pp. 17–31 survive), 17–18; *Het Leger des Grooten Godts* . . . (Dec. 1673: not in Knuttel, but in *Works*), 23; *Zeedige en Christen Beantwoordinge*, 55, 63–4; *Eenige Fragmenta*, 19–20; *Eenige Prophetien en Revelatien Godts*, 56–7.
[2] *Eenige Prophetien en Revelatien Godts*, 34–9.
[3] *Eenige Briefen van hoogen gewichte*, 18.

that he had had to warn them that God Almighty might change his plans and promises for them if they were hard of heart.[1] Hamburg was their destination, for it was in the north, and sufficiently tolerant for Rothe to expect that they might be left unmolested. Indeed, the Labadists had already settled down near by at Altona. Rothe took up an old quarrel, and three times vainly summoned his rivals to appear before the face of the Lord at six o'clock in the morning on the field in front of the Hamburg gate, for a prayer contest. He also wrote to the King of Denmark and, receiving no reply, called down war, famine, and pestilence on his lands.[2] Apart from these diversions, he waited eagerly for news from home. Some was not pleasant. He learned that criminal proceedings had been instituted against him for his print; that he had been sentenced to perpetual banishment and confiscation of his property (24 June); and, bitterest of all, that on 16 July a petition had been presented to the court, in the name of his wife and friends, asking for leniency on the ground that he had not been right in the head from youth on. But his confidence was not shaken. In July he published a *Summons unto the People of God to repair to the Banner of Christ which should be set up in several provinces of Europe* before Christmas. Copies appeared in English and he summoned several people by name to join him, 'and delivered unto them apostleships over nations, and sent some into England, Scotland and other provinces'.[3] And the great day seemed to be approaching, when reports reached him of great storms devastating town and countryside alike. These culminated in the tempest of 1 August 1674 which wrecked the nave of the great cathedral of Utrecht, leaving the tallest church tower in the Republic standing in isolation.[4] Surely the millennium must now be close at hand. Advancing to Emden he wrote a batch of defiant letters. One went to William, accusing him of being more a tyrant than a prince, and

---

[1] Kühlmann, *Böhme*, 108–9; *Schrift tegens allen, die met een Geest van twijfelinge en misduydinge tegens mijn Persoon en Schriften ingenomen zijn* [? early 1675] in *Works*, 5–6.

[2] *Provisioneel Oordeel* (Nov. 1675), 31–9; Knuttel, no. 11366.

[3] 'Jean de Pré' [W. Carr] to Arlington, 10 Oct. 74, Coventry Papers at Longleat, vol. 43, fol. 118.

[4] Cf. E. Schrijver, ' "Een Schrickelyk Tempeest" ' in *History Today*, xxv (1975), 287–9.

recommending him, if he wanted to banish anyone, to banish all murderers, adulterers, whore-mongers, and frauds, beginning with himself as the biggest murderer and fraud of the lot. 'Your other sins,' Rothe added forbearingly, 'are best known to yourself.' Other letters promised fire from the heavens for Amsterdam, Haarlem, Leyden, and The Hague, while poisonous adders and serpents would crawl through the streets and toads would enter all the dining-halls.[1]

So he approached the frontiers—and there was complete anticlimax. No fire or tempest, no snakes or toads; no one to welcome him; nothing. As he waited in Friesland, he continued to have visions; he saw himself seated on a throne next to Jesus to judge all political, religious, and military differences.[2] Slowly, as his small band of followers drifted away, he came to realize, not that his ideas were wrong, but that God had changed his plans; so at least he answered the taunt that the forty weeks had come and gone without anything happening.[3] More and more he came to feel that the reason for the postponement of the millennium was the Dutch people's idolatry of William. Instead of turning to God they had turned to an earthly ruler. And in November 1674 the Earls of Arlington and Ossory came over to The Hague in order (so it was rumoured) to arrange for William to marry Princess Mary. In the Whig tradition this marriage was to be the basis of Protestant liberties in England and Ireland; but for Rothe it was the taking of a Popish wife from the godless house of Stuart, and a prelude to Popish domination of Dutch and English alike. In this spirit he wrote a series of anti-Orangist pamphlets, much more directly political than anything that he had published before.

He began by republishing his print of William as the great idol of Holland, with commentary. He complained about the violence and rioting of 1672 when the young prince was raised to power and 'the wild and unfit people ruled everything like a ferocious animal, devouring its rulers without distinguishing between good regents and bad'; for Rothe was plainly no democrat. He accused William of using every possible means to

[1] *Eenige Briefen*, 18–31; *Een Brief van hoogen gewichte voor Nederlandt* and *Een Brief aan het Leger van de Prins van Oranje* (in *Works*).
[2] *Eenighe Prophetien en Revelatien Godts*, 62–4.
[3] *Schrift tegens allen*, 1–8.

get his foot on the neck of the States-General, and to rule like a sovereign. Was he not filling the country with foreign troops and seizing every chance to replace a Dutch commander by a foreigner? Was he not arranging that almost all the generals, governors of fortresses, colonels, etc. were Papists, as well as adulterers, drunkards, and murderers? Had the Prince not been busy introducing an episcopal government into the Church, and so opening the way for Popery, until the death of the clergy intended for this work? Had they not a disloyal and dissimulating ruler, who would willingly surrender old rights to England knowing that what he did for England he would be doing for himself, since he hoped to succeed to the English throne?¹ This pamphlet attracted more attention, and William even told Sir William Temple that he had received intelligence of a plan for a rising of 3,000 Fifth Monarchists in The Hague on Christmas Day, but the time came and went without violence.² The context of *Het Bedrogh en verkeert voornemen van de Prins van Orange ontdeckt* (printed according to the title-page in Antwerp and dated 31 March, 1675³) was the proposal of the province of Gelderland to revive the old title of Count of Gelderland in William's favour. Orangist influences, including that of the Pensionary Fagel, were strong in the province, and the general assumption was that the offer was not spontaneous. How much William in fact knew about it before it was made is uncertain. He would in all probability have welcomed the title, but eventually declined it in the face of opposition from Holland in particular. Rothe's pamphlet, however, gave him no credit for the renunciation. The seven provinces should join in a new Union and make the Prince promise to be content with the titles and offices of his ancestors: and a careful eye should be kept on his creatures, whom he had put into all the governorships of the frontier towns. In Gelderland, Overijssel, and Utrecht almost all the magistrates had been put in by William, and Friesland also favoured him; but there was hope for 'the good party' in Groningen, Zeeland, and Amsterdam. Rothe offered to come and talk to the States-General; in the

¹ The copy in the *Works* bears only the heading 'De Prins van Orange', over the print.
² [? Wicquefort to Sir Joseph Williamson], 5/15 Nov., PRO, SP101/58/142; Temple to Williamson, 10/20 Nov., SP 84/197, fol. 21.
³ Knuttel, no. 11334; cf. W. Carr to Williamson, 7 May, SP 84/199, fol. 60.

meantime burghers must obey their magistrates and the preachers must encourage them to do so.

At almost the same time he denounced William's letter to the States of Zeeland protesting that he had never had any improper aims in Gelderland as an attempt to stir up the people of Zeeland against the States.[1] William's statement that he had done everything possible to preserve the country in its privileges and liberties was a shameless lie, he said. It was obvious William was no true Protestant from the company he kept, the preachers to whom he listened, and the planned marriage to the Popish daughter of a Popish father and mother: his associates, courtiers, and servants were mostly Papists as were most of the governors and generals in his army, where men were openly summoned to Mass by a kettle-drum, and wandered through the camp saying Paternosters.

A further pamphlet[2] maintained that the traditional government of the Republic was moderate, middle-class (*burgerlijk*), and well suited to people's needs: the only drawback was the heavy taxation made necessary by the wars. Monarchy on the other hand was the form of government in hell, sometimes sent by God as a chastisement. If William did not spare the lives of his soldiers, what would he care about civilians? The foreign troops brought in by the Prince to impoverish the citizens and make them easy prey should be sent home, because a reasonable peace with France would be possible but for William's opposition. If he could be forced to content himself with the same powers as his ancestors, the intolerable taxes could be softened, particularly those on grain, and poverty reduced. He accused William of plotting with his uncle Charles II, during his visit to England in 1671, to make himself a sovereign and to bring in Popery.

Moving secretly from one city to another to escape arrest he prophesied, when the magistrates of Enkhuizen did not respond to his complaint against the seizure of some of the tents used by the children of Israel, that 'God will let your children be sold to other nations'; and great was his triumph a few weeks

---

[1] *Refutatie of Wederlegginge*, Knuttel, no. 11333.

[2] *Debat of Overweeginge Wat Regeeringe van Nederlant de Salutariste en beste is* (n.d.; in *Works*); cf. also *Het Verdwaalt en verkeert verstant van de meeste gedeelte der Regenten en het gemeyne Volck* (also in *Works*) attacking Orangist supporters everywhere.

later when an East Indiaman with 200 men of Enkhuizen was captured by the Turks. A letter to the States of Holland attacking Fagel as the Prince's slave he sent to Fagel himself, and naïvely called upon him to do his duty and put it before the States. Yet another was addressed to the House of Commons summoning them to defend Protestantism against the tyranny, superstition, and abomination of the Pope of Rome. The King had put his conscience in the lap of whores who did what they liked with him. The Prince and Charles were plotting to trample the laws of the two countries under foot, with the aid of the Popish faction, if Parliament and States-General did not oppose it together. In printing these letters, Rothe added one from an anonymous English gentleman, expressing surprise that the Dutch were blind to their danger.[1]

The Dutch authorities could not fail to respond to these challenges, not least because the English ambassador had already been complaining to the rulers of Amsterdam about the circulation of false and damaging rumours. On 19 September 1675, Pensionary Fagel carried out Rothe's 'instructions' and produced his letters before the States of Holland, who condemned Rothe and his friends as enemies of the state and disturbers of the public peace, ordered his arrest, and published a rejoinder describing the assertion that the Prince aimed at 'sovereignty' as 'false, fictitious, slanderous, calumnious, rebellious and seditious'. In December the *advokaat-fiscaal* called for Rothe's punishment, the confiscation of his property, and the burning of his pamphlets by the public hangman. But, because of the private intervention of Rothe's influential relatives, on 15 January 1676 the hue and cry against him was called off.[2]

Probably under restraint from his relatives, Rothe kept silence for several months, until in November 1676 he exhausted the patience of the authorities by publishing *Een kort en grondigh Verhaal*.[3] This alleged that on the Prince's visit to England in 1670–1, there had been an agreement that France should attack the Republic, with the support of an English fleet, on

[1] *Copye van een Brief*, in *Works*, not in Knuttel.
[2] De Boer, 'Johannes Rothe', 216–17; Resolutions of the States of Holland, 19 Sept. 1675, 15 Jan. 1676; *Hollandtse Mercurius* (1677), 94, 96; newsletters, 31 Aug./10 Sept., 10/20 and 14/24 Sept. 1675, PRO, SP 101/59, nos. 240, 273, 281.
[3] Knuttel, no. 11406.

condition that Louis XIV would help Charles II to become an absolute ruler free from parliamentary restrictions, and 'on this Popery must follow'. The Prince was to be made Count of Holland and raised to absolute power, without any need to consult the States and able to make war and peace and raise taxes as he chose; and a marriage with the Duke of York's daughter was part of the agreement, with the refinement that if there were several sons each should be sovereign in one of the Dutch provinces. William's father-in-law would strengthen his ambition, 'and if Parliament wages war against the King (as it did thirty years ago, and is very likely now) the Prince will want to assist his father-in-law, as his grandfather and his father did Charles I'. Ever since William II's marriage to Charles I's daughter, the Stuarts had been a disaster for the United Provinces, for their pride had infected the House of Orange. In *Eenige sware beschuldinge rechtmatigh tegen de Prins van Oranje ingebracht,*[1] Rothe complained of William's secret correspondence with the Jesuits and the Court of Rome; and alleged that William had stirred up the people against their rulers, 'just as we know that the servants of Zuylestein, Prince [Frederick] Henry's bastard, and other such villains were used for the massacre of the de Witts'.

Rothe sent copies to the *advokaat-fiscaal* of the Court of Holland on 8 November 1676 with an admonition to accuse the Prince of high treason. But enough was enough. William's campaigns were making no progress, desires for peace were growing, and Rothe's statement that in five years since his coming to power William had shed more blood and spent more money than his ancestors in twenty was uncomfortably close to the bone. Moreover the best chance of tipping the balance against Louis XIV was by enlisting Charles II in the coalition; and the idea of a Popish conspiracy against Protestant liberties was bound to be offensive to Charles, whose ministers were aware of Rothe's dangerous connection with the former Fifth Monarchist preacher in Leyden, Dr. Edward Richardson, and pressed for action against him.[2] A price was put on Rothe's head, and before the end of 1676 he was arrested by a former

---

[1] Knuttel, no. 11407.

[2] Cf. Sir W. Temple to Henry Coventry, 9/19 Oct., 27 Oct./6 Nov. 1674, 21/31 May 1675, Coventry Papers at Longleat, vol. 29, fols. 125, 127, 161.

employee of Lord Arlington named Herne and other Englishmen with the aid of only two of the *schout*'s men, who otherwise
might have left him alone even now. Asked whether he was
Rothe, he made himself known by saying 'I am a servant of
the Lord.' 'Thousands of libels' were said to have been seized,
including some printed in English in readiness for the next
session of Parliament. Rothe made no difficulty about
confessing his authorship, and Herne was promised 5,000
guilders by the States of Holland and employment by the
Prince.[1]

Rothe was confined in the *tuchthuis* at Amsterdam until his
relatives successfully petitioned for his release in 1691. He was
not immediately forgotten, either in Holland or in England;
indeed, William's journey to England in the autumn of 1677
revived interest in his later pamphlets. Copies of the *Kort en
grondigh Verhaal* seem to have been distributed in London, and
it was presumably people with knowledge of it who burned an
effigy of the Pope with a string of symbolic oranges round his
neck and a placard to indicate that the marriage of William
and Mary was part of a Popish conspiracy.[2]

But in 1691, with William and Mary established as the
saviours of Protestant liberties from the Popery of James II, his
pamphlets were no longer dangerous or even relevant to the
situation. This was, too, the world of Baltasar Bekker and the
'father of scepticism', Pierre Bayle, and the raising of a standard, even if Rothe had retained his old ideas, would no longer
have attracted much attention. Accordingly he was freed on
condition that he published nothing further. His wife had died
in 1679, and his son—christened Samuel in the expectation that
he too would be a servant of the Lord—had found being the
son of an unsuccessful prophet too much of a burden and taken
to drink, so that he had to be packed off to the East Indies; but
Rothe spent his own last years in comfort in his house on
the Keizersgracht, according to Bayle, completely 'normal' in

[1] De Boer, 'Johannes Rothe', 217–18; *Hollandtse Mercurius* (1677), 96; Newsletters, 7/17 Nov., 19/29 Dec. 1676, 22 Dec./1 Jan. 1677, SP 101/60, nos. 13, 118,
120; R. Meredith to Williamson, 19/29 Dec., SP 84/203, fol. 229; W. Carr to the
same, 19/29 Dec., ibid., fol. 232.

[2] *CSPD, 1677–8*, 385–6, 477, 547; K. H. D. Haley, 'No-Popery in the Reign of
Charles II' in *Britain and the Netherlands*, ed. J. S. Bromley and E. H. Kossmann,
v (1976), 102–3.

mind until his death in ripe old age in 1702.[1] Others who were deluded by his wrong-headed conviction that he was called by God did not end their days so well. Dr. Edward Richardson, for instance, claimed to have come to serve the English church in Leyden at considerable sacrifice in 1669; to have preached 574 sermons in $2\frac{1}{4}$ years for an official salary of only £100 p.a.; only to be expelled from his ministry, with his wife and seven children, for answering Rothe's call.[2]

There is a short postscript to the curious tale of Sir Johannes Rothe. His grandson, named after him, became a member of the Amsterdam city council in 1748, and after serving for seventeen years, died worth 386,000 florins.[3] For an Amsterdam regent family the world obstinately refused to turn upside down.

[1] De Boer, 'Johannes Rothe', 218; Elias, *Vroedschap*, ii. 896.
[2] Petition to the Burgomasters and Council of Leyden, 27 Oct. 1674, in the Gemeentelijk Archief at Leyden, Secretarie Archief 2147.
[3] Elias, *Vroedschap*.

The Catholic Puritans
Jansenists and Rigorists in France

ROBIN BRIGGS

ENGLISH Puritan divines seem to have found no difficulty in dismissing Roman Catholics *en bloc* as superstitious and idolatrous.[1] If they looked across the Channel, their sympathies naturally went to the Protestant minority in France, whose churches exemplified a much purer Calvinist organization and discipline than that favoured by Anglican episcopalians. The divisions within the French Catholic church were obscured, in Protestant eyes, behind the one issue which came near to uniting it, the desire for an early abrogation of the Edict of Nantes and the elimination of 'la religion prétendue réformée'. Puritans and Jansenists could never have understood one another directly in any case, because they belonged to different epochs as well as different faiths. Historians have nevertheless drawn close parallels between the two movements, with their predestinarian, Augustinian theology, their desire to revive the virtues of the primitive church, and their strict moral standards. One particularly tiresome characteristic shared by Puritanism and Jansenism is their resistance to any attempt at close definition. Both were terms of opprobrium, often violently denied by those to whom they were applied, changing their meaning with circumstances and periods. This is no good reason for abandoning the terms, for we should not expect to find labels with which we can classify men's beliefs like jam-pots, but it does impose some caution in their use. Officially Jansenism consisted in the Five Propositions censured by the Papal bull *Cum occasione* in 1653, yet the inadequacy of such a definition was already recognized by Fénelon, when he wrote 'Les cinq propositions ne réalisent nullement le jansénisme, parce que

[1] C. Z. Weiner, 'The Beleaguered Isle. A Study of Elizabethan and early Jacobean Anti-Catholicism', *P. and P.* 51 (1971); R. Clifton, 'The Popular fear of Catholics during the English Revolution', *P. and P.* 52 (1971).

le parti les condamne'.¹ The Archbishop of Cambrai's own attempt to mount a comprehensive attack on Jansenism produced the bull *Unigenitus* of 1713, which erred in the opposite direction. The censure of 101 propositions from Quesnel's *Réflexions morales* covered so many aspects of theology and practice, in so ambiguous a fashion, that it merely created greater confusion. One reason for these difficulties, of course, was the insistence of the Jansenists that they were the heirs of the real tradition of the church, whereas their opponents were the innovators. Like the Puritans, they stood on their right to remain in full membership of the church, trying to argue away the relevance of any measures taken against them.

Puritan hostility to separatists was reflected in the way many Jansenists denounced Protestantism; both reactions must to some extent have been an unconscious defence against dangerously plausible attacks. While it would be a gross caricature to describe Jansenism as a kind of Protestantism *manqué*, such accusations were frequent, and not necessarily insincere. Richelieu was plainly telling less than the whole truth when he justified the arrest of Saint-Cyran to Hardouin de Beaumont with the remark 'On aurait remédié à beaucoup de malheurs et de désordres si l'on avait fait arrêter Luther et Calvin dès qu'ils commencèrent à dogmatiser', but the insinuation was typically shrewd.² In a later period we find Joachim Colbert, Bishop of Montpellier, complaining in 1717 of the provincial intendant Basville: 'Lui et ses amis travaillent avec succès à me décrier dans le public, et l'on dit hautement que je veux établir une religion nouvelle, détruire les sacrements, faire marier les prêtres et me marier moi-même.'³ In a more spontaneous episode three years later, the parishioners of Quernes refused the benediction offered by the Bishop of Boulogne, shouting 'nous ne voulons point de bénédiction d'un hérétique, d'un appelant . . .'.⁴ After a visitation of his parish by the rigorist Bishop Coislin of Orléans in 1682, the prior of

---

¹ L. Ceyssens, 'Le jansénisme. Considérations historiques préliminaires à sa notion', *Analecta Gregoriana*, lxxi (1954), 8.

² References for this and similar statements in J. Orcibal, *Jean Duvergier de Hauranne, abbé de Saint-Cyran, et son temps* (Paris, 1947), 573.

³ V. Durand, *Le Jansénisme au 18ᵉ siècle et Joachim Colbert, évêque de Montpellier (1696–1738)* (Toulouse, 1907), 43–4.

⁴ J. Carreyre, *Le Jansénisme durant la Régence* (Louvain, 1929–33), iii. 50–3.

Sennely tried to carry out his instruction to remove a statue of Saint Antoine, judged 'ridicule et indigne', only to find himself confronted by 'toute la paroisse soulevée jusque là que quelques femmes dirent insolemment que Monsieur l'Evêque n'aimoit pas les Saints parce qu'il étoit d'une race d'huguenots . . .'.[1] Far-fetched though these attacks were, such slurs were still effective enough, so that hostile polemicists never tired of portraying the Jansenists as thinly disguised Calvinists.[2]

Any credibility such claims ever possessed has been destroyed by the work of modern scholars, who have demonstrated abundantly that the Jansenists were an integral part of the great movement for reform within the Gallican church. Practically every one of their individual views can be found in authors of unquestioned orthodoxy, and one of the reasons for the duration of the disputes was the ease with which Jansenist sympathizers could use respected authorities in their own defence. The most important of all was naturally St. Augustine, the ultimate authority on grace and predestination. The keen eye of Pierre Bayle saw to the heart of the Catholic predicament:

Il est certain que l'engagement où est l'Eglise Romaine de respecter le système de St. Augustin, la jette dans un embarras qui tient beaucoup de ridicule. Il est si manifeste à tout homme qui examine les choses sans préjugé, et avec les lumières nécessaires, que la doctrine de St. Augustin et celle de Jansenius Evêque d'Ipre sont une seule et même doctrine, qu'on ne peut voir sans indignation que la Cour de Rome se soit vantée d'avoir condamné Jansenius, et d'avoir néanmoins conservé à St. Augustin toute son autorité et toute sa gloire. Ce sont deux choses tout à fait impossibles.

Bayle went on to praise the Arminians for having at least had the honesty to bracket Augustine with Calvin as a *Prédestinateur* to be rejected, commenting 'les Jésuites en auroient fait autant sans doute, s'ils avoient osé condamner un Docteur que les Papes et les Conciles ont aprouvé'.[3] Although he may not have been entirely 'sans préjugé', Bayle knew very well that in the decades following the Reformation Rome had taken a number

---

[1] G. Bouchard, *Le Village immobile* (Paris, 1972), 299.

[2] Examples from the 1640s in A. Adam, *Du mysticisme à la révolte. Les Jansénistes du 17ᵉ siècle* (Paris, 1968), 175–6.

[3] Pierre Bayle, *Dictionnaire historique et critique* (1702 edn.), art. 'Augustin'.

of steps, of which the decrees of the Council of Trent and the condemnation of Baius in 1567 were the most important, to assert a 'central' doctrinal position against the extreme Augustinianism of Calvin. The reformer had asserted of Augustine's views on election: 'Il s'accorde si bien en tout et partout avec nous, il est tellement nôtre que, s'il me fallait écrire une confession sur cette matière il me suffirait de la composer des témoignages écrits de ses livres.'[1] Pascal and others tried to dissociate themselves from Calvin by rejecting the doctrine of 'double predestination', under which the reprobate are as positively chosen by God as the elect, and by maintaining a tenuous element of free will. Although such distinctions are perfectly valid, they are also very fine; paraphrasing Bayle, I think an honest reader must conclude that Calvinists and Jansenists were far closer to one another than they were to the 'new theology' of the Molinists.

The Council of Trent had reacted to the Protestant challenge by reasserting the value of the sacraments and of good works, but had not succeeded in clarifying the knotty theological problems associated with predestination and grace. The effrontery of the heretics in claiming part of the Christian tradition for their own had not helped, but in any case the Council would have risked tearing the church apart if it had ventured too far. A degree of equivocation had worked well enough in the past; unfortunately new standards of critical scholarship, combined with the effects of printing, were fast making old compromises untenable. A much clearer sense of historical time, something of a mania for legalistic definitions, and the beginnings of textual criticism were all threatening to upset the authority of tradition, less by denying it than by fragmenting it. The Protestants had found at least a temporary escape route by emphasizing the Bible, as God's direct message to his people. Although an appeal to Scripture could support some alarming innovations, on a conscious level it was still possible to treat the Bible as the repository of absolute truth, so that in combination with the theory of predestination it could produce a very rigid and seemingly watertight theology. The psychological appeal of such devices was probably enhanced by the growing intellectual uncertainties of early

[1] P. Sellier, *Pascal et saint Augustin* (Paris, 1970), 299.

modern Europe, and by the division of Europe into warring confessions. There was no real consumer choice in religion, so that within each creed the characteristic polarities remained: personal faith against institutional practice; moral rigour against the need to win back sinners; divine obligations against secular; individual holiness against the saving power of the sacraments; austerity against ceremonies. As long as men believed that there was some absolute answer to these conundrums, they were bound to generate endless conflicts; in a sense the intensity of these struggles was a sign of the vitality of the churches, and of their involvement with the real problems of their time.

Whereas the Protestants had radically simplified the ecclesiastical structure, the Catholics had added a whole range of new orders to the complex medieval heritage. Among these the Jesuits were outstanding, for their rapid success, for the violent feelings they aroused, both positive and negative, and for the boldness of their approach to the great problems of the day. Without the Jesuits the Jansenist quarrel seems almost unthinkable, although this is not to make them solely or even primarily responsible for it. Few contemporaries realized the extent of the divisions within the Society, which became more serious as its expansion inevitably slackened.[1] Just as fearful Protestants credited the Jesuits with superhuman powers, so their Catholic opponents saw deep-laid designs behind what was often mere confusion.[2] It remains true that the Jesuits had produced a distinctive new theology; the doctrines of Molina and Lessius sought to take the sting out of predestination, by detaching it from God's will, to make it merely a statement of divine foreknowledge. This device, by giving man back control over his own fate, made it possible to mount a much more positive defence of Catholic doctrines on works, penance, and the sacraments. It reflected the Society's missionary role, for it could also help to justify the teaching of a simplified, even rather formalized religion to the ignorant masses, in the hope of leading them into something better in due course. Immediately

[1] M. de Certeau, 'Crise sociale et réformisme spirituel au début du 17ᵉ siècle: une "Nouvelle Spiritualité" chez les Jésuites français', *Revue d'ascétique et de mystique*, 41 (1965).
[2] Wiener, 'Beleaguered Isle', 42–4.

denounced as semi-Pelagian, these theories were never formally condemned by Rome; the Popes disliked them, but valued the services of the Jesuits too highly to risk humiliating them. The new theology was also very much in keeping with the Tridentine defence of the efficacy of the sacraments *ex opere operando*, while in pastoral terms it was doing little more than make explicit the practice of the medieval church, always potentially at odds with the stricter interpretations of Christian teaching. Saint-Cyran seemed to admit as much when he praised St. Bernard as the last defender of true faith, and in some of his comments on the corruption of the church.[1] Many Catholics, among them the Jansenists, implicitly rejected any idea of the organic development of tradition, looking instead for an absolute, fixed truth. Pascal wrote that theology consisted simply in knowing 'ce que les auteurs ont écrit . . . d'où il est évident que l'on peut en avoir la connaissance entière, et qu'il n'est pas possible d'y rien ajouter'.[2] The differing attitudes of the opponents to the permitted mode of discourse itself made dialogue impossible, and encouraged the contestants to lapse into mutual abuse.

In France the Jesuits had to contend with a powerful indigenous movement for religious reform, attached to the Gallican traditions, whose most prominent leader was perhaps Pierre de Bérulle, the founder of the French Oratory. A convinced Augustinian, and a defender of the rights of the bishops, Bérulle was no friend to the Jesuits. Operating through the networks of friendship and influence which were characteristic of the period, he became a dominant personality among the Catholic enthusiasts known as the *dévots*. These clerics and pious laymen wanted the crown to put religion first in making policy decisions, but were also active in initiating new foundations and good works across the country. Jansenism can only be properly understood, in its first phase at least, as one of the expressions of the *dévot* movement, and as a reaction to the terrible crisis it underwent during the ministry of Cardinal Richelieu. In 1624 Richelieu still had strong links with the *dévots*; he was a protégé of Bérulle and the Queen Mother,

---

[1] Orcibal, *Duvergier de Hauranne*, 533, 655–6; *Lettres inédites de Jean Duvergier de Hauranne*, ed. A. Barnes (Paris, 1962), 105.

[2] Sellier, *Pascal*, 304.

a friend of Saint-Cyran, a bishop known for his reforming zeal. Soon, however, his ambition and his political realism led to a parting of the ways, as he grappled with the major issues of policy in Europe and towards the Huguenots. While the English Puritan preachers were calling for intervention in the Thirty Years War, the *dévots* wanted France to remain neutral, leaving the Habsburgs a free hand in Germany and the Netherlands. Both groups saw the struggle as primarily one over religion, in which the fate of Christendom might be decided; the pursuit of secular interest by their respective governments baffled and dismayed them. On this issue at least the *dévots* might hope to make common cause with the Jesuits, themselves leading advocates of a Counter-Reformation crusade against the heretics. Richelieu himself attributed the two pamphlets *Mysteria Politica* and *Admonitio*, which attacked his policy in 1625, to a Jesuit, commenting '. . . la pernicieuse doctrine qu'ils renferment étant la doctrine particulière de leur Ordre'.[1] In practice the Cardinal managed the Society so well, by offering protection against its numerous enemies, that he was able to secure its compliance. In his doctrinal works Richelieu had already shown himself to favour a laxist position similar to that of the Jesuits, and adapted to the needs of the ordinary believer, especially in his views on the vexed issue of attrition and contrition. Now the apologists for his foreign policy put forward theories the *dévots* could only regard as Machiavellian exercises in sophistry, bearing a strange resemblance to the morality of the casuists. While their opponents appealed to arguments from analogy, assuming the existence of an absolute, God-given natural order, the Cardinal's publicists used secular rationalism to draw endless distinctions for use in the real world.[2]

The political defeat of the *dévots* in the great crisis of the 'Day of Dupes' (November 1630) threw the leaders of the Catholic Reform into disarray. Many, like Vincent de Paul and Condren, felt that they must preserve their own orders and foundations, and that to oppose Richelieu directly would be disastrous for them and for the whole reform movement. Their submission, and the servility of most of the bishops, left the way open for

[1] E. Thuau, *Raison d'état et pensée politique à l'époque de Richelieu* (Paris, 1966), 110.
[2] Ibid. 148.

other leaders who might crystallize the widespread disquiet of the traditionalists. This was the role in which Saint-Cyran found himself cast, probably quite against his will, for nothing in his career suggests personal or political ambition. His reputation for learning and piety, his known refusal of favours from Richelieu, and his association with the abbey of Port-Royal were enough to make him the object of grave suspicion, even if he had been less given to imprudent sallies and paradoxes. His friend Cornelius Jansen was the author of the *Mars Gallicus*, a bitter attack on Richelieu's declaration of war in 1635. M. Orcibal has shown how Saint-Cyran's arrest and imprisonment in May 1638 was the culmination of a series of episodes in which he had been identified as a potential centre of disaffection.[1] Ironically, one of the most crucial was the imprudence of a Jesuit, Father Caussin, dismissed from the key post of royal confessor in November 1637 for trying to make the King's policies a matter of conscience. Another was the appearance of the *solitaires* attached to Port-Royal; the government's reaction to these apparently harmless religious enthusiasts ceases to be puzzling when it is realized how far they defied social conventions. The alienation of property, the rejection of careers in the service of the state, and the willing assumption of manual labour—regarded as humiliating and degrading by *les gens aisés*—all seemed a direct defiance of the social order.[2] The simple existence of the *solitaires* was a kind of blueprint for a new order based on religion, which the French government treated much as Parliament would the Diggers.

Like Richelieu's investigators, the historian must admit that Saint-Cyran was largely innocent of the charges brought against him. He held an extreme version of the Bérullian position on the way to individual salvation, regarding retreat from the world as the ideal, to which even those who remained in the world should approach as nearly as possible. In his defence of Gallicanism, under the pseudonym of Petrus Aurelius, he had already objected to the works of the Jesuit casuists, in which he saw a prime example of the errors introduced by the excessive rationalization of faith.[3] He thought that the true value of

---

[1] Orcibal, *Duvergier de Hauranne*, 435–594.

[2] L. Cognet, 'Le mépris du monde à Port-Royal et dans le Jansénisme', *Revue d'ascétique et de mystique*, 41 (1965).   [3] Orcibal, *Duvergier de Hauranne*, 348.

the sacraments was being lost, because 'le monde est devenu corrompu . . . on a mis presque toute la piété de la Religion Chrétienne dans les seules choses extérieures, comme sont les confessions et les communions . . .', whereas in contrast 'Dieu a réduit toute la Religion à une simple adoration intérieure faite en esprit et en vérité. . . .'[1] In such passages from his letters Saint-Cyran may strike a note reminiscent of many Puritans, and he went even further with remarks such as 'on ne se sauve que rarement et avec mille difficultés dans le mariage . . . et dans les grandes conditions'.[2] In practice, however, he seems to have been a relatively moderate *directeur de conscience*, and to have accepted the corruption of the world as beyond repair. His arbitrary imprisonment was a matter of politics, not of theology; it did, however, set the stage for the Jansenist quarrel, by preparing a small group of his sympathizers centred on Port-Royal to employ any weapon they could find against the enemies of the 'truth'.

Saint-Cyran's experience foreshadowed a repeated pattern, which would see the Jansenist movement created, as an independent entity, by the efforts of anti-Jansenists. The posthumous publication of Jansen's *Augustinus* in 1640 led to another attempt to find heresies, which trawled up so pathetically small a catch that it only enraged the Augustinians; the blatant partisanship of Jansen's critics made them determined to defend his book. Saint-Cyran's own most partisan act was in response to Isaac Habert's violently hostile sermons, which led him to suggest that Antoine Arnauld should denounce the trivialization of the sacraments and 'la dévotion facile'. The celebrated *De la Fréquente Communion* (1643) was the result, setting off another round of polemic which did more to popularize the book than anything else could have done. Later in the same year Arnauld repeated the trick with his *Théologie morale des Jésuites*, whose criticisms of propositions drawn from the casuists elicited yet more unwise replies from his adversaries. By raising major issues of commonplace religious practice, which affected laymen as well as clerics, Arnauld had shifted the revolt of the traditionalists towards a more fruitful ground than that of the abstruse debates over grace and predestination.

[1] Barnes, *Lettres inédites*, 247, 298.
[2] J. Orcibal, *La Spiritualité de Saint-Cyran* (Paris, 1962), 45.

The conflicts of the 1640s and 1650s would be all the more intense as a result, widening the divisions within the church, and creating parties which threatened to fight one another interminably.

The formal persecution of Jansenism began with the papal condemnation of the Five Propositions in 1653, the expulsion of Arnauld from the Sorbonne in 1655, and the imposition of the Formulary in 1656. Throughout the complex manœuvres leading to these events the Popes themselves seem to have remained consistently ill-informed about French affairs. Preoccupied with defending their rather limited sovereignty over the Gallican church, they repeatedly misunderstood the likely results of their interventions, falling easy victims to a variety of misrepresentations. On the other hand, Cardinal Mazarin exploited the dispute with cynical skill; he kept the pot boiling, to give him another ploy for use in his elaborate diplomatic game.[1] Identified with opposition to the government from the start, the Jansenists had seen their position worsened as a result of the Fronde, and their marginal but highly damaging association with the fugitive Cardinal de Retz. Memories of the Fronde would remain a major element in Louis XIV's thinking, and half a century later his confessor reported:

J'ai souvent entendu dire à Sa Majesté que cette cabale de gens révoltés contre les décisions et les sentiments de l'Église n'était pas moins nuisible à l'État qu'à la Religion; qu'il savait, par une fâcheuse expérience, qu'un certain esprit d'indépendance se glissait partout où ce parti de novateurs trouvait quelque accès et que, généralement parlant, cette secte était ennemie de toute domination, tant spirituelle que temporelle.[2]

Those who put religion before political expediency could expect a rough ride in seventeenth-century France, except when it suited the Most Christian King to agree with them. The only effective defence against the hostility of the crown lay in an appeal to public opinion, the tactic brilliantly exploited by Pascal. The *Provincial Letters* did not create mistrust of Jesuit casuistry, but they exploited it to devastating effect. In 1694 the Jesuit Gabriel Daniel admitted that Pascal had 'given the

[1] P. Jansen, *Le Cardinal Mazarin et le mouvement janséniste français* (Paris, 1967).
[2] G. Gutton, *Le Père de la Chaize* (Paris, 1959), ii. 206.

Jesuits' reputation a terrible wound . . . That book alone has made more Jansenists than all Mr. Arnauld's books together.' Equally bad, it had also created a third party in France, 'almost as numerous as the other two', of those who submitted to the church, but reproved Jesuit laxity.[1] The existence of such a party was already evident in the same Assembly of the Clergy which decided to enforce the Formulary, when in February 1657 it approved the printing and circulation of a French translation of Borromeo's *Instructions aux confesseurs*, to serve as a barrier 'pour arrêter le cours des opinions nouvelles, qui vont à la destruction de la Morale Chrétienne'.[2] The whole tone of Borromeo's crisp and practical guide was very much in line with Jansenist thinking; he advocated public penitence, full restitution of wrongs, the turning-away of those who appeared improperly dressed, and the deferment of absolution until there had been a genuine amendment of life. Such ideas must have found a ready audience among the large group of Parisian *curés* who joined in the hunting of the casuists, much aided by the appearance of Pirot's *Apologie pour les casuistes*, a damningly honest defence of the extreme Jesuit position. Bayle would later remark, 'Ceux qui ont lu le livre du Père Pirot m'avouëront qu'il est plus aisé de le censurer, et de sentir qu'il contient une mauvaise doctrine, que de résoudre ses objections'.[3] To a modern eye Pirot often seems to take a thoroughly sensible position, pointing out that Jansenism could discourage men from making any effort, that such impossibly high standards would mean denuding the church of priests, and that the kind of cases discussed by the casuists would have the ordinary parish priest in great difficulties.[4] Hardened sinners who were refused absolution risked being deprived of it to the end of their lives, when the grace of the sacraments could have helped them to overcome their temptations.[5] Less sympathetically, although in an equally common-sense fashion, Pirot attacked extreme views on almsgiving, for 'les conditions et le partage des biens, ont esté introduits par le droit des gens, afin de rendre les

---

[1] [Gabriel Daniel], *The Discourses of Cleander and Eudoxus on the Provincial Letters* (Cullen, 1694), 13–14 (French original same year).
[2] Procès-verbal de l'Assemblée, cited in contemporary editions.
[3] *Dictionnaire*, art. 'Loyola'.   [4] *Apologie* (1659 edn.), 5, 13, 73.
[5] Ibid. 49.

particuliers laborieux, car si toutes choses estoient communes, personne ne voudroit travailler: La maxime des Jansenistes fomente cette fainéantise, parce que personne ne se soucieroit d'aquerir du superflu; si les riches estoient obligez de donner à ceux qui sont en grande nécessité, tout leur superflu . . .'.[1] Although Pirot's *Apologie* is often maladroit or unfair, it is not the absurd work it is often assumed to be; behind it there lies the vision of a pastoral method adapted to the needs of the ordinary parishioner. The strict Augustinians could never admit the kind of compromises this involved, and remained blind to the psychological insight the Jesuits had shown in developing their missionary techniques. The majority of the French church seems to have agreed that absolute standards had to be enforced at every level, an attitude which must make the Jesuit doctrines suspect.

The theology of the Jansenists might have been condemned, but their rigorous conception of Christian morality was on the way to becoming the official position of the French church. There were good reasons for this apparent illogicality on the part of the church's leaders, which was far from being the direct result of the *Provincial Letters*, and might well have happened without them. The dispute between regulars and seculars still smouldered on, and nowhere were the bishops more jealous of their authority than over control of the confessional. The whole century resounded with the complaints of *curés* against the interference of the various orders, always ready to tempt penitents away with the promise of easy absolution. The accusations brought against a congregation of Penitents in the diocese of Paris in 1672 are typical: 'tous indifféremment entendent les confessions de tous ceux qui se présentent et mesme donnent l'absolution à ceux dont on a différé l'absolution pour des cas de conséquence, comme pour des scandales, pour ne pas vouloir restituer le bien de l'Eglise, en ayant le pouvoir et autres, ce qui fait un grand désordre à la Pasque'.[2] The Jesuits' policy, virtually admitting that the ends might justify the means, naturally included the toleration, even the encouragement, of the multifarious forms of popular devotion.

[1] *Apologie* (1659 edn.), 59.
[2] J. Ferté, *La Vie religieuse dans les campagnes parisiennes (1622–1695)* (Paris, 1962) 319.

Most of the bishops, sharing the prejudices common to the educated classes of their time, were coming to see popular customs as unwanted accretions, offensive to morality, good taste, and reason. This trend was to culminate in the great compilations of popular superstitions by the *curé* Jean-Baptiste Thiers and the Oratorian Father Le Brun.[1] The widespread sympathy for such censorious views was sufficient to ensure that the Jesuits, although they continued to play an important part in the great movement for pastoral reform, would never dominate it as they had once hoped. Many reforming bishops, even if they were not Jansenists, would look for a more rigorist approach, aimed at producing a revolution in both the outer and the inner man. It was probably an appreciation of the extent to which such ideas were winning acceptance that led some Augustinians to break with the leaders of 'le parti Janséniste'. When the intransigence of the latter frustrated an attempt at a compromise settlement in 1662, Jacques de Sainte-Beuve, whose support for Arnauld had earlier lost him his chair at the Sorbonne, commented despairingly: 'Le feu est aux quatre coins de l'Eglise, et au lieu de l'éteindre, on y jette toujours plus d'huile. Ils ne peuvent s'empêcher d'écrire.'[2] The reforms which Sainte-Beuve thought more important than the doctrinal issues depended crucially on the parish clergy, so the first essential was to create or expand the seminaries necessary to train them properly. A great deal would depend on who ran these institutions, and what they taught.

The organization of a seminary was one of the many responsibilities of a bishop, who was free to invite any suitable order or group of clerics to run it. There was always a small group of avowed Jansenists among the bishops, for the obscurity, not to say unreality, of the distinction between orthodoxy and heresy was such that the government periodically miscalculated in its selection of prelates. More important for the general tone of the church, however, were the numerous bishops who belonged to no party, while looking for high moral standards and strict discipline. Neither group was likely to call on the Jesuits to run their seminaries; often their eye fell on the

---

[1] Jean-Baptiste Thiers, *Traité des superstitions selon l'Ecriture sainte* . . . (Paris, 1679); Pierre Le Brun, *Histoire critique des pratiques superstitieuses* . . . (Paris, 1702).

[2] Adam, *Mysticisme*, 250.

Oratorians, if they did not simply appoint individual clerics of whom they approved. Despite repeated attempts to purge it of Jansenists, the Oratory remained Augustinian in its basic attitudes, so that the clerics it trained were likely to feel a certain sympathy for the Jansenist position. In 1678 and again in 1684 the government considered the suppression of all Oratorian colleges and seminaries, as the result of a number of individual imprudences.[1] The congregation had a dangerous knack of producing troublesome and independent minds; apart from Quesnel and the pioneering biblical scholar Richard Simon (both eventually expelled), there was the Cartesian Bernard Lamy, disgraced and exiled by *lettre de cachet* in 1675. In his moral theology course he had dared to suggest disapproval of the social order, for 'Dans l'état d'innocence, il n'y aurait point eu d'inégalité des conditions: c'est par une suite du péché qu'il y a maintenant une différence parmi les hommes, dont les uns commandent et les autres obéissent'.[2] Despite these various embarrassments, in the early eighteenth century the Oratory still ran sixteen seminaries, while another eight were under the control of small orders holding similar opinions. Allowing for seminaries not directed by a specified order, perhaps a quarter of these institutions were in the hands of clerics with a strong Augustinian bias.[3] Before 1700, when a more tolerant attitude towards such doctrines prevailed, the number had been greater. At La Rochelle, for example, the seminary was directed between 1667 and 1694 by Michel Bourdaille, author of a *Théologie morale de S. Augustin*; after his death the new bishop called in the Jesuits, who introduced major changes in the teaching.[4] The opposing parties had become increasingly aware of the need to woo young priests, and in 1682 the king's confessor, Père de la Chaize, persuaded the Jesuits to relax the rule under which they would only direct seminaries in towns where they already had a college. He argued that although seminarists did not spend very

[1] P. Lallemand, *Essai sur l'histoire de l'éducation dans l'ancien Oratoire de France* (Paris, 1887), 135–6.

[2] Ibid. 126–7.

[3] E. Préclin, *Les Jansénistes du 18ᵉ siècle et la constitution civile du clergé* (Paris, 1928), 84–8.

[4] L. Pérouas, *Le Diocèse de La Rochelle de 1648 à 1724* (Paris, 1964), 260–1, 365–6, 378–9.

long under training, 'L'expérience cependant, nous apprend que, pendant ce peu de temps, les ecclésiastiques qui nous étaient les plus attachés et qui n'avaient qu'une saine doctrine changent entièrement de sentiment dans ces séminaires où nous n'avons point d'accès'.[1] In many respects the personal rule of Louis XIV (1661–1715) was a decisive period for the pastoral orientation of the French church.

Obligatory training in the seminaries, periodic visitations, a flood of episcopal orders and publications, all helped to transform the parish clergy into a relatively orderly and respectable group. The attitudes and ideas which became current during these decades of reform would subsequently be hard to change completely, even if they were liable to some slow evolution. The *dévot* movement might have lost the political battle, but at the parish level, where the government's power was so much less, it had gained a degree of compensation. The imposition of strict moral standards on the people had an obvious appeal, not least as a method of social control; the government itself subscribed to something of a double standard, wishing to deprive its subjects of the moral liberty it claimed for itself. One result of the doctrinal quarrels over Jansenism was to make anything that hinted at laxism suspect to a great number of people; even the Jesuits became highly sensitive to possible attacks, so that from the 1660s there are far fewer instances of 'scandalous' propositions being advanced by their casuists. The austere Pope Innocent XI condemned 65 propositions tending towards moral laxity in 1677, as a result of a new Jansenist campaign which had begun with the publication of *La Morale pratique des Jésuites*,[2] while in 1700, at the prompting of Bossuet and others, the Assembly of the Clergy censured no less than 127 similar propositions. Helped by the influence of Mme de Maintenon over ecclesiastical appointments, a party of *dévot* rigorists had become the most powerful force in the church; their success was signalled by the appointment of Cardinal Noailles as archbishop of Paris in 1695. Strongly Gallican and Augustinian in their sympathies, the leaders of this group were behind the attempt to discredit the Jesuits through accusations that their missionaries in China had

---

[1] Gutton, *La Chaize*, 171–2.
[2] First vol. Cologne, 1669, by Nicolas Perrault and others.

tolerated paganism. Although they were themselves quite clear in their stand against Jansenism as defined by the previous condemnations, they commonly promoted clerics and approved books whose orthodoxy was more disputable. The support many of them had given to Quesnel was a primary reason for the choice of his *Réflexions morales* as the target for the bull *Unigenitus*. Catechisms were among the most important instruments of pastoral reform, and here too the rigorist school seems to have had the upper hand. While the variety was immense, Bossuet's catechism of Méaux and Colbert's catechism of Montpellier were very popular; as has been remarked, these manuals had a striking tendency to emphasize the all-present, all-seeing nature of God as judge, creating a negative image of a church based on prohibitions.[1]

The association between the *dévot* movement and moral repressiveness was inevitable, and had already found expression in the *Compagnie du Très-Saint Sacrement*, a secret association of pious laymen and clerics founded in 1627, only to be proscribed by Mazarin in 1660.[2] The dissolution of the national organization did not, however, mean the end of the local groups it had encouraged, which continued with their well-meant but odious work of searching out abuses for denunciation to the authorities. The minute-book of the Company in Marseille reveals a good deal of genuinely charitable work, alongside an apparently continuous battle to eliminate abuses from processions, dancing and drinking on Sundays and feast-days, and the misbehaviour of travelling players or the scandalous poor. Even though the bishop and the municipality probably agreed in disapproving mixed bathing, 'ceste grande immodestie des nudités des femmes', or the use of images of saints as tavern signs, it was clearly an uphill battle to achieve more than a temporary result.[3] A cosmopolitan port like Marseille was not very promising ground for such endeavours, but there was no lack of resistance in the remoter dioceses where individual bishops tried to introduce the new spirit. Caulet's episcopate at Pamiers (1645–80) saw a great improvement in the standards

[1] J. C. Dhôtel, *Les Origines du catéchisme moderne* (Paris, 1967).
[2] R. Allier, *La Cabale des dévots* (Paris, 1903).
[3] Idem, *La Compagnie du Très-Saint-Sacrement de l'autel à Marseille* (Paris, 1909), 68–9 and *passim*.

of the clergy, but this was partly at the cost of keeping their numbers down, for when the brothers Foreau visited Caulet's diocese in 1669 they reported him to be short of thirty 'bons ouvriers', so that the people 'crient sans cesse après lui pour avoir des prêtres et que même on lui chante injure'.[1] Prohibitions against dancing resulted in repeated gestures of defiance; despite a campaign of preaching and missions at Foix, Caulet himself was serenaded by revellers for three nights, from St. John's Eve 1663 to the night after the feast-day.[2] The *curés* were encouraged to impose public penances, while delaying absolution for habitual sinners until there was evidence of a genuine change of life, and in an attenuated form such practices are reported to have persisted in the Ariège well into the nineteenth century.[3] There is a certain irony in the way the population responded to such ferocious methods of evangelization; instead of reforming their conduct, they treated Caulet as a thaumaturge—once he was safely dead. Despite the hostility of the authorities, his tomb became a centre for miraculous cures and pilgrimages, which continued at least thirty years after his death.[4] Caulet's neighbour, Bishop Pavillon of Alet (1639–1677), ordered his *curés* to keep registers recording 'les qualités et les défauts de chacun des paroissiens', backing up the confessional itself with an annual visit to each household to interrogate both inmates and neighbours.[5] One can only agree with another rigorist, Cardinal Le Camus of Grenoble, who judged Pavillon's policy 'sèche et peu propre à convertir le monde, et il [Pavillon] n'a aucune ouverture pour les expédients et les tempéraments nécessaires. Il y a donc dans sa discipline quelque chose du temps des Goths'.[6]

Le Camus nevertheless described Pavillon as 'un saint sur terre', while he had earlier lamented of his own diocese; 'En vérité je suis bien combattu entre les règles que je lis dans tous les Pères et la nécessité dans la pratique, que l'expérience nous fait voir, ou qu'il faut tout rompre ou qu'il faut des condescendances qui passent l'imagination.'[7] In his own corner of

---

[1] J.-M. Vidal, *François-Étienne de Caulet, évêque de Pamiers (1610–80)* (Paris, 1939), 106.   [2] Ibid. 149–51.
[3] Ibid. 285, 292.   [4] Ibid. 601.   [5] Ibid. 288–9.
[6] B. Neveu, 'Le Camus et les jansénistes français' in *Le Cardinal des Montagnes*, ed. J. Godel (Grenoble, 1974), 102.
[7] Ibid. 102.

the Alps he fought a similar, if less impossibly idealistic, battle between 1671 and 1707. While he seems to have achieved a considerable reform of clerical morals, the visitation records of his last years still emphasize the high level of sexual misconduct, profanation of the Sabbath, drunkenness, and other disorders. It can hardly have been worth the Cardinal's while to condemn so mild a deviation as winter sports for women, even 'attendu l'indécence et le danger de cette sorte de divertissements'.[1] Another bishop who had to combat the popular attitudes of a mountainous diocese was Soanen of Senez (1695–1740), the victim of the Council of Embrun in 1727. An isolated and exceptional figure in the region, he evidently had little permanent effect on the deeply rooted culture and life-style of its inhabitants, failing to create a wide following even among the clergy. A study of wills demonstrates the modest and ephemeral nature of his influence over an aspect of religious practice which was more easily influenced than most, because it was relatively uncontaminated by secular concerns. Requests for funeral processions of penitents declined sharply, while those for simple funerals rose, but both trends were quickly reversed once Soanen had been confined to a distant abbey.[2] Similar limitations emerge from the journals of two *curés* in very different areas of France, Christophle Sauvageon at Sennely-en-Sologne in the diocese of Orléans (1675–1710), and Alexandre Dubois at Rumegies, in the northern frontier diocese of Tournai (1686–1739). Both were confronted by parishioners who were assiduous in their attendance at church, and charitable towards the poor, but saw no reason to alter their life-style in any other respect. Troublesome over the tithes, they were subject to all the normal human frailties; at Sennely their sexual morality was particularly dubious, while at Rumegies personal violence ran high. The *curés* had to yield ground everywhere, using their journals to record their dismay, and to warn their successors of the problems they would face.[3]

[1] J. Solé, 'La crise morale du clergé du diocèse' in *Le Cardinal des Montagnes*, 204 and *passim*.
[2] R. Collier, *La Vie en Haute-Provence de 1600 à 1850* (Digne, 1973), chs. vi–vii; M. Vovelle, *Piété baroque et déchristianisation en Provence au 18e siècle* (Paris, 1973), 463–97.
[3] G. Bouchard, *Le Village*; H. Platelle, *Journal d'un curé de campagne au 17e siècle* (Paris, 1965).

In practice there is little doubt that the aims of the rigorist bishops and seminary teachers disintegrated at parish level, because they were so remote from the behaviour and beliefs of ordinary people. Many *curés* managed some kind of compromise, but it was hardly in the best interests of the church for much of its painfully constructed system of clerical education to be inculcating notions which could only prove counterproductive.

Resistance was not confined to the lower classes or the uneducated; superstition may have been declining in polite society, but the other great sticking points were at least as much in evidence. The theatre, dancing, concupiscence, gambling, and usury were the targets of repeated denunciations, with the most minimal effect. Despite numerous threats from the newly devout Louis XIV, and Noailles's efforts to set up a kind of moral policing, Parisian society moved steadily towards the free and easy Deism which would characterize the eighteenth century.[1] The church was treading on particularly delicate ground when it intervened over the economic relations between rich and poor; one of Pavillon's most outrageous breaches of convention occurred when he collected a series of problems of casuistry which had arisen in his diocese. After obtaining opinions from the celebrated Parisian experts Sainte-Beuve and Porcher he published them, apparently without permission.[2] Most of the twenty-nine cases were concerned with economic misbehaviour by the local landowners, including depriving peasants of their customary rights, evading taxes, using false measures, imposing unjust sharecropping contracts, and making usurious loans of grain.[3] The rigorist doctors faithfully condemned a vast range of abuses, demanding restitution in almost every case. Had such standards ever been successfully imposed, they would have effected a revolution in economic life; one is hardly surprised to find that in cases XXII–XXIV the doctors had to consider situations in which these offenders, refused absolution, appealed to secular courts, or appeared with a notary and witnesses to demand a public statement of

[1] J. de Saint-Germain, *La Reynie et la police au 17ᵉ siècle* (Paris, 1962); O. A. Ranum, *Paris in the Age of Absolutism* (N.Y., 1968).

[2] *Résolutions de plusieurs cas importants pour la morale et pour la discipline ecclésiastique* (Paris, 1666).

[3] Ibid. esp. cases I, II, VII, XIV–XVI, XVIII.

the *curé's* reasons for excluding them from the sacraments. After Sainte-Beuve's death his brother collected hundreds of his individual consultations, which appeared in a monumental three-volume work, forming a kind of encyclopedia of rigorist casuistry to set against the laxist manuals of the Jesuits.[1] The church had certainly got into a frightful tangle over the question of usury, where established doctrine and general practice clashed head-on. The Jesuits were uncertain themselves; in 1677 La Chaize intervened to obtain the suppression of a book by Jacques Tiran, which virtually legitimized lending at interest, for fear of 'troubles graves', presumably protests over laxism.[2] The kind of embarrassed justification offered by Gabriel Daniel was not going to convince many critics:

But if these learned men, who are but Schoolmen, Canonists, or Casuists, be deceived in a matter, so subject to error, what shall become of an infinite number of Christians, of all estates, conditions, and employments, who daily either give, or take money, at this kind of interest? . . . But in a word, when once any doctrine makes an universal trouble and disorder in civil affairs, that very disorder ought to pass for a moral demonstration that it is false, and that it is against the order of Divine Providence, and, by consequence, against the eternal verities, of which common sense and reason are but the expressions which make part of the rules, God has given us for our conduct.[3]

Many dioceses were apparently unaffected by Jansenism as such, yet here too the rigorist current often left its mark, while all reforming bishops seem to have aimed at a more personalized religion, which should have manifested itself in changed lifestyles. Some Jesuits become remarkably strict, like Father Paul-Gabriel Antoine, whose *Théologie morale* of 1726 advocated delaying absolution, opposed probabilism, and won the approval of rigorist bishops.[4] Some of his colleagues in Lorraine, however, under the patronage of Stanislas of Poland, embarked on a missionary campaign after 1739 which used all the methods of 'la dévotion facile', stirring up widespread clerical opposition.[5] Such missions were far more popular than the attempts

[1] Jacques de Sainte-Beuve, *Résolutions de plusieurs cas de conscience touchant la morale et la discipline de l'Eglise* (Paris, 1689–1704).
[2] Gutton, *La Chaize*, ii. 120–3.   [3] Daniel, *Cleander and Eudoxus*, 114.
[4] R. Taveneaux, *Le Jansénisme en Lorraine* (Paris, 1960), 674–5.
[5] Ibid. 687–90.

of the rigorists to repress popular festivities and superstitions, which led to endless struggles, rarely successful outside the towns.[1] Faced with the people's desire to extend the faith, as a matter of communal practice, the élites reacted by seeking to limit and restrict it. This did not exclude aiming at a high pitch of exaltation; for the Jansenists this was to be obtained through love of a God one was condemned to ignore, with no assurance the affection was reciprocal. It also involved a rigorous self-discipline which limited life as well as faith. The extension of such high standards to the people, under the cover of a return to tradition, may have been partly the unconscious imposition of class-determined moral views; in this sense rigorism perhaps represented the subjection of the poor and unruly to bourgeois values. Inevitably this fell short of real success, and detailed research has cast doubt on some of the assumptions made earlier about the church's effectiveness in tightening up sexual morality.[2] The preoccupation of some Jansenists with sexual pollution is certainly striking, if few went as far as Pavillon's catechism, which warned that a simple conversation between two people of opposite sex was never without sin.[3] Confessional manuals like those of Habert and Treuvé worried obsessively about the attachments that might develop between priest and penitent, the 'chutes effroyables' caused by immodest dress, and the illicit habits of the married.[4] Such dangers loomed larger as the church moved from providing a mechanism for reconciling disputes (once the dominant function of the confessional) to trying to reinforce and intensify man's personal relationship with God.[5]

Although Jansenism and rigorism shared many characteristics with English Puritanism, their rejection of the world seems to have been more sweeping and more absolute. Unlike the Puritans, they never indulged in dreams of an 'elect nation', preferring a radical pessimism which even excluded

---

[1] Y.-M. Bercé, *Fête et révolte* (Paris, 1976), chs. iv–v.

[2] J.-L. Flandrin, *Les Amours paysannes (16ᵉ–19ᵉ siècle)* (Paris, 1975), and *Familles* (Paris, 1976).   [3] Vidal, *Caulet*, 284.

[4] Louis Habert, *Pratique du sacrement de pénitence, ou methode pour l'administrer utilement* (Paris, 1691); Simon Michel Treuvé, *Instructions sur les dispositions qu'on doit apporter aux sacremens de penitence et d'eucharistie* (Paris, 1676).

[5] J. Bossy, 'The social history of Confession in the Age of the Reformation', *TRHS* 5th ser., 25 (1975).

millenarian hopes, until the belated appearance of the abbé Vaillant, 'figurism', and the *convulsionnaires*.[1] These deviations only appeared after Fleury had made *Unigenitus* a law of the state in 1730, following this up with a renewed persecution. More positive elements in Jansenism, like the opening of the Bible to the faithful in such translations as that of Mons, ran into determined obstruction from the authorities. In this area, as in the case of attacks on 'superstitious' devotion to the Virgin and the saints, the likenesses between Jansenism and Protestantism proved uncomfortably obvious even at the time.[2] The retreat into Richérism, with its assertion of the apostolic role of the *curés*, is also reminiscent of Presbyterianism, especially when one finds it being pursued through the meetings of *curés* in the regular *conférences ecclésiastiques*.[3] Jansenism never succeeded in becoming a popular religious movement; the evidence is rather that it was disliked by the majority of those subjected to attempts to enforce its teachings. The doctrine of the elect and the reprobate might rationalize this situation, but it was no basis for a sustained pastoral campaign. The narrower forms of Jansenism were too highly intellectualized to relate closely to the demands of the everyday world, dominated as they were by a vision of the primitive church as a small community of true believers. Yet somehow Jansenism did come to incorporate many of the positive elements in the Catholic reform, so that the attempts to eradicate it proved highly damaging to the church. Louis XIV's crude persecution allowed the movement to acquire the prestige attaching to a doctrine of opposition, while no Laudian supporter of dumb dogs could have improved on Massillon's complaint against the Jansenists 'd'avoir mis dans la bouche des femmes et des simples laïques les points les plus relevés et les plus incompréhensibles de nos mystères et d'en avoir fait un sujet de conversation et de dispute. C'est ce qui a répandu l'irréligion, et il n'y a pas loin pour les laïques de la dispute au doute et du doute à l'incrédulité.'[1] Such defeatism was hardly much of an alternative.

---

[1] Préclin, *Jansénistes*, 112 et seq.
[2] See esp. Adrien Baillet, *De la dévotion à la Sainte Vierge* (Paris, 1694).
[3] Taveneaux, *Lorraine*, 703–4; Platelle, *Journal d'un Curé*, 140–1.
[4] Letter of 1724 in E.-A. Blampignon, *L'Épiscopat de Massillon . . . suivi de sa correspondance* (Paris, 1884), 256–7.

Social Mobility and Business Enterprise in Seventeenth-century England

RICHARD GRASSBY

THE relatively high rate of social mobility within the propertied class is sometimes invoked as one explanation of the difference in the rate of economic growth between England and other pre-industrial economies in the seventeenth century. The free movement of capital and labour in and out of business is contrasted with the divorce of business from landed society on the continent, where capital was immobilized and the bourgeoisie preferred public office in a parasitic bureaucracy. The process of 'mutual conversion' which William Harrison noticed in 1586[1]—the movement of younger sons of the landed class into trade and the parallel movement of merchants and their children into landed society and the professions—was certainly of great social significance. The apprenticing of gentlemen's sons was a much more radical step than joint-stock investment by landowners because it cut the children off from their social roots and put them on an equal footing with City merchants with whom they lived and served their time; it made them men of business not men of leisure. But the mechanism by which social fluidity generated economic benefits requires clarification. What was the real impact of social mobility on the private business sector and what effect did commercial expansion and prosperity have on the social structure of England?

Business certainly drew on the whole propertied class. The

---

* Because of limitations on space it has been necessary to omit from the notes all references to printed secondary sources and to refer to some printed sources in general categories.

[1] William Harrison, *Description of England*, ed. F. J. Furnivall (New Shakespere Soc., 1877–9), 131; Lewis Roberts, *Merchants Map of Commerce* in *Early English Tracts on Commerce*, ed. J. R. McCulloch (Cambridge, 1954), 85.

peerage, with a few notable exceptions among the lesser barons and Scottish and Irish peers, did not normally indulge. But baronets, knights, and esquires were prepared to put their children into trade as permanent, self-employed, full-time managers as well as passively investing in privateering, mining, colonial, and drainage schemes. Apprenticeship lists, registers of freemen, indentures, and family papers reveal substantial numbers of sons of country, urban, and professional gentry in business. Although less numerous than yeomen and husbandmen—the two other main status categories—they constituted a significant proportion of apprentices of non-mercantile origins.[1] In London entry varied from Company to Company but in the more prestigious mercantile guilds which have been studied, between 16 and 30% were sons of gentlemen. In the Leathersellers Company, which sheltered Merchant Adventurers as well as humble glovers, for example, of 4,387 apprentices admitted between 1629 and 1673, 139 were sons of knights, esquires, and baronets and 562 were sons of gentlemen, 48 of whom were also citizens of London.[2] Of those taking the freedom of the City in 1690, 179 or just under 10% were sons of knights and gentlemen. In the provincial towns the percentage varied from 15% in Southampton to 33·2% for the Shrewsbury Drapers, 40·8% for the Newcastle Hostmen, and only 2·5% for Leicester, Kingston, and Norwich; in Bristol 25·5% of the Merchant Venturers and 22–23% of the apprentices were sons of gentlemen in the first and last decades of the century.[3] Most of the children came from minor gentry families, some bordering on yeomen status, and some were of

[1] Data on the social and geographical origins of apprentices in many of the major London Livery Companies are available for several decades of the seventeenth century; there are also valuable studies of the Court of Aldermen, of Common Council, and of heraldic visitations. Apprentices from Newcastle and those bound to the Stationers, Skinners, Butchers, Carpenters, Longbowstringmakers, and Scriveners have been the subject of individual monographs. Very few registers have been printed. Many styled gentlemen in seventeenth-century documents were not armigerous and would not have been recognized as gentlemen in the previous century.

[2] These figures have been calculated from the apprenticeship registers of the Leathersellers Company, for access to which I am indebted to the Master and Wardens.

[3] Evidence has been published for the following counties and towns: Lancashire, Yorkshire, Warwickshire, Norfolk, Southampton, Shrewsbury, Bristol, Norwich, Newcastle, Great Yarmouth, Kingston-upon-Thames, Chester, and Halifax.

course merchant and professional families recently turned rentiers and parochial gentlemen. But the apprenticeship lists show a relatively small number of sons of practising business men entering by servitude or patrimony and a surprisingly large number—often several brothers[1]—from landed families with names familiar in local if not national history. Very few were eldest sons and many had been orphaned at time of binding—a sign that they were among the younger children.[2]

All branches of business, apart from minor handicrafts, were affected. London masters in the export and colonial trades were the most popular. But a substantial number of gentlemen entered the wholesale, distributive, and even the retail shop-keeping trades as well as small-scale manufacture of textiles and iron goods, particularly as the century progressed.[3] In the provincial towns, gentlemen entered the dominant local trades and crafts; in the rural counties, the returns of the 1709 Act reveal an extraordinary variety of forms of livelihood.[4] All regions were involved. Roughly half of the London apprentices came from the south-east, and possibly some 20 per cent from the City itself and its immediate environs. But every county in England sent children of local gentry, though numbers decreased from the remote north-west, Scotland, and Ireland. Most provincial towns drew heavily on their hinterland with a small entry from other counties. This participation by the gentry continued after the Restoration. Indeed the peak period of mobility between land and trade appears to have been 1650–90.

---

[1] Nat. Lib. of Wales, Wynn MS. 5830; *The Oxinden Letters, 1607–1642*, ed. D. Gardiner (1933), xxiv. 117; F. R. Raines and C. W. Sutton, *Life of Humphrey Chetham* (Chetham Soc., 1903), i. 6–8; ii. 42–4; *The Diary and Autobiography of Edmund Bohun*, ed. J. W. Rix (Beccles, 1853), 87, 129; Lincs. AO, Nelthorpe MSS.; Sir James Whitelocke, *Liber Famelicus*, ed. J. Bruce (Camden Soc., 1858), vi. 11; Sir John Reresby, *Memoirs*, ed. A. Browning (Glasgow, 1936), 22; *The Diary of William Lawrence*, ed. G. E. Aylmer (Beaminster, 1961), xi. Other examples will be found in the families of Bowles, Myddleton, Rawdon, Jeffries, Barnardiston, and Isham.

[2] Lancs. RO, DDB/58–60.

[3] *The Ferrar Papers*, ed. B. Blackstone (Cambridge, 1938), 67; *The Shiffren Archives*, ed. F. W. Steer (Lewes, 1959), ix, xi, xv; *The Travels of John Sanderson*, ed. Sir W. Foster (Hakluyt Soc., 1931), x.

[4] The registers for Bedfordshire, Wiltshire, Surrey, Sussex, and Warwickshire have been published. Participation by the gentry was most frequent in counties which had the most opportunities and a large number of gentry families.

Migration from business is not so easily quantified and doubts have been expressed about merchants buying their way into the landed gentry. Many business families, both in London and in the provincial towns, did indeed remain in city life and combined an active trade with landownership and suburban residence.[1] Genealogies, admission registers, and family papers show substantial continuity in trade within the same family, though not necessarily through the eldest son.[2] Between 1620 and 1720 sixteen Carys became merchants alongside soldiers and clerics. Nonconformity made it difficult for some families to leave business and most marriages occurred within business society. The large landed estate was normally beyond the resources of even a prosperous business and few bought estates far from their home town or place of business. When land was acquired, the motive was often economic: to provide for retirement, widows and dependants, to settle charities, to avoid partible inheritance, to recover debts, to escape the heat and the plague.

None the less the three-generation rule frequently applied, and it is among the papers of gentry families that most private business records of the period now survive. 'The merchant', wrote Gainsford, was wrong to 'speake evill of gentlemen when all that he labours for is to be esteemed so or at least to leave his sonne so both in name and libertie.'[3] Thomas Mun's son, to whom *England's Treasure* was dedicated, ignored his father's diatribes and became a country gentleman.[4] The migration from business occurred primarily in the second generation. Sir Gilbert Heathcote did not live at the estate which he purchased from the Cony family, but his son took up residence. Commercial capital was frequently employed on land for the eldest son and attractive portions for daughters. Since marriage was the most rapid social elevator, merchants, as Stow put it, 'being satisfyed with gaine doe for the most part marry their

---

[1] Bodl., MS. Eng. lett. c. 192 (27 May 1700).

[2] *Wills and Inventories from the Registry at Durham*, ed. H. M. Wood (Surtees Soc., 1929), 160–3; Ipswich and East Suffolk RO, Acc. 787; Guildhall Lib., MS. 10822; Leeds Central Lib., MS. NH 2926; Salop RO, MS. 1224, letter to William Sharpe, 12 Oct. 1664; A. F. W. Papillon, *Memoirs of Thomas Papillon* (Reading, 1827), 11, 37; Lincs. AO, Holywell MSS.

[3] Thomas Gainsford, *The Rich Cabinet* (1616), fol. 90ᵛ.

[4] Samuel Hartlib, *His Legacy*, repr. in *Directions of a Gentleman to his Son* (1670), Epistle.

children into the Countrey'.[1] Younger sons were not as favoured. One was usually put to trade and the others were educated at the Inns or universities and distributed among the professions.[2] Incompetent and idle sons without managerial skills were not allowed to take over the family business, but were found sinecures or rental incomes. Like their brothers in the professions, they swelled the ranks of the urban gentry. Whatever the aspirations of merchants to landownership and gentility, it was inevitable that the personal character of business and the fragility of business assets would force merchants to transfer capital into urban property, private mortgages, and public loans as they grew older and provided for their children.

It was the desire of gentry families to consolidate and extend their estates in the main line which created a demand for employment. Primogeniture made paid employment essential for younger sons. Several sons were necessary to guarantee the male succession, but if all survived to maturity, as in the Hudleston family, the younger were obliged to work. The aristocracy often provided for their younger children, as they normally had greater resources and were sensitive to their prestige. But John Verney claimed, 'I doe know Lords sones which must be apprintices and theire elder brother is worth 5 thousand pounds a yeare, as for example my Lord Cosselton'.[3] Among the middling and lesser gentry, however, and especially if provision was left to the eldest brother,[4] the younger children could at best expect an education and training. When John Verney asked his father about his prospects, he received a stiff reply that he was expected to recoup the cost of his apprenticeship.[5] Practice varied according to region and parental preference. One extraordinary example is Sir Ralph Radcliffe,

[1] John Stow, *Survey of London*, ed. C. L. Kingsford (Oxford, 1971), ii. 208.
[2] *The Autobiography of William Stout*, ed. J. D. Marshall (Manchester, 1967), 134–5; *The Travels of Peter Mundy*, ed. R. C. Temple and L. M. Anstey (Hakluyt Soc., 1919), appx. B; 'Memorials of the Knapp Family' in S. Grimaldi, *Miscellaneous Writings* (1874–81), iii. 315, 329; *James Claypoole's Letter Book, 1681–1684*, ed. M. Balderston (San Marino, 1967), 4.
[3] *Memoirs of the Verney Family*, ed. F. P. Verney (1892–4), iii. 366; *HMC, Var. Coll.* ii, pp. xvi, 172.
[4] For contrasting attitudes of elder brothers see J. Ap Roberts, *The Younger Brother his Apologie* (Oxford, 1634), and *The Flemings in Oxford*, i (1650–1680), ed. J. R. Magrath (Oxford Hist. Soc., 1903), 453.
[5] Verney, *Memoirs*, iii. 379; Ipswich and East Suffolk RO, Acc. 331, Box 23, letter 9 Aug. 1658.

who used the provision set aside for his two youngest grandsons to start the eldest two in business. Most families, however, were reluctant to provide even a small rent charge or annuity (the cheapest method if a son died young) and certainly would not bequeath land. Families pressed to find delinquency fines, land taxes, and daughters' portions expected their younger sons to achieve complete economic independence.

Fortunately there were no legal barriers to gentlemen entering business. Roman Law proscribed trade on the grounds of unfair competition for the *plebs* and the corruption of money, but it never had enough influence in England to create a threat of derogation. Nothing came of the various proposals in the 1530s and 1550s to restrain mobility by restricting purchase of land by merchants. The status of gentleman depended fundamentally on personal qualities rather than on birth or occupation; gentility was ambiguously defined and conferred no exemptions from taxation. As Selden put it, 'In other countrys he is known by his priviledges; in Westminster Hall he is one yt is reputed one; in ye Court of Honor he yt has arms'.[1] Apprenticeship and retailing did present problems. An apprentice could not marry or leave service and his master acted *in loco parentis*.[2] He lacked independence and the higher status of a university or legal education. Chamberlayne in 1669 echoed Sir Thomas Smith's view that apprenticeship extinguished gentility. But this passage was omitted from the 1704 edition of his work and the dominant opinion was that apprenticeship was a civil contract.[3] Business, moreover, had a hierarchy of trades and offices to meet all social needs.[4] The retail trades were not, for most of the century, considered suitable for either gentlemen or wholesale merchants by sea. But, in practice, gentlemen were excluded only from portering, hawking, peddling, and mechanic crafts—activities normally distinct

---

[1] John Selden, *Table Talk*, ed. Sir F. Pollock (1927), 50.

[2] *The Ledger of John Smythe, 1538–1550*, ed. J. Vanes (Bristol Rec. Soc., 1975), 12–14; *Relief of Apprentices* (1687), 8.

[3] Edward Chamberlayne, *Angliae Notitia* (1669), 435, 480, 492; Richard Braithwait, *A Survey of History* (1638), 314; Stow, *Survey of London*, ii. 331–2; Edmund Bolton, *The Cities Advocate* (1629), repr. with a different title in 1674 and also attributed to J. Phillimore, John Philpot, and Sir W. Segar; Thomas Fuller, *The Holy State*, ed. M. G. Walten (N.Y., 1938), ii. 48–9.

[4] PRO, P.C. 2/55, fol. 159; P.C. 2/45, fol. 171; SP For. 105/153, fol. 37; BL Add. MS. 9365, fols. 23, 31.

from shopkeeping and the domestic trades, which they entered
without loss of status. The *Complete Tradesman* claimed, with
some exaggeration, that 'the shopkeepers trade is esteemed
creditable enough for the preferment of the best mens sons in
the kingdom next unto the Nobility;—but so is not the Pedlars
trade'.[1] Although there was widespread fear of vertical integration, wholesalers did have retail outlets. Access to the business
élite depended simply on wealth and scale of enterprise.
Younger sons of gentlemen always had a lower status than the
heirs to estates, but this was more a cause than a consequence
of being in business.

The absence of legal prohibitions did not make a business
career universally popular with the gentry, particularly when
trade was identified with republicanism and Puritanism, land
taxes and usury, utilitarianism, pretension, and moral repression. Since status depended on social acceptance, convention
often had the force of law. Thomas Wilson, an impoverished
younger son, did not even consider trade as a livelihood and
Sir Thomas Baines, a physician and companion of Sir John
Finch, said, 'Without question the being made an apprentice,
according to our custom . . . is a blott at least in every man's
scutcheon'.[2] Henry Belayse said that 'nothing argues the ill
breeding of our gentlemen so much as the low employments
they betake themselves to as not knowing themselves fitt for
higher ones. To be apprentises in a shop, sitt bare head, sweep
the shop and streets is the life of thousands'.[3] Nathaniel Harley,
a younger son in business remarked, 'no merchants are wrote
Esq. but fools, coxcombs and cuckolds'.[4] Some merchants
suffered from a sense of inferiority and devalued their occupation; others defensively closed their ranks, provoked by the
arrogance and snobbery of the gentry and the Court and by
fear of competition.[5] The intellectuals identified profit with
exploitation, as their own status depended on elevating
academic virtues above wealth. The economic writers, mainly
in government service and obsessed with production and the

[1] H. N., *The Complete Tradesman* (1684), 45.
[2] *HMC, Finch*, ii. 32; Thomas Wilson, 'The State of England, 1601', *Camden Misc.* xvi (1936).
[3] Henry Belayse, 'An English Traveller's First Curiosity' (1657) in *HMC, Var. Coll.* ii. 204.
[4] *HMC, Portland*, ii. xi.　　　　　[5] Stow, *Survey of London*, i. 287.

balance of trade, condemned all middlemen as parasitic and all private interests as injurious to the public good. The courtesy books adopted the Renaissance ideal of education, which directed talent away from business. Peacham, in 1634, recognized the value of merchants to the community, but he added, 'the exercise of merchandise hath been (I confess) accounted base and much derogating from nobility except it be exercised and undertaken by a general estate or the deputies thereof'.[1] The Court dramatists never favoured the City, and Restoration comedy emphasized the social and sexual inferiority of the citizen; no merchant was considered a suitable subject for tragedy until Lillo in 1731. Journalists, poets, satirists, novelists, divines, character writers, antiquarians, and essayists all rejected business values.[2] Society did not recognize the values and skills of trade and thereby encouraged merchants to seek recognition in other ways than through business.

On the other hand, as the English economy grew, the anti-acquisitive attitudes, which reflected lack of opportunity, also declined. Some gentlemen, like Gervase Holles, proudly acknowledged their commercial origins; others, like Edmund Bohun, believed passionately that trade was an instrument of civility as well as prosperity.[3] The growth of cities and an urban gentry, the institutionalization of business in undying corporations, and the self-confidence engendered by the obvious utility of trade, all helped to increase the prestige of business. Some merchants used their marks like coats of arms[4] or, as in Bristol, left the world in ebullient and aggressive funerals. Spokesmen for the merchants, from Thomas Mun to Daniel Defoe, elevated the status of trade by encouraging participation by the gentry.[5] Blanch regarded trade as a more

---

[1] Henry Peacham, *The Compleat Gentleman*, ed. V. B. Heltzel (Ithaca, 1962), 21–2.

[2] Ambrose Rigge, *A Brief and Serious Warning* (1678), 4; Immanuel Bourne, *The Godly Man's Guide* (1620), 20; Tom Brown, *Amusements Serious and Comical*, ed. A. L. Hayward (1927), 21; Thomas Lodge, *Complete Works* (N.Y., 1963), iv. 5; Bartholomew Ashwood, *The Heavenly Trade* (1679), Epistle; *The Sermons of John Donne*, ed. G. R. Potter and E. Simpson (Berkeley and Los Angeles, 1953–62), iv. 277; Thomas Cooper, *The Worldings Adventure* (1619), 62.

[3] Bodl., MS. North (Caesar Papers) a 2, fols. 71–2; Gervase Holles, *Memorials of the Holles Family*, ed. A. C. Wood (Camden Ser., 1937), 19; *Diary of Bohun*, 132.

[4] William Scott, *Essay on Drapery* (1635), ed. S. L. Thrupp (Boston, 1953), 8.

[5] Daniel Defoe, *The Complete English Gentleman*, ed. K. D. Bulbring (1890), 262;

noble profession than arms for the gentry.[1] Even among the clergy, business had its defenders. Many clergymen, like Richard Hakluyt the younger, were related to merchant families and comparisons between religion and 'merchandising' were a common theological vogue after 1660.[2] Bishop Sprat thought that 'trafic and commerce have given mankind a higher degree than any title of nobility, even that of civility and humanity itself'.[3] Some political economists, like the author of *Britannia Languens*, emphasized the role of labour in production and contrasted the unproductiveness of office-holders, physicians, and an inflated clergy with the utility and productiveness of trade, industry, and agricultural management; those 'intitled to so much a year in Land do consider Trade as no otherwise necessary in a Nation than to support younger brothers'.[4] Other economists attacked the social pressures which elevated leisure above work and the respect for intellectual and military skills which implied the superiority of the leisure class. Even some professional authors supported trade. Thomas Fuller and Nicholas Breton patronized trade and merchants. Dramatists like Thomas Heywood and Thomas Deloney wrote plays for city audiences. To professional travellers, like Richard Flecknoe, the merchant mastered wealth, 'making it only serve to noble ends'.[5] At the end of the century Addison and Steele romanticized trade, while Nehemiah Grew urged the gentry to find in trade 'a durable satisfaction beyond that of any vaine and transient pleasure'.[6] In England *mésalliance* was a subject for comedy, not tragedy. Even the courtesy books were prepared to compromise. Doderidge agreed that the gentry could trade as long as their profits returned to the land and 'so long as they did not undertake common buying and selling'.[7]

The Character and Qualifications of a Merchant (1686), 91 ff.; *Early English Tracts*, ed. McCulloch, 85; BL, Hargeaves MS. 321, fol. 94ᵛ; C. Molloy, *De jure maritimo* (1676), 430–1.

[1] John Blanch, *The Interest of England Considered* (1694), 39; *A Discourse of the Necessity of Encouraging Mechanic Industry* (1689), 21.
[2] Edward Reynolds, *Works* (1826), iv. 432.
[3] Thomas Sprat, *History of the Royal Society* (repr. 1959), 408.
[4] *Tracts*, ed. McCulloch, 285.
[5] Richard Fleckno, *Relations of ten years* (1653), 89; Fuller, *Holy State*, ii. 113–16.
[6] Huntington Lib., MS. 1264, fols. 147, 160; *The Spectator*, ed. D. F. Bond (Oxford, 1965), i. 294, ii. 188–9; *The Tatler*, ed. G. A. Aitken (1899), iv. 72.
[7] Sir John Doderidge, *Honours Pedigree* (1652), 152–3.

Braithwait emphasized the independence of the younger son in trade and Westcote cited Anglo-Saxon precedents for ennobling merchants.[1]

If the social difficulties of entering trade have sometimes been exaggerated, the financial obstacles have often been underestimated. In order to enter a trade, a man had to be trained, to obtain his freedom of his city and trade, and to find his maintenance during his training. Apprenticeship was not the only method of entry. Admission to a trade and to chartered Companies could be purchased by redemption by established merchants; sons of freemen could enter by patrimony.[2] Entry was also possible through the merchant marine and through joint-stock companies. But the normal initial expense for parents consisted of apprenticeship and entry fees. Neither early schooling nor entrance fees were too costly. The apprenticeship fee normally included the cost of replacing clothing, food and lodging, as well as training, but additonal pocket money and gifts were usually needed to maintain a reasonable standard.[3] Sureties for good behaviour were also more frequently demanded. Slingsby Bethel's father had to offer £500, and by the end of the century sureties of £1,000 were quite common. The major capital outlay, however, was the fee charged by the master. It is difficult to generalize about the level of fees, because they were fixed by individuals and not by institutions and recorded in the indentures and not in the registers of apprenticeship. Friendship, kinship, and incompetence in a master could bring down a particular fee below the general level. But the high and rising level of premiums during the century is well attested. In the Levant trade fees rose from £200–£300 in the 1640s to £300–£400 in the 1650s, £500–£800 in the 1680s and 1690s, and £1,000 by 1700.[4] As

[1] Richard Braithwait, *The Turtle's Triumph* (1641), 26; Thomas Westcote, *A View of Devonshire in 1630*, ed. G. Oliver and P. Jones (Exeter, 1845), 52; *English Historical Documents c. 500–1042*, ed. D. Whitelock (1955), 432; Richard Blome, *The Art of Heraldry* (2nd edn. 1693), 254.

[2] Henry Parker, *Of a Free Trade* (1648), 22; *Select Charters of Trading Companies*, ed. C. T. Carr (Selden Soc., 1913), xli; Mundy, *Travels*, xxx; Guildhall Lib., MS. 11741/1–2, fol. 214; PRO, SP For. 105/153, fols. 31, 343; P.C. 2/55, fol. 159; *The Spanish Company*, ed. P. Croft (London Rec. Soc., 1973), 83–7.

[3] It is sometimes difficult to determine whether maintenance is included in the price quoted. See PRO, SP 46/84, No. 93; University of London, MS. 553, letter Aug. 1675.

[4] Bodl., MS. D. D. Ashurst c. 1, letter 12 July 1680; *HMC, House of Lords*,

Henry Hunter remarked, 'here masters ask so great rates and its so hazardous the falling upon a good one, that moderate fortunes can scare afford the venture'.¹ Other trades were more varied and reflected fashion, opportunity, and demand for places. Although the Merchant Adventurers charged £300–£400 in the early seventeenth century, Sir John Wynn found a master for £100 and £50 on going abroad.² In the London drapery trade, premiums seem to have risen from under £100 to £300³ and in the Mediterranean trade up to £400 and £600.⁴ In the provinces and in retail trades, premiums were distinctly lower and ranged from £50 to £150. Bristol seems to have had a level of fees around £100–£200, Manchester around £60 with sureties, Newcastle £30–£40.⁵ Stout paid only £20 in Lancaster, whereas Sir John Pettus paid £300 to put his son to a Leeds clothier.⁶ If the traditional export trades were virtually confined to the wealthy, no profitable trade was cheap to enter without favouritism and the charges were not recoverable.

The cost of setting-up as an independent merchant even in a partnership was also considerable. As Maurice Wynn, who never received the £100 promised by his father, remarked in 1621, 'one without money (which is the essence of a merchant) is but a cipher in arithmetick, for of nothing (as the saying is) nothing can be produced'.⁷ Even a factor working on commission had to pay his expenses and overheads. Thomas French told Nathaniel Harley in 1686 to allow £50–£60 for expenses. One younger son in Aleppo, in 1689, having spent most of his capital on his apprenticeship, found the remainder

1695–1697, ii. 43; Lincs. AO, Heathcote MS. 1/11; Sheffield Public Lib., Pye MS. 7 (b); BL, Add. MS. 32523, fol. 39; Corporation of London RO, Misc. Inventories, Bundle 52, roll 15; Guildhall Lib., MS. 10823/1; *The Norris Papers*, ed. T. Heywood (Chetham Soc., 1846), 10; Lancs. RO, D/DB/58/4.

¹ Berks. RO, D/EZ56/1, letters 21 & 24 Apr. 1701.
² *Calendar of the Wynn (of Gwydir) Papers, 1515–1690* (Aberystwyth, 1926), 80.
³ *The Commonplace Book of Sir John Oglander*, ed. F. Bamford (1936), 235.
⁴ Bodl., MS. Dep. c. 23, fol. 11; *HMC, Var. Collns.* ii. 175; Berks. RO, MS. D/ED/F 41.
⁵ *Records of the Company of Hostmen of Newcastle*, ed. F. W. Dendy (Surtees Soc., 1901), liv.
⁶ Stout, *Autobiography*, 73; Lincs. AO, Whichcote MS. 21/18; Ipswich and East Suffolk RO, H.E. 30, will of William Blois, 6 Feb. 1621.
⁷ Nat. Lib. Wales, Wynn MSS. 896; 964; 1023.

swallowed up in living: 'it was hard', he wrote, 'upon a younger brother of a mean fortune to be putt so much back in the work instead of improving with God's blessing'.[1] The cost varied of course according to type and area of trade. Businesses with a fast turnover, with established marts and a sound credit structure for producers and consumers, demanded less outlay than long-distance trades with seasonal fluctuations, fixed investments, and transport delays. Despite differences between individuals, £1,000 seems to have been about the required sum in foreign trade in the second half of the century. Merchants like Daniel Harvey and Humphrey Chetham did begin and prosper with small sums of £40–£50;[2] £50–£60 was probably sufficient in most towns and £100 for a London shop. Others managed in the internal and coasting and retail trades on £200–£300 initial capital with additional loans. But whereas Thomas Cullum began with £200 and a loan of £100, he set up his younger son as a draper with £5,000. In 1701, Henry Hunter thought £860 'a pretty tolerable bottom' for a man investing in a partnership rather than an apprenticeship.[3] Sir William Turner in 1686 spent £1,000 to set up his nephew Richard and Streynsham Master provided the same sum for his son.[4]

Sums of this magnitude could not normally be accumulated from profits and savings, and the absence of limited liability made sleeping partnerships difficult. Some merchants could draw on charitable foundations, like the Sutton bequest in London, or from Orphans' Funds to provide capital at low or zero rates of interest.[5] Others, like George Boddington, took on

[1] PRO, SP For. 110/16, letters 15 Feb. 1688/89, 28 Nov. 1689, 14 Jan. 1689/90; BL, Loan MS. 29/223, letter 15 June 1686; Sheffield Public Lib., Pye MS. 7 (b); Bodl., MS. D. D. Ashurst c. 1, letter 12 July 1675; Bodl., Rawlinson MS. 1483; Lincs. AO, DDC/a1/45.

[2] Chetham, *Life*, 11; *The Trade of England Revived* (1681), repr. in *Seventeenth-Century Economic Documents*, ed. J. Thirsk and J. P. Cooper (Oxford, 1972), 395–6; Warwickshire RO, C.R. 314, No. 123; Papillon, *Memoirs*, 14.

[3] Berks. RO, D/EZ5/B1 fol. 37; B. 2, 2 Apr. 1701; Guildhall Lib. MSS. 10187 and 10823/1, fol. 41; PRO, C. 104/44, letter June 1684; *Diary of William Hedges*, ed. Col. H. Yule and R. F. Barlow (Hakluyt Soc., 1889), iii, cviii; H. N., *Complete Tradesman*, 37; Warwickshire RO, C.R. 314.

[4] Guildhall Lib., MS. 5105, fol. 31; MS. 10823/1, fols. 38, 41; BL, Stowe MS. 219, fol. 220.

[5] Corporation London RO, Rep. 79, fol. 328; *Acts and Ordinances of the Eastland Company*, ed. M. Sellers (Camden Ser., 1906), xxxvi; *The Compleat Solicitor* (1683), 452.

other jobs as clerks and book-keepers or purchased their freedom and used as working capital what they saved on an apprenticeship premium. A little capital could support a great turnover, when the proportion of fixed capital was small. Others married their masters' daughters or widows, became partners with their masters or other merchants, or bought on time and borrowed funds.[1] But in good years, loan funds were short; in bad years, borrowing and overtrading could not be financed by low turnover and profits. 'Next time you send orders for the buying any things for you,' wrote one London merchant to his factor, 'pray send a certain commodity called Money along with 'em.'[2] The only satisfactory source of capital were parents and relations through legacies, gifts, or special provision. When even established merchants had difficulty funding their children, sons of gentlemen had an uphill task. Trading gentlemen, like Peregrine Pelham, Marmaduke Rawdon, and Richard Bagnall, did marry commercial capital, and a few parents, like Sir Robert Filmer, Sir Edward Master, and Sir George Sondes, provided some funds.[3] But most gentry either underestimated the capital needs of trade or were unwilling to divert funds from their estates. Short of liquid assets, they expected their outlay to be limited to the cost of binding. Consequently gentlemen in trade were 'pigmies in Stocks and experience',[4] liable to be forced to withdraw from business or to take dangerous risks and ruin themselves. The high cost of apprenticeship reduced the capital available for private trade, and the more popular an area of trade with the gentry, the higher rose the cost of admission. It was rare for an outsider to achieve take-off into a mature and self-generating business.

The trading gentleman also lacked the contacts within the business world which were so essential to success. The kinship group was the basis of all business dealings. Family cartels, cemented by intermarriage, dominated certain areas of trade,

---

[1] *HMC, Sackville*, ii. 75; PRO, C. 114/55; PRO, SP For. 105/152, fol. 169.
[2] PRO, SP For. 110/16, letter 25 Aug. 1684.
[3] *Blundell's Diary and Letter Book, 1702–1728*, ed. M. Blundell (Liverpool, 1952), 40; *Abstracts of Yorkshire Wills*, ed. J. W. Clay (Yorks. Arch. and Topog. Assoc. Rec. Ser., 1890), 51, 66, 133.
[4] Sir Josiah Child, *Brief Observations* (1668), repr. by W. Letwin, *Sir Josiah Child* (Boston, 1959), 51; Joseph Hill, *The Interest of these United Provinces* (1673), sect. vi, 5; Fynes Moryson, *An Itinerary* (Glasgow, 1907–8), iii. 101.

and most merchants preferred to employ and deal with relations they could trust. Merchants could provide accurate advice about suitable trades for their sons and nephews; they could act as masters and, most important of all, they could provide business. It was crucial for a young merchant to have clients and commissions, particularly as principals increasingly preferred to use commission agents rather than factors.[1] Only family connections on 'Change and in the coffee-houses and City companies of London could generate business. The trading gentleman could, and did, employ his kin and exploit family patronage. But families which did not have a tradition of placing children in business often fell prey to incompetent, dishonest, or indifferent masters. When Dudley Foley's business career was launched, he complained that his father was 'a country gentleman . . . not understanding much of the merchant's business'.[2] Many gentlemen, without relations in trade, found it impossible to obtain business, once out of their time. One younger son records how in eleven years he 'never raised enough from Gabriel Roberts consignments to pay a third part of his charges tho he has been always a very good Husband . . . the Estate he has raised here has been from the business of friends that have come in meerly by accident and who never had the least obligation to employ him'.[3]

The kinship group was also necessary as a defence against insecurity. The risks of trade cannot be underestimated, particularly for a young man starting on his own. Most factors never became merchants, just as most apprentices never became freemen. All trades were subject to arbitrary factors—both human and acts of God—seasonal fluctuations, disruptions through weather or war, fire, earthquake, piracy, price movements, fiscal exactions, the failures of other merchants, the condition of the currency, sudden shifts in demand. The speed with which a ship reached a market could turn on the

[1] PRO, C. 104/44, letter 12 Aug. 1682.

[2] Ipswich and East Suffolk RO, Acc. 331, Box 19, letter from Dudley Foley to John Normansell. On the use and abuse of kinship see Guildhall Lib., MS. 6645, Henry Morse to George Radcliffe, 28 May 1715, and PRO, Requests 2/390/595, 15 Chas I.

[3] PRO, SP For. 110/16, letters from Aleppo, 30 Mar. 1689, 4 May 1690; Kent AO, U. 119/C4, Feb. 1704; PRO, SP For. 110/10, letter 24 Sept. 1684; C. 104/44, letter 13 Apr. 1685.

wind or the temperature and the timing of arrival could mean profit or ruin on a cargo. The unpredictable nature of events could be modified to a certain extent by insurance, by distributing cargoes between several ships, by adjusting profit margins and prices to risk. But as Michael Blackett wrote, 'I never yet Adventured anything but which I durst trust God withall to let his will be done'.[1] Time and good luck were essential. Since it took ten years to establish a business, those who began during a depression were fortunate to escape the living death of a debtor's prison. A merchant who died young died poor. Most gentlemen entering business probably had a better chance of succeeding to the family estate than of making a fortune in business.

Success also demanded technical skill. 'In all sciences and occupations', wrote Henry Parker, a younger son, 'breeding is necessary but among merchants it is more than ordinarily necessary.'[2] 'Most tradesmen are ruined for want of skill in arithmetic', wrote Aubrey; merchants had to read and write neatly, legibly, briefly, and with exactness.[3] Several languages were essential for foreign trade. Although the specialist teachers exaggerated the tasks of business, the range of skills was much wider than contemporaries educated at grammar schools, the universities, and the Inns were willing to admit.[4] Knowledge of weights and measures, of commodities and credit instruments, of currencies and bills of exchange, of commercial and international law, of port and customs procedures, invoicing and contracts, transport, packing and marketing, and above all mastery of accounts were essential. Primary education was supplemented by practical experience and exposure to competition in an apprenticeship. George Wansey sent his servant

[1] Cambridge Univ. Lib., MS. Add. 91 C, fol. 120ᵛ, letter 11 July 1676; BL, Loan MS. 29/223, letter 20 July 1694; Essex RO, D/DU 457/7, letter 2 Dec. 1665; BL, Add. MS. 24107, fol. 149; Bodl., Rawlinson MS. lett. 66, fol. 110; William Bagwell, *The Distressed Merchant* (1645).
[2] Parker, *Free Trade*, 15; Thomas Powell, *Tom of all Trades* (1631), ed. F. J. Furnivall (New Shakespere Soc., 1876), 162.
[3] John Aubrey, *On Education*, ed. J. E. Stephens (1972), 103; *The Educational Writings of John Locke*, ed. J. L. Axtell (Cambridge, 1968), 268, 319–20; John Pollexfen, *Discourse of trade and coyn* (1697), 49; Kent AO, U 145/C1, letter 20 Sept. 1661; Lincs. AO, Monson MSS., Misc. Books 21; Bodl., MS. Dep. c. 23, fol. 1.
[4] Ipswich and East Suffolk RO, Acc 331 /H. A. 49.

to help in the packhouse and learn languages and accounts; while abroad he was expected to send monthly reports to his master.[1] Gentry families frequently regarded education as a substitute for provision. At home and at school they received adequate instruction and business literature was often to be found in noble households. But academic learning, particularly a training in classical syntax, was irrelevant and often imbued with values antipathetic to business.[2] Ignorant masters selected for their low premiums could not compensate for a gentleman's education.[3] When the *Complete Tradesman* recommended business for younger sons without the intelligence demanded by the Church, it voiced a common attitude that business, as a socially subordinate occupation, required lesser qualities than the Law or Medicine.[4] Yet to put the clever children into the professions and the dunces into business was a grave error.

The economic virtues of frugality, industry, chastity, and honesty were also essential to success. Thrift was the prime virtue because reducing consumption (if not taken to the extreme of avarice) helped to reduce debts and accumulate capital.[5] Industry, punctuality, and concentration ensured the completion of routine chores, but work was very irregular in most businesses. 'Better doe something to noe purpose then be idle', wrote Peter Mundy,[6] but such advice was really relevant to periods of inactivity, at sea or between shipments, when boredom could become intolerable. Moderation in eating, drinking, and fornication reduced expenditure and preserved health; in the case of some guilt-stricken merchants, like Ambrose Barnes and Francis Rogers, self-denial intensified their dedication to business. Honesty and integrity, said Yarranton, played the role in trade that discipline played in

---

[1] PRO, SP 46/85/66; July 1641; *Yorkshire Diaries and Autobiographies*, ii, ed. C. Jackson (Surtees Soc., 1883), 19.

[2] Thomas Watts, *An Essay on the proper method of forming the man of business* (1716), ed. A. H. Cole (Boston, 1946); Sir Francis Brewster, *Essays on Trade* (1695), Preface, p. vi; *The Advice of W.P. to Mr Samuel Hartlib* (1647–8).

[3] Verney, *Memoirs*, iii. 369; iv. 340; *The Norris Papers*, 11.

[4] H. N., *Complete Tradesman*, 36.

[5] One of the earliest printed handbooks, John Browne, *The Marchants Avizo*, ed. P. McGrath (Cambridge, Mass., 1957), states the orthodox view on thrift, which changed little over the centuries.

[6] Mundy, *Travels*, v, xxiii; *The Art of Good Husbandry* (1675), repr. in *Harleian Miscellany*, ed. T. Park (1808–13), i. 387.

an army.[1] Thomas Palmer, when a client delayed his account, wrote that 'every man's credit but especially a merchant's should be dearer to him than his estate';[2] rational self-interest combined with religious and moral sanctions to enjoin the keeping of covenants, even when legal remedies were expensive and inadequate.[3] The whole structure of credit rested on trust and a self-enforcing morality.

Of the numerous theories of gentility which circulated, one certainly favoured the adoption of frugality, industry, self-control, and reputation. Isaac Barrow, son of a London linen-draper, wrote his tract on Industry for the gentry, though it was later reprinted for businessmen. Many gentlemen responded well. Marmaduke Rawdon 'did allwayes endeavour to taike time by the foretop', and Nathaniel Harley and John Verney took their apprenticeships very seriously. The gentleman's code of honour fortified other pressures to make a man's word his bond. But the Newcastle Merchant Adventurers' records are illuminating on the difficulties of turning gentlemen into merchants. Many broke their indentures, were dismissed, married, entered the army, or were guilty of fornication, improper dress, and absence from service.[4] Laziness, libertinism, and a taste for leisure and comfort, all threatened the gentleman apprentice. The Presbyterian, Ambrose Barnes, commented on his fellow-apprentice, a Durham gentleman, that 'men of large abilities, relying upon their wit and neglecting application suffer meaner capacities to go beyond them'.[5] Richard Elder, apprenticed at high cost to a linen draper in 1680, was too fond of horse-racing, talked back to his master, and though 'witty and ingenious' was discharged. George Boddington remarked of his apprentice, Horace Rossiter, that 'he did not behave himself well, so . . . I offered the Earl of

[1] Andrew Yarranton, *England's Improvement* (1677), 6.
[2] PRO, C. 114/55, draft of a letter by Thomas Palmer.
[3] BL, Add. MS. 22781, fol. 12. Cf. the marginal note in the Yale University Lib. copy of Thomas Milles, *The Misterie of Iniquity* (c. 1611); Daniel Defoe, *Complete English Tradesman* (1727), i. 229, 234; ii. 205, 209; Gerard Malynes, *Lex Mercatoria* (1622), 22; Matthew Hale, *Works moral and religious* (1805), ii. 280. Some merchants preferred the Civil Law to the Common Law; see BL, Add. MS. 5489, fol. 83, and BL, Add. MS. 34218, fol. 95ᵛ.
[4] *Records of the Merchant Adventurers of Newcastle* (Surtees Soc., 1899), 184–342.
[5] *Memoirs of the Life of Ambrose Barnes* (Surtees Soc., 1866), 37.

Clare to return the money he had with him and discharge him'.[1] Gentlemen's sons, wrote Donaldson, 'cannot apply themselves to mean imployments or Boorish Drudgerie' without being miserable.[2] Of course the attitudes and behaviour of sons of yeomen and artisans may have been no better. The wastage rate among all apprentices was high, and the ambitious and conscientious younger son of a landed family was probably better fitted for commerce than sons of merchants with inherited wealth and security, anxious to cut a dash in society.[3] Henry Whichcote, a merchant, told Robert Hedges that his son's letters 'give but little encouragement of any inclination in him to apply himself to business, for his thoughts are upon long perewigs, silk stockings and such like fopperies as if his voyage to India was only to learn to dress and not one sylable of business'.[4] Where dislike of occupation combined with a taste for leisure, the prospects of success were small.

What were the alternatives to business? Low status and low income eliminated all manual and craft skills and some semi-professional posts, like schoolmastering, were probably not considered suitable until the eighteenth century. Other alternatives, like marrying widows and heiresses, cannot be measured exactly. The cost of jointures and children has to be offset against the value of portions, and gentlemen faced competition from other propertied men in the marriage market.[5] The basic opportunities lay in the Law, Medicine, the armed services, the Church, and public office. The growing complexity of a richer society in the seventeenth century created greater demand for lawyers, and the status of even the lower ranks remained unaffected by the universal distrust felt towards them.

[1] Guildhall Lib., MS. 10823/1, fol. 44; Nicholas Blundell, *The Great Diurnal, I, 1702–1711*, ed. J. J. Bagley (Lancs. and Cheshire Rec. Soc., 1968), 46–8.
[2] James Donaldson, *The Undoubted Art of Thriving* (Edinburgh, 1700), 114; Robert Burton, *The Anatomy of Melancholy*, ed. F. Dell and P. Jordan-Smith (1931), 439.
[3] Leeds Central Lib., Brotherton Collection Tr. v., Memoirs of Capt. Aptall; Aphra Behn, *The Younger Brother* in *Works*, ed. M. Summers (1915), iv. 327; Samuel Butler, *Characters*, ed. A. R. Waller (Cambridge, 1908), 149.
[4] Lincs. AO, I.B. /48–50, 22 Jan. 1705.
[5] *The Letters of John Pinney, 1679–1699*, ed. G. F. Nuttall (Oxford, 1939), 80; Kent AO, U 145/18, letters of Thomas Hill; U. 119/C4 Masters correspondence; Guildhall Lib., MS. 507; Verney MSS. at Claydon House, letters 2 Aug., 3 Sept. 1674; Cambridge Univ. Lib., MS. Dd vii 26, fol. 38, letter 16 June 1677; Yorkshire North Riding RO, ZK 11126 and ZCG 6.

Entry into the Law was relatively cheaper than entry into business and had more secure prospects. Conveyancing and settlements provided a reasonable living for those not destined for high legal office. In the early seventeenth century the cost of training at an Inn may have been around £40 p.a. and the profession became more structured as the legal bureaucracy grew. The demand for physicians also surged and the status of apothecary and surgeon, although technically retailer and manual craftsman respectively, benefited from the genuine services they provided in contrast to the academic physicians, who had inherited the status of the learned clerk. Medicine was relatively cheap to enter and its practitioners seem to have prospered at all levels.[1] The physician had the cost of a university; the apothecary had to find around £50 for an apprenticeship and the capital to set up shop. The major drawbacks seem to have been unpaid bills and exposure to infection.

Military service, in contrast, attracted those who sought glory rather than money. Even when a standing army was created, with better prospects for employment in European and colonial wars, it was not a properly salaried profession. Pay was usually in arrears, and in peacetime it was difficult for a soldier to make a decent living, unless he was well connected and fortunate enough to secure a lucrative office or enjoy a private income. The hazards to life and limb were higher than in business, and a hard campaign could reduce a man's investment in men and equipment to nothing. But war was the very essence of nobility and the army demanded much the same qualities of courage, stamina, organizing ability, and risk-taking as did business. Many apprentices, like Richard Oxinden, turned to soldiering, which was similar to self-employment in business. The regiment was an unlimited Company; promotion was achieved by money and influence, and payment was by perquisites and daily allowances rather than by salary. A professional soldier bought his commission and earned his income by contracting for supplies. The cost of entry, moreover, was comparable with foreign trade. In Anne's reign, an ensign of the line cost £200–£500, a company £250, a regiment £400–£500. The standing navy had equal status and a longer history, but it demanded greater technical

[1] PRO, C. 104/130–131 and C. 114/59.

skill. Unemployment in peacetime was a problem and conditions of service at sea were less attractive than army life. On the other hand, the prospect of income from prizes was high and supplemented salaries and freight money. The initial outlay was very small and special methods of entry were available for landed gentlemen.

The Church and public office also compared favourably with business, especially after 1660. In many benefices after the last purge of the Restoration, an orthodox incumbent enjoyed security of tenure with an adequate stipend (augmented by plurality and promotion) and consequently improved status. The landed class could exercise its patronage and rights of presentation; intellectual interests could be indulged; duties were light and marriage permitted. The great offices of state, the lucrative fiscal posts, and the diplomatic service were, like bishoprics, reserved for those with estates. Major offices were expensive to obtain and risky investments. According to the Duke of Newcastle, the sale of offices reduced vacancies for younger sons and forced them into trade. But the gradual expansion of the lower ranks of the bureaucracy did provide some opportunities for careers in government—in revenue posts, on regulatory and advisory bodies, in the provincial Customs. The main outlay for parents was for education.

The salaried posts in private business institutions, like the overseas Companies, also became more attractive. The joint-stock Companies allowed their employees to function as individual entrepreneurs in order to compensate for low salaries. Offices in these Companies were offices of profit under the shareholders. Business administration attracted the gentry because gentlemen without capital could enter simply by furnishing a bond for good behaviour—£500 in the case of a writer of the East India Company. After 1669, the latter recruited systematically and established a proper hierarchy of posts with grades of salary and a promotion structure facilitated by high mortality.[1] Successful men needed luck, contacts, good

[1] India Office Lib., Home Misc. MS. 78; *The English Factories in India, 1618–1669*, ed. Sir W. Foster (Oxford, 1906–27), xi; *English Factories, 1670–1677*, ed. Sir C. G. H. Fawcett (1936–52), i. 273; *Court Minutes of the East India Company, 1671–3*, ed. E. B. Sainsbury (Oxford, 1907–38), ix. 82; *The Diaries of Streynsham Master*, ed. R. C. Temple (Indian Rec. Soc., 1911), 193.

health, and the skills of seeking office.[1] Nor was capital irrelevant. John Marshall told William Atwood in 1669 that at Metchepatnam, 'is noe money to be gotten honestly except a man hath a good stock of his own'.[2] Salaries varied from £5 for writers to £500 for the President of a Factory and conditions were extremely dangerous. But transport, food, and lodging were included, and the private trade, corruption, money-lending, and provisioning made the Company so attractive that by the 1680s there was an 'irresistible importuning of friends' for posts.[3] On a smaller scale the same was true of other Companies.[4]

What therefore determined the distribution of children between careers and how well could business compete with alternative forms of employment? Although opinion cannot be quantified, it seems clear that there was no dominant system of anti-business values. Each family decided for itself how to rank business as a career for their younger sons. Status based on birth, wealth, and conspicuous consumption gradually gave way to a theory based on personal qualities and on assimilation. Snobbery became a substitute for effective social barriers and the dividing line in English society was drawn between those who had to earn and those to whom all activity was a leisure occupation.

Business was not as highly regarded as the Law and Office by many families, but it was largely a question of taste and fashion. The difference between the top and bottom of any occupation was always greater than the difference between occupations at the same level. Church livings, military commands, and public office were all regarded as private property, and fees and salaries enjoyed no moral superiority over profits. To parents, the opportunity in relation to the ability, health, and temperament of their children was probably more important than prestige. Most families probably inclined towards employment outside business, but they were influenced less by social prejudice

[1] *English Factories, 1670–1677*, i, p. vii; ii, p. vi.
[2] PRO, C. 109/10.
[3] *Diary of Hedges*, lxxv, cclviii; John Fryer, *A New Account of East India and Persia*, ed. E. W. Crook (Hakluyt Soc., 1909), 89–90, 216–17; *English Factories, 1670–1677*, ii. 143; PRO, C. 110/87; Bodl., Rawlinson MS. A 303, fols. 145–6; Rawlinson MS. D. 747, fols. 139, 164.
[4] Salop RO, Walcott and Bittersly MSS., Case of Humphrey Walcott.

than by education and upbringing, by family patronage and conditions of work, by the prospect of residence in England, even by their children's preferences. John Verney rejected (wrongly as it turned out) his father's choice of the Law and apologized for 'your worme for desiring to bee an apprentice'.[1] Prestige often carried less weight than earning power and the decision was made by individuals, not by society.

It was economic rather than social factors which determined the type of employment. The cost of setting-up in relation to a family's size and income, and the level and security of return expected, were decisive. As Mandeville put it:

> most people look out for some warrantable employment . . . But some of these employments being vastly more creditable than others, according to the great difference of the charges required to set up in each of them, all prudent parents in the choice of them chiefly consult their own abilities and the circumstances they are in. A Man that gives three or four hundred pounds with his son, to a great merchant and has not two or three thousand pounds to spare against he is out of his time to begin the world with, is much to blame not to have brought his child up to some thing that might be followed with less money.[2]

Parents expected their children to acquire financial independence and they spread them between careers, like investments in a portfolio. But, on a strict economic comparison, business had lower returns and higher entry costs and risks than other occupations. Roger North, in 1698, wrote that soldiering was a most dishonourable trade, that 'the parson's trade was as good as ever', that the Law could not bear more than one of a family; but a merchant, he added, is 'now the most chargeable of all'.[3] Optimism and ignorance no doubt misled parents and children, but the failure rate in business was so high that merchants did not wish their children to follow in their footsteps. It is not surprising, therefore, that parents preferred careers

---

[1] Verney MSS. at Claydon, letter 15 May 1659; Verney, *Memoirs*, iii. 367; Ben Jonson, *Works*, ed. C. H. Herford, P. and E. Simpson (Oxford, 1925–52), viii. 504; Edward Gibbon, *Memoirs of my Life*, ed. G. A. Bonnard (1966), 7.

[2] Bernard Mandeville, *The Fable of the Bees*, ed. F. B. Kaye (Oxford, 1924), i. 58–9.

[3] BL, Add. MS. 32500, fols. 84, 168, 175–178, 184, 192–193, 501; Ipswich and East Suffolk RO, Acc. 331, Box 19; Hereford RO, F/iv/1a/110, 116–18, 135–9; BL, Add. MS. 4224, fol. 37; HMC, *Fortescue*, i. 18.

which provided security and a regular income for a low outlay. Salaried posts, with some private trade on the side, were the ideal, and rational economic interests often dictated against a business career. Why therefore did so many younger sons of gentlemen nevertheless enter business? The answer is that only business could accommodate their number. On average two male children survived to each peerage and gentry family in the seventeenth century. If every landed family had at least one younger son, there would, on Gregory King's figures for 1688, have been some 16,500 younger sons compared with some 55,000 merchants and tradesmen and 65,000 posts in the Law, the Church, the Army, the Navy, and public office combined, only a proportion of which would be vacant at any one time and most of which also attracted eldest sons, aliens, and children from the non-gentry class.[1] Sir William Petty in 1690 thought that younger sons would starve without agricultural improvement, that offices, the Army and Navy, the Church, Law and Physic, and service in noble households could not accommodate more than 3,000 of the 10,000 younger sons, who must live by trade or depend on the charity of elder brothers.[2] Although precise statistics are lacking, there is little doubt that most younger sons without provision had to choose between business and emigration to the colonies. Many younger children must have been forced to remain as managers on the family estate. Other professions were equally restricted in their rate of growth. Population pressure thus ensured recruits for business even though rewards were inadequate for the risk.

It is, however, doubtful whether either individual merchants or the national economy benefited from a socially comprehensive flow of new men. Sir William Petty might claim that 'it is not improbable that since the generality of Gentlemen and some Noblemen do put their younger sons to merchandising, they will see it reasonable as they increase in the number of merchants, so to increase the magnitude of Trade and

---

[1] *Seventeenth-Century Economic Documents*, 780; Edward Waterhouse, *The Gentleman's Monitor* (1665), 75.

[2] *The Economic Writings of Sir William Petty*, ed. C. H. Hull (Cambridge, 1899) i. 313.

consequently to increase stock'.[1] But the large number of children from non-mercantile families could not compensate for the loss of capital created by merchants retiring from trade or setting up their dependants and heirs with land, urban property, and offices. The premiums paid to masters of apprentices and the starting capital provided for their children by landowners and farmers distributed assets towards business. But the children were placed in trade precisely because the parents did not wish to make more than minimal provision for them. Most new merchants were short of working capital and unable to finance an adequate volume of business at viable rates of interest. Some speculative and unfashionable areas of trade, particularly those in the hands of small partnerships, may have benefited from an influx of funds which would not have reached them through joint-stock investment and the new institutions of credit. But it was the willingness of passive investors to put their savings into business as well as into better secured loans to landowners and the state which eventually relieved shortages of liquid capital and funded long-term investment. Business investment was maintained more by an excess of capital in relation to opportunities than by new recruits.

The movement of children of the propertied class into business increased the percentage of the educated population engaged in the creation of new wealth rather than in the administration and defence of existing assets. But the economic effects may have been extremely limited in an economy whose principal characteristic was underemployment. What business needed was quality, not quantity. Most trades tried to restrict entry as demand exceeded opportunities for expansion. Business could always use more men of real talent. Brilliant entrepreneurs no doubt languished unseen among the underprivileged or had to make their way in new trades or in the New World. But the demographic forces which allowed business to compete for recruits could not ensure that the most able and energetic of those in a position to choose would prefer business and the weakest choose office and the professions. Many entered trade *faute de mieux*, not because they had a talent for commerce. Indeed to some contemporaries, business

---

[1] *The Economic Writings of Sir William Petty*, ed. C. H. Hull (Cambridge, 1899), 312.

was a support for the gentry, not the gentry a support for trade.[1]

The economic advantages of social mobility were more indirect. The landed interest gained primarily from the freedom it acquired to practise primogeniture. Without the possibility of employment in private business, younger sons would have imposed a major financial burden on landed estates. Slingsby Bethel, a young son in business, exaggerated when he claimed that noble wealth was preserved by careers similar to his own.[2] But estates were rescued from amorcellation by business opportunities. In a few cases, younger sons could even make a fortune. These advantages offset the potential friction, prophesied by Matthew Wren and Thomas Hobbes,[3] between landed and moneyed wealth, between those who paid and those who escaped the land tax. Suspicion of mercantile ambitions and hostility to the growing power of financial interests could easily have dried up passive investment by the gentry in commerce and industry and affected government policy in a political system dominated by landed men. The gentry had to remain persuaded that agricultural prosperity and their credit facilities depended on the expansion of trade. The interchange of gentry and merchants, bolstered by intermarriage, did help to publicize mutual economic interests. Younger sons in business advised their parents on purchase of urban property, acted as agents for the sale of minerals and agricultural produce, and served as contacts for future migrants into business. The family links between town and country permitted innovation within a stable framework and generated a continuing interest in economic growth. Agriculture, industry, and trade were more closely integrated without endangering the prestige and distinctiveness of the landed class.

The business community also benefited. Even if the merchant-turned-gentleman faced snobbery and other difficulties of adjustment to landed life, his children were easily absorbed into landed society. Without some gentlemen in business, there would have been no space for new gentlemen from urban society. As Defoe noted, 'Trademen become Gentlemen by

[1] Henry Robinson, *England's Safety in Trades Increase* (1641), repr. in *Select Tracts*, ed. W. A. Shaw (1935), 48–9.
[2] Slingsby Bethel, *The Interest of the Princes and States of Europe* (3rd edn. 1689), 8.
[3] Matthew Wren, *Considerations on Mr Harrington's Oceana* (1657), 14–15, 86–9.

Gentlemen becoming Tradesmen.'[1] It was, moreover, self-perpetuating. By recruiting so widely, business accentuated the process of mobility which made social interchange possible. Because social divisions were vertical as well as horizontal, merchants of non-gentle origin had a powerful incentive to make their fortune. If the gentry had been excluded from trade by their own prejudices or by the hostility of the commercial interest, it would have been difficult for business men to improve their own status except through the bureaucracy. The high turnover in the commercial companies and the City offices constantly introduced new blood into what was theoretically a socially static, oligarchic system. English society had enough elements of distinction to make the pursuit of gentle status worth while and enough opportunities for self-made men to rise. A closed society would have spelt poverty for many gentry and restless frustration for the bourgeoisie. In Tokugawa Japan, for example, the prohibition on the purchase of land by townsmen seems to have diverted commercial profits into conspicuous consumption and riotous living. A completely open society, on the other hand, would have reduced the exclusiveness which access to an élite eventually brings and which served to inflame the ambitions of business men. In England incentives never reached saturation point, as the long haul to the top of the social ladder stimulated change without provoking revolution or reaction.

Another consequence of this dynamic social equilibrium was the absence of an independent, urban aristocracy or a legal and office-holding nobility. The absence of privilege made the gentry no economic threat to the merchants, and the wish to identify with the upper class made the gentry more sympathetic to the social pretensions of business. The gentry were able to accept a free land market, a programme of economic growth, and the specialization and division of labour within the propertied class. The merchants were able to accept the social order and the traditional habits and authority of the landed class because they had some chance of rising in the world. Progress was possible because both stood to gain by change. Free movement within the social hierarchy allowed for individual merit

---

[1] D. Defoe, *A Plan of the English Commerce* (1728) in *Novels and Selected Writings* (Oxford, 1927–8), xiii. 9.

without endangering social order. Because of this process of assimilation, no powerful and hostile social order arose to challenge the gentry, and new business wealth did not transform social institutions. Business did not create a self-conscious class, but a functional group. The ambivalence towards business created by the identification, in some quarters, of mobility with original sin and with repudiation of an inherited calling, fortified the acquisitive spirit. The merchants imitated the values, attitudes, and habits of landed society, but in return the gentry were exposed to the cosmopolitan ideas and behaviour of urban society. Those cut off from traditional society by religious belief were able to resist pressures to assimilate; business, like other occupations, was subdivided into closed interest groups. But social compromise and wordly success created a relatively homogeneous society, in which the propertied class had more to share than to dispute, where economic growth was possible without government intervention or social coercion.

Christopher Hill
A Select Bibliography, 1938–1977

COMPILED BY M. F. ROBERTS

THIS is not intended as a definitive bibliography. It includes Christopher Hill's books (but not their numerous foreign translations), and some of his articles, reviews, and published correspondence. The compiler is grateful to Professor Ivan Roots for his help.

1938

[As C. E. Gore], '250th Anniversary of the "Glorious" Revolution of 1688', *Communist International* (Nov.), 22–9.

'Soviet Interpretations of the English Interregnum', *EcHR* viii. 159–67.

'A Whig Historian' (H. A. L. Fisher), *Modern Qtly.* i. 275–84.

Reviews:

S. J. Madge, *The Domesday of Crown Lands*: *EcHR* viii. 203–4.

G. Davies, *The Early Stuarts 1603–1660*: *Modern Qtly.* i. 91–4.

1939

Reviews:

D. L. Keir, *The Constitutional History of Modern Britain 1485–1937*, and M. A. Thomson, *A Constitutional History of England, iv: 1642–1801*: *Modern Qtly.* ii. 198–205.

N. Riches, *The Agricultural Revolution in Norfolk*: *Sci. and Soc.* iii. 261–3.

1940

The English Revolution, 1640: Three Essays, ed. C. Hill (Lawrence and Wishart). [2nd edn. 1949.] [Hill's own essay published separately as *The English Revolution 1640* in 1955.]

'The Agrarian Legislation of the Interregnum', *EHR* lv. 222–50. [Revised in *Puritanism and Revolution* (1958).]

Reviews:

R. B. Schlatter, *The Social Ideas of Religious Leaders 1660–88*: *EcHR* x. 162–4.

H. B. Parkes, *Marxism: A Post-Mortem*: *Scrutiny*, ix. 277–84.

1942
Reviews:
V. M. Lavrovsky, *Parliamentary Enclosure of the Common Fields in England at the end of the Eighteenth and the beginning of the Nineteenth Centuries*: EcHR xii. 92–5.

The Works of Gerrard Winstanley, ed. G. H. Sabine: EHR lvii. 384–8.

[Unsigned] E. Ecclestone, *Sir Walter Raleigh: Our Time*, i. 7–9.

1943
Review:
W. K. Jordan, *Men of Substance*: EcHR xiii. 120–2.

1944
Introduction to *Gerrard Winstanley: Selections from his Works*, ed. L. Hamilton (Cresset Press).

1945
[As 'K. E. Holme'], *Two Commonwealths: The Soviets and Ourselves* (Harrap).

1946
'Professor Lavrovsky's Study of a Seventeenth-Century Manor', *EcHR* xvi. 125–9.

'Society and Andrew Marvell', *Modern Qtly.* new ser. i. 6–31. [Revised in *Puritanism and Revolution* (1958).]

Review:
G. M. Trevelyan, *English Social History (from Chaucer to Queen Victoria)*: *Communist Rev.* (Mar. 1946), 26–9.

1947
Lenin and the Russian Revolution (English Univ. Press).

Revised and edited version of M. E. Gow's translation of S. I. Arkhangelsky, *Agrarian Legislation of the English Revolution (1643–8)* [typescript deposited in Bodl.].

'Lenin: Theoretician of Revolution', *Communist Rev.* (Feb. 1947), 59–64.

'England's Democratic Army', *Communist Rev.* (June 1947), 171–8.

'The Restoration Spirit', *New Theatre*, iv. 16–17.

Reviews:
M. Dobb, *Studies in the Development of Capitalism*: *Modern Qtly.* new ser. ii. 268–72.

A. Toynbee, *A Study of History* (vols. i–vi), and D. C. Somervell, *A Study of History* (abridgement): *Modern Qtly.* new ser. ii. 290–307.

1948

'The Fight for an Independent Foreign Policy', *Communist Rev.* (Feb. 1948), 46–52.

'Marxism and History', *Modern Qtly.* new ser. iii. 52–64.

'The English Civil War Interpreted by Marx and Engels', *Sci. and Soc.* xii. 130–56.

Review:

D. B. Quinn, *Raleigh and the British Empire*: *Daily Worker* (1 Jan. 1948).

Letter: 'The Minsk Manifesto': *TLS* (10 Apr. 1948), 205.

1949

Ed. [with E. Dell], *The Good Old Cause. The English Revolution of 1640–60. Its Causes, Course and Consequences* (Lawrence and Wishart). [2nd edn. with new Introduction by C. Hill: Frank Cass, 1969.]

'The English Revolution and the State', *Modern Qtly.* new ser. iv. 110–28.

'Hobbes and English Political Thought' in *Philosophy for the Future. The Quest of Modern Materialism*, ed. R. W. Sellars, V. J. McGill, M. Farber (New York: Macmillan), 13–32. [Revised, in *Puritanism and Revolution* (1958).]

'Land in the English Revolution', *Sci. and Soc.* xiii. 22–49.

Reviews:

G. Soloveytchik, *Potemkin: A Picture of Catherine's Russia*: *Anglo-Soviet Journ.* x. 45–6.

W. Schenk, *The Concern for Social Justice in the Puritan Revolution*, and M. A. Gibb, *John Lilburne*: *Communist Rev.* (Mar. 1949), 475–80.

A. L. Morton, *A People's History of England* (revised edn.): *Daily Worker* (24 Feb. 1949).

R. T. Davies, *Four Centuries of Witch Beliefs*: *History*, new ser. xxxiv. 138–9.

G. H. Turnbull, *Hartlib, Dury, and Comenius: Gleanings from Hartlib's papers*: ibid. 140–1.

V. G. Childe, *History*: *Modern Qtly.* new ser. iv. 259–62.

G. H. Dodge, *The Political Theory of the Huguenots of the Dispersion*: *Sci. and Soc.* xiii. 273–5.

1950

'The Myth of Western Civilisation', *Modern Qtly.* new ser. v. 172–4.

'Historians and the Rise of British Capitalism', *Sci. and Soc.* xiv. 307–21.

Reviews:

V. F. Semeonov, *Enclosures and Peasant Revolts in England in the Sixteenth Century*: *EcHR* new ser. iii. 138–9.

The Life and Letters of Sir Lewis Dyve 1599–1669, ed. H. G. Tibbutt: *History*, new ser. xxxv. 156.

[with A. Calder-Marshall, J. Lindsay, and A. Rothstein] Letter: 'Russia and Civilized Values': *TLS* (21 July 1950), 453.

1951

'The Materialist Conception of History', *University*, i. 110–14.

Comment on review of M. Dobb, *Studies in the Development of Capitalism*: *Revue Historique*, ccv. 174–7.

1952

'Cavaliers, Roundheads—or Neither?', *Amateur Historian*, i. 13–17.

'Puritans and the Poor', *P. and P.* 2. 32–50. [Revised in *Puritanism and Revolution* (1958).]

Reviews:

M. M. Barg, *Cromwell and His Time*: *Communist Rev.* (May 1952), 155–9.

S. O'Faolain, *Newman's Way*: *Daily Worker* (27 Nov. 1952).

Patriarcha and other political works of Sir Robert Filmer, ed. P. Laslett: *History*, new ser. xxxvii. 166.

B. Farrington, *Francis Bacon, Philosopher of Industrial Science*: *Modern Qtly.* new ser. vii. 55–8.

G. R. Cragg, *From Puritanism to the Age of Reason*: *Sci. and Soc.* xvi. 70–4.

J. H. Gleason, *The Genesis of Russophobia in Great Britain*: ibid. 281–3.

Letter: on Marxism and historical teaching: *TLS* (19 Dec. 1952), 837.

1953

'Clarendon and the Civil War', *History Today*, iii. 695–703.

'The Barebones Parliament: a Revaluation', *Listener* (23 July 1953), 142–3.

'Stalin and the Science of History', *Modern Qtly.* new ser. viii. 198–212.

Communication: on 'Puritans and the Poor' and William Perkins: *P. and P.* 3. 53–4.

'The English Revolution and the Brotherhood of Man', *Rekishigakukenkyu* (The Journal of Historical Studies) clxv. [Translated in *Sci. and Soc.* xviii. 289–309. Revised in *Puritanism and Revolution* (1958).]

'The Transition from Feudalism to Capitalism, II', *Sci. and Soc.* xvii. 348–51.

Reviews:

L. N. Nikiforov, *Russko-Angliskie Otnoshenia Pri Petre I*: *Anglo-Soviet Journ.* xiv. 34–5.

T. S. Willan, *The Muscovy Merchants of 1555*: ibid. 40.

L. and M. Harder, *Plockhoy from Zurik-zee*: *EHR* lxviii. 480–1.

A. H. Dodd, *Studies in Stuart Wales*: ibid. 642–3.

H. Jenkins, *Edward Benlowes (1602–1676)*: *Essays in Criticism*, iii. 143–51.

386   *Christopher Hill*

J. Lindsay, *Byzantium into Europe: Modern Qtly.* new ser. viii. 186–9.
F. S. Siebert, *Freedom of the Press in England 1476–1776: Sci. and Soc.* xvii. 180–3.
C. Brinton, *The Anatomy of Revolution*: ibid. 270–3.

1954

'The Norman Yoke', in *Democracy and the Labour Movement. Essays in honour of Dona Torr*, ed. J. Saville (Lawrence and Wishart), 11–66. [Revised in *Puritanism and Revolution* (1958).]

Reviews:
D. Brunton and D. H. Pennington, *Members of the Long Parliament*: *Daily Worker* (25 Feb. 1954).
I. Morley, *A Thousand Lives*: ibid. (25 Nov. 1954).
R. P. Stearns, *The Strenuous Puritan*: *EHR* lxix. 666–7.
S. F. Mason, *A History of the Sciences*: *Oxford Left* (Michaelmas 1954), 49–51.
P. Hazard, *The European Mind: The Critical Years 1680–1715*: *Sci. and Soc.* xviii. 253–5.

1955

'Clarissa Harlowe and Her Times', *Essays in Criticism*, v. 315–40. [Revised in *Puritanism and Revolution* (1958).]
'The University of Moscow, II: The Teaching of History', *Universities Qtly.* ix. 332–41.

Reviews:
A. French, *Charles I and the Puritan Upheaval*: *Daily Worker* (29 Dec. 1955).
The Correspondence of Bishop Brian Duppa and Sir Justinian Isham 1650–1660, ed. Sir G. Isham: *EHR* lxx. 668–9.
T. L. Coonan, *The Irish Catholic Confederacy and the Puritan Revolution*: *Sci. and Soc.* xix. 275–8.

1956

Economic Problems of the Church. From Archbishop Whitgift to the Long Parliament (Oxford: O.U.P.) [with corrections, 1963 and 1968].
'Die gesellschaftlichen und ökonomischen Folgen der Reformation in England' in *Beiträge zum neuen Geschichtsbild*, ed. F. Klein and J. Streisand (Berlin: Rütten and Loening), 88–104. [Revised and trans. in *Puritanism and Revolution* (1958).]
'Recent Interpretations of the Civil War', *History*, new ser. xli. 67–87. [Revised in *Puritanism and Revolution* (1958).]
'A Propos d'un Article Récent sur Cromwell' [by H. R. Trevor-Roper]: *Annales E. S. C.* xi. 490–2.

Reviews:
W. Haller, *Liberty and Reformation in the Puritan Revolution*: *EHR* lxxi. 286–8.

Angliyskaya Burzhuaznaya Revolyutziya XVII Veka, ed. E. A. Kosminsky: ibid. 458–62.

C. V. Wedgwood, *The King's Peace 1637–1641*, T. L. Coonan, *The Irish Catholic Confederacy and the Puritan Revolution*, and P. Zagorin, *A History of Political Thought in the English Revolution: History*, new ser. xli. 230–2.

C. de Grunwald, *Peter the Great*: *Spectator* (17 Feb. 1956), 221–2.

C. Price, *Cold Caleb*, and D. Ogg, *William III*: ibid. (6 Apr. 1956), 454–5.

From Donne to Marvell, ed. B. Ford, and *The Poetical Works of Robert Herrick*, ed. L. C. Martin: ibid. (6 Apr. 1956), 454–5.

L. Stone, *An Elizabethan: Sir Horatio Palavicino*: ibid. (20 Apr. 1956), 553–4.

J. W. F. Hill, *Tudor and Stuart Lincoln*: ibid. (27 Apr. 1956), 594.

L. G. Pine, *The Story of the Peerage*: ibid. (18 May 1956), 696.

R. T. Petersson, *Sir Kenelm Digby*: ibid. (25 May 1956), 734–6.

Sir W. W. Greg, *Some Aspects and Problems of London Publishing between 1550 and 1650*: ibid. (15 June 1956), 835.

The Thought and Culture of the English Renaissance: An Anthology of Tudor Prose, ed. E. M. Nugent: ibid. (29 June 1956), 893–4.

E. Wingfield-Stratford, *The Squire and His Relations*: ibid. (6 July 1956), 24–7.

M. 'Espinasse, *Robert Hooke*: ibid. (27 July 1956), 152.

P. G. Rogers, *The First Englishman in Japan*: ibid. (31 Aug. 1956), 301.

J. Farrow, *The Story of Thomas More*: ibid. (14 Sept. 1956), 361.

The Phanseys of William Cavendish, Marquis of Newcastle, Addressed to Margaret Lucas, and her Letters in Reply, ed. D. Grant: ibid. (21 Sept. 1956), 396.

G. Botero, *The Reason of State* and *The Greatness of Cities*, ed. D. P. Waley: ibid. (5 Oct. 1956), 458–9.

R. Tyler, *The Emperor Charles the Fifth*: ibid. (2 Nov. 1956), 617–18.

They Saw it Happen: An Anthology of Eye-Witness Accounts of Events in British History 1485–1688, ed. C. R. N. Routh: ibid. (9 Nov. 1956), 658–60.

B. Little, *The Monmouth Episode*: ibid. (16 Nov. 1956), 687.

E. M. W. Tillyard, *The Metaphysicals and Milton*: ibid. (23 Nov. 1956), 750–2.

A. L. Rowse, *The Early Churchills*: ibid. (14 Dec. 1956), 880–1.

The Works of John Dryden, vol. I: *Poems 1649–80*, ed. E. N. Hooker, H. T. Swedenberg, Jr., *et al.*: ibid. (21 Dec. 1956), 914.

1957

'The Mad Hatter', *History Today*, vii. 672–5. [Revised in *Puritanism and Revolution* (1958).]

'John Mason and the End of the World', ibid. 776–80. [Revised in *Puritanism and Revolution* (1958).]

[With P. Cadogan and M. MacEwen]: Minority Report of the Commission on Inner Party Democracy presented to the Twenty-Fifth (Special) Congress of the Communist Party, April 1957.

Reviews:

The Registers of the Church of St. Augustine the Less, Bristol 1577–1700, ed. A. Sabin: *EcHR* new ser. ix. 506.

A. Simpson, *Puritanism in Old and New England*: *EHR* lxxii. 173–4.

J. Bohatec, *England und die Geschichte der Menschen- und Bürgerrechte*: ibid. 750–1.

The Diary of John Evelyn, ed. E. S. de Beer: *History*, new ser. xlii. 12–18.

J. Frank, *The Levellers*: *Sci. and Soc.* xxi. 172–8.

W. P. Holden, *Anti-Puritan Satire 1572–1642*, and G. Davies, *The Restoration of Charles II*: ibid. 172–8.

D. Bahlman, *The Moral Revolution of 1688*: ibid. 378–81.

E. Lampert, *Studies in Rebellion*: *Sociological Rev.* new ser. v. 308–9.

W. Notestein, *Four Worthies*: *Spectator* (4 Jan. 1957), 26–7.

The Great Tudors, ed. K. Garvin, and D. Meadows, *Elizabethan Quintet*: ibid. (11 Jan. 1957), 55–6.

Sir J. E. Neale, *Elizabeth I and Her Parliaments. 1584–1601*: ibid. (1 Feb. 1957), 148.

M. Whinney and O. Millar, *English Art 1625–1714*: ibid. (15 Mar. 1957), 352.

J. Marlowe, *The Puritan Tradition in English Life*: ibid. (19 Apr. 1957), 522.

C. D. Bowen, *The Lion and the Throne: The Life and Times of Sir Edward Coke*: ibid. (24 May 1957), 682.

C. Wilson, *Profit and Power: A Study of England and the Dutch Wars*: ibid. (7 June 1957), 786.

G. R. Cragg, *Puritanism in the Period of the Great Persecution*: ibid. (21 June 1957), 817–18.

P. Caraman, *Henry Morse, Priest of the Plague*: ibid. (28 June 1957), 856.

P. Hughes, *A Popular History of the Reformation*: ibid. (19 July 1957), 112–14.

N. Cohn, *The Pursuit of the Millennium*: ibid. (9 Aug. 1957), 196–7.

C. Dawson, *Dynamics of World History*, and F. Stern, *The Varieties of History*: ibid. (20 Sept. 1957), 370.

M. Ashley, *The Greatness of Oliver Cromwell*: ibid. (4 Oct. 1957), 446.

H. R. Trevor-Roper, *Historical Essays*: ibid. (25 Oct. 1957), 551–2.

English Historians, Selected Passages, ed. B. Newman: ibid. (6 Dec. 1957), 810–11.

1958

Puritanism and Revolution. Studies in Interpretation of the English Revolution of the 17th Century (Secker and Warburg).

Oliver Cromwell 1658–1958 (Historical Assn. Pamphlet G 38).

Letter: 'Storm over the Gentry': *Encounter*, xi. 76.

Reviews:

E. S. Morgan, *The Puritan Family*: *EHR* lxxiii. 156–7.

G. F. Nuttall, *Visible Saints: the Congregational Way, 1640–1660*: ibid. 157.

A. M. Everitt, *The County Committee of Kent in the Civil War*, and D. H. Pennington and I. A. Roots, *The Committee at Stafford 1643–1645*: ibid. 157–9.

I. M. Calder, *Activities of the Puritan Factions of the Church of England, 1625–33*: ibid. 351–2.

I. Morgan, *Prince Charles's Puritan Chaplain*: ibid. 719–20.

A. Gramsci, *The Modern Prince and Other Writings*, trans. and ed. L. Marks: *New Reasoner*, 4. 107–13.

A. Cornu, *Karl Marx et Friedrich Engels: Leur Vie et Leur Œuvre*, i, ii: *1818–1844*: ibid. 5. 115–18.

H. Warrender, *The Political Philosophy of Hobbes*: *Sci. and Soc.* xxii. 177–82.

G. L. Mosse, *The Holy Pretence*: ibid. 273–5.

T. L. Moir, *The Addled Parliament*: *Spectator* (28 Feb. 1958), 270.

Sir C. Petrie, *The Stuarts*: ibid. (21 Mar. 1958), 368.

R. Tuve, *Images and Themes in Five Poems by Milton*: ibid. (4 Apr. 1958), 436.

T. Woodrooffe, *The Enterprise of England*: ibid. (2 May 1958), 566.

R. L. Mackie, *King James IV of Scotland*: ibid. (30 May 1958), 708.

A. Tindal Hart, *The Country Clergy in Elizabethan and Stuart Times, 1558–1660*: ibid. (6 June 1958), 741.

J. P. Kenyon, *Robert Spencer, Earl of Sunderland, 1641–1702*: ibid. (13 June 1958), 780.

Richard Hakluyt, Voyages and Documents, ed. J. Hampden: ibid. (20 June 1958), 809.

G. Yule, *The Independents in the English Civil War*: ibid. (4 July 1958), 21.

M. Roberts, *Gustavus Adolphus*, ii: *1626–1632*, and W. McElwee, *The Wisest Fool in Christendom*: ibid. (8 Aug. 1958), 199.

J. Merrien, *Christopher Columbus: The Mariner and the Man*: ibid. (29 Aug. 1958), 285.

M. Bottrall, *Every Man a Phoenix: Studies in 17th-Century Autobiography*: ibid. (5 Sept. 1958), 318.

H. C. Porter, *Reformation and Reaction in Tudor Cambridge*: ibid. (26 Sept. 1958), 412.

G. R. Elton, *Star Chamber Stories*: ibid. (3 Oct. 1958), 460.

R. H. Tawney, *Business and Politics under James I: Lionel Cranfield as Merchant and Minister*: ibid. (10 Oct. 1958), 493.

J. P. Kenyon, *The Stuarts: A Study in English Kingship*: ibid. (24 Oct. 1958), 558.

The Reformation 1520–59, ed. G. R. Elton: ibid. (7 Nov. 1958), 618.

Saint-Simon at Versailles, ed. L. Norton: ibid. (21 Nov. 1958), 706.

C. Ferguson, *Naked to Mine Enemies: The Life of Cardinal Wolsey*, and P. A. Welsby, *Lancelot Andrewes, 1555–1626*: ibid. (5 Dec. 1958), 824–5.

Sir J. E. Neale, *Essays in Elizabethan History*: ibid. (5 Dec. 1958), 836.

C. V. Wedgwood, *The King's War, 1641–1647*: ibid. (12 Dec. 1958), 870.

H. W. Chapman, *The Last Tudor King: A Study of Edward VI*: ibid. (19 Dec. 1958), 900.

1959

'La Révolution Anglaise du XVIIᵉ siècle (Essai d'interprétation)', *Revue Historique*, ccxxi, 5–32.

Reviews:

P. Williams, *The Council in the Marches of Wales under Elizabeth I*: EcHR new ser. xii. 128–9.

R. Schlatter, *Richard Baxter and Puritan Politics*: EHR lxxiv. 157–8.

J. D. Eusden, *Puritans, Lawyers and Politics in Early Seventeenth-Century England*: ibid. 732–3.

R. H. Tawney, *Social History and Literature*: Spectator (2 Jan. 1959), 22.

L. Hanke, *Aristotle and the American Indians*: ibid. (9 Jan. 1959), 53.

V. Klyuchevsky, *Peter the Great* (trans. L. Archibald), and R. Charques, *A Short History of Russia*: ibid. (13 Feb. 1959), 233.

V. Cronin, *A Pearl to India: the Life of Roberto de Nobili*: ibid. (27 Feb. 1959), 304.

R. W. K. Hinton, *The Eastland Trade and the Common Weal in the Seventeenth Century*: ibid. (6 Mar. 1959), 334.

Lt.-Col. A. H. Burne and Lt.-Col. P. Young, *The Great Civil War 1642–46*: ibid. (20 Mar. 1959), 414.

A History of the County of Cambridge and the Isle of Ely, vol. III: *The City and University of Cambridge*, ed. J. P. C. Roach: ibid. (3 Apr. 1959), 481.

W. T. MacCaffrey, *Exeter 1540–1640*: ibid. (10 Apr. 1959), 516.

E. C. Williams, *Bess of Hardwick*: ibid. (8 May 1959), 668.

G. Huxley, *Endymion Porter: The Life of a Courtier, 1587–1649*: ibid. (22 May 1959), 740–1.

K. M. Briggs, *The Anatomy of Puck*: ibid. (29 May 1959), 784.

R. C. Bald, *Donne and the Drurys*: ibid. (19 June 1959), 900.

P. M. Handover, *The Second Cecil: The Rise to Power, 1563–1604*, of Sir Robert Cecil: ibid. (10 July 1959), 43.

A. G. Dickens, *Lollards and Protestants in the Diocese of York 1509–1558*: ibid. (31 July 1959), 144–5.

M. Lee, Jr., *John Maitland of Thirlestone and the Foundation of the Stewart Despotism in Scotland*: ibid. (21 Aug. 1959), 234.

The Life of Girolamo Savonarola by Roberto Ridolfi, trans. C. Grayson: ibid. (28 Aug. 1959), 277.

R. Pilkington, *Robert Boyle: Father of Chemistry:* ibid. (11 Sept. 1959), 342.

J. B. Black, *The Reign of Elizabeth 1558–1603*: ibid. (18 Sept. 1959), 381.

A. L. Rowse, *The Elizabethans and America*: ibid. (16 Oct. 1959), 528–9.

G. Mattingly, *The Defeat of the Spanish Armada*: ibid. (23 Oct. 1959), 564–5.

The Campden Wonder, ed. Sir G. Clark: ibid. (27 Nov. 1959), 776.

N. O. Brown, *Life against Death*, and E. H. Erikson, *Young man Luther*: ibid. (4 Dec. 1959), 831.

Sir L. Namier, *Charles Townshend: His Character and Career*: ibid. (11 Dec. 1959), 884.

1960

'The Start of a Great Myth: The Restoration of Charles II', *Guardian* (25 May 1960), 8.

'Republicanism After the Restoration', *New Left Rev.* iii. 46–51.

Communication [with R. Hilton]: on the XIth International Congress of Historical Sciences, *P. and P.* 18. 4–5.

Reviews:

C. Robbins, *The Eighteenth-Century Commonwealthman*: *Commentary*, xxix. 90–2.

John Eachard, *Mr Hobbs's State of Nature Considered in a Dialogue between Philautus and Timothy*, ed. P. Ure: *Durham Univ. Journ.* lii. 134–5.

Samuel Daniel, *The Civil Wars*, ed. L. Michel: *Essays in Criticism*, x. 207–11.

W. M. Mitchell, *The Rise of the Revolutionary Party in the English House of Commons 1603–29*: *P. and P.* 18. 111–12.

A. G. Dickens, *Thomas Cromwell and the English Reformation*: *Sci. and Soc.* xxiv. 364–7.

I. Deutscher, *The Prophet Unarmed. Trotsky, 1921–1929*: *Soviet Studies*, xi. 317–23.

The Diary of John Evelyn, ed. E. S. de Beer: *Spectator* (8 Jan. 1960), 47–8.

C. V. Wedgwood, *Truth and Opinion: Historical Essays*, and *Poetry and Politics under the Stuarts*: ibid. (19 Feb. 1960), 259.

C. Read, *Lord Burghley and Queen Elizabeth*: ibid. (4 Mar. 1960), 326.

H. Pearson, *Charles II*: ibid. (6 May 1960), 670–1.

H. Chapman, *Two Tudor Portraits*: ibid. (27 May 1960), 777–8.

R. Unwin, *The Defeat of John Hawkins*, and P. K. Kemp and C. Lloyd, *The Brethren of the Coast*: ibid. (3 June 1960), 807–8.

M. Irwin, *That Great Lucifer: A Portrait of Sir Walter Raleigh*: ibid. (24 June 1960), 922.

G. Donaldson, *The Scottish Reformation 1560*: ibid. (15 July 1960), 107–8.

F. Bengtsson, *The Life of Charles XII, King of Sweden, 1697–1718*: ibid. (22 July 1960), 139.

The Royal Society: Its Origins and Founders, ed. Sir H. Hartley, and *History of the Royal Society*, by Thomas Sprat, ed. J. I. Cope and H. W. Jones: ibid. (29 July 1960), 190.

Locke's Two Treatises of Government, ed. P. Laslett: ibid. (9 Sept. 1960), 379.

J. G. Crowther, *Founders of British Science*: ibid. (14 Oct. 1960), 570–1.

W. K. Jordan, *The Charities of London, 1480–1660*: ibid. (18 Nov. 1960), 789.

Sir A. Bryant, *Restoration England*: ibid. (25 Nov. 1960), 867.

G. R. Cragg, *The Church and the Age of Reason (1648–1789)*: ibid. (9 Dec. 1960), 961–2.

The Tudor Constitution: Documents and Commentary, ed. G. R. Elton: ibid. (30 Dec. 1960), 1052.

G. F. Nuttall, *The Welsh Saints, 1640–1660*: *Welsh Hist. Rev.* i. 99–100.

1961

The Century of Revolution, 1603–1714 (Edinburgh: Nelson).

Ed., H. N. Brailsford, *The Levellers and the English Revolution* (Cresset Press).

'Protestantism and the Rise of Capitalism' in *Essays in the Economic and Social History of Tudor and Stuart England In Honour of R. H. Tawney,* ed. F. J. Fisher (Cambridge: C.U.P.), 15–39. [Reprinted in *Change and Continuity* (1974).]

'Richard Pares', *P. and P.* 20. 4–5.

Reviews:

Suffolk and the Great Rebellion 1640–1660, ed. A. Everitt: *EcHR* new ser. xiv. 148–9.

Sredniye Veka (The Middle Ages), xvii and xviii: ibid. 385–6.

Z. I. Roginsky, *Poyezda Gontsa Gerasima Semyonovicha Dokhturova v Angliyu v 1645–1646 gg*: *EHR* lxxvi. 332–4.

Conflict in Stuart England: Essays in Honour of Wallace Notestein, ed. W. A. Aiken and B. D. Henning: ibid. 681–2.

R. A. Marchant, *The Puritans and the Church Courts in the Diocese of York, 1560–1642*: *History*, new ser. xlvi. 53–4.

Sir George Clark, *Three Aspects of Stuart England*: ibid. 142–3.

W. B. Gallie, *A New University: A. D. Lindsay and the Keele Experiment*: *Oxford Mag.* (16 Feb. 1961), 245–7.

R. Garner, *Henry Vaughan, Experience and the Tradition*: *Sci. and Soc.* xxv. 280–3.

Elizabethan Government and Society: Essays Presented to Sir John Neale, ed. S. T. Bindoff, J. Hurstfield, and C. H. Williams: *Spectator* (3 Feb. 1961), 158.

G. E. Aylmer, *The King's Servants: The Civil Service of Charles I, 1625–42*: ibid. (3 Mar. 1961), 303–4.

The Autobiography of Thomas Whythorne, ed. J. Osborne: ibid. (24 Mar. 1961), 420.

V. Pearl, *London and the Outbreak of the Puritan Revolution*: ibid. (21 Apr. 1961), 572.

A. J. Toynbee, *A Study of History*, vol. xii: *Reconsiderations*: ibid. (12 May 1961), 685–6.

The Ascendancy of France, 1648–88, ed. F. L. Carsten: ibid. (23 June 1961), 924.

A. Woolrych, *Battles of the English Civil War*: ibid. (27 Oct. 1961), 591–2.

C. V. Wedgwood, *Thomas Wentworth, First Earl of Strafford, 1593–1641*: ibid. (24 Nov. 1961), 780–1.

1962

'Intellectual Origins of the English Revolution':

'1. Science in Seventeenth-Century London', *Listener* (31 May 1962), 943–6.

'2. Emergence of the Scientific Method', ibid. (7 June 1962), 983–6.

'3. Sir Walter Raleigh and History', ibid. (14 June 1962), 1023–6.
'4. Raleigh and the Revolutionaries', ibid. (21 June 1962), 1066–8.
'5. Sir Edward Coke', ibid. (28 June 1962), 1107–9.
'6. A Single Revolution', ibid. (5 July 1962), 17–19.
'A. B. Rodger', *Balliol Coll. Record* (1962), 35–7.

Communication: on the Anglo-Dutch Historical Conference 1962, *P. and P.* 23. 84.

Reviews:

T. G. Barnes, *Somerset, 1625–40*: *EcHR* new ser. xv. 156–8.

London 1645–1646 gg. ed. Z. I. Roginsky: *EHR* lxxvii. 373–4.

K. Samuelsson, *Religion and Economic Action*, ed. D. C. Coleman: ibid. 765–6.

H. F. Kearney, *The Eleven Years 'Tyranny' of Charles I*: *P. and P.* 22. 94.

The Complete Prose Works of John Milton, ii: *1643–8*, ed. E. Sirluck: *Sci. and Soc.* xxvi. 248–50.

C. H. and K. George, *The Protestant Mind of the English Reformation, 1570–1640*: ibid. 501–3.

W. H. G. Armytage, *Heavens Below: Utopian Experiments in England 1560–1960*: *Spectator* (5 Jan. 1962), 19–20.

The Memoirs of James II: His Campaigns as Duke of York, 1652–1660, ed. A. Lytton Sells: ibid. (9 Mar. 1962), 311.

A. L. Rowse, *Raleigh and the Throckmortons*: ibid. (13 Apr. 1962), 484.

F. Smith Fussner, *The Historical Revolution, 1580–1640*: ibid. (6 July 1962), 28.

N. L. Williams, *Sir Walter Raleigh*: ibid. (21 Sept. 1962), 406.

1963

'Propagating the Gospel' in *Historical Essays, 1600–1750, Presented to David Ogg*, ed. H. E. Bell and R. L. Ollard (Black), 35–59. [Revised in *Change and Continuity* (1974).]

'The Politics of John Milton', *Listener* (12 Sept. 1963), 383–5.

'Puritans and "the Dark Corners of the Land" ', *TRHS* 5th ser. xiii. 77–102. [Revised in *Change and Continuity* (1974).]

[with E. J. Hobsbawm and J. Thirsk]: Communication: on the Anglo-Russian Conference 1963, *P. and P.* 26. 4.

Reviews:

J. R. Jones, *The First Whigs: the Politics of the Exclusion Crisis, 1678–1683*: *Durham Univ. Journ.* lv. 32–3.

The Diurnal of Thomas Rugg, 1659–1661, ed. W. L. Sachse: *EHR* lxxviii. 175–6.

The Diary of William Lawrence, ed. G. E. Aylmer: ibid. 176–7.

J. Frank, *The Beginnings of the English Newspaper, 1620–1660*: *EHR* lxxviii. 780–1.

P. A. Welsby, *George Abbott: the Unwanted Archbishop, 1562–1633*: *History*, new ser. xlviii. 215–16.

J. H. Parry, *The Age of Reconnaissance*: *New Statesman* (24 May 1963), 798–800.

Historical Studies IV, ed. G. A. Hayes-McCoy: ibid. (9 Aug. 1963), 172–4.

G. R. Elton, *Reformation Europe*: ibid. (18 Oct. 1963), 529–30.

P. Geyl, *Encounters in History*: ibid. (1 Nov. 1963), 620–1.

Prescott's Histories: The Rise and Decline of the Spanish Empire, ed. I. Blacker: ibid. (27 Dec. 1963), 945–6.

Advice to a Son: Precepts of Lord Burghley, Sir Walter Raleigh and Francis Osborne, ed. L. B. Wright: *N. and Q.* new ser. x. 318–19.

C. B. Macpherson, *The Political Theory of Possessive Individualism: Hobbes to Locke*: *P. and P.* 24. 86–9.

J. A. van Dorsten, *Thomas Basson, 1555–1613: English Printer at Leiden*, and id. *Poets, Patrons and Professors: Sir Philip Sidney, Daniel Rogers and the Leiden Humanists*; A. G. H. Bachrach, *Sir Constantine Huygens and Britain, 1596–1687*, vol. i: ibid. xxv. 90–2.

A. Simpson, *The Wealth of the Gentry, 1540–1660: East Anglia Studies*: *Sci. and Soc.* xxvii. 120–1.

Sir L. Namier, *England in the Age of the American Revolution* (2nd edn.): ibid. 497–9.

[Unsigned] E. P. Thompson, *The Making of the English Working Class*: *TLS* (12 Dec. 1963), 1021–3.

1964

Society and Puritanism in Pre-Revolutionary England (Secker and Warburg). [Revised edn. with new Preface: Panther, 1969.]

'Seventeenth-Century English Society and Sabbatarianism' in *Britain and the Netherlands II*, ed. J. S. Bromley and E. H. Kossmann (Groningen: J. B. Wolters), 84–108. [Revised as ch. v of *Society and Puritanism* (1964).]

'William Harvey and the Idea of Monarchy', *P. and P.* 27. 54–72.

'Puritanism, Capitalism and the Scientific Revolution' (Debate), *P. and P.* 29. 88–97.

Reviews:

Acts of the Privy Council of England, 1630 June–1631 June, ed. T. A. Penfold: *EcHR* new ser. xvii. 410–11.

R. Peters, *Oculus Episcopi: Administration in the Archdeaconry of St. Albans, 1580–1625*: *History*, new ser. xlix. 72.

Luis Vaz de Camoens, *The Lusiads*, ed. G. Bullough: *New Statesman* (17 Jan. 1964), 89.

O. Chadwick, *The Reformation*, and S. Neill, *A History of Christian Missions*: ibid. (3 Apr. 1964), 530–1.

M. Ashley, *Life in Stuart England*, and R. J. White, *Life in Regency England*: ibid. (8 May 1964), 734–5.

N. Williams, *Thomas Howard, Fourth Duke of Norfolk*, M. Dewar, *Sir Thomas Smith*, and J. Buxton, *Elizabethan Taste*: ibid. (26 June 1964), 998–9.

V. Cronin, *Louis XIV*: ibid. (7 Aug. 1964), 185.

C. V. Wedgwood, *The Trial of Charles I*: ibid. (28 Aug. 1964), 283–4.

K. R. Andrews, *Elizabethan Privateering*: ibid. (16 Oct. 1964), 580.

D. Duran, *The Aztecs*, ed. D. Heyden and F. Horcasitas, and *The Conquistadors*, ed. P. de Fuentes: ibid. (20 Nov. 1964), 796–7.

S. Lehmberg, *Sir Walter Mildmay and Tudor Government*, P. Caraman, *Henry Garnet and the Gunpowder Plot*, A. Lee, *The Son of Leicester*, and P. Barbour, *The Three Worlds of Captain John Smith*: ibid. (4 Dec. 1964), 889–90.

F. Raab, *The English Face of Machiavelli*: ibid. (25 Dec. 1964), 998–9.

S. I. Mintz, *The Hunting of Leviathan: Seventeenth-Century Reactions to the Materialism and Moral Philosophy of Thomas Hobbes*: *Sci. and Soc.* xxviii. 240–2.

A. Ogle, *The Tragedy of the Lollards' Tower*; N. O. Brown, *Life Against Death*, and C. B. Macpherson, *The Political Theory of Possessive Individualism: Twentieth Century*, clxxii. 148–9.

Herbert Correspondence: the Sixteenth and Seventeenth-Century Letters of the Herberts of Chirbury, ed. W. J. Smith: *Welsh Hist. Rev.* ii. 192–4.

1965

Intellectual Origins of the English Revolution (Oxford: Clarendon P.).

Introduction to *Crisis in Europe, 1560–1660. Essays from Past and Present*, ed. T. Aston (Routledge), 1–3.

'William Harvey (No Parliamentarian, No Heretic) and the Idea of Monarchy', *P. and P.* 31. 97–103.

'Science, Religion and Society in the Sixteenth and Seventeenth Centuries' (Debate), ibid. 32. 110–12.

'Colonel John Hutchinson, 1615–1664: A Tercentenary Tribute', *Trans. Thoroton Soc.* lxix. 79–87.

Reviews:

   C. W. Chalklin, *Seventeenth-Century Kent. A Social and Economic History*: *EcHR* new ser. xviii. 648–9.

   J. R. Powell, *The Navy in the English Civil War*: *EHR* lxxx. 171–2.

   W. M. Lamont, *Marginal Prynne, 1600–1669*: ibid. 397–8.

   The Letter Book of Sir Samuel Luke, 1644–1645, ed. H. G. Tibbutt: ibid. 594–6.

   P. Geyl, *History of the Low Countries: Episodes and Problems*: *New Statesman* (7 Feb. 1965), 204.

   The Itinerary of John Leland, ed. L. T. Smith: ibid. (12 Mar. 1965), 407–8.

   W. McNeill, *The Rise of the West* and *Europe's Steppe Frontier*: ibid. (16 Apr. 1965), 614.

   L. Stone, *The Crisis of the Aristocracy*: ibid. (21 May 1965), 803–4.

   H. Holborn, *A History of Modern Germany*, and C. Wilson, *England's Apprenticeship*: ibid. (3 Sept. 1965), 325–6.

1966

'The Many-Headed Monster in Late Tudor and Early Stuart Political Thinking' in *From the Renaissance to the Counter-Reformation. Essays in*

Honour of Garrett Mattingly, ed. C. H. Carter (Jonathan Cape), 296–324. [Revised in *Change and Continuity* (1974).]

'The Master's Letter', *Balliol College Record*, 4–7 [and annually thereafter].

Reviews:

P. Legouis, *Andrew Marvell. Poet, Puritan, Patriot*: *EHR* lxxxi. 596.

M. H. Armstrong Davison, *The Casket Letters*, and G. Donaldson, *Scotland: James V–James VII*: *New Statesman* (21 Jan. 1966), 93–4.

C. R. Boxer, *The Dutch Seaborne Empire*, and J. H. Parry, *The Spanish Seaborne Empire*: ibid. (11 Mar. 1966), 340–2.

J. Simon, *Education and Society in Tudor England*: ibid. (29 Apr. 1966), 619–70.

N. Robb, *William of Orange*, vol. ii, and S. B. Baxter, *William III*: ibid. (17 June 1966), 898.

M. Walzer, *The Revolution of the Saints*: ibid. (22 July 1966), 135.

1967

Reformation to Industrial Revolution. A Social and Economic History of Britain, 1530–1780 (Weidenfeld and Nicolson). [Revised edn. Pelican, 1969.]

'History and Denominational History', *Baptist Qtly.* new ser. xxii. 65–71.

'Marx's Virtues', *Listener* (10 Aug. 1967), 172–3.

'Pottage for Freeborn Englishmen: Attitudes to Wage Labour in the Sixteenth and Seventeenth Centuries' in *Socialism, Capitalism and Economic Growth. Essays Presented to Maurice Dobb*, ed. C. H. Feinstein (Cambridge: C.U.P.), 338–50. [Revised in *Change and Continuity* (1974).]

'Sir Isaac Newton and His Society', *Texas Qtly.* x. 30–51. [Revised in *Change and Continuity* (1974).]

[with Bridget Hill], 'Catherine Macaulay and the Seventeenth Century', *Welsh Hist. Rev.* iii. 381–402.

Reviews:

A. M. Everitt, *The Community of Kent and the Great Rebellion*: *EcHR* new ser. xx. 167–9.

P. Collinson, *The Elizabethan Puritan Movement*: ibid. 389–91.

R. Howell, *Newcastle upon Tyne and the Puritan Revolution. A Study of the Civil War in North England*: ibid. 557–8.

Ship Money Papers and Richard Grenville's Note-Book, ed. C. G. Bonsey and J. G. Jenkins: *EHR* lxxxii. 166–7.

The Correspondence of Henry Oldenburg, vol. I: *1641–1662*, ed. A. R. and M. B. Hall with E. Reichmann: ibid. 795–7.

P. Laslett, *The World We Have Lost*: *History and Theory*, vi. 117–27. [Printed with additional material in *Change and Continuity* (1974).]

I. Roots, *The Great Rebellion*: *New Statesman* (3 Feb. 1967), 154–6.

The Chronicle and Political Papers of King Edward VI, ed. W. K. Jordan; D. T. Witcombe, *Charles II and the Cavalier House of Commons*, and H. Chapman, *Privileged Persons*: ibid. (5 May 1967), 624–5.

The Shorter Poems of Ralph Knevet: A Critical Edition, ed. A. M. Charles: *N. and Q.* new ser. xiv. 113–14.

The Journal of the Friends' Historical Society, li(2): ibid. 403.

1968

'The Intellectual Origins of the Royal Society—London or Oxford?', *Royal Soc. Notes and Records*, xxiii. 144–56.

Reviews:

M. A. Barg, *Narodnyie Nizy v. Angliyskoy Burzhuaznoy Revelyutsii XVII veka, Dvizhenie i ideologiyoi istinnykh Levellerov*: *Agric. Hist. Rev.* xvi. 75–7.

H. R. Trevor-Roper, *Religion, the Reformation and Social Change*: *EcHR* new ser. xxi. 183–5.

Privy Council Registers . . . in facsimile, vol. i: *June 1631–31 October 1637*, vol. ii: *1 November–28 February 1638*: ibid. 394–5.

The Stuart Constitution: Documents and Commentary, ed. J. P. Kenyon: *EHR* lxxxiii. 125–7.

The Correspondence of Henry Oldenburg, ii: *1663–1665* and iii: *1666–1667*, ed. A. R. and M. B. Hall: ibid. 176–7.

Elias Ashmole (1617–1692). His Autobiographical and Historical Notes, His Correspondence, and Other Contemporary Sources Relating to His Life and Work, ed. C. H. Josten: ibid. 355–7.

P. G. Rogers, *The Fifth Monarchy Men*: ibid. 397.

M. A. Barg, *The Lower Orders in the English Bourgeois Revolution*: *P. and P.* 41. 213.

R. B. Knox, *James Ussher, Archbishop of Armagh*: *Welsh Hist. Rev.* iv. 191–2.

1969

'Plebeian Irreligion in 17th Century England' in *Studien über die Revolution*, ed. M. Kossok (Berlin, 1969).

' "Reason" and "Reasonableness" in Seventeenth-Century England', *British Journ. of Sociology*, xx. 235–52. [Revised in *Change and Continuity* (1974).]

Reviews:

J. Dunn, *The Political Thought of John Locke*, and *Two English Republican Tracts*, ed. C. Robbins: *Durham Univ. Journ.* lxii. 127–30.

H. A. Lloyd, *The Gentry of South-West Wales, 1540–1640*: *EcHR* new ser. xxii. 128–9.

A Calendar of Southampton Apprenticeship Registers, 1609–1740, ed. A. L. Merson: *EHR* lxxxiv. 178.

J. M. Wallace, *Destiny His Choice: the Loyalism of Andrew Marvell*: ibid. 613.

S. Butler, *Hudibras*, ed. J. Wilders: *Essays in Criticism*, xix. 78–84.

F. Braudel, *Civilisation Matérielle et Capitalisme (XVᵉ–XVIIIᵉ siècle)*, vol. i: *History and Theory*, viii. 301–3.

W. M. Lamont, *Godly Rule: Politics and Religion, 1603–60*: *New Statesman* (12 Dec. 1969), 868–9.

Journal of the Friends' Historical Society, li: *N. and Q.* new ser. xvi. 2.
The Genealogists' Magazine, xvi(2): ibid. 364.
R. Overton, *Mans Mortalitie*, ed. H. Fisch: ibid. 389–90.

1970

God's Englishman. Oliver Cromwell and the English Revolution (Weidenfeld and Nicolson). [Revised edn. Pelican, 1972.]

Reviews:

Sredniye Veka Nº32: *EcHR* new ser. xxiii. 594.
The Correspondence of Henry Oldenburg, vol. IV: *December 1667–January 1668*, ed. A. R. and M. B. Hall: *EHR* lxxxv. 615–16.
P. W. Thomas, *Sir John Berkenhead, 1617–1679: a Royalist Career in Politics and Polemics*: *Essays in Criticism*, xx. 243–51.
P. Zagorin, *The Court and the Country*: *The Nation*, ccx. 698–700.
C. S. Hensley, *The Later Career of George Wither*: *N. and Q.* new ser. xvii. 267–8.
T. J. Pickvance, *George Fox and the Purefeys*: ibid. 402.
A. A. Garner, *Colonel Edward King*: ibid. 435.
J. T. Cliffe, *The Yorkshire Gentry from the Reformation to the Civil War*: *Oxford Mag.* (16 Oct. 1970), 11–12.

1971

Antichrist in Seventeenth-Century England (O.U.P.).

'Alexander Dunlop Lindsay', *Dictionary of National Biography: 1951–1960*, ed. E. T. Williams and H. M. Palmer (O.U.P.), 641–4.

[with D. Pennington], 'Science and Society' and 'Cromwell', *Sussex Tapes*: record H 3.

Reviews:

R. A. Marchant, *The Church Under the Law: Justice, Administration and Discipline in the Diocese of York, 1560–1640*: *EHR* lxxxvi. 842–3.
The Genealogists' Magazine, xvi(7): *N. and Q.* new ser. xviii. 2.
P. S. Seaver, *The Puritan Lectureships: The Politics of Religious Dissent 1560–1662*, and A. Macfarlane, *The Family Life of Ralph Josselin*: *Renaissance Qtly.* xxiv. 410–14.

1972

The World Turned Upside Down (Maurice Temple Smith). [Revised edn. Pelican, 1975.]

'Partial Historians and Total History', *TLS* (24 Nov. 1972), 1431–2.

'The Radical Critics of Oxford and Cambridge in the 1650s' in *Universities in Politics*, ed. J. W. Baldwin and R. Goldthwaite (Baltimore: John Hopkins U.P.). [Revised in *Change and Continuity* (1974).]

Reviews:

M. Cole, *The Life of G. D. H. Cole: Balliol Coll. Rec.* (1972), 28–30.

B. S. Capp, *The Fifth Monarchy Men: Cambridge Rev.* xciv. 32–5.

Seventeenth-Century Economic Documents, ed. J. Thirsk and J. P. Cooper: *EcHR* new ser. xxv. 706–7.

A. Everitt, *Change in the Provinces: the Seventeenth Century: EHR* lxxxvii. 188–9.

Puritans, the Millennium and the Future of Israel: Puritan Eschatology 1600 to 1660, ed. P. Toon: ibid. 415–16.

M. A. Judson, *The Political Thought of Sir Henry Vane the Younger:* ibid. 416.

G. R. Elton, *Policy and Police: The Enforcement of the Reformation in the Age of Thomas Cromwell: Guardian* (23 Mar. 1972), 17.

W. R. Prest, *The Inns of Court under Elizabeth I and the Early Stuarts, 1590–1640: History of Education Qtly.* xii. 543–50. [Revised in *Change and Continuity* (1974).]

Samuel Hartlib and the Advancement of Learning, ed. C. Webster: *N. and Q.* new ser. xix. 399–400.

A. L. Rowse, *The Elizabethan Renaissance: the Cultural Achievement: Oxford Mag.* (3 Nov. 1972), 10–11.

K. Thomas, *Religion and the Decline of Magic: Welsh Hist. Rev.* vi. 105–8.

1973

Ed., *Winstanley. The Law of Freedom and other Writings* (Harmondsworth: Penguin Books).

'Christopher Hill and Lawrence Stone discuss with Peter Burke the English Revolution of the 17th Century', *Listener* (4 Oct. 1973), 448–51.

'The Levellers' in *People for the People,* ed. D. Rubinstein (Ithaca Press), 30–6.

Reviews:

A. G. Debus, *Science and Education in the Seventeenth Century: EHR* lxxxviii. 185.

V. A. Rowe, *Sir Henry Vane the Younger: A Study in Political and Administrative History:* ibid. 186.

The Correspondence of Henry Oldenburg, v: *1668–9;* vi: *1669–70;* vii: *1670–1;* viii: *1671–2,* ed. A. R. and M. B. Hall: ibid. 383–5.

F. A. Yates, *The Rosicrucian Enlightenment: New York Rev. of Books* (4 Oct. 1973), 23–4.

The Correspondence of John Morris with Johannes de Laet (1634–1649), ed. J. A. F. Bekkers: *N. and Q.* new ser. xx. 195.

K. L. Carroll, *John Perrot: Early Quaker Schismatic:* ibid. 196.

The English Essays of Edward Gibbon, ed. P. B. Craddock: *Oxford Mag.* (1 June 1973), 12.

1974

Change and Continuity in Seventeenth-Century England (Weidenfeld and Nicolson).

Irreligion in the 'Puritan' Revolution (The Barnett Shine Foundation Lecture, Queen Mary College, London. Dept. of Economics).

'John Pym', *Encyclopaedia Britannica: Macropaedia*, xv. 312–13.

'Milton the Radical', *TLS* (29 Nov. 1974), 1330–2.

Reviews:

R. Terrill, *R. H. Tawney and His Times: Socialism as Fellowship*: *Balliol Coll. Rec.* (1974), 28–32.

J. N. Wise, *Sir Thomas Browne's Religio Medici and two Seventeenth-Century critics*: *EHR* lxxxix. 669.

J. Miller, *Popery and Politics in England 1660–1688*: ibid. 894–5. *The Origins of the English Civil War*, ed. C. Russell: *History* new ser. lix. 470–1.

B. Worden, *The Rump Parliament 1648–1653*: *New Statesman* (22 Mar. 1974), 410–12.

E. Broxap, *The Great Civil War in Lancashire 1642–1651*, new edition, intro. by R. N. Dore, and D. Underdown, *Somerset in the Civil War and Interregnum*: ibid. (2 Aug. 1974), 159–60.

R. C. Tucker, *Stalin as Revolutionary 1879–1929*, and A. B. Ulam, *Stalin: The Man and His Era*: *New York Rev. of Books* (24 Jan. 1974), 9–13. [Reply to letters critical of review, ibid. (21 Mar. 1974), 41–2.]

J. H. Parry, *The Discovery of the Sea*, D. B. Quinn, *England and the Discovery of America 1481–1620*, S. E. Morison, *The European Discovery of America: The Southern Voyages 1492–1616*, M. Foss, *Undreamed Shores: England's Wasted Empire in America*: ibid. (14 Nov. 1974), 17–21.

The Journal of the Friends' Historical Society, liii: *N. and Q.* new ser. xxi. 82–3.

I. Waters, *Henry Marten and the Long Parliament*: ibid. 403.

O. C. Watkins, *The Puritan Experience*: ibid. 434.

1975

Forward to *Freedom in Arms: A Selection of Leveller Writings*, ed. A. L. Morton (Lawrence and Wishart), 12–13.

[with D. Pennington], 'Seventeenth-Century England: Change and Revolution', *Audio Learning Ltd.*, cassette: English History No. 4.

Letter: 'Milton the Radical' *TLS* (24 Jan. 1975), 84.

Letter: 'The Burden of Proof', ibid. (7 Nov. 1975), 1333.

Reviews:

F. A. Yates, *Astraea: The Imperial Theme in the Sixteenth Century*: *La Cultura*, xiii. 244–6.

C. Holmes, *The Eastern Association in the English Civil War*: *Durham Univ. Journ.* new. ser. xxxvii. 87–8.

Tai Liu, *Discord in Zion: The Puritan Divines and the Puritan Revolution*: *History*, new ser. lx. 298.

The University in Society, ed. L. Stone: *History of Education Qtly.* xv. 93–5.

M. Spufford, *Contrasting Communities: English Villages in the Sixteenth and Seventeenth Centuries*: *Literature and History*, i. 104–6.

E. Rose, *Cases of Conscience: Alternatives open to Recusants and Puritans under Elizabeth I and James I*: *New Blackfriars* lvi. 190.

R. Spalding, *The Improbable Puritan: A Life of Bulstrode Whitlocke 1605–75*: *New Statesman* (24 Jan. 1975), 114–15.

M. van Cleave Alexander, *Charles I's Lord Treasurer: Sir Richard Weston, Earl of Portland (1577–1635)*: ibid. (15 Aug. 1975), 202.

C. Webster, *The Great Instauration: Science, Medicine and Reform 1626–1660*: ibid. (14 Nov. 1975), 613–14.

Winstanley, a film directed by K. Brownlow and A. Mollo: *P. and P.* 69. 132.

1976

'La Revolución Inglesa', *Historia*, 16. i. 100–9.

[with Michael Shepherd], 'The Case of Arise Evans: a historico-psychiatric study', *Psychological Medicine*, vi. 351–8.

Reviews:

The Records of a Church of Christ in Bristol 1640–1687, ed. R. Hayden: *EHR* xci. 426.

The Correspondence of Henry Oldenburg, ix: *1672–3*; x: *1673–4*, ed. A. R. and M. B. Hall: ibid. 645–6.

J. Bossy, *The English Catholic Community 1570–1850*: *New Statesman* (2 Apr. 1976), 436–7.

A. C. Dobbins, *Milton and the Book of Revelation*: *English*, xxv. 38–42.

First Images of America: The Impact of the New World on the Old, ed. F. Chiappelli and H. Koning, *Columbus: His Enterprise*: *New York Rev. of Books* (25 Nov. 1976), 43–6.

L. Miller, *John Milton Among the Polygamophiles*: *N. and Q.* new ser. xxiii. 27–8.

A. Cowley, *The Civil War*, ed. A. Pritchard: ibid. 192.

J. A. Wittreich, Jr., *Angel of Apocalypse: Blake's Idea of Milton*: ibid. 461–2.

The Diary of Sir Simonds D'Ewes 1622–1624, ed. E. Bourcier: ibid. 574–5.

H. M. Richmond, *The Christian Revolutionary: John Milton*: *Renaissance Qtly.* xxix. 144–5.

B. Manning, *The English People and the English Revolution*: *Spectator* (3 July 1976), 21–2.

P. Burke, *Venice and Amsterdam: a study of seventeenth-century élites*: *Urban History Yearbook* (1976), 59–60.

1977

Milton and the English Revolution (Faber).

'Occasional Conformity' in *Reformation, Conformity and Dissent: Essays in Honour of Geoffrey Nuttall*, ed. R. B. Knox, (Epworth P.), 199–220.

'Inglaterra: Puritanos en familia', *Historia*, 16. ii. 105–15.

'Forerunners of Socialism in the Seventeenth-Century English Revolution', *Marxism Today*, xxi. 270–6.

'John Morris', *P. and P.* 75. 3–4.

Letter: on disease and the New World, *New York Rev. of Books* (17 Feb. 1977), 48.

Reviews:

W. R. Foster, *The Church Before the Covenants: the Church of Scotland 1596–1638*: *EHR* xcii. 435–6.

J. Bunyan, *The Doctrine of Law and Grace Unfolded* and *I will pray with the Spirit*, ed. R. L. Greaves: ibid. 438–9.

M. J. Lasky, *Utopia and Revolution*: *Guardian* (27 Jan. 1977), 16.

J. S. Bromley and E. H. Kossmann, eds. *Britain and the Netherlands*, v: *Some Political Mythologies: Literature and History*, 5. 113–14.

S. E. Ozment, *The Reformation in the Cities: The Appeal of Protestantism to Sixteenth-Century Germany and Switzerland*: ibid. 109–10.

M. McKeon, *Politics and Poetry in Restoration England: The Case of Dryden's Annus Mirabilis*: ibid. vi. 262–4.

W. G. Hoskins, *The Age of Plunder: The England of Henry VIII 1500–1547*: *New Statesman* (7 Jan. 1977), 24–5.

G. Mann, *Wallenstein: A Life*: *New York Rev. of Books* (17 Mar. 1977), 33–5.

R. Howell, Jr., *Cromwell*: ibid. (9 June 1977), 39–40.

M. F. Alvarez, *Charles V: Elected Emperor and Hereditary Ruler*; G. Dethan, *The Young Mazarin*; P. Pierson, *Philip II of Spain*, and R. Strong, *The Cult of Elizabeth: Elizabethan Portraiture and Pageantry*: ibid. (8 Dec. 1977), 42–5.

Der Deutsche Bauernkrieg 1524–1526, ed. H.-U. Wehler: *Social History*, 4. 530–1.

Index

Index 415

poverty, 52, 59, 60, 65. *See also* poor
Powell, Vavasor, 235, 236, 238, 244, 245, 247, 248, 249, 250, 254, 277
preachers, 107, 239, 244, 256, 277. *See also* clergy
predestination; predestinarianism, 81, 336. *See also* Calvinism
Presbyterians; presbyterianism, 101, 103, 107, 112, 121, 125, 147–60, 195–6, 197, 217, 218, 220, 276–81
Price, John, 236, 253
Pride, Col. Thomas, 227
Prideaux, Sir Edmund, 194, 227, 293, 303
Pride's Purge, 121, 133, 227, 301
primogeniture, 359. *See also* younger sons
Privy Council; Privy Councillors, 104, 110, 134, 163, 167, 168, 177, 178, 206, 232
professions, 355, 372–7
Propagation of the Gospel: in England, 241, 276; in Wales, 234–56; in Ireland, 276
prostitution, *see* brothels
Protestant cause, 96, 112
Protestants, 261; and marriage, 259. *See also* Reformers
Protestant Union, 314
Protestation, 169, 182, 265
Prussia, 313
Prynne, William, 64, 126, 271
Ptolemy, 78
Pullar, Isaac, 193
Puritans, Puritanism: definition, 73–4, 81, 333; and adultery, 258, 271, 273, 274; and alehouses, 47, 53, 59, 60, 67, 69; and the church, 61; and Jansenism, 333, 334, 341, 353–4; and law, 95; and marriage, 259 n.; and poor-relief, 201–19; and radicalism, 159–60; and science, 74, 77, 78, 79; and the Thirty Years War, 339; in Wales, 233, 249; individuals, 97, 142, 145, 148, 204, 215, 217. *See also* Fifth Monarchists, Independents, Presbyterians, sectaries, separatists
Pye, Sir Robert, 164, 165, 166, 167, 172, 185
Pym, John, 118, 120, 123, 131, 133–4, 164–5, 177–80, 182, 184, 188, 190
Pyne, John, 201, 203, 205

Quakers, 126, 128, 224, 310, 319

Quarter Sessions, 206, 266. *See also* alehouses, licensing of
Quernes, 334
Quesnel, Pasquier, 334, 346, 348

Raab, Felix, 34
Raadt, Alhardt de, 319
Radcliffe, Sir Ralph, 359–60
radicalism, 186–206; religious, 65, 187, 193. *See also* people, petitions, Puritans
Radnorshire, 255
Rainsborough, Thomas, 40
Ralegh, Sir Walter, 23 n., 91
Ramus, Peter; Ramism, 95–8, 102, 106, 107, 109, 117
Ranters, 41, 67, 277, 278
Rathborne, Aaron, 76
Rawdon, Marmaduke, 367, 371
Rawley, William, 92
Rawlidge, Richard, 47
Recognition, *see* Cromwell, Richard
recusants, *see* Catholics, Roman
Reformatio Legum Ecclesiasticarum, 264
reformation of manners, 72 n.; societies for, 205, 276, 282
Reformers, and sexual offences, 259, 270
republicanism; republicans, 67, 120, 132–4, 136–8, 202, 204, 251, 285, 300. *See also* Commonwealthsmen
Restoration, *see* Charles II
Richard II, 307
Richards, Dr. T., 236 n., 241
Richardson, Dr. Edward, 317, 330, 332
Richelieu, Armand-Jean du Plessis, duc de, Cardinal, 334, 338, 339, 340
Richérism, 354
Riddens, Franciscus, 319
Ridley, Mark, 76, 85
rigorists, rigorism, 351, 353
rites de passage, 62
Roberts, Gabriel, 368
Rochester, John Wilmot, 2nd Earl, 36 n.
Roe, Sir Thomas, 82
Rogers, Francis, 370
Romans; Rome, 268, 282, 303, 319
Root and Branch Petition, 264
Rossiter, Horace, 371
Rothe, Hans, 311; Sir Johannes, 311–32; Samuel, 331; Thomas, 311; Zacharias, 311
Rotterdam, 319